Law of Contract

THE FOUNDATION STUDIES IN LAW SERIES

Series Adviser – Paul Richards, LLB, PhD, PGCE

The books in this series are written for law students for the foundation subjects required to be studied on both law degrees and postgraduate common professional examination courses. Each text concentrates on developing a basic framework for the subject and as such is designed to be accessible and readable, a format especially suitable for part-time courses, CPE and distance-learning courses, as well as more traditional full-time courses where teaching is becoming increasingly student-centred and modularised. These basic texts are intended to be used in conjunction with other sources, such as law reports, case books and statutory materials.

Law of Contract

Criminal Law

Land Law

Law of Tort

Trusts and Equity

Constitutional and Administrative Law

European Community Law

Law of Contract

Second Edition

Paul Richards

Senior Lecturer in Law,
University of Huddersfield

PITMAN
PUBLISHING

PITMAN PUBLISHING
128 Long Acre, London WC2E 9AN

A Division of Pearson Professional Limited

First published in 1992
Second edition 1995

© Pearson Professional Limited 1995

A CIP catalogue record for this book can be obtained
from the British Library.

ISBN 0 273 614126

10 9 8 7 6 5 4 3

Typeset by Land & Unwin (Data Sciences) Ltd
Printed in England by Clays Ltd, St Ives plc

The Publishers' policy is to use paper manufactured from sustainable forests.

Contents

Preface

The truism in the statement that the law does not stand still is amply evidenced from the changes made in this second edition. Over fifty new cases have been dealt with, including *Barclays Bank plc* v *O'Brien* and *CICB Mortgages plc* v *Pitt*, both of which promise to open up a new rich vein of legal development in relation to undue influence. Also discussed, and equally important, is the European Directive on Unfair Terms in Contracts (now SI 3159 The Unfair Terms in Consumer Contracts Regulations 1994 to be implemented on 1 July 1995), the Commercial Agents Regulations 1993 and the Sale and Supply of Goods Act 1994.

The object, as set out in the first edition, has been to produce a textbook that presents the law of contract in a readable and accessible form. Responses from students and colleagues have confirmed this need. Whilst the book has been primarily prepared for those studying the subject at undergraduate level, others studying the law of contract as a single subject may also find it useful.

The general movement in higher education towards student-centred learning programmes continues. For first-year students new to such methods of learning and with no previous knowledge of law, the jump from lecture notes to the traditional authoritative text is often too wide a gap to produce a sound understanding of the subject. Such problems have been encountered for many years by correspondence students and, indeed, by anyone faced with a new subject who is required to obtain a good knowledge and understanding of it in the absence of the more formal educational structures. Such students often have a need for some half-way house which sets out the law to the required depth but without the number of footnotes and minor cases that tend to obscure rather than clarify the principles behind the subject.

Whilst this book has been written with the above matters in mind, it has to be stressed that it is not intended to be a substitute for further and wider reading on the part of the student if he or she is to be fully aware of the wider issues surrounding this increasingly complex subject. Students other than law undergraduates who are studying the law of contract as a single subject in other courses may also find this work of some use.

No work of this nature could be written without references to those books which are recognised as the authoritative works on this subject, in particular: Treitel, *The Law of Contract*; Cheshire, Fifoot and Furmston, *The Law of Contract*; and *Anson's Law of Contract*. The contribution of these to the subject has been immense and it is only correct that acknowledgement should be given to this fact and to the help each one of these works has given me over the years and, in particular, with the writing of this book. These works are often the recommended texts on law degree courses and, as a consequence, the opportunity has been taken to refer readers to them when necessary for the further elucidation of the material.

Whilst the writing of the original book, and the amendments made to it in this edition, are my responsibility, it could not have been produced without the help and support of others. On the academic side I must express my thanks and gratitude to Martin Murphy of the Department of Law of the University of Huddersfield for kindly allowing me to make use of his work on the Commercial Agents Regulations. Continued thanks must also go to Muriel Naylor who again typed the manuscript. Her comments on the readability of the text were invaluable, especially as this was a central aim of the book. Thanks must also go to David Sagar, of the Department of Law of the University of Huddersfield, whose suggestions and constructive criticism of the text (both solicited and unsolicited!) were warmly welcomed. On the production side, I would like to thank the publishers and, in particular, Pat Bond and Elizabeth Tarrant, for their continued support and belief, not only in relation to this book but for the series as a whole. I had anticipated that preparing the second edition would be a relatively straightforward task. How wrong I was! That this new edition is appearing at all can only be ascribed to their dedicated hard work and professionalism.

On a personal level my thanks and gratitude go to my mother and father for their dedication, help and support over many years.

Finally, I dedicate this book to three very special people whose love, affection and companionship is of paramount importance to me. Firstly, my wife, Val, without whose patient support and encouragement the original book and this second edition would never have been completed. Secondly, to my sons, Phillip and William, who have now succeeded in evicting me from my study. Their constant energy and enthusiasm provided ample excuses for me to lay my pen down!

Paul Richards
January 1995

Table of cases

Table of statutes

Other legislative enactments

Part I
THE FORMATION OF A CONTRACT

1 | The evolution and definition of the modern contract

EVOLUTION

The Early Development

The law of contract in England has a long history which dates back to the thirteenth and fourteenth centuries. Its early development was connected closely with the growth and expansion of the jurisdiction of the common law courts over the myriad of courts that evolved from before and after the Norman Conquest. Some local courts in the Middle Ages exercised a limited jurisdiction based on custom that was very similar to that of the law of contract. This jurisdiction was termed the 'law merchant' and was often administered at local fairs, markets and ports. It was however the common law courts that evolved a more generalised jurisdiction.

The evolution of contract began initially with forms of action based on covenant and debt, roughly equivalent to what we know today as contracts under seal and simple contracts. Under 'covenant' some agreements were regarded as so important that they were formalised in writing. In addition to this, and no doubt because of widespread illiteracy, the parties were required to acknowledge the written document by sealing it. Initially the action was based on the need to enforce a specific promise to do something, such as ploughing a field, but it evolved into an action for damages for a sum of money, awarded by a jury for breach of the 'covenant' or agreement.

The informal contract evolved in a very different way since the action based on covenant could not be used in a parol (oral) contract. Here the action began on the basis of debt and detinue whereby specific sums of money lent or otherwise owed (debt) or chattels sold or lent (detinue) could be recovered. These forms of action revolved around a fiction that the plaintiff was recovering his own money or property. The main deficiencies with these actions were that they could not be used to enforce a positive obligation, the only remedy being the recovery of the debt in all property. Further the trial procedures were based on compurgation or wager of law, whereby a defendant could evade liability by producing a number of oath-swearers (usually 12) to swear his innocence in respect to the money or property alleged to be held by him. An action could be lost merely by the incorrect enunciation of the oath by one of the oath-swearers. Other rules made these actions inappropriate and often unjust, and it was at this time that the jurisdiction of the courts of chancery began to intervene to correct the inadequacies of the common law and evolve their own particular remedies applicable to agreements.

Whilst the actions of debt and detinue were the earliest recognition of the enforcement of agreements, the modern law of contract in relation to informal agreements does not originate from these actions. As already stated, at this time there were a large number of different courts all vying to expand their own jurisdictions. The common law courts developed a jurisdiction over wrongs in which the king had a special interest. These were known as pleas of the Crown and involved actions relating to breaches of the king's peace. Such actions were founded on actions in trespass (i.e., actions in tort) which were particularly useful in that the form of the writ was flexible and allowed the writ to be developed and used in many different situations. It is for this reason that Maitland called trespass 'the mother of all torts'. These types of writ were called 'actions on the case' and were tried by a jury who themselves awarded damages as a remedy. Eventually the bringing of these actions ceased to be the sole prerogative of the Crown and could be used to remedy purely civil wrongs. Those torts that did not evolve in this way went on to form the basis of the criminal law. Among the torts that evolved at this time was an action in which the plaintiff alleged that the defendant had entered an informal agreement with him and then by a defective performance caused the plaintiff some damage. One particular anomaly in this early trespass on the case, known as 'assumpsit', was that it lay only for a *misfeasance*, that is performing one's obligations badly, rather than a *nonfeasance*, that is not performing one's obligations at all, though this restriction was removed after *Thoroughgood*'s case (1584) 2 Co Rep 92. The lifting of this anomaly was significant in the development of a law of contract since it meant that any breach of promise could be actionable, even though the agreement was merely informal.

The only remaining blot on the development of assumpsit was the relation of this action to debt. Again the significant factor was the competition for jurisdiction between the courts. With assumpsit the Court of the King's Bench was prepared to allow the action to be used instead of the action on debt. The Court of Common Pleas regarded this use of assumpsit as improper, with the result that it would not allow a plaintiff to recover a specific sum of money by way of an action in assumpsit. It required such a claim to be brought in debt with all its incumbent defects. The dispute between the two courts was resolved in *Slade*'s case (1602) 4 Co Rep 92a when the views of the Court of the King's Bench was upheld. The result of the case was to produce a single form of action for the enforcement of informal agreements and potentially produced an action that held no bounds in the enforcement of promises.

The open-ended scope of assumpsit needed to be controlled. The controlling element as to what types of promise fell within the general scope of assumpsit emerged also in the sixteenth and early seventeenth centuries when the doctrine of consideration evolved. How this doctrine arose in English law is unclear, but what is clear is that by the seventeenth century a principle had emerged that not only had a promise to be shown, but also some motivating reason for the existence of the promise. Put another way, a promise may be regarded as a statement of will but for that statement to have legal effect it had to be supported by a motive for the exercise of that will or consideration. The establishment of the need to show consideration produced a broad form on which the modern law is now based and one which was not to be subject to radical reformulation until the nineteenth century.

The nineteenth century

The nineteenth century is regarded as the golden age of contract since it was at this time that the law of contract evolved into the structure that we have today. Perhaps just as important was the fact that the significance of contract changed within the legal psyche of lawyers since it emerged as a subject in its own right.

The emergence of the law of contract at this time has often been put down to the Industrial Revolution, though this development owes more to coincidence than to a substantive causative link. As Atiyah (1989) points out in *An Introduction to the Law of Contract*, the emergence of the law of contract is really the result of the adoption of the theories of natural law, which propounded the idea of an inalienable right of men to own and deal with property, and that the state via the law should interfere as little as possible with the affairs of individuals. The effect of these two approaches was to elevate the law of contract to a higher plane and produce the notion of the sanctity of the contract, the function of the law being to uphold the contract and only to become involved when things went wrong, not concerning itself with the fairness or social justice of the situation.

This latter comment is of course too simplistic and creates an imbalance when the reality of the situation is assessed since the courts of chancery did attempt to protect individuals who found themselves bound by an onerous contract. Nevertheless the protection offered by the court of chancery was limited and probably even reduced during this period, which was a time of great corruption within the court as is graphically illustrated by Charles Dickens in *Bleak House*.

The result of the above changes produced by the early part of the nineteenth century a new concept of individualism, whereby the man in the street was regarded as self-sufficient and imbued with a new notion of self-reliance, in being able to control his own destiny. Given this development one then had to consider at what point the courts should become involved to settle any dispute that might arise from a contract, though central to this question was whether a contract had been entered into in the first place.

The answer here lies in the perhaps obvious statement that a contract materialises where there is an agreement between the parties. Again the statement is far too simplistic, since the stereotypical response where any breach of the contract is alleged is: 'I did not agree to that'. The problem is one of measuring the existence of the agreement. Further, in many situations, a party may not have expressly 'agreed' to anything. Thus, the act of buying a ticket and getting on a train shows no agreement on the face of things, the same being true of any standard form of contract, in that one has no option but to sign and accept; there is no question of 'agreement' here.

It is at this point that the notion of freedom of contract shows its frailty since the law imposes an objective test to find for the existence or not of an agreement, the court representing the so-called reasonable man. At the end of the day then the idea of individualism fails and the courts have to find for the existence of a contract based on the intention of the parties. That intention is found by reference to a legal rule rather than the intention of the individuals themselves, despite the fact that some judges at this time considered that *consensus ad idem* (total agreement) was an essential feature of the existence of an enforceable contract.

A further misconception of the notion of freedom of contract is the idea that it provides the parties with freedom of choice as to the terms on which the agreement is entered into. Such an idea holds good where there is equality of bargaining power but is plainly false where this is not the case. Indeed it is the fact of the powerful imposing terms on the weak that led to the notions of collectivisation, the growth of the trade union movement, the intervention of government and the weakening of the notion of freedom of contract, with its *laissez-faire* basis, as the underlying principle on which the modern law of contract is based.

The classical theory of contract, as we have seen, played an important part in the early economic and social development of the country, when modern economic theory and power were still in their infancy and true freedom of choice existed. Once large powerful industrial units developed, as in the railways for instance, where there was no competition or freedom of choice, then the chinks in the armour of the classical theory began to open up, allowing interventionism and a new dawn of state paternalism to develop.

The modern era

The nineteenth century saw great social, economic and political change in Britain which heralded a swing away from the classic theory of freedom of contract. Britain became firmly established as an industrial leader and this brought with it large industrial concerns, mass production with a wide selection of goods readily available and the dawn of a new consumerism. While previously an individual was free to negotiate an agreement, now he was faced with standard-form contracts, large companies carrying great financial power and products which required a scientific knowledge beyond that of the man in the street. Political and social changes were also occurring, taking the form of a widening of the franchise and a movement towards a more socialist society, the result of which was a change from, as Atiyah puts it, 'a corrective form of justice to one which was distributive'.

The modern era then became one of protectionism and a subsequent decline in the freedom of contract caused by the fettering of negotiating discretion. This decline was only partial and in many aspects of business freedom still persisted, particularly in the manufacturing industry. The new protectionism evolved in three ways, all of which often interacted with each other.

Social protectionism

The industrial revolution, culminating in the 1880s, the 'Golden Age' of Britain's economic and industrial transformation, produced a society dependent on earning a living since the population now became centred around major areas of industrial activity. The movement from the country to the towns presented massive social and infrastructure problems. The worker was treated by his employer as a commodity that without careful financial control could be a considerable liability. The effect of this was to produce slum dwellings, jerry-built with little or no sanitation, and working conditions that had the appearance of the devil's cauldron, with unsafe working practices and widespread pollution. These conditions could be seen to be the result of the need to further the profit motive, to produce housing and a work-force that allowed for the greatest maximisation of profit, this objective in turn being achieved by the negotiation of the contract between the manufacturer and the distributors of his goods. Freedom of contract in the classical theory could be seen as being at the centre of the exploitation of the most vulnerable members of society. It was to curtail these excesses that Parliament and the law were called in, and this they did, imposing planning controls, prohibiting certain types of contracts and imposing terms into contracts.

So far we have seen how protectionism began but this process has also continued right through the twentieth century. Thus there has developed a whole network of institutions designed to act as a safety net for the individual, to protect him from the extremes of commercial and industrial life, such as a system of national insurance, a national health service, statutory recognition of trade unions, a compensation scheme for those made redundant and a whole battery of legislation to protect tenants from the excesses of their landlords. There has also been a recognition of the dangers of the concentration of economic power with the development of restrictions on the development of monopoly power.

Consumer protection

As already stated, the industrial revolution brought with it mass production, a great deal more freedom of choice and the development of goods of a complexity never before available. Britain had also become a consumer society, one where an individual generally had to work to earn a living to buy not only essentials such as food and clothing, but also those items which had hitherto been luxuries and beyond the aspirations of the ordinary person to acquire and which were available because of mass production techniques.

With this development the common law and Parliament imposed conditions on the parties to contracts, particularly sellers of goods, to comply with certain basic standards. Such legislation generally protected the individual against the vagaries of the commercial enterprise, though more limited protection was also imposed on contracts made between commercial enterprises. In contracts between private individuals the idea of freedom of contract encapsulated in the maxim *caveat emptor* (let the buyer beware) still persisted – as it does today.

Consumer-protection legislation not only imposed civil liability, which left it to the individual himself to enforce the terms imposed by way of statute in an action for breach of contract, but also imposed criminal liability in some areas. Thus the Trade Descriptions Act 1968 made it a criminal offence to describe falsely goods offered for sale.

Contracts of adhesion

Contracts of adhesion, generally known today as standard-form contracts, have now become part and parcel of the commercial life of the country. They derive from the time of the development of the passenger-carrying train when, for the first time, large numbers of contracts were entered into on any one day and it would clearly have been nonsensical to have to negotiate every single contract. The railway companies thus produced a standard contract which applied to everyone, the terms of which were not open to negotiation.

It must not be thought, therefore, that such contracts are of recent origin, as they are not, and their history goes back to the very beginnings of mercantile enterprise. Initially they could be found in trade usage, and eventually they were transformed into documents such as charterparties, insurance policies and bills of lading. Their purpose here was to save time and expense since clearly in complex matters such as those indicated it would be commercially wasteful to have to sit down and negotiate each contract separately. A further purpose was to indicate where particular risks lay in carrying out the contract, so enabling a party to insure or guard against the risk becoming a loss. In contracts for export sales, for example, a strict free on board (or FOB) contract requires the seller to place the goods, at his own expense, on a ship nominated by the buyer. The price quoted on such a contract does not include the price of the freight or insurance, both of which must be provided for by the buyer.

Such contracts are quite legitimate when entered into between men of business at arm's length. Indeed this might also be the case where a contract negotiated with a private individual can assume that the individual himself would normally insure against a particular risk, as for example, the cancellation of a holiday. Such contracts become illegitimate where the standard-form contract seeks to impose harsh and onerous terms on an individual who has no option but to accept them. Very often the weaker party will be unable both to renegotiate the contract and, very often, to go elsewhere since such contracts may be common to all operators within a particular industrial activity. A further criticism of such contracts is that they are often drafted in such a way as to be virtually incomprehensible to the ordinary person and often impose wide-ranging exemption clauses which preclude the stronger party from being liable for breach of the contract in almost any circumstances.

In the twentieth century such contracts became all pervasive and while the courts attempted to curtail the operation of such contracts – and in particular the effect of the exemption clause – by means of various rules regarding the construction of such clauses, a more radical step was required. This reform developed in a piecemeal fashion in various statutes until the passing of the Unfair Contract Terms Act in 1977.

The present day

Sir George Jessel in 1875 in *Printing and Numerical Registering Co v Sampson* (1875) LR 19 Eq 462 stated:

> if there is one thing more than another which public policy requires, it is that men of full age and competent understanding shall have the utmost liberty in contracting, and that their contracts, when entered freely and voluntarily, shall be held sacred and shall be enforced by the Courts of Justice.

Such a view is clearly not one which sums up the evolution of the law of contract in the latter quarter of the nineteenth century or in the twentieth century. The notion of freedom of contract lives on, but the reality is that it persists only in very limited areas of commercial life. The courts and Parliament have made substantial inroads into limiting the powers of those who exercise economic dominance.

In the 1980s, however, the notion of freedom of contract was given a new lease of life in the form of so-called Thatcherism, the idea that the controls that had evolved over the past hundred years had now become so restrictive and so protectionist that they had dulled the cutting edge of competitiveness which Britain required to succeed in the modern commercial world. The result of this dramatic policy change has been to privatise the once publicly owned utilities which had become dilatory, safe in the knowledge that they were state owned and protected monopolies which governments had to support no matter how inefficient. On a more individualistic level the government argued that the population was now better educated and more sophisticated, and that individuals were more able to look after their own interests.

The result of this change of policy has been to reduce the levels of protection offered and to allow the individual to have greater freedom of choice, thereby inducing a new competitive order to the economy. Thus the previously state-owned industries now had to become more efficient in order to make profits and to keep their customers. Failure to do so meant not only loss of business but also the asking of questions at the annual general meeting of the newly privatised company in question, since now their privatised customers, or at least some of them, were shareholders to whom the board was answerable.

Such changes occurred not only in relation to the old state-owned utilities, but also in relation to some of the benefits previously enjoyed and protected by the state. Thus individuals now became free to choose how to organise their pensions rather than being dependent on the state. Further, in the private sector, tenants had their rights to security of tenure reduced since it was recognised that the wide-ranging protection previously afforded had the effect of reducing investment in the rented housing market with a consequent reduction in the stock of rented accommodation throughout the country.

This new era of freedom of contract is not a complete one; some level of protection will always be required to protect those less able to look after themselves. It is of course not desirable to revert to the slums and deprivations that existed prior to the protectionist era and therefore some level of protection will be maintained. What that level should be is a matter of political debate, though it seems unlikely that, whatever the political colour of future governments, there will be a reversion to the protectionism prevalent prior to the 1980s. All political parties recognise that the competition prevalent in the notion of freedom of contract is essential to a sound national economy.

DEFINITION

Treitel (1991) in *The Law of Contract* defines a contract as:

> an agreement giving rise to obligations which are enforced or recognised by law. The factor which distinguishes contractual from other legal obligations is that they are based on the agreement of the contracting parties.

Anson, in *Principles of the Law of Contract*, takes his definition a little further than this, defining it as:

> A legally binding agreement made between two or more persons, by which rights are acquired by one or more to acts or forbearances on the part of the other or others.

Objectivity

The notion of agreement is central to both definitions and the question has to arise as to at what point an agreement actually materialises. The problem of measuring the existence of the agreement has already been looked at in our discussions on the concept of freedom of contract. Nevertheless, it is worth restating the fact that the law requires more than some subjective indication of agreement between the parties. There is a clear need for some degree of evidence of the fact of agreement, otherwise there would be great uncertainty when one attempts to reconcile the theoretical basis of the law of contract with the actual intentions of the parties. An individual could escape his obligations merely by stating that he had no intention of being bound by any agreement. The courts thus require some outward objective evidence of the existence of an agreement. Any subjective element is subordinate to the objective one and is, to a large degree, of no consequence except where it corresponds with the intentions of the parties as ascertained by objective means.

In the case of *The Leonidas D* [1985] 1 WLR 925, Goff LJ, in analysing the discussions on the objective test that took place in *The Hannah Blumenthal* [1983] AC 854, preferred the assertion of Lord Brightman in defining the objective test, stating:

In his speech Lord Brightman was, as we understand it, asserting that if one party (O) so acts that his conduct, objectively considered, constitutes an offer, and the other party (A), believing that the conduct of O represents his actual intention, accepts O's offer, then a contract will come into existence, and on those facts it will make no difference if O did not in fact intend to make an offer, or if he misunderstood A's acceptance, so that O's state of mind is, in such circumstances, irrelevant.

The concept of objectivity in this context has, however, to be given some balance, since it is clearly not desirable for the law to impose an agreement where none existed simply because some hypothetical reasonable man says that there is such an agreement!

In the case of *The Golden Bear* [1987] 1 Lloyd's Rep 330 at 341 it was stated that the objective test would not apply, for instance, where X knows that Y's actual state of mind was not in accordance with the objective appearance created by Y's conduct. Moreover the objective test will not apply when the result would be to cause hardship to the other party where, for instance, the apparent acceptance of one party is based on a mistake which has been induced by the negligent acts of the other.

For the most part this apparent conflict between finding for an agreement in objective or subjective terms will not materialise since in the vast majority of contracts there will be *consensus ad idem* between the parties, i.e., subjective agreement *and* an agreement as seen objectively. In such circumstances there is unlikely to be a dispute as to the existence of an agreement *per se*.

The notion of a bargain and legal relations

So far we have been discussing the need to establish an agreement before a contract becomes established, and certainly evidence must be submitted to prove this fact. English law of contract requires that there be not only an agreement but also the presence of a bargain since otherwise any promise could give rise to a binding obligation. Thus for the purposes of English law a promise is not binding unless it is either made under seal or supported 'by consideration'.

Whilst the doctrine of consideration will be examined in more depth later in this book, one has to consider it briefly here as an essential element in finding for the mere existence of a contract. This requirement can be seen in Anson's definition, where he indicates that there must be a degree of *quid pro quo* to establish the contract, or – to put it simply – the parties are each required to 'buy' the promise of the other party, as, for example, 'I promise to give you £500 if you promise to give me your car'.

In simple contracts, therefore, one must establish the existence of a bargain, and a bare promise, such as: 'I promise to give you £500', is not enforceable, being simply a bare promise or *nudum pactum*. The only way such a promise is binding is if it is made in writing under seal as in a deed. However here we are in the territory of speciality contracts and for the most part this book is about simple contracts.

A further factor in determining what sort of agreements are binding is the requirement of an intention to create a legal relationship. Even if evidence of an agreement is proven, together with consideration, not every such bargain will give rise to a legally enforceable contract. If X says to his neighbour: 'If you give me a lift to work, I will cut your lawns' and the neighbour agrees to this, there is prima facie no binding contract despite the clear existence of a bargain. The reason for this is that such a social arrangement is not one which a reasonable person would consider as giving rise to legally enforceable obligations. The law thus draws a line between agreements of a commercial nature and those of a social or domestic nature.

Further reading

Atiyah, 'The Hannah Blumethal and Classical Contract Law', 102 *Law Quarterly Review* 363, 1986

Atiyah, *The Rise and Fall of the Freedom of Contract* 1979, Oxford University Press

Atiyah, *An Introduction to the Law of Contract* 4th ed. 1989, Oxford University Press

Beale, Bishop and Furmston, *Contract – Cases and Materials* 2nd ed. 1990, Butterworths

Cheshire, Fifoot and Furmston, *The Law of Contract* 12th ed. 1991, Butterworths

Guest, *Anson's Law of Contract* 26th ed. 1984, Oxford University Press

Howarth, 'The Meaning of Objectivity in Contract', 100 *Law Quarterly Review* 265, 1984

Treitel, *The Law of Contract* 8th ed. 1991

Vorster, 'A Comment on the Meaning of Objectivity in Contract', 103 *Law Quarterly Review* 274, 1987

2 | The fact of agreement

It has already been stated that there must be an intention to enter into a binding agreement, and that this intention is usually established by some outward objective indication of the existence of an agreement, rather than a subjective assessment of the actual intentions of the parties. On a practical level, however, the question arises as to what evidence of objective intention the law requires in deciding whether or not an agreement has been entered into.

Two very different approaches have been used to assess the presence of an agreement. The first is a liberal *laissez-faire* approach under which virtually anything at all could potentially be used in assessing the presence of an agreement. Such an approach almost invariably results in a subjective assessment of the parties' actions taking place and has the disadvantage of rendering the law uncertain and unpredictable. This approach has found favour with Lord Denning who, in *Butler Machine Tool Co Ltd* v *Ex-Cell-O Corporation (England) Ltd* [1979] 1 All ER 965, stated:

> In many cases our traditional analysis of offer, counter offer, rejection, acceptance and so forth is out of date . . . . The better way is to look at all the documents passing between the parties and glean from them or from the conduct of the parties, whether they have reached agreement on all material points . . .

Similarly, in *Gibson* v *Manchester City Council* [1979] 1 All ER 972, he also stated that one ought to:

> look at the correspondence as a whole and at the conduct of the parties and see therefrom whether the parties have come to an agreement on everything that was material.

In both these cases Denning's approach was rejected in favour of the second, more traditional, approach which is to find the objective intention of the parties to enter into an agreement by reducing the agreement in terms of offers, counter-offers, acceptances, revocations and rejections. This method of finding whether an agreement has come into existence or not provides a more predictable, certain and objective means of assessment, though one which is artificial. One should always bear in mind that this process of breaking an agreement down into smaller, more manageable units is simply an evidential device and in difficult cases where this process of analysis is not possible the courts may well adopt Denning's approach. Lord Diplock in the *Gibson* case certainly considered it was a legitimate method of analysing a set of circumstances 'which do not fit easily into the normal analysis of offer and acceptance'.

This legitimacy of Lord Denning's approach has since been affirmed in *G Percy Trentham Ltd v Archital Luxfer* [1993] 1 Lloyd's Rep 25. The facts of the case were that the plaintiffs (Trentham) were engaged by Municipal Mutual Insurance as main contractors to design and build industrial units in two phases. Trentham employed Archital to design, supply and install the doors and window frames for the development. This work was eventually completed and, indeed, paid for by Trentham. The sub-contracts were thus fully executed. Subsequently claims were made against Trentham by Municipal Mutual under the main contract for alleged delays and defects in carrying out the work. In order to obtain an indemnity against the damages that it had to pay out Trentham began proceedings against several sub-contractors, including Archital, alleging defects in the window works in both of the phases. In their defence Archital denied that any binding contracts had come into existence between themselves and Trentham. It was common ground in the dispute that no integrated written sub-contacts had come into existence; instead there had been a series of exchanges of letters and telephone conversations but no corresponding offer and acceptance. The picture presented then was of two parties jockeying for position in a scenario very similar to a 'battle of forms' type of situation (see p 31 below) where the parties both attempt to impose their own terms and conditions on a contract by the use of offers and counter offers. The case is unusual in that the issue is not one concerning whose standard terms and conditions predominate, but whether any contract at all has come into existence out of the exchange of correspondence. At first instance the judge held that a contract had been formed when the defendant carried out the work, basing his decision on *Brogden* v *Metropolitan Railway Co* (1877) 2 App Cas 666 (see p 27 below). In other words the plaintiff had made an offer which the defendants had accepted by conduct in carrying out the work. Archital appealed from this decision.

  In the Court of Appeal the only judgment was given by Steyn LJ, the two other members concurring. Steyn LJ agreed with the judge at first instance that there was a contract in existence. In arriving at this decision Steyn LJ considered that there were four matters which were of importance to the case. Firstly, English law generally adopts an objective test to the issue of contract formation. As we have already seen, the law generally ignores a subjective assessment of the 'expectations and unexpressed mental reservations of the parties'. He stated that the governing criterion was 'the reasonable expectations of honest men', which he translated in the present case as the 'reasonable expectations of sensible businessmen'. Secondly, whilst in the vast majority of cases the presence of offer and acceptance will be the means of deciding the matter of contract formation, 'it is not necessarily so in the case of a contract alleged to have come into existence during and as a result of performance', citing *Brogden* v *Metropolitan Railway Co* (1877) 2 AC 666; *New Zealand Shipping Co Ltd* v *A M*

Satterthwaite & Co Ltd [1974] 1 Lloyds Rep 534 at p 539; [1975] AC 154 at p 167; *Gibson* v *Manchester City Council* [1979] 1 WLR 294, as supporting this proposition. Thirdly, he stated that the fact that the contract in the case was executed (i.e. performance of the contract was completed) rather than executory was important since the fact that the transaction has been performed by both parties will make it very difficult for an argument to be sustained that there was no intention to create legal relations or that the contract is void for uncertainty. Indeed on the specific matter of uncertainty Steyn LJ considered that the fact that the contract was executed 'makes it easier to imply a term resolving any uncertainty, or, alternatively, it may make it possible to treat a matter not finalised in negotiations as inessential. Fourthly, Steyn LJ stated that 'if a contract only comes into existence during and as a result of performance of the transaction it will frequently be possible to hold that the contract impliedly and retrospectively covers pre-contractual performance' as indicated in *Trollope and Colls Ltd* v *Atomic Power Construction Ltd* [1962] 3 All ER 1035.

On the basis of these points Steyn LJ concurred with the decision at first instance that there was sufficient evidence to conclude that there was a binding contract; the parties had clearly intended to create a legal relationship between each other. In arriving at this position Steyn LJ stated that 'one must not lose sight of the commercial nature of the transaction', that is one party carrying out work for which he expected to be paid, and this is what had occurred. There was no suggestion that there was a continuing stipulation that a contract would only be created if a written agreement was concluded. Thus Steyn adopted an approach that was very similar to Denning's in that he looked at the overall effect of what had been said and done by the parties, although he did not refer to Denning's approach. He stated:

> The contemporary exchanges, and the carrying out of what was agreed in those exchanges, support the view that there was a course of dealing which on Trentham's side created a right to performance on the work by Archital, and on Archital's side it created a right to be paid on an agreed basis…The Judge (at first instance) analysed the matter in terms of offer and acceptance. I agree with his conclusion. But I am, in any event, satisfied that in this fully executed transaction a contract came into existence during performance even if it cannot be precisely analysed in terms of offer and acceptance.

Does this decision suggest an abandonment of offer and acceptance as central pillars in the formation of contracts? The answer to the question is clearly in the negative, since Steyn himself states that 'the coincidence of offer and acceptance will, in the vast majority of cases, represent the mechanism of contract formation'. What the decision does is to broaden the opportunity to find for a contract by examining the 'commercial reality' of the situation coupled with evidence of the parties' intentions and to this extent a level of uncertainty may have been created as to when a contract has actually been formed.

Despite the decision of Steyn it should be borne in mind that the judge at first instance was able to find for a contract on the basis of offer and acceptance, that is by adopting the classical approach. More often than not, therefore, the courts will continue to go to great lengths to analyse the facts in terms of the classical approach.

As Lord Wilberforce stated in *New Zealand Shipping Co Ltd* v *A M Satterthwaite and Co Ltd* [1975] AC 154:

> English law, having committed itself to a rather technical and schematic doctrine of contract, in application takes a practical approach, often at the cost of forcing the facts to fit uneasily into the marked slots of offer, acceptance and consideration.

Whilst one must always bear in mind Denning's approach the classical analysis is far more important and has to be considered in a great deal more depth. The basic proposition of the classical analysis may be summed up as:

offer + acceptance = agreement

OFFER

The nature of an offer

An offer is an expression of a willingness to contract on certain terms made with the intention that a binding agreement will exist once the offer is accepted.

The task of a plaintiff seeking to enforce a contract is to prove the existence of an offer. An offer may be made either orally or in writing, or implied by the conduct of the person making the offer, namely, the offeror. Furthermore, the offer may be made to a specific person or group of persons or to the world at large. In the now famous case of *Carlill* v *Carbolic Smoke Ball Co* [1892] 2 QB 484, it was argued that it was not possible to make an offer to the world at large.

In this case the plaintiff bought a medical preparation called 'The Carbolic Smoke Ball' on the basis that the defendants advertised that they would pay £100 to any person who contracted influenza after using the smoke ball in the prescribed manner and for a specified period. Further, the defendants stated that, 'to show their sincerity' they had deposited £1,000 with the Alliance Bank. The plaintiff bought one of the smoke balls and used it in the manner prescribed and promptly caught influenza! She sued for the £100. The defendants contended that there was no agreement between them and used considerable ingenuity in promoting this contention. One of the defences used was that it was not possible to make an offer to the whole world since this would enable the whole world to accept the offer, which was clearly beyond the realms of commercial reality. The Court of Appeal had no difficulty in rejecting this defence. Bowen LJ stated the position very clearly as follows:

> It was also said that the contract is made with the whole world – that is, with everybody and that you cannot contract with everybody. It is not a contract made with all the world. There is the fallacy of the argument. It is an offer made to all the world; and why should not an offer be made to all the world which is to ripen into a contract with anybody who comes forward and performs the condition? . . . Although the offer is made to the world, the contract is made with that limited portion of the public who come forward and perform the condition on the faith of the advertisement.

In the *Carlill* case the defendants also contended that the plaintiff had not accepted their offer and therefore there was no *consensus ad idem* and thus no agreement. This defence, which was rejected, exposes the fact that offers may arise in two forms, either bilateral or unilateral. A bilateral offer arises where one party promises to do something in return for a promise made by the offeree. Both parties are agreeing to do something in return for some reciprocal promise from the other. An example of such an offer would be if A promises to sell his car in return for B promising to pay him £5,000. The vast majority of offers are of this type.

A unilateral offer occurs where one party, the offeror, promises to pay for the act of another, that is, a conditional promise. The acceptance of the offer takes place when the offeree performs the act in question. The offer here is said to be unilateral because only one party is making a promise. The facts of the *Carlill* case provide an obvious example of such an offer.

Two further features of offers to be noted are that the terms of an offer must be clear and that the offer is made with the intention that it should be binding. In connection with the latter requirement, a further defence propounded in the *Carlill* case was that the advertisement was a 'mere puff' and not intended to form the basis of a binding agreement. Such 'puffs' are very much part of commercial life today, particularly in the advertising industry. Clearly statements that allude to certain soap powders 'washing whiter than white' or certain types of beers working untold miracles are not intended to be taken seriously but to 'puff up' the propensities of the product to induce the all-suffering public to buy. In the *Carlill* case the allegation that the offer was a 'mere puff' was rejected on the basis that the advertisement also stated that the defendants had deposited £1,000 with the Alliance Bank 'to show their sincerity'. It was clear in this case that this fact indicated that they intended the promise to form the basis of a legal relationship.

So far everything presented is fairly straightforward, but unfortunately the situation is not so simple. There are many types of statement which, on the face of things, appear to be offers but in fact do not so comprise.

Offers compared with other types of transaction

Offers distinguished from invitations to treat

It has been seen that, according to one definition, an offer is an expression of a willingness to be bound by the terms of the offer should the offer be accepted. Clearly the implication here is that the statement of offer is the final statement of an individual who wishes to be bound by those terms; it is a person's final declaration of his readiness to be bound. It follows that if an individual is not willing to implement the terms of his promise but is merely seeking to initiate negotiations then this cannot amount to an offer, such statements being termed 'invitations to treat'.

The distinction between an offer and an invitation to treat is not an easy one to make since it very often revolves around that elusive concept of intention. It may be that a statement amounts to an invitation to treat even though the statement is said to make an 'offer' and vice versa. The easiest way of making the distinction is by analysing how the law deals with the problem within certain stereotypical transactions, bearing in mind that the courts will look at the surrounding circumstances and the intention of the parties and will not necessarily have regard to the actual wording of the statement.

(a) Advertisements and other notices. It has already been seen that the advertisement in the *Carlill* case amounted to an offer, though a unilateral one. In the words of Bowen LJ:

It is not like cases in which you offer to negotiate or you issue advertisements that you have got a stock of books to sell, or houses to let, in which case there is no offer to be bound by any contract. Such advertisements are offers to negotiate – offers to receive offers – offers to chaffer . . .

The decision in the *Carlill* case that the advertisement was an offer is peculiar to a situation where the statement is a conditional promise, a unilateral offer. A similar situation would result if an individual placed an advertisement offering a reward to the finder of a lost wallet. In such a case there is clearly a conditional promise and the advertisement would amount to an offer.

Most advertisements do not fall into this category and hence they are held not to be offers but statements inviting further negotiations or invitations to treat. An example of such a situation can be seen in the case of *Partridge* v *Crittenden* [1968] 2 All ER 421, where the appellants placed an advertisement in a periodical for bird fanciers stating, 'Bramblefinch cocks and hens 25s.'. They were charged under the Protection of Birds Act 1954, s. 6(1), in that they were unlawfully 'offering for sale' a certain live bird, a brambling, contrary to the provisions of the Act. At first instance the appellants were convicted but on appeal the conviction was quashed by the divisional court.

This decision affirms the much earlier decision of *Harris* v *Nickerson* (1873) LR 8 QB 286, where an auctioneer advertised that certain goods would be sold at a certain location on a certain date. The plaintiff went to the sale but all the lots he was interested in had been withdrawn. He sued the auctioneer for his loss of time and expenses. It was held that the claim must fail as the advertisement of the auction was merely a declaration of intent to hold a sale and did not amount to an offer capable of being accepted and thus forming the basis of a binding contract, that is, that the advertisement merely amounted to an invitation to treat.

The same conclusion was also reached in the case of a price list circulated by a wine merchant (*Grainger and Son* v *Gough* [1896] AC 325) though a notice declaring that deck-chairs were for hire was held in *Chapelton* v *Barry UDC* [1940] 1 KB 532 as amounting to an offer. The moral of the story is clear that in this type of case, whilst one can draw on certain generalisations, as in advertisements, one must treat each case on its own merits, assessing the intentions of the parties.

(b) Displays of goods for sale. By far the most common example of the occurrence of invitations to treat is in the case of goods displayed either in shop windows or within a shop itself. The issue that arises here is that if the display of the goods in question amounts to an offer then a customer may enter the shop and purport to accept that offer, thus creating a binding obligation on the shopkeeper to sell the goods at the stated price. If, however, the display of goods only amounts to an invitation to treat then it is the customer who makes the offer to the shopkeeper, who is free to accept or reject that offer as he wishes. Almost invariably it is the latter approach that is adopted by the courts, though the reasoning behind the general rule is somewhat obscure and lost in the mists of time – some think the rule is a throw-back to the time of the market-place when bargaining and haggling were commonplace, a notion that is not particularly appropriate today. The rule could

nevertheless produce some startling effects. For instance, a shopkeeper could refuse to sell the goods to a customer even if he offered certain goods for sale and wrote the words 'Special Offer' across his windows. The words 'Special Offer' import no specific legal meaning here and do not necessarily mean an offer at law. Such a conclusion may be somewhat unfair, however, if those words had induced a person to wait outside the shop all night, only to be told the next morning that his offer to buy had been rejected. Nevertheless, even if the goods subject to the 'Special Offer' were regarded as an offer at law, an offeror in any event is free to withdraw that offer at any time up to acceptance.

The general rule as regards goods displayed in shop windows is well illustrated in the case of *Fisher* v *Bell* [1961] 1 QB 394, where a price-marked flick-knife was displayed for sale in a shop window. The seller was prosecuted under the now repealed Restriction of Offensive Weapons Act 1961, which made it an offence to offer to sell such items, and was acquitted. Lord Parker stated:

> It is clear according to the ordinary law of contract that the display of an article with a price on it in a shop window is merely an invitation to treat. It is in no sense an offer for sale, the acceptance of which constitutes a contract.

A more problematical situation occurred in the case of *Pharmaceutical Society of Great Britain* v *Boots Cash Chemists (Southern) Ltd* [1952] 2 All ER 456; [1953] 1 All ER 482, where the status of goods on the shelves of a self-service shop was called into question. The facts of the case were that the defendants were being prosecuted under the Pharmacy and Poisons Act 1933, s. 17, in that they had allowed the sale of a listed poison to be effected without the supervision of a registered pharmacist. The arrangement in the shop was that a customer on entering was given a basket and he was then free to walk around the shop selecting items from the shelves. When he had selected such items as he required they were taken to the cash desk, where the customer was required to pay for them. Near to the cash desk was a registered pharmacist who was authorised to prevent a customer removing any drug from the shop. The Pharmaceutical Society alleged that the goods on the shelves were offers to sell which the customer accepted by placing the goods in the basket, and that thus the sale took place at that point and not at the cash desk under the supervision of the registered pharmacist. In such a situation, it was alleged, Boots were clearly in breach of the provision and had committed a criminal offence. The court however decided that the goods on the shelves were only invitations to treat and that it was the customer who made an offer to buy when he presented the goods for payment at the cash desk. At this point the person at the cash desk or the registered pharmacist could accept or reject that offer. The effect of this reasoning was that the sale did take place under the supervision of the registered pharmacist and no criminal offence had been committed.

Some authorities, particularly American ones, dispute such a conclusion as regards the status of goods on display in a self-service shop. In *Lasky* v *Economy Grocery Stores*, 65 NE 305 (1946), it was stated that the goods displayed constituted offers but that the acceptance took place, not on the placing of the goods in the basket, but on the customer's presenting them at the cash desk for payment. Alternatively, in *Sheeskin* v *Giant Food Inc.*, 318 A 2d 894 (1974), it was stated that acceptance took place before the goods were presented at the cash desk, though the customer could cancel his acceptance before payment if he wished. Contradiction also exists in English law though, since in *R* v *Morris* [1984] AC 320, it was held that the taking of goods from a shelf and changing the price tags amounted to an 'appropriation' within the Theft Act 1968.

(c) Auction sales. The status of the call for bids by an auctioneer was considered in the case of *Payne* v *Cave* (1789) 3 Term Rep 148. In the case it was decided that a call for bids amounts to an invitation to treat, the bids themselves amounting to offers which the auctioneer is free to accept or reject as he wishes. This situation is given implied authority in the Sale of Goods Act 1979, s. 57(1), which provides that a sale in an auction is completed by the fall of the hammer and each party is allowed to withdraw up to this time.

Auction sales can take two forms, in that goods may be sold with or without a reserve price. Where the goods are put up for sale with a reserve price, it was held (in *McManus* v *Fortescue* [1907] 2 KB 1) that no contract results if the auctioneer purports to accept a bid that is lower than the reserve price. Where the auction is held without reserve no contract of sale materialises between the owner of the property and the highest bidder if the auctioneer either refuses or otherwise fails to accept the highest bid. In *Warlow* v *Harrison* (1859) 1 E & E 309 it was stated, *obiter dicta*, that in such a case there is a collateral contract between the auctioneer and the highest bidder, whereby the auctioneer in calling for bids is offering to accept the highest bid and that this offer is accepted by bidding. Thus if the auctioneer refuses to sell to the highest bidder he, himself, may be sued for breach of contract.

(d) Tenders. It was held in *Spencer* v *Harding* (1870) LR 5 CP 561 that a statement that goods are to be sold by tender is not normally an offer, and that thus no obligation is created to sell to the person making the highest tender. Similarly, an invitation for tenders for the supply of goods or services is not generally an offer, but an invitation for offers to be submitted which can be accepted or rejected as the case may be.

In some circumstances, however, an invitation to tender may be held to be an offer.

In the recent case of *Blackpool and Fylde Aero Club Ltd* v *Blackpool Borough Council* [1990] 3 All ER 25, the Council owned and managed an airport, raising money by granting a concession to an operator to run pleasure flights from the airport. Shortly before the concession was about to expire in 1983 the Council invited tenders for the right to run the concession, invitations being sent to the plaintiffs and six other interested parties. The terms of submission of bids were that they were to be submitted in an envelope provided, which was to bear no mark which could identify the sender. Furthermore the tender had to be submitted no later than 12 noon on 17 March 1983. The plaintiffs' tender was put in the Town Hall letter-box at 11.00 a.m. on 17 March. However, although the box should have been cleared at noon, this did not occur. The plaintiffs' tender was subsequently marked down as being submitted late and was therefore not considered. The plaintiffs sued the Council for breach of contract on the basis that it had warranted that had a tender been submitted by the deadline it would be considered and that the Council had acted in breach of that warranty. It was held, on appeal, that in certain circumstances an invitation to tender could give rise to binding obligations. This was such an instance since tenders had been sought from a number of parties, all of them known to the Council, who had also imposed strict rules of compliance on them. It was thus implied that a person submitting a tender in compliance with those rules had the right to have his tender opened and considered along with the others.

Tenders may take two possible forms. They may be specific tenders or standing-offer tenders. The former comprises a tender for a definite quantity of goods to be delivered or sold at a specified time. Here the person requiring or selling the goods makes an invitation to tender, the person wishing to deliver or buy them making the offer, which will be converted into a trading contract when accepted by the first party.

The second type of tender arises when a person invites tenders for the supply of goods or services which *may* be required within a specified time at some future date. An example of such a tender may be where a company invites tenders for the supply of stationery as and when, or if and when, required. Here acceptance of the tender (i.e. the offer) does not create a binding contract. The supplier whose bid is successful is in fact making a standing offer which is accepted every time an order is placed for stationery. At this point the supplier is obliged to meet the order or be in breach of contract, though he is free to revoke his standing offer at any time prior to an order being placed with him, though he is bound to fulfil orders already received.

The problem of standing offers was considered in the case of the *Great Northern Railway Co* v *Witham* (1873) LR 9 CP 16 where the plaintiffs invited tenders for the supply of goods, including iron, for a period of 12 months. The defendant submitted a tender to supply the goods over the period at a fixed price in such quantities as may be ordered from time to time. The tender was accepted but before the expiry of 12 months the defendant refused to supply any more goods and was sued for breach of contract. It was held that just as the plaintiffs were not bound to order goods, the defendant was only bound to supply goods actually ordered and that he could revoke his standing offer at any time provided that revocation was communicated to the other party.

The revocation thus only operated to free him from future obligations, not those which had actually accrued by virtue of the placing of an order. The case thus affirmed the earlier decision of *Offord* v *Davies* (1862) 12 CBNS 748.

In recent years a new development has occurred in the area of tenders, namely, the referential bid. A referential bid occurs in a competitive tender situation where one party attempts to win the order by reference to a bid submitted by another party. An example of a referential would be where X offers to pay £100,000 for a concession or £10,000 more than any other offer. The latter part of this bid is a referential bid.

The status of referential bids was considered in the case of *Harvela Investments Ltd* v *Royal Trust Co of Canada (CI) Ltd* [1986] AC 207 where an invitation was made to two persons to submit 'offers' for the purchase of a quantity of shares. The first defendants, who were disposing of the shares, also agreed to accept the highest offer received provided it met with other stipulated conditions. The plaintiffs bid $2,175,000 whilst the second defendant bid $2,100,000 or '$10,000 in excess of any other offer which you may receive which is expressed as a fixed monetary amount whichever is higher'. The first defendants accepted the second defendant's offer. The House of Lords held that the referential bid was ineffective and that the fixed bid of the plaintiffs should have been accepted. The reasoning for this decision was that the House of Lords considered that the idea behind a competitive tender was that the bids were to be confidential and that no bidder would know the amount bid by the other person. The effect of a referential bid would be to defeat the notion of a confidential competitive tender.

(e) Ticket cases. One problem that has recurred time and time again concerns the giving of a ticket during the course of entering into the contract. The problem revolves around whether the ticket is a contractual document, thereby rendering the parties subject to the terms and conditions printed or referred to on the ticket, or not. Two factors can influence the role of tickets in contracts; first, whether it was intended that the ticket should amount to a contractual document and, secondly, the mode and timing of the issue of the ticket.

In *Chapelton* v *Barry UDC* [1940] 1 KB 532 the Court of Appeal considered that a sign by some deck-chairs for hire constituted an offer, which the plaintiff accepted when he took two of the chairs. The tickets amounted to no more than mere receipts with the result that the terms and conditions on them formed no part of the contract since they were handed out after the contract was concluded.

With regard to timetables and passenger tickets, however, the law is not at all certain. Tickets have been held to be contractual documents on the basis that the proffering of the ticket by a bus conductor or ticket office clerk is an offer which is accepted by the taking of the ticket, as suggested in *Cockerton* v *Naviera Aznar SA* [1960] 2 Lloyd's Rep 450. Another view is that a timetable amounts to an offer which is accepted by a passenger either by applying for a ticket or by boarding the bus. The latter problem was discussed in the case of *Wilkie* v *London Passenger Transport Board* [1947] 1 All ER 258. In the *Wilkie* case Lord Greene considered that on a bus a contract is made when the intending passenger 'puts himself either on the platform or inside the bus'. The implication here is that the company makes an offer of carriage by running the bus which the passenger accepts by boarding. The fact that a contract arises here despite the fact that no fare has been paid, nor ticket issued, renders the statement open to doubt. A better solution would surely be that the company makes an invitation to treat by virtue of its advertisement or sign on the front, the passenger making an offer when he gets on the bus, which is accepted by the conductor's taking his fare and issuing the ticket. The question then arises as to whether the ticket issued is a contractual document or a mere receipt, but no doubt this is one for the court to answer in the circumstances of a particular case.

The question of the status of tickets also arose in *Thornton* v *Shoe Lane Parking Ltd* [1971] 1 All ER 686, which concerned the issue of a ticket by an automatic issuing machine in a car-park. This case will be discussed more fully when exemption clauses are analysed later in the book, but in relation to offer and acceptance the case also has a contribution to make. Broadly speaking the facts are that the plaintiff went to park his car in the defendant's car-park. At the entrance there was a sign which set out the charges and which stated: 'all cars parked at customer's risk'. As customers drove in, a light changed from red to green and a ticket was ejected from the machine. Lord Denning discussed the transaction as follows:

The customer pays his money and gets a ticket. He cannot refuse it. He cannot get his money back. He may protest to the machine, even swear at it; but it will remain unmoved. He is committed beyond recall. He was committed at the very moment when he put his money in the machine; the contract was concluded at that time. It can be translated into offer and acceptance in this way. The offer is made when the proprietor of the machine holds out as being ready to receive the money. The acceptance takes place when the customer puts money in the slot. The terms of the offer are contained in the notice placed on or near the machine, stating what is offered for the money. He (the customer) is not bound by the terms printed on the ticket because the ticket comes too late. The contract had already been made.

The decision in the case is certainly a better solution to the status of tickets than Lord Greene's statement in the *Wilkie* case which would appear to be wrong.

Offers distinguished from requests for information

Very often, particularly in commercial transactions, substantial negotiations may take place before the terms of the contract are agreed by the parties concerned and the contract itself is entered into. During the period of negotiation one of the parties may simply require further information before he can place himself in the position of being able to enter the contract. Such a situation is very common where negotiations for the sale of land take place since there may be many questions of detail to be investigated before a formal contract can be entered into.

In *Harvey* v *Facey* [1893] AC 552, for example, where the appellants sent a telegram to the respondent which read, 'Will you sell us Bumper Hall Pen? Telegraph lowest cash price', the respondent replied, 'Lowest price for Bumper Hall Pen, £900'. The appellants then telegraphed, 'We agree to buy Bumper Hall Pen for £900 asked by you. Please send us your title deeds in order that we may get early possession'. The appellants received no reply and thereupon brought an action for specific performance. It was held that the action must fail since the respondent's reply was not an offer to sell but simply a statement as to the minimum price required should he decide to sell; his reply was a mere response to a request for information. The appellant's final telegram amounted to the offer to buy, which was not accepted by the respondent.

A similar case is that of *Clifton* v *Palumbo* [1944] 2 All ER 497, where the defendant was negotiating the purchase of a large estate owned by the plaintiff who wrote, 'I am prepared to offer you . . . my . . . estate for £600,000 . . . I also agree that a reasonable and sufficient time shall be granted to you for the examination and consideration of all the data and details necessary for the preparation of the Schedule of Completion'. It was held that, in the circumstances, this letter did not amount to an offer to sell but a mere preliminary statement as to price to enable negotiations to proceed.

So far the distinction between offers and requests for information is fairly straightforward, though one wonders if some of the earlier decisions can be considered correct. Would the decision in *Harvey* v *Facey*, for instance, be the same today? If A walks up to B and says, 'How much do you want for your car?' and B replies, '£3,500', is this not a contract? Surely the situation is likely to be that if B does not wish to sell he will reply, '£3,500, but it is not for sale' or simply, 'The car is not for sale'. The surrounding circumstances of the case will be important in this type of situation but on the face of things there would appear to be a binding contract today.

The courts in any event are not consistent or predictable in this type of case. In *Bigg* v *Boyd Gibbons Ltd* [1971] 2 All ER 183, negotiations were taking place for the sale of some freehold property belonging to the plaintiffs. The plaintiffs wrote to the defendants, stating: 'As you are aware that I paid £25,000 for this property, your offer of £20,000 would appear to be at least a little optimistic. For a quick sale I would accept £26,000 . . .'. The defendants replied: 'I accept your offer' and asked the plaintiffs to contact the defendants' solicitors. In their final letter the plaintiffs said: 'I am putting the matter in the hands of my solicitors . . . my wife and I are both pleased you are purchasing the property'. The plaintiffs alleged that this exchange of correspondence constituted an agreement for the sale of the property and sought specific performance. The Court of Appeal stated that an agreement on price did not necessarily mean an agreement for sale and purchase, nor did the use of the word 'offer' always amount to an offer in law; however, on the facts it was clear from the correspondence that the plaintiffs' first letter constituted an offer, the acceptance of which by the defendants constituted a binding contract. In this case the parties had gone so far down the road of negotiations that a binding agreement had resulted.

Communication of offers

Clearly an offer cannot take effect until it has been received by the offeree, since he cannot accept something of which he is not aware. The principle can be seen in the case of *Taylor* v *Laird* (1856) 1 H & N 266, 25 LJ Ex 329, where the plaintiff, the captain of a ship, was employed to command a steamer 'for an exploring and trading voyage up the river Niger . . . at a rate of £50 per month'. The plaintiff took this ship as far as Dagbo, but refused to go further and resigned his command. He later helped to work the ship home and he claimed his wages for this work. It was held that the owners of the vessel were entitled to refuse payment as the plaintiff's offer to help to bring the ship back to its home port was not communicated to them. In other words they were given no opportunity to either accept or reject his offer.

The timing of the communication of the offer can be of importance when determining the time within which it can be accepted by the offeree. From the above case it is clear that acceptance can only take place when the offer has been received; however, if the offer specifies some date by which the offer must be accepted and that date has passed when the offer is received, then the offeree is not able to accept the offer. Similarly, it may be that there has been a very long delay in the transmission of the offer to the offeree, and in these circumstances it may well be the case, depending on the subject matter of the offer, that the offer has in fact lapsed, rendering it incapable of acceptance.

One problem that arises in the latter context is what happens where the delay in the transmission of the offer is the fault of the offeror himself. In *Adams* v *Lindsell*

(1818) 1 B & Ald 681, the defendants offered to sell wool to the plaintiffs. Their letter of offer was wrongly addressed so that it reached the plaintiffs two days later than the defendants could, in normal circumstances, have expected it to arrive. The plaintiffs, on receiving the letter, immediately accepted the offer and it was held that they were entitled to do so, creating a binding contract, despite the fact that the defendants had considered that the offer had lapsed by the delay and sold the wool to a third party. It would seem from the case that the significant factor was the negligence of the defendants in addressing the letter and that if the delay had been caused by some other factor then it is possible that the decision could have been the reverse.

ACCEPTANCE

The definition of acceptance

Treitel (1991) defines acceptance as 'a final unqualified expression of assent to all the terms of an offer'. The objective test, which was examined above in regard to offers, applies in the same manner to acceptance. In other words, evidence must be produced from which the courts can adduce an intention by the offeree to accept the offer communicated to him. Two principles evolve from the definition of acceptance and the requirement of its objective existence. First, the expression of intention to assent to the offer must, as seen in *Taylor* v *Laird* above, be in response to the offer and match the terms of the offer precisely. The acceptance, therefore, must be unequivocal and unconditional. Secondly, where acknowledgement of the offer is insufficient, there must be a communication of the acceptance to the offeror.

These two factors can, however, lead to peculiar results in certain types of case, in particular where cross-offers materialise. The problem here occurs when two identical offers cross in the post, as, for example, where X offers to buy Y's car from him for £5,000, whilst at the same time Y offers to sell his car to X for £5,000. In such an instance no contract will be found to exist since, although the parties may undoubtedly be in subjective agreement, there must be an objective outward indication of the agreement, even if one could say there has been adequate communication of acceptance. In *Tinn* v *Hoffman and Co* (1873) 29 LT 271, Blackburn J stated:

> When a contract is made between two parties, there is a promise by one in consideration of the promise made by the other; there are two assenting minds, the parties agreeing in opinion and one having promised in consideration of the promise made by the other – there is an exchange of promises. But I do not think exchanging offers would, upon principle, be at all the same thing . . . The promise or offer made on each side in ignorance of the promise or offer made on the other side, neither of them can be construed as an acceptance of the other.

The American case of *Fitch* v *Snedaker* 38 NY 248 (1868) allegedly supports the judgment of Blackburn. Indeed in that case Woodruff J asked, 'How can there be consent or assent to that of which the party has never heard?' Further support is also alleged in *R* v *Clarke* (1927) 40 CLR 227, where a reward of £1,000 was offered 'for such information as shall lead to the arrest and conviction of' the murderers of two police officers. The offer also added that if the information was given by an accomplice, he, not being one of the murderers, should receive a free pardon. Clarke saw the offer and later gave the necessary information and claimed the reward. In attempting to enforce his claim he admitted that at the time he gave the information he acted to save himself and that the reward was not at the forefront of his mind. The High Court of Australia held that his claim must fail. Isaacs CJ stated that Clarke was in the same position as if he had never heard of the reward:

> An offer of £100 to any person who should swim a hundred yards in the harbour on the first day of the year would not in my opinion be satisfied by a person who was accidentally or maliciously thrown overboard on that date and swam the distance simply to save his life, without any thought of the offer.

Similarly Higgins J stated:

> Clarke had seen the offer, indeed, but it was not present to his mind – he had forgotten it and gave no consideration to it in his intense excitement as to his own danger. There cannot be assent without knowledge of the offer, and ignorance of the other is the same thing, whether it is due to never hearing of it or to forgetting it after the hearing.

Although these cases seem to support the decision of *Tinn* v *Hoffman*, Cheshire, Fifoot and Furmston (1991) believe that there are significant differences between the cases, pointing out that whilst the actions of the parties in *Tinn* v *Hoffman* are not 'in direct relation to that of the other and that the strict requirements of offer and acceptance are unsatisfied . . . each party does, in truth, contemplate legal relations upon an identical basis, and each is prepared to offer his own promise as consideration for the promise of the other'. Cheshire and Fifoot also refer to the need for a coincidence of acts and a unanimity of mind in the case; the problem, however, is that whilst there is communication in the form of the transmission of the offer there is, in truth, no communication that conveys the idea of unanimity between the parties, the result being an absence of agreement in both subjective and objective terms.

The requirements of the transmission of unanimity might seem unduly harsh on the facts of *Tinn* v *Hoffman*, though it should be borne in mind that no more than a small act of performance by one of the parties would have been enough to bring about acceptance by conduct. It should also be borne in mind that without such a requirement a large element of uncertainty and confusion would be introduced into the case. Thus in *Henkel* v *Pape* (1870) LR 6 Ex 7, the defendant had previously intimated that he would have liked to buy as many as 50 rifles from the plaintiff. He sent a telegram to place an order for three but the telegraph clerk made a mistake and the telegram read, 'Send . . . the rifles', whereupon the plaintiff sent 50. It was held that the plaintiff could not recover the price of the extra 47. The acceptance was valid in the form as sent, not in the form as received. Without the requirement of the transmission of unanimity, who is to say what this contract is for, 50 or three rifles? There is no contract in this case since the manifestations of each party's willingness to enter a contract are not conjoined. The same is also true in *Tinn* v *Hoffman*, even though the parties' intentions are similar.

The fact of acceptance

The mode of acceptance

Acceptance of the offer may be communicated either orally or in writing or inferred from conduct. Generally speaking the first two methods of accepting an offer present little difficulty; however, where one attempts to infer acceptance by conduct, difficulties arise as to the nature and precise moment of the inferred conduct. It has been held in *Weatherby* v *Banham* (1832) 5 C & P 228 that where an offeror offered to supply goods to the offeree by sending the goods to him, acceptance of the offer arose when the offeree began using the goods. Such a set of circumstances must, however, be treated guardedly today. First, under the Unsolicited Goods and Services Act 1971, if an offeror sends unsolicited goods to an individual in certain circumstances, as stipulated by the Act, that individual may treat those goods as a gift and is able to treat the goods as his own, without incurring contractual liability. Secondly, it was stated in *Taylor* v *Allon* [1966] 1 QB 304, in true objective principle terms, that acceptance inferred from conduct can only have this effect if the offeree performed the act in question with the intention of accepting the offer. In that case it was held that an offeree did not accept an offer by an insurance company to provide car insurance merely by taking the vehicle out on the road where there was evidence that the offeree intended to take out insurance with another company.

The main difficulty concerning inferring acceptance from conduct usually arises where there have been protracted negotiations between the parties or where the negotiations have been so tentative that it is difficult to find when or if an agreement has been reached between the parties.

Such a situation arose in the case of *Brogden* v *Metropolitan Railway Company* (1877) 2 App Cas 666 where Brogden had supplied the respondent railway company with coal for a number of years and then suggested that a formal contract should be entered into. A draft contract was submitted to Brogden who completed certain details on it, introduced a new term on it by adding the name of an arbitrator and then signed it, writing 'approved' at the end of the contract before returning it to the respondents. The company's agent put the contract in a drawer and nothing else was done to execute the contract. For some time afterwards coal was supplied and paid for on the basis of the draft agreement. Eventually a dispute arose and Brogden denied that any binding long-term contract on the basis of the written contract had come into existence. The difficulty facing the court was to determine when, if ever, any mutual assent could be found. Because Brogden had introduced a new term into the contract his signature and return of the agreement could not amount to acceptance since, as we shall see later, qualified acceptance is no acceptance. The return of the contract could, however, amount to an offer on Brogden's part to supply coal, but where was the acceptance of this offer? Clearly the putting of the document into a drawer could not amount to acceptance by conduct, so where did the contract arise? In fact a court has considerable power to resolve uncertainties and in this case the court decided to exercise this discretion. To find that there was no contract would clearly be wrong since the parties had contracted on the basis of the agreement for a number of years and it was this conduct, which was explicable only on the basis of a mutual acceptance of the terms of the approved contract, that the court relied on. Subsequently the House of Lords held that a contract came into existence either when the company ordered its first load of coal upon the terms of the approved contract or at least when Brogden first supplied the coal on those terms.

One final point must be made in relation to acceptance by conduct and that is that it is found most commonly in unilateral contracts. It has already been seen in *Carlill* v *Carbolic Smoke Ball Co* that Mrs Carlill accepted the company's offer merely by buying and using the smoke balls in the prescribed manner and subsequently catching influenza. Usually there will be some sort of communication of the fact that acceptance has been performed in order, as in Mrs Carlill's case, to claim the reward, but this is only notification of the fact that acceptance has taken place. It does not amount to acceptance itself. The act of acceptance must be completely performed for it to be valid. For instance in Mrs Carlill's case the mere using of the smoke balls would not be enough – she had to use them in the prescribed manner and catch influenza. This requirement of complete performance was emphasised in *Daulia* v *Four Millbank Nominees Ltd* [1978] 2 All ER 557 by Goff LJ, who stated:

> I think the true view of a unilateral contract must in general be that the offeror is entitled to require full performance of the condition he has imposed and short of that he is not bound . . .

A related point is that very often an offer may prescribe a particular mode of acceptance; in such a case conduct cannot amount to acceptance until the mode stipulated is complied with, as stated in *Wettern Electric Ltd* v *Welsh Development Agency* [1983] 2 All ER 629, unless the offeror acquiesces in allowing the conduct to amount to acceptance.

Counter-offers

It has already been stated when defining acceptance that there must be an unqualified expression of assent. It follows that any attempt to introduce a new term amounts not to an acceptance of an offer, but in fact itself becomes a counter-offer. Such a result is manifestly fair since otherwise the offeror would be bound by a new term which he would not have had the opportunity to peruse and consider. The effect of a counter-offer is to destroy the original offer, that is, it operates as a rejection of the original offer. In *Hyde* v *Wrench* (1840) 3 Beav 334, the defendant offered to sell his farm for £1,000. The plaintiff at first made a counter-offer of £950, but two days later agreed to pay £1,000 and attempted to accept the original offer. The defendant refused to complete the sale and the plaintiff brought an action against him for a decree of specific performance. It was held that no contract existed since by his letter offering £950 the plaintiff had made a counter-offer, the effect of which was to reject and destroy the original offer, so that the latter was therefore not available for him to accept two days later.

Some care needs to be taken when discussing this whole area of counter-offers since the fact that acceptance needs to be unqualified does not by the same token mean that it needs to be precise. Very often communications take place which present themselves as counter-offers in that there appears to be a qualified acceptance when in fact there is nothing of the sort. Examples of such communications are as follows.

(a) Conditional acceptances. On the face of things this may seem to be an exercise in pedantry but in fact the law makes a distinction between a conditional acceptance and a qualified acceptance. A conditional acceptance is neither a full acceptance of the original offer nor a counter-offer. Very often before an individual enters into a contract he might wish to consult a third party for advice as to the nature of the contract or the wisdom of entering into a particular contract. Further, in some contracts there are many other ancillary matters to be arranged before an individual feels able to comply with the requirements of the contract. Such a situation commonly occurs in the purchase of a house, which is essentially a contract to purchase land. In this type of contract there are many factors to be considered by a purchaser before he can commit himself to a formal contract, such as obtaining a surveyor's report on the property, obtaining a mortgage, making land registry or land charges searches, and so on. The result of these circumstances is that any agreement is usually arrived at 'subject to contract'.

The term 'subject to contract' now has a precise legal significance in that it raises a presumption that the parties do not intend to enter a legally binding contract. It is an expression of future intention to enter into a contract providing the offeree is satisfied as to any factors that may be of concern to him. It renders the entering of a formal contract, usually written, a condition precedent to a legally binding agreement. The words, however, do not invariably have this effect and in *Alpenstow Ltd* v *Regalian Properties plc* [1985] 2 All ER 545, the courts found for a legally binding contract despite the use of the expression, though it should be stated that this was an exceptional case.

From time to time attempts are made to adopt other language to indicate that any agreement is merely tentative and not meant to be final. The task facing the court here is to attempt to interpret the intention of the parties from their negotiations, correspondence and other surrounding circumstances of the case. It may be that the court will find that there is no condition precedent intended and that any further document is merely needed to formalise an already legally binding contract. In *Branca* v *Cobarro* [1947] KB 854, a vendor agreed to sell the lease and goodwill of his mushroom farm. The parties signed a document which contained the terms of their agreement. The document concluded, 'This is a provisional agreement until a fully legalised agreement drawn up by a solicitor and embodying all the conditions herewith stated is signed'. The purchaser sued for the return of his deposit and the vendor contended that their agreement was a binding contract despite the use of the expression 'provisional'. The court held that there was an immediately binding contract 'until' the document was replaced by one couched in more precise and formal language. The court commented that the decision would probably have been different if the parties had used the expression 'tentative' rather than 'provisional', though each case had to be decided on its own facts. This latter point can be seen in the earlier case of *Chillingworth* v *Esche* [1924] 1 Ch 97, where the plaintiffs agreed to purchase the defendant's nursery for £4,800 'subject to a proper contract to be prepared by the vendor's solicitors'. The purchasers then refused to sign a contract prepared by the solicitors and executed by the vendor and failed to complete the transaction. It was held in this case that consent was conditional upon a 'proper contract' being signed and the plaintiffs could therefore recover their deposit.

In commercial contracts the instinct of a judge is to find that the document indicates an intention to be bound, especially where trade usage forms the background to the transaction. In *Hillas & Co Ltd* v *Arcos Ltd* (1932) 38 Com Cas 23, there was an agreement in writing for the supply of wood during 1930, together with an option to buy more wood the following year. The option clause did not specify the kind or size of timber required, nor the ports to which it had to be shipped or indeed the manner of shipment. The suppliers argued that the option clause was not binding and the fact of the absent factors was evidence that it was only to provide a basis for future negotiation and agreement. It was held that as the 1930 agreement had been expressed in a similar way and had been complied with, the option thus showed a sufficient intention to be bound and could create a binding obligation. With regard to the omissions the court held that these could be resolved by reference to the previous dealings between the parties and the trade usage of the timber trade.

The courts will not find for a binding contract if the agreement between the parties is too speculative, usually requiring some sort of previous course of dealings between the parties or some common business practice or usage before exercising discretion. Since the first instinct of the court is to exercise this discretion in commercial transactions it follows that the courts will often allow retrospective acceptance to legitimise past informal arrangements between the parties as illustrated in *Trollope and Colls Ltd* v *Atomic Power Constructions Ltd* [1962] 3 All ER 1035 and restated by Steyn LJ in *G Percy Trentham Ltd* v *Archital Luxfer* [1993] 1 Lloyds Rep 25. The approach of the courts is summed up by Lord Tomlin in *Hillas* v *Arcos* where he stated:

> The problem for a court of construction must always be so to balance matters that without the violation of essential principle, the dealings of men may as far as possible be treated as effective, and that the law may not incur the reproach of being the destroyer of bargains.

(b) Clarifying the terms of the offer. Just as the courts have difficulty in construing a particular contract, businessmen in lengthy or complex contracts often have similar problems when attempting to arrive at a finite and settled agreement. For this reason there may be many communications between the parties which are not intended to operate as counter-offers but merely as attempts to clarify the extent and terms of the offer, or to ascertain whether the offeror would consider changing certain aspects of the offer. The courts view such correspondence as mere requests for information which do not operate as a counter-offer to destroy the original one.

A typical such case is that of *Stevenson, Jacques & Co v McLean* (1880) 5 QBD 346, where the defendant offered to sell iron to the plaintiffs at 40s. per ton. The plaintiffs sent a telegram to the defendant, 'Please wire whether you would accept forty for delivery over two months, or if not, the longest limit you could give'. Later that day a further telegram was sent to the defendant by which the plaintiffs accepted the original offer. The defendant maintained in the action brought by the plaintiffs for breach of contract, that the first telegram amounted to a counter-offer which destroyed the original offer so that it subsequently became incapable of acceptance. It was held that the first telegram was a mere request for information not a counter-offer. There was no attempt here to introduce new terms into the contract as in *Hyde v Wrench*, but a genuine enquiry by the plaintiffs to see if the defendant would be willing to modify his terms.

A further refinement of this problem can occur where a person in accepting the offer makes reference to some other term. Ostensibly this would amount to a counter-offer. However, if this term would be implied into the contract in any event by operation of law, there would be a valid acceptance of the offer. Similarly Treitel indicates that where the acceptance 'adds new provision by way of indulgence to the offeror', then the acceptance will still be valid. In other words the acceptance should still be valid provided any new term introduced is by way of benefit or concession to the offeror. He further indicates that should the offeree attempt to introduce a new term, which is not by way of concession to the offeror in his acceptance, that acceptance would still be valid if the offeree makes it clear that he will accept the offer even if the new term is rejected. This proposal was rejected in *Global Tankers Inc v Amercoat Europa NV* [1975] 1 Lloyd's Rep 666, and indeed it is difficult to envisage the courts enabling the offeree to accept an offer once a counter-offer had been made. Clearly on a classical analysis the introduction of the new term must invariably destroy the original offer. In *Global Tankers* it was suggested that the test as to whether an offeree is replying with a counter-offer or not is whether a reasonable person would regard the 'acceptance' as 'introducing a new term into the bargain and not as a clear acceptance of the offer'. The question is then reduced to one of the chicken or the egg – which comes first, the counter-offer or the acceptance?

(c) The 'battle of the forms'. It has already been stated that one of the hallmarks of the modern environment of the law of contract is the use made of the standard form of contract. Most companies adopt such forms since it is clearly more efficient and convenient than to have to discuss and negotiate each contract with a customer on an individual basis, quite apart from the administrative nightmare created by having hundreds, possibly thousands, of individual contracts to supervise. It is not surprising therefore that in the offer, acceptance and counter-offer situation conflicts are likely to result when companies attempt to impose on the other party their own standard conditions of contract. This scenario arises when company X offers to, say, sell certain goods to company Y on company X's standard terms and conditions. Company Y replies, accepting company X's offer, but on company Y's terms and conditions – which could be materially different from company X's. The conflict now arises as to whose terms and conditions the contract is based on.

If the conflict is to be resolved by reference to the classical theory then it is clear, as Megaw J stated in *Trollope & Colls Ltd* v *Atomic Power Construction Ltd*, that 'the counter offer kills the original offer'. This being the case, the person who wins the 'battle of the forms' is the person who last submits the counter-offer which is accepted by the other party. This principle is sometimes referred to as the 'last shot' principle.

The classic modern case illustrating this conflict is that of *Butler Machine Tool Co Ltd* v *Ex-Cell-O Corporation (England) Ltd* [1979] 1 All ER 965. The facts of the case were that on 23 May 1969, in response to an enquiry by the buyers, the sellers made a quotation offering to sell a machine tool to the buyers for £75,535, delivery to be made in 10 months' time. The terms and conditions given in the quotation contained a price variation clause. The terms and conditions were also stated to 'prevail over any terms and conditions in the buyer's order'. On 27 May the buyers replied by placing an order for the machine. This order was subject to terms and conditions that were materially different from those of the sellers, and in particular there was no price variation clause. At the end of the buyer's order there was a tear-off acknowledgement of the receipt of the order stating, 'We accept your order on the terms and conditions stated thereon'. On 5 June the sellers completed and signed the acknowledgement and returned it to the buyers with a letter stating that the buyers' order was entered into in accordance with the sellers' quotation of 23 May. On delivering the machine the sellers claimed the price had increased by £2,892. The buyers refused to pay and the sellers brought an action for the increase based on the price variation clause. It was held that the buyers' communication of 27 May was a counter-offer which was accepted by the sellers' returning the tear-off acknowledgement slip. The contract being thus made on the buyers' terms and conditions meant that the buyers were not subject to the price variation clause and were consequently not liable to pay the extra £2,892. The letter accompanying the acknowledgement slip, though the 'last shot' in the series, did not prevail because the reference in it to the sellers' original offer was not made with the intention of reiterating the terms and conditions contained in the original quotation/offer, but to identify the subject matter of the contract only.

The decision is clearly correct when analysed on the lines of the classical approach, given the interpretation of the letter accompanying the acknowledgement slip returned by the sellers. At first instance, though, the judge thought the additional monies were recoverable because of the emphatic statement in the quotation of 23 May that the sellers' terms and conditions were to prevail. In the Court of Appeal the majority of the judges decided the case on classical lines though Lord Denning expressed sympathy for the views of the judge at first instance. He considered the classic view of offer, counter-offer, rejection and acceptance and so on to be out of date in the high-pressure commercial life of the twentieth century, reiterating Lord Wilberforce's view in *New Zealand Shipping Co Ltd* v *A. M. Satterthwaite*, which we have already considered. Denning thought the better approach was to examine all the documents passing between the parties and glean from them and the conduct of the parties whether agreement exists on the material terms. He thought that very often the end result may be no different, the man who fires the last shot being the winner. He puts forward his terms and conditions which are not objected to by the other, who is thus regarded as having agreed to those terms and conditions. Denning went further, however, and considered that in appropriate cases different approaches may be justified. He stated:

> In some cases, however, the battle is won by the man who gets the blow in first. If he offers to sell at a named price on the terms and conditions stated on the back and the buyer orders the goods purporting to accept the offer on an order form with his own different terms and conditions on the back, then, if the difference is so material that it would affect the price, the buyer ought not to be allowed to take advantage of the difference unless he draws it specifically to the attention of the seller. There are yet other cases where the battle depends on the shots fired on both sides. There is a concluded contract but the forms vary. The terms and conditions of both parties are to be construed together. If they can be reconciled so as to give a harmonious result, all well and good. If differences are irreconcilable, so that they are mutually contradictory, then the conflicting terms may have to be scrapped and replaced by a reasonable implication.

Denning's approach can clearly be seen to be a subjective one which attempts to find for a consensus between the parties. We have already seen that such a view is not adopted today, the law preferring an objective approach. For this reason the other judges in the Court of Appeal, Lawton and Bridge LJJ, decided the case on classical objective lines. Where does the above situation leave the modern businessman? Clearly, in order to avoid losing the 'battle of the forms', it is essential that if he is to take part in a contract based on his own conditions he must ensure that he is the one who fires the last shot. Even here he cannot ensure that he will be the winner because of the possibility of a counter-offer coming from the other party. The only real certainty that can be achieved is a stalemate and this is not a satisfactory state of affairs since it might be the case that the court will find that there is no contract at all in such a situation! For this reason this approach was rejected in both *Johnson Matthey Bankers Ltd* v *State Trading Corporation of India* [1984] 1 Lloyd's Rep 427 and *Interfoto Picture Library Ltd* v *Stilletto Visual Programmes Ltd* [1988] 1 All ER 348. While such a solution may be possible where the contract is purely executory with no or only a limited performance having taken place, it is neither desirable nor convenient in executed contracts where, as in the *Butler* case, an expensive custom-made machine has been produced and delivered. The idea of restitution here, that is, a handing back of what has been received by both sides, is clearly nonsensical. In such a case a contract will be found to exist and the courts would then attempt to impose terms and conditions on the parties. This may not be a particularly elegant way for the courts to resolve the problem, but it fulfils an exigency. Such an approach was adopted in the case of *British Steel Corporation* v *Cleveland Bridge and Engineering Co Ltd* [1984] 1 All ER 504. One should also take into account the approach taken by Steyn LJ in *G Percy Trentham Ltd* v *Archital Luxfer* [1993] 1 Lloyds Rep 25, as examined earlier.

Another method that can be used to attempt to avoid the battle of the forms scenario is for a party to a contract to steadfastly maintain his bargaining proposals come what may. The effect of this can be seen in the case of *Nissan UK Ltd* v *Nissan Motor Manufacturing (UK) Ltd* (1994) *The Independent*, 26 October, where the Court of Appeal stated that if one of two contracting parties to-ing and fro-ing with offers and counter-offers has maintained a proposal to the last, and has received no comeback from the other party, it could naturally be inferred that any subsequent conduct by that other party that was referable to the existence of some contract between the parties denoted the acceptance of the proposal.

The communication of acceptance

The general rule

A further aspect of our analysis of the definition of acceptance is concerned with the communication of acceptance. The general rule here, as restated in *Holwell Securities Ltd* v *Hughes* [1974] 1 WLR 155, is that some objective or external manifestation of acceptance must be communicated to the offeror. The principle is also well illustrated in the case of *Powell* v *Lee* (1908) 99 LT 284, where the defendant decided to appoint the plaintiff as headmaster of a school. The terms of the appointment were never communicated to the plaintiff. It was held that there was no contract since the defendant's acceptance of the plaintiff's offer of service had not been communicated to him.

The need for communication of acceptance has raised several problems in this area of the law, to the extent that one really wonders why English law insists on such a requirement. One does not have to go very far to find compelling reasons for its need. First, substantial hardship would result for the offeror if he were to be held to be bound by the terms of his offer without first knowing that his offer had been accepted. It should be noted that communication of acceptance to the offeror's agent would be sufficient, provided that the agent has the authority to receive the acceptance, even though the offeror was unaware of that communication. On the other hand communication, whether to the offeror directly or to his authorised agent, will not be effective if it was made by an agent of the offeree who had no authority to communicate such acceptance, this being expressed in the case of *Powell* v *Lee* above. Secondly, as a simple matter of practical expediency, some outward sign of acceptance has to be present in order for it to be possible to decide whether a contract exists or not. Since this outward sign, of necessity, has to be measured in objective terms, it is easier to prove such existence by requiring the assent of the offeree to be communicated to the offeror.

It should be noted that acceptance has to be not only communicated to but also received by the offeror. In *Entores* v *Miles Far East Corporation* [1955] 2 QB 327, Lord Denning illustrated this principle by describing a situation where A shouts an offer to B across a river and A does not hear the reply because of the noise of an aircraft flying overhead. In such a situation there is no contract. A similar state of affairs could also exist if a person's reply was so indistinct that the offeror could not hear or understand what was being stated. This position does have to be qualified however since, if the acceptance would have been communicated and received by the offeror but this has not occurred because of the conduct of the offeror, then he will be precluded from denying that he received the acceptance. In the *Entores* case, which will be examined in more detail later, Lord Denning explained the rule by stating that an offeror cannot deny receipt of the acceptance if 'it is his own fault that he did not get it', for example, 'if the listener on the telephone does not catch the words of acceptance but nevertheless does not . . . ask for them to be repeated'. Presumably the same principle applies if a message of acceptance is sent by telex but this is unread by the offeror, although Lord Cairns in *The Brimnes* [1975] QB 929 denied this. So far the general rule is fairly straightforward, but unfortunately such rules are rarely so simple and this aspect of acceptance is no exception to that principle.

The exceptions to the general rule

(a) The effect of silence. Is it possible to impose contractual liability on an individual, within the terms of the offer, by not requiring him to communicate his acceptance before becoming a party to the contract? On the basis of the general rule the answer to this question must be in the negative. Such a conclusion can be seen in the case of *Felthouse* v *Bindley* (1862) 11 CBNS 869.

The case is rather unusual since it was based not on an action in contract but on an action in tort. The facts of the case were that the defendant was an auctioneer who had been instructed to sell the farming stock of John Felthouse. John's uncle was interested in one of the horses that was being sold and some negotiation took place between the parties. During the course of the negotiations a misunderstanding arose as to the price of the horse, namely whether it was for sale for £30 or 30 guineas. The uncle then wrote to John offering to split the difference and concluded: 'If I hear no more about him, I consider the horse mine at £30 15s.'. John did not reply but instructed the defendant to withdraw the horse from the auction. By mistake the horse was put up for sale and sold. The uncle began an action against the defendant for the tort of conversion and failed. The court held that the uncle had no property in the horse and as the silence of his nephew could not amount to acceptance of the uncle's offer. As Cheshire, Fifoot and Furmston (1991) state at p.48:

> Silence is usually equivocal as to consent and the uncle's letter did not render the nephew's failure to reply unequivocal since failure to reply to letters is a common human weakness.

Such a view found more recent support in *Allied Marine Transport Ltd* v *Vale Do Rio Doce Navegacao SA, The Leonidas D* [1985] 2 All ER 796 where, in the Court of Appeal, Goff LJ stated:

> In the absence of special circumstances, silence and inaction by a party to a reference [to arbitration] are, objectively considered, just as consistent with his having inadvertently forgotten about the matter; or with his simply hoping that the matter will die a natural death. . . . If so, there should, on ordinary principles, be no basis for the inference of an offer. Exactly the same comment can be made of silence and inaction of the other party, for the same reasons, there appears to be no basis for drawing the inference of an acceptance in response to the supposed offer, still less of the communication of that acceptance of the offeror . . . it is difficult to imagine how silence and inaction can be anything but equivocal.

It is an over-simplification to say that silence can never amount to acceptance since, as Goff LJ indicates, there may well be 'special circumstances' that will render silence as constituting acceptance of the offer. Treitel also discusses certain exceptions to the rule, arguing that:

> if an offer has been solicited by the offeree, the argument that he should not be put to the trouble of rejecting it loses much of its force, especially if the offer is made on a form provided by the offeree and that form stipulates that silence may amount to acceptance.

Further he states that a previous course of dealing between the offeror and offeree might also give rise to acceptance by way of silence. An example of the operation of such a course of dealing may be seen in the American case of *Ammons* v *Wilson* 176 Miss 645 (1936) where the offeror regularly ordered certain goods from the offeree. His order was usually given to the offeree's representative who would transmit the order to his head office, at the same time giving the offeror a booking. A dispute arose when the offeror was given a booking but not told until some 12 months later that the offeree had not accepted his order. The court held that a contract had been created since, given the previous course of dealing, it was reasonable that the offeree should notify the offeror if he did not intend to accept.

Whilst English courts might be willing to adopt such a stance it would be essential for there to be a previous course of dealing present since any attempt to render an offeror liable for a contract for goods or services which are not requested by him amounts to a criminal offence under the Unsolicited Goods and Services Act 1971, and indeed, such goods or services can be enjoyed as an outright gift provided the provisions of the Act are complied with.

Although an offeror cannot impose liability on an offeree by not requiring him to communicate his acceptance, subject to the exceptions discussed, it is possible for the offeror to waive the need for acceptance so that he runs the risk of having contractual liability thrust upon himself. This waiver of the need to communicate acceptance may be express or implied from the circumstances of the case. Such a situation occurs in the case of unilateral contracts. Thus in *Carlill* v *Carbolic Smoke Ball Co* there was no need for Mrs Carlill actively to communicate her acceptance of the company's offer. The company assumed such liability by Mrs Carlill's purchasing the smoke balls, using them in the prescribed manner and subsequently catching influenza. The company had impliedly waived the need for communication of acceptance. Similarly if one offers £100 to anyone who finds a certain lost dog, everyone who reads the advertisement does not have to write to the owner and accept the offer. The owner has impliedly waived the need for such communication and anyone who finds and returns the dog is regarded as having accepted the offer, imposing a contractual obligation on the owner, whether or not acceptance has been communicated.

(b) The postal rule. The rule that acceptance must be communicated to the offeror is overturned when acceptance is sent via the post since here the rule is that acceptance takes place as soon as the letter is validly posted.

In *Adams* v *Lindsell* (1818) 1 B and Ald 681, the defendants wrote to the plaintiffs on 2 September offering to sell them some wool on certain terms and requested a reply 'in course of post'. The letter containing the offer was wrongly addressed and only received on 5

September. As a result the letter of acceptance was received on 9 September, two days later than it should have been reasonably expected by the defendants. On the day before the letter of acceptance was received the defendants sold the wool to a third person, no reply having been received from the plaintiffs. The question which arose was whether a contract of sale had been entered into before 8 September when the wool was sold to the third party. Clearly if the acceptance was only effective when it arrived at the address or, at the latest, when it was brought to the attention of the defendant, then no contract would have been entered into, revocation of the offer being effected at that time by the later sale to the third party. The court held, however, that the offer had been accepted as soon as the letter of acceptance had been posted. The contract was thus in existence before the sale of the wool to the third party even though the letter of acceptance had not been received by the defendant, who was thus liable for breach of contract.

Adams v *Lindsell* was one of the earliest cases in this area of the law but any doubts as to its correctness or not were dispelled in *Household Fire and Carriage Accident Insurance Co* v *Grant* (1879) 4 Ex D 216 where the defendant applied for shares in the plaintiff's company. The shares were allotted to him but the letter of allotment was never received. The company then went into liquidation and the liquidator claimed the balance of the purchase monies from him. The defendant disputed the fact that he was a shareholder on the basis that he had not received an acceptance, in the form of the letter of allotment, to his offer to purchase the shares. It was held that the contract had been entered when the letter of allotment had been posted to him despite the fact that it had never arrived.

Today it has become firmly established in *Brinkibon Ltd* v *Stahag Stahl und Stahlwarenhandelsgesellschaft mbH* [1983] 2 AC 34 that acceptance is effective when it is placed in the control of the Post Office, that is, put into a post-box, or handed to an officer of the post authorised to receive or collect letters. A postman delivering letters is not so authorised and the handing of a letter of acceptance to such an individual would only take effect when actually communicated to the offeror, as stated in *Re London and Northern Bank* [1900] 1 Ch 220. One conclusion that may be drawn from the above is that the letter must go into the post-box to be effective and if one arrives at the post-box just as it is being emptied it would not be a valid posting to place the letter directly into the postman's bag – he is not authorised to receive mail in this way. The letter must go into the box to be valid, even if this means that the postman simply has the door open and catches it as it falls in and places it in his bag! It also seems that the rules as regards letters apply equally to a telegram, the acceptance being valid as soon as its wording is communicated to a person authorised to receive it for transmission to the offeror. Treitel also suggests that the same rules apply to telemessages since there is nothing to doubt why these should be treated any differently.

Both Treitel (1987) and Cheshire, Fifoot and Furmston (1991) put forward theories to justify the existence of the rule but do not fully and conclusively provide an answer. One theory is that the rule prevents an offeree from accepting by post and then nullifying his acceptance by communicating his rejection of the offer by a quicker means of communication, such as telex, thereby preventing the letter of acceptance from being effective on receipt by the offeror. Another theory is that without the rule an offeree would not be able to know for certain whether he had actually entered into a contract or not. The truth of the matter is that the rule is one of expedience since whatever approach is adopted one of the parties is bound to suffer hardship. The law, by taking a particular stance, is merely providing for certainty, though in *Holwell Securities Ltd v Hughes* it was stated that the rule would have no application if this would result in 'manifest inconvenience and absurdity'.

One theory often promoted as a reason for the existence of the postal rule is that if the offeror, either expressly or impliedly, indicates that postal acceptance is sufficient then he should bear the consequences of the postal rule. This proposition leads us on to a discussion of whether it is possible for the offeror to circumvent the operation of the rule.

In *Henthorn v Fraser* [1892] 2 Ch 27 it was stated that the postal rule only applies where it was reasonable for the offeree to use the post as a means of communication. Indeed, in the case of *Quenerduaine v Cole* (1883) 32 WR 185, the view was taken that an offer by way of telegram was an indication that an equally expedient mode of acceptance was required, so that acceptance by post was held not to be valid. In these cases the required mode of acceptance was inferred from the prevailing circumstances of the offer but, in the earlier case of *Household Fire and Carriage Accident Insurance Co Ltd v Grant* Bramwell LJ considered that the postal rule could be avoided by the prudent offeror saying, 'Your answer by post is only to bind if it reaches me'. The position has been supported in modern times by *Holwell Securities Ltd v Hughes* where there was an option said to be exercisable only by 'notice in writing'. It was held that these words were sufficient to negate the effects of the postal rule, so that a letter of acceptance posted but not received by the offeror was insufficient to form a contract.

From the latter cases it is clear that the offeror may also prevent the operation of the postal rule by expressly prescribing a particular mode of communication. The leading case in this area is *Manchester Diocesan Council for Education v Commercial and General Investments Ltd* [1969] 3 All ER 159, where Buckley J stated:

> An offeror may by the terms of his offer indicate that it may be accepted in a particular manner . . . an offeror, who by the terms of his offer insists on acceptance in a particular way is entitled to insist that he is not bound unless acceptance is effected or communicated in that precise way, although it seems probable that, even so, if the other party communicates his acceptance in some other way, the offeror may, by conduct or otherwise, waive his right to insist on the prescribed method of acceptance. Where, however, the offeror has prescribed a particular method of acceptance, but not in terms insisting that only acceptance in that mode shall be binding, I am of opinion that acceptance communicated to the offeror by any other mode which is no less advantageous to him will conclude the contract . . . . If an offeror intends that he shall be bound only if his offer is accepted in some particular manner, it must be for him to make this clear.

The position then is that if the offeror requires acceptance by a particular mode and stipulates that only that mode will be sufficient, the offeree must comply with that stipulation, though the offeror can waive his requirement if he so wishes. Where, however, the offeror merely asks for acceptance by a particular mode, an acceptance by the offeree will be sufficient even if it is by a different mode, provided that mode is more expeditious than (or equally as expeditious as) the method requested by the offeror. The latter position occurred in *Tinn* v *Hoffman and Co* (1873) 29 LT 271 where the offeree was asked 'to reply by return of post' and the court held that an equally expeditious method would suffice.

(c) Instantaneous forms of communication. The postal rule as an exception to the general principle requiring communication is confined to communications through the post, telegrams and probably also telemessages. Modern technology however provides other methods of communication which are instantaneous in their operation to the extent that the parties are, as it were, in each other's presence. Such was the reasoning in *Entores* v *Miles Far East Corporation* [1955] 2 QB 327.

Here the plaintiffs were a company based in London who were dealing with the defendants, an American company, with agents in Amsterdam. Both parties possessed telex equipment. The plaintiffs offered to buy goods from the defendants' agents using the equipment. The agents accepted the offer also by telex. Subsequently a dispute arose between the parties and the plaintiffs wished to serve a writ on the defendants alleging breach of contract. This was only possible if the contract had in fact been made in England and it was this question that arose before the court. The Court of Appeal held that the parties were in the same position as they would have been if they had been in each other's presence. The consequence of this was that the contract was entered into when the acceptance by the agents was received in London by the plaintiffs, not when the telex was sent in Amsterdam, which would have meant that the contract would be subject to Dutch law. Lord Denning confirmed, *obiter*, that the same principles also apply to acceptances by telephone.

The decision in the *Entores* case was confirmed in *Brinkibon Ltd* v *Stahag Stahl . . . mbH* where the facts were very similar except that the offer was made by telex in Vienna and accepted by telex sent in London. It was held that the contract was made in Vienna. In the two cases both the telex messages were sent during ordinary office hours but what would happen if the acceptance had been sent out of office hours? Would the acceptance take place when received at the offeror's office or when it was read the next morning or the next time the office was open? Similarly if the acceptance had been sent by telephone and recorded on an answering machine, would the acceptance take place when received or when the recording was next played back? What would happen if the recording was accidentally erased?

In *The Brimnes* case the Court of Appeal held that a notice of withdrawal that had been sent during office hours, but not seen by the office staff until the next Monday, was effective when received. One factor that may have influenced the decision here was a possibility of negligence on the part of the office staff. Such a solution may be appropriate where the erasing of a message on the telephone-answering machine could be regarded as a negligent act of the offeror or his agents/servants. The problems in such circumstances were discussed by Lord Wilberforce in the *Brinkibon* case, where he stated:

> Since 1955 the use of telex communications has been greatly expanded, and there are many variants on it. The senders and recipients may not be the principals to the contemplated contract. They may be servants or agents with limited authority. The

message may not reach, or be intended to reach, the designated recipient immediately: messages may be sent out of office hours, or at night, with the intention, or on the assumption, that they will be read at a later time. There may be some error or fault at the recipient's end which prevents receipt at the time contemplated and believed in by the sender. The message may have been sent and/or received through machines operated by third persons. And many other variations may occur. No universal rule can cover all such cases; they must be resolved by reference to the intentions of the parties, by sound business practice and in some cases by a judgment where the risks should lie.

In this electronic age of instantaneous communications, whether one talks of telephones, telexes, electronic mailing systems or facsimile and telephone-answering machines, it is regrettable that Lord Wilberforce did not address the problem of when acceptance is effective more precisely. The result is that at the present time the law in this area is in a state of uncertainty.

THE TERMINATION OF OFFERS

So far it has been seen that, for a legally binding agreement to arise, an unconditional acceptance must be communicated and there must be the intention of being legally bound. It follows, therefore, that if the offer has ceased to exist there can be no such acceptance. In this section relating to the fact of the agreement we examine the ways in which an offer ceases to exist. It should also be borne in mind that, apart from the methods examined here, acceptance of an offer also terminates the offer, though to some extent this depends on the nature of the offer. Clearly, however, if A offers his car for sale to members of his office and B accepts that offer, no other member of the office can accept the offer.

An offer ceases to exist in the following circumstances:

Revocation

Bilateral contracts

In *Payne* v *Cave* (1789) 3 Term Rep 148, it was first established that it is possible to revoke an offer at any time before the offer is accepted since no legal obligation exists until this event occurs. Any attempt to revoke an offer after acceptance must of necessity be a prima facie breach of contract. Furthermore, there is no obligation on an offeror to keep his offer open for or until a specified date or time. Thus in *Routledge* v *Grant* (1828) 4 Bing 653, it was held that where a defendant made an offer to purchase the plaintiff's house and gave him six weeks to accept the offer, he was free to revoke and withdraw his offer before the six weeks had passed. The only way the plaintiff could have held the defendant to his promise is if he had actually purchased an option, whereby the defendant would be bound by a separate, binding contract to keep his offer open for the stipulated period. Any attempt to revoke within the period in this instance would give rise to an action for breach of the option contract.

In order for the revocation to be effective notice of the withdrawal of the offer must be communicated to the offeree. It should be noted here that the postal rule as seen in the context of acceptance has no application here.

In *Byrne v Van Tienhoven* (1880) 5 CPD 344, the defendants posted a letter in Cardiff on 1 October offering to sell a quantity of tinplate to the plaintiffs in New York. The offer was received by the plaintiffs on 11 October, and they immediately accepted it by telegram and confirmed their acceptance by a letter posted on 15 October. On 8 October the defendants had posted a letter withdrawing their offer but this was not received by the plaintiffs until 20 October. It was held that a contract had come into existence when the telegram was sent on 11 October and that the letter of revocation sent on 8 October had no effect on the validity of the contract since it was only effective when received on 20 October, after a legally binding contract had already come into existence.

This rule relating to communication of revocation clearly flies in the face of the earlier thinking of judges since here a contract has come into existence when the parties are patently not in agreement. The rule, nevertheless, is correct, as otherwise no one would be able to rely on any offer since it might have been revoked before it had been received by the offeree, a result which would undoubtedly lead to inconvenience and uncertainty.

There are two principal exceptions to the rule that revocation must be communicated to the offeree. First, the rule may be overturned where the revocation would have been received by the offeree but for his being negligent in some way, as, for example, by the offeree failing to inform the offeror of a change of address. This exception also raises the spectre of when communication takes place, that is, when received or when actually read by the offeree. It would be a nonsense for the offeree, for instance, knowing that a letter might contain a revocation to ignore opening that letter and reading it until he had actually sent his letter accepting the offer. The logic contained in *The Brimnes*, as already discussed, is clearly appropriate here in that communication of the revocation would be deemed to have taken place when the letter was opened in the ordinary course of business or would have been so opened and read if the normal course of business had been followed.

A second exception occurs where an offer has been made to the general public. For example, if an offer had been placed in a newspaper it would be clearly impossible to communicate the revocation to every person who had read the offer. In these circumstances it would seem that revocation will be effective if the offeror takes all reasonable steps to bring the notice of the revocation to all those who potentially may have read the offer. In the case of our example of the offer in the newspaper it might be that a similar sized notice in the same newspaper on the same day might well pass this test of reasonableness. Unfortunately no English authority exists at this point but such was the decision in the American case of *Shuey v US* 92 US 73 (1875).

A final point relating to communication of revocation is that whilst the revocation must be communicated to the offeree it is thought that it need not be communicated by the offeror. For revocation to be effective in such circumstances, however, the revocation must be communicated to the offeree via a reliable third party. Notice of the revocation would not be effective if it came to the offeree's attention by way of mere rumour or supposition.

The case often quoted as being the authority for this principle is that of *Dickinson v Dodds* (1876) 2 Ch D 463 where on 10 June the defendant offered to sell his house to the plaintiff for £800 adding, 'This offer to be left over until Friday 12th June, 9 a.m.'. On Thursday 11 June the defendant sold the house to someone else and that evening the plaintiff was informed of that sale to another individual named Berry. That same evening the plaintiff delivered a formal letter of acceptance to the defendant's house and followed this up with a duplicate at 7 a.m. the next morning, that is, before the 9 a.m. deadline. When the defendant failed to complete the contract the plantiff sued him for a decree of specific performance. It was held by the Court of Appeal that the plaintiff should fail in his application since he was aware at the time that he accepted the offer that Dodds, the defendant, no longer intended to sell the house to him. The principle established in the case places a substantial onus on the offeree to decide whether the source of the revocation is reliable or not, or indeed the precise time at which the revocation is deemed to have been communicated to him. To a large degree the case reflects the traditional and defunct consensus approach to establishing a legally binding agreement, but therein lies an anomaly, since there would be no consensus even if the withdrawal of the offer had not been communicated to him. A further weakness lies in the case in that the third party, Berry, subsequently became the agent of Dickinson, thus calling into question the notice of revocation being communicated by an independent third party. Perhaps, as Treitel suggests, the rule should simply be that the revocation must be communicated to the offeree by the offeror.

Unilateral contracts

It has already been seen earlier in this chapter that a unilateral contract occurs where a person, the promisor, binds himself to perform a stated promise when the promisee fulfils some condition stipulated by the promisor, such being the situation in our example of *Carlill v Carbolic Smoke Ball Co.*

In the context of the revocation of offers, unilateral contracts present particular difficulties because of the fact that acceptance takes place when the condition is completed. It has been established in our study of revocation that it is possible to revoke an offer at any time until it has been accepted by the offeree. In terms of unilateral contracts this rule can lead to abuse and injustice. For example, A may make an offer stating that he will pay £1,000 to anyone who walks from Manchester Town Hall to Nelson's Column in Trafalgar Square arriving on 6 June. B sets out and arrives in Trafalgar Square on 6 June but just as he is about to touch Nelson's Column, A revokes his offer. On the basis of the general rule relating to revocation of offers A is entitled to do this, since, as Goff LJ stated in *Daulia Ltd v Four Millbank Nominees Ltd* [1978] 2 All ER 557:

> the true view of the unilateral contract must in general be that the offeror is entitled to require full performance of the condition that he has imposed and short of that he is not bound . . .

Such an approach is undoubtedly intolerable and unjust, and indeed, this has been recognised as such in a number of cases.

In *Luxor (Eastbourne) Ltd* v *Cooper* [1941] AC 108, an owner of a piece of land promised to pay an estate agent a £10,000 commission if he introduced someone who was willing to purchase the property. The agent did in fact introduce someone and a sale was agreed subject to contract. Whilst the third party was always ready and willing to purchase the property the owner decided not to proceed with the sale. The result of the decision was that the agent could not complete the act he was employed to do. He nevertheless claimed the £10,000 which the owner refused to pay. The agent then brought an action for breach of contract alleging that there was an implied undertaking that he would not do anything to prevent completion of the sale. The House of Lords held that the owner could revoke his offer at any time up to exchange of contract and, therefore, the agent's action failed since the commission only became payable on completion. On the face of things the case supports the proposition that an offer in a unilateral contract is freely revocable by the offeror until performance by the offeree. The House of Lords, however, was not so definite in its judgment, preferring to decide that *in the circumstances of the case* it would not be proper to infer an undertaking on the part of the owner not to withdraw from the sale and thereby revoke his offer. Presumably, however, if such an undertaking could be implied in a particular case the court would find such an implication justifiable and the undertaking would be binding on the offeror. In the *Luxor* case, for instance, the House of Lords would not imply such an undertaking, on the basis that the reward was very substantial for comparatively little effort on the part of the agent and therefore the agent was taken to have assumed that it was possible that the offeror would wish to withdraw from the sale. If, to effect the sale, the agent had been required to undertake an obligation or task that was substantial and onerous in comparison to the fee level promised, the House of Lords might have been prepared to imply such an undertaking.

In *Errington* v *Errington and Woods* [1952] 1 KB 290, a father purchased a house in his own name and then allowed his son and daughter-in-law to live in the house provided they paid the mortgage instalments. He told them that the house would be theirs when the mortgage was paid off. The couple lived in the house and paid the instalments. They were not contractually obliged to do this, though if they did, the house would be theirs. The father eventually died and his widow claimed possession of the house. It was held that the agreement amounted to a contract which could not be revoked, provided the couple continued to pay the instalments.

Lord Denning summed the situation up as follows:

> The father's promise was a unilateral contract – a promise of a house in return for their act of paying the instalments. It could not be revoked by him once the couple entered a performance of the act, but it would cease to bind him if they left it incomplete and unperformed, which they have not done. . . . They have acted on the promise and neither the father nor his widow, his successor in title, can eject them in disregard of it.

Whilst the above view was supported in *Daulia Ltd* v *Four Millbank Nominees Ltd*, the basis of the decisions in all three cases is conceptually elusive. Not surprisingly Denning, as very much the father of the modern doctrine of promissory estoppel, tends to rely on this as justification for the rule. The doctrine of estoppel, however, cannot provide a complete answer since its application is deficient in that there needs to be an existing legal relationship for it to apply. Very often such a relationship is not present where an offer of a unilateral contract is being revoked. Another justification for disallowing revocation of the offer once the offeree has begun to perform his side of the agreement can be found in the idea of collateral contracts. In other words, in fact two offers are presented in the offeror's statement. The first is the one which expressly presents itself to the offeree, and in which the offeror promises to pay once the offeree has performed the act in question. The second offer is an implied one, namely that that offeror shall not withdraw his offer once the offeree has begun to perform the act in question. If the offeror attempts to revoke his first offer he will be in breach of the second collateral contract. Such a view finds much favour with Cheshire and Fifoot. Treitel, however, tends to favour the idea that acceptance of the offer takes place when the offeree begins to perform the act required by the offeror thus rendering any attempt at revoking the offer impossible. The main flaw here is that a binding contract will materialise and the offeree will be in breach of contract if he fails to fully perform the act in question. It is submitted that such a consequence would be unacceptable to the offeree.

Different arguments can be found justifying the rule and it may be that there is a degree of probity in all of them. It is regrettable that the courts have been so reluctant to define the theoretical basis behind the rule that the courts will treat an offer of a unilateral contract as irrevocable once performance by the offeror has commenced.

Rejection

The rules relating to rejection have largely been dealt with in our discussion of counter-offers since these operate as a rejection of the original offer, as seen in *Hyde v Wrench*.

On the matter of communication it would seem that a rejection is ineffective until it is communicated to the offeror. Treitel suggests that, this being the case, it is possible for an offeree to post a letter of rejection and subsequently accept the offer – provided the communication of the acceptance is brought to the attention of the offeror before he receives the letter of rejection. Such a conclusion would seem fair, though it would also seem to be valid to apply the postal rule to a letter of acceptance sent subsequent to the sending of the letter of rejection. Such a conclusion, however, whilst being legally correct, would be grossly unfair to the offeror who might, whilst relying on the letter of rejection received by him, sell the goods (for instance) to someone else, being unaware that in fact there was a valid contract between himself and the original offeree. The point is undecided to date.

Lapse of time

An offer cannot last indefinitely and a point must arise at some time when the offer ceases to exist. It may be that the offer is expressed to last only for a certain period and that if not accepted within that period the offer will lapse. Where no express provision is contained in the offer it will in any event lapse after a reasonable time.

What constitutes a reasonable time depends largely on the subject matter of the offer. For example, an offer to sell a quantity of perishable goods, say tomatoes, would lapse after a fairly short period of time compared to the time reasonable for a quantity of steel. Some items, whilst they are not perishable in that sense, may, nevertheless, be highly volatile in other respects and this again would cause the offer to lapse in a fairly short period of time. An example may be seen in the case of *Ramsgate Victoria Hotel Co Ltd* v *Montefiore* (1866) LR 1 Ex 109 where the defendant applied for shares on 8 June but none was allotted to him until 23 November. It was held that the company could not accept the defendant's offer to purchase the shares since that offer had lapsed. Any acceptance had to take place within a reasonable time and in the case of a highly volatile commodity such as shares lapse occurred after a comparatively short period of time. The delay from June to November was unreasonable and therefore the action for breach of contract for failure to accept and pay for the shares failed.

Failure of a condition precedent

Apart from an offer only being effective for a stated or reasonable period of time, as discussed above, the offer may only be effective whilst certain conditions exist. An offer may expressly provide that it will determine on the occurrence of some condition. Any acceptance subsequent to the occurrence of the stated condition will therefore be ineffective. Such conditions precedent may also be implied in an offer. For example, it is implied in an offer to purchase goods that they will remain in substantially the same condition as they were in when the offer was first made.

In *Financings Ltd* v *Stimson* [1962] 3 All ER 386 the defendant, having seen a car at the premises of the dealer, decided to buy it on hire purchase. He signed a form supplied by the dealer which stated that the hire purchase agreement only became binding when signed by the plaintiffs, the finance company. The defendant paid a first instalment of £70 and took the car away on 18 March. On 20 March the defendant returned the car dissatisfied with its performance and stated to the dealer that he no longer wished to purchase it. On 25 March the plaintiffs signed the agreement, thereby purporting to accept the offer of the defendant. On the night of the 24/25 March the car was stolen from the premises of the dealer and badly damaged. The plaintiffs eventually sold the car and claimed damages from the defendant, who counter-claimed for his first instalment of £70. It was held that the defendant would succeed since by returning the car to the dealer the defendant had revoked his offer and there was thus no concluded contract between the parties. Further, on the facts of the case, there was an implied condition in the offer of the defendant that the car would remain in substantially the same condition until the time of acceptance. Since the damage occurred before acceptance the plaintiffs were not in a position to accept the offer which had lapsed due to the fact that the implied condition had not been complied with.

Death

The effect of death on an offer is, unlike death itself, not quite so certain, at least where it concerns the death of the offeror. Where the contract requires the personal services of the offeror then death will automatically terminate the offer. Thus an offer by a film star to open a gala will clearly lapse on the death of the film star. Where, however, the contract does not require the personal services of the offeror then it may be the case that the personal representatives will have to employ some other person to carry out those services. What is a relevant consideration here is whether notice of the death of the offeror was brought to the attention of the offeree. If the death of the offeror was brought to the attention of the offeree prior to his accepting the offer then the offer will cease to exist. Where the offeree has no notice of the death of the offeror then, on acceptance, the offeror's estate will be bound by the ensuing contract.

The principles in relation to the death of the offeror can be found *obiter dicta* in *Bradbury* v *Morgan* (1862) 1 H & C 249. No authority exists, however, in the case of the death of the offeree, though in the context of a bilateral contract it would seem reasonable to suggest that very often the terms of the offer apply specifically to a particular offeree, and that as a result the death of the offeree terminates the offer.

CERTAINTY OF TERMS

Despite the fact that one can find a valid offer and acceptance leading to an agreement, the courts may nevertheless fail to find for a binding contract between the parties. Such a conclusion may be reached where one party has raised, as a defence to an action for breach of contract, the fact that some essential element has been omitted from the agreement, or that some terms are so vague that the contract as a whole is rendered unenforceable. Not surprisingly this problem is all too common since the vast majority of contracts are negotiated and entered into by businessmen with no legal knowledge. It is, of course, for this very reason that standard-form contracts have been, and continue to be, so popular. Where such a device is not used the businessman is more concerned with the general round of negotiating and obtaining a contract in principle, leaving certain issues such as pricing or delivery arrangements to be negotiated at a later date.

It is the loosely drafted contract that creates the problem and here the courts are faced with a difficult task. The judge must do all he can to preserve the contract, if indeed there is one, but what he must not do is to write the contract for the parties. The question as to whether the contract is enforceable or unenforceable largely revolves around the level of vagueness, ambiguity or incompleteness in the contract for it is this which, combined with the uncertainty of the willingness of the judge to save or sacrifice the contract, creates substantial uncertainty for the parties. With this level of overall uncertainty it is impossible to draw up a precise set of rules since each case revolves very much on its own facts. It is nevertheless possible to develop a broad set of guidelines which may give some indication as to the possible direction a judge might opt for in any particular case.

The contract is uncertain but has yet to be performed

The attitude of the courts here may be seen in the case of *Scammell and Nephew Ltd* v *Ouston* [1941] AC 251, where the respondents agreed to purchase a new van from Scammell. The order was given 'on the understanding that the balance of purchase price can be had on hire purchase terms over a period of two years'. Scammell accepted the offer though the term 'hire purchase terms' was never determined. It was held that no precise meaning could be attributed to the clause as hire purchase agreements varied widely and there was thus no contract. The level of vagueness here was such as to render the contract unenforceable, since it was impossible for the court to determine either the meaning or intention of the parties with regard to the expression 'hire purchase terms'. There was, for instance, no previous course of dealings between the parties to rescue the contract, nor was there any performance of the contract which might have given the court guidance as to the meaning of the term.

Where there is no performance of the contract the courts, in the absence of any aids, will much more readily find that the contract is unenforceable. A further example of this attitude can be found in *May & Butcher* v *R* [1934] 2 KB 17n.

The contract is uncertain but performance has commenced

In this situation, the courts, as a matter of expediency, are much more likely to uphold the contract as enforceable. Perhaps it is an oversimplification of the process to suggest that expediency forces the arm of the courts to find for a contract, since very often the courts will have more information on which to resolve the uncertainty within the contract once some performance has been rendered. Nevertheless the reluctance of the courts to unravel a contract that is partly, or perhaps even substantially, performed should not be underestimated either.

In *Hillas & Co Ltd* v *Arcos Ltd* (1932) 38 Com Cas 23, the facts of which have already been considered, the court was able to determine the meaning of the option clause by reference to the previous course of dealings of the parties in the contract of which the option clause was part and parcel. Further, the position of the court was aided by the existence of well-established trade usage.

A more striking example can be seen in the case of *Foley* v *Classique Coaches Ltd* [1934] 2 KB 1 where the plaintiff, who was a retail dealer in petrol, contracted to supply the defendants, who ran a coach business, with all the petrol they required 'at a price to be agreed by the parties in writing and from time to time'. No such agreement as to the price was ever concluded and three years later the defendants purported to repudiate the contract. It was held that they were not entitled to do so since in the absence of an express agreement a term would be implied that the petrol supplied by the plaintiff should be of reasonable quality and sold at a reasonable price. Undoubtedly the fact of the contract having been performed was a major factor in the Court of Appeal's decision.

A further factor that is often taken into account by the courts in resolving problems of uncertainty is the provision for arbitration or some other means of resolving disputes within the contract. Such a clause existed in the *Foley* case and was another factor taken into account by the Court of Appeal in coming to its decision. Such a provision is always prudent if any terms, such as price or terms of delivery, are to be left open by the parties. In the past the machinery set up by the parties for resolving disputes or such matters have nevertheless also been held to be ineffective because of the machinery itself being vague, ambiguous or defective in some other way. In *Sudbrook Trading Estate Ltd* v *Eggleton* [1983] 1 AC 444, the House of Lords adopted a means whereby such decisions should now be reduced. In the case there was an agreement by which a tenant could purchase his premises 'at such a price . . . as may be agreed upon by two valuers . . .' One valuer was to be appointed by the tenant and one by the landlord. The tenant decided to purchase his premises and appointed his valuer according to the agreement. The landlord refused to appoint the other valuer, thus nullifying the provision. The House of Lords interpreted the provision as being an agreement to sell at a fair and reasonable price to be assessed by the valuers. Since the landlord, by his conduct, had rendered this process ineffective and inoperable, the court was able to assess a price by reference to expert opinion as to what might be regarded as a fair and reasonable price.

The fact that there has been some degree of performance of the contract or that the contract contains a means of resolving any uncertainty within it does not necessarily mean that the courts will invariably treat the contract as enforceable.

In the case of *British Steel Corporation* v *Cleveland Bridge & Engineering Co Ltd* [1984] 1 All ER 504, where a contract was entered into concerning a major construction project, work on the project started before all the terms had been agreed, though negotiations proceeded in the expectation that a full and final agreement would eventually be forthcoming. At the heart of the negotiations were matters relating to delivery, price and certain other terms. Eventually a dispute broke out whereby BSC claimed a reasonable price for the items delivered so far, whereas CBE counter-claimed for damages for non-delivery of certain items. BSC's claim was based on a claim in *quantum meruit* and since it alleged that there was no contract between the parties, the effect would be to preclude CBE's claim. The court held that, despite the fact that substantial performance had taken place and the fact that there was a submission on CBE's part that a letter of intent sent to BSC constituted a subcontract, there was no contract in existence. It was stated that there was so much left unsaid that one could not find that a contract had been formed and, consequently, BSC could claim a reasonable sum for work done on a *quantum meruit* basis. As Cheshire, Fifoot and Furmston (1991) point out, the decision creates difficulties in that either party could have abandoned the project with impunity without giving notice to the other party since there was no contract – no matter how 'commercially unacceptable' the result. Further it is pointed out that the finding of no contract could present difficulties in determining whether goods delivered and accepted, but later found to be defective, could be rejected or not. Despite these difficulties and the cases already examined with regard to certainty, the case indicates that the courts still retain substantial discretion to find for no contract despite performance of the contract where the terms are uncertain. However, in *G Percy Trentham Ltd* v *Archital Luxfer* [1993] 1 Lloyds Rep 25 Steyn LJ suggested that, where a transaction is executed, it is easier to imply a term resolving any uncertainty, or alternatively make it possible to treat as non-essential a matter not finalised in negotiations.

Further reading

Beale, Bishop and Furmston, *Contract – Cases and Materials* 2nd ed. 1990, Butterworths

Cheshire, Fifoot and Furmston, *The Law of Contract*, 12th ed. 1991, Butterworths

Evans, 'The Anglo-American Mailing Rule: Some Problems of Offer and Acceptance in Contracts by Correspondence', 15 *International and Comparative Law Quarterly* 553, 1966

Fried, *Contract as Promise, A Theory of Contractual Obligations*, 1981

Gower, 'Auction Sales of Goods Without Reserve', 68 *Law Quarterly Review* 457, 1952

Guest, *Anson's Law of Contract* 26th ed. 1984, Oxford University Press

Stone, 'Forming a Contract without Offer and Acceptance', *Student Law Review* 12, Spring 1994

Stone, 'The Postal Rule in the Electronic Age', *Student Law Review* 15, Spring 1992

Winfield, 'Some Aspects of Offer and Acceptance', 55 *Law Quarterly Review* 499, 1939

Treitel, *The Law of Contract*, 8th ed. 1991, Sweet & Maxwell

3 | Consideration

INTRODUCTION

Consideration is one of the principal ingredients of an enforceable simple contract in English law. It was not always such a requirement and it is largely regarded as having originated in the sixteenth century, though the technical reasons for its evolution are not clear. One theory is that it evolved as a means of restricting the development of assumpsit, in that only promises supported by consideration could be enforced; gratuitous promises were, therefore, not enforceable. The law thus evolved in simple contracts in such a way as to enforce bargains rather than promises. The concept of speciality contracts evolved separately from assumpsit at a time when the law was very much more formulary in its approach. In this situation an agreement made under seal could be enforced despite the lack of consideration.

The difference between a simple contract and a speciality contract may be illustrated by reference to gifts. As we will see, consideration broadly means a *quid pro quo* on the part of the participants to the contract, a reciprocal giving and taking by both parties or 'something for something'. In the case of a promise by A to give B £10, this is clearly a bare gift, a *nudum pactum*, and as such is unenforceable as a simple contract since there is clearly no reciprocity between the parties. If this gift is embodied, however, in a deed, a deed being a document made under seal, then such an agreement is enforceable as a speciality contract.

In this chapter we are thus considering what, in law, amounts to consideration that will support a simple contract. Before we approach this task three further points need to be made. First, the question as to what constitutes consideration has to be addressed to each party's promise in relation to the contract, as each party must provide this element to enforce the contract. In other words, the validity or otherwise of consideration is assessed in relation not to the contract as a whole but to its provision by an individual participant to the contract. Secondly, although textbook writers often refer to this area as the doctrine of consideration, and whilst this might originally have been true, it is erroneous to think of it as a single concept today. Consideration has evolved into a body of rules developed by the courts in order to place limitations on the enforceability of the contracts that come before them. Thirdly, an agreement in which consideration is lacking is not necessarily unenforceable, as we shall see in our analysis of promissory estoppel later in this chapter. Here the courts will, in certain circumstances, enforce a contract even though there is a lack of consideration. Similarly the courts will on occasion return a finding of no contract despite the apparent existence of consideration, the basis for such a decision being that only certain types of consideration are recognised by the law. Whilst the notion of consideration is concerned with a giving of value by both parties, only 'something of value in the eyes of the law' is regarded as amounting to consideration.

THE DEFINITION OF CONSIDERATION

Consideration is the price for which the promise of the other is bought. It must be of 'something of value' which is recognised by the courts as amounting to consideration. Traditionally the doctrine of consideration has been defined in terms of either a detriment to the promisee or a benefit to the promisor. In *Currie* v *Misa* (1875) LR 10 Ex 153 consideration was defined as:

> A valuable consideration in the sense of the law, may consist either in some right, interest, profit or benefit accruing to one party, or some forbearance, detriment, loss or responsibility given, suffered or undertaken by the other.

This approach to defining consideration develops deficiencies when seen in contracts based purely on an exchange of promises. Thus if A promises to buy a car from B for £2,000 and B on his part promises to sell the car to A for £2,000 there is clearly a binding contract which can be enforced, should one of the parties decide not to carry on with the contract. Until the date for performance arrives there is clearly no detriment or benefit undertaken by either party, the consideration within the contract presenting itself via the exchange of promises made by the parties. The definition is therefore meaningless in this context. Indeed this and other criticisms have meant that it has become preferable today to think in terms of consideration amounting to a plaintiff buying a defendant's promise by performing some act in return for it. Alternatively, the plaintiff may purchase the defendant's promise by the furnishing of a counter-promise. This modern approach was summed up by Sir Frederick Pollock (1950) in *Principles of Contract*, where he defined consideration as:

> An act or forbearance of one party, or the promise thereof, is the price for which the promise of the other is bought, and the promise thus given for value is enforceable.

This definition was approved by the House of Lords in *Dunlop Pneumatic Tyre Co Ltd* v *Selfridge Ltd* [1915] AC 847 and is regarded as being more representative of the doctrine of consideration in the modern commercial contract than the nineteenth-century concept of benefit and detriment.

So far our definition has been very straightforward and simple but, as indicated earlier, it is erroneous to think of it as a single coherent principle. In truth, the definition is an expression of a body of rules or sub-principles which, together with their exceptions, make up the doctrine as we know it today. The sub-principles may be expressed as follows:

(a) consideration may be executed or executory but not past;
(b) consideration must move from the promisee but not necessarily to the promisor;
(c) consideration must be sufficient though not necessarily adequate.

CONSIDERATION MAY BE EXECUTED OR EXECUTORY BUT NOT PAST

Executory and executed consideration

The above principle reflects the methods by which the plaintiff purchases the promise of the defendant. In executory consideration the form of the consideration arises by way of a promise by the defendant in return for a promise by the plaintiff. In other words, the whole agreement is one which is to take place in the future. An example of this type of consideration would arise where A promises to purchase B's car on credit, delivery to take place next week. Here both A's and B's consideration is to be performed in the future – it is executory. Executed consideration occurs when one of the parties has done all that he is required to do under the contract, that is, he has 'executed' his side of the bargain. The other party's consideration which is still unperformed remains executory in that it remains to be completed in the future.

Past consideration

The rule in English law is that 'past consideration is no consideration'. In defining consideration we have seen that consideration for a promise has to be given in return for a promise, in other words, there has to be a causal link between the two promises in order for the contract to be enforceable. If a party makes a promise subsequent to some action carried out by the other party, then that promise can only be regarded as an expression of gratitude, a gift, and nothing more. An example of past consideration may be seen where A paints the outside of B's house as a voluntary act while B is on holiday. When B returns from holiday he is pleasantly surprised by A's kindness and promises to pay A £50. If B refuses to pay, can A claim his £50? The answer here must be that his action will fail since A's consideration of painting the house is past in relation to the promise to pay made by B and, of course, past consideration is no consideration. Put another way, there is no causal link between the actions of A and B in that the act of painting the house was not made in response to a promise to pay for that act.

It should be noted carefully that past consideration means past in relation to the promise that the plaintiff is seeking to enforce and not in relation to the time at which the plaintiff is seeking to enforce the defendant's promise. In the above example, if B had promised A £50 if he painted his house, then A can only claim the £50 once he has carried out his part of the bargain, that is, his consideration is executed in that it has been carried out in response to a promise to pay by B. It is true, however, that A's consideration here is past in that it has already been completed but here it is past in relation to the time of enforcement rather than to the promise made by B.

Two cases traditionally illustrate the principle as regards past consideration, *Roscorla* v *Thomas* (1842) 3 QB 234 and the modern authority of *Re McArdle* [1951] Ch 669. In the former case the plaintiff had negotiated the purchase of a particular horse from the defendant for a certain price. Subsequent to the agreement the defendant promised the plaintiff that 'the said horse was sound and free from vice'. In fact the horse proved to be particularly vicious and the plaintiff sued for breach of the promise. It was held that his action would fail since the consideration provided by the plaintiff was already past when the promise of the defendant that the horse was sound and free from vice was made. In truth, the warranty as regards the horse was not induced by the payment made for the horse and was, as such, purely gratuitous.

In *Re McArdle* [1951] Ch 669, by virtue of a father's will, his children were to be left his house on the death of their mother. Whilst the mother was alive, one of the children and his wife lived in the house with her. The wife, during this period, made substantial alterations and improvements to the property. In gratitude the children later signed a document which stated 'in consideration of your carrying out certain alterations and improvements to the property, we hereby agree that the executors shall repay to you from the estate, when distributed, the sum of £488 in settlement of the amount spent on such improvements'. The Court of Appeal held that the alterations and improvements completed before the signing of the undertaking by the children amounted to past consideration and that, when the executors refused to pay the £488, the wife was unable successfully to sue for those monies. The wife had furnished no consideration for the promise to pay the money for the alterations and improvements.

Exceptions to the past consideration rule

The principle in Lampleigh *v* Braithwait

The facts of *Lampleigh* v *Braithwait* (1615) Hob 105 were that Braithwait had killed another man and asked Lampleigh to secure a pardon from the king. Lampleigh went to considerable effort and expense to secure the pardon for Braithwait who subsequently promised to pay Lampleigh £100 for his trouble. Braithwait then failed to pay the £100 and was sued on his promise by Lampleigh. Clearly on the basis of the rule relating to past consideration, the efforts of Lampleigh were in the past in relation to the promise to pay by Braithwait and therefore he should have failed in his action. The court, however, held that the original request by Braithwait in fact contained an implied promise that he would reward and reimburse Lampleigh for his efforts. Thus the previous request and the subsequent promise were part of the same transaction and as such were enforceable against Braithwait by Lampleigh once he had secured the pardon for him.

It should be noted that the principle only applies if the plaintiff's services had been rendered at the defendant's request and that it was implicit that both parties must have understood that the plaintiff's services would have to be paid for. Further, the implication of the promise to pay normally only arises in a commercial relationship between the parties. It is often considered that the exception did not apply in the case of *Re McArdle* above because of the absence of a request from the defendant to his wife to maintain the property and the lack, therefore, of an implied promise to pay as a result. In truth, however, if this case had been a commercial one, an implied promise might have been found, despite the lack of a previous request.

An example of such a finding can be seen in the case of *Re Casey's Patents* [1892] 1 Ch 104, where there were joint owners of certain patent rights who wrote to the plaintiff, 'In consideration of your services as the practical manager in working our patents, we hereby agree to give you one-third share of the patents'. It was contended by the defendants that the promise was made in respect of the plaintiff's past services and therefore the plaintiff could not enforce the promise against them because he himself had supplied no consideration for it. Bowen LJ found for the plaintiff, stating that there was an implied promise that the plaintiff's services would be paid for and that the share of the patents would be regarded as such payment, despite the lack of a previous request by the defendants for the plaintiff to supply his services.

The principle in *Lampleigh* v *Braithwait* has been affirmed and restated by Lord Scarman in *Pao On* v *Lau Yiu Long* [1975] 3 All ER 65 as follows:

> An act done before the giving of a promise to make a payment or to confer some other benefit can sometimes be consideration for the promise. The act must have been done at the promisor's request, the parties must have understood that the act was to be remunerated further by a payment or the conferment of some other benefit and payment, or the conferment of a benefit must have been legally enforceable had it been promised in advance.

So far we have expressed the principle in *Lampleigh* v *Braithwait* as an exception to the rule of past consideration, and on the face of things this certainly appears to be the case. A different viewpoint is that it is not such an exception but merely reflects the normal requirement of the need for consideration. If, for example, one asks a mechanic to repair one's car, but at the time no mention is made as regards payment, this is clearly not a question of past consideration but a question of normal commercial practice. There is no question, usually at least, of the mechanic not being paid (or doing something for nothing) once the car has been fixed. What is at issue is the amount he is to be paid, this matter being resolved in the subsequent promise.

Statutory exceptions

(a) Limitation Act 1980, s. 27(5). This provides that if a debtor acknowledges a debt it shall be deemed to accrue, for the purpose of calculating the commencement of the limitation period, from the date of the acknowledgement and not before. The acknowledgement need not necessarily be a promise to pay the debt by the debtor, though if it should take on this form the effect will still be to extend the period, despite the fact that the consideration for the promise is the antecedent debt and is thus in the past. See *Dungate* v *Dungate* [1965] 3 All ER 818 for an application of the provision. The provision does not have the effect of renewing the enforceability of a debt that is already statute-barred.

(b) Bills of Exchange Act 1882, s. 27. An antecedent debt, whilst normally regarded as past consideration, though not invariably so, will be good consideration for a bill of exchange.

CONSIDERATION MUST MOVE FROM THE PROMISEE THOUGH NOT NECESSARILY TO THE PROMISOR

The rule that consideration must move from the promisee means that a person can only enforce a promise made to him if he himself can show that he has provided consideration for that promise. An example of the principle can be seen in *Price* v *Easton* (1833) 4 B & Ad 433 where Price owed the defendant £13 and agreed to work for the defendant who promised to pay Price's wages to the plaintiff, but in the event failed to do so. It was held that the plaintiff could not recover the £13 from the defendant as no consideration had moved from the plaintiff.

In truth, the principle is a corollary of the rule requiring privity of contract between the parties to a contract. In other words, only parties to a contract can enforce the contract against the other, but in order to be a party to a contract one must be a party to the bargain and therefore also provide consideration. The decision in *Price* v *Easton* was decided on both grounds, one judge, Lord Denman, stating that the plaintiff would not succeed as he could not 'show any consideration for the promise moving from him to the defendant'. Another judge, Littledale J, based his decision on the fact that 'no privity is shown between the plaintiff and the defendant'.

The reasonings of the two judges in *Price* v *Easton* can be seen clearly in the case of *Tweddle* v *Atkinson* (1861) 1 B & S 393 which also illustrates the second part of the principle, that consideration need not move to the promisor. In the case the plaintiff's father and prospective father-in-law agreed with each other that they would pay the plaintiff £100 and £200 respectively in consideration of the plaintiff's intended marriage and, in fact, confirmed that agreement in writing after the marriage. The father-in-law died before he paid his £200 and the plaintiff sued the executors to recover the monies. It was held that his action would fail as he had not furnished any consideration and he was not a party to the contract, even though it was made for his benefit. He could not enforce the contract since no consideration had moved away from him. The only person who could enforce the contract would have been the plaintiff's father, since he could show that consideration had moved away from him, though, of course, he would not benefit from the contract. It was not required of him that he show that the promisor, the father-in-law, had received the consideration but merely that something had moved away from himself.

CONSIDERATION MUST BE SUFFICIENT THOUGH NOT NECESSARILY ADEQUATE

Consideration must be valuable

The principle we are examining is sometimes simply referred to as a principle requiring the consideration to have some value, namely, economic value, and there is nothing erroneous in this expression of the rule, though it fails to make the distinction between 'adequate' and 'sufficient' consideration. To the lay person there is no distinction between these terms but in a legal context the distinction is profound. The expression 'adequacy' of consideration is used to describe the reciprocal elements of the bargain, that is, the *quid pro quo* of the contract. This is the aspect that is most important to the parties to the contract since it is the factor that decides whether an individual has made a 'good' sale or purchase in economic terms. The term 'sufficiency' of consideration is the aspect that is of most concern to the lawyers since this expression describes not the economic value or otherwise of the consideration, but whether the consideration can exist as such in the eyes of the law as supporting a simple contract.

Adequacy of consideration

It has been settled for many years that the courts will not make any enquiry as to whether the consideration given by the parties is adequate or not. In other words, the courts will not make a comparative economic evaluation of the consideration proffered by each party to the contract. The courts seek merely to establish that the consideration has a degree of economic value and do not enquire into the relative values of the consideration contained in the contract. The law is not concerned, barring allegations of fraud, with bad bargains where the relative values of consideration are disproportional. There is adequate consideration in a contract for the sale of a Rolls-Royce for a hairpin since both items have an economic value, albeit widely disparate, and, in the absence of fraud, there is a good contract here.

A modern example of the principle can be seen in *Chappell & Co Ltd* v *Nestlé Co Ltd* [1960] AC 87 where the plaintiffs owned the copyright to a piece of music entitled 'Rockin' Shoes'. X made records of the tune which they sold to Nestlé, the defendants, for 4d. each, who then offered them to the public for 1s. 6d. each plus three wrappers from Nestlé 6d. chocolate bars. The wrappers were thrown away on receipt. The main object of Nestlé Ltd was to promote and sell their chocolate, though a profit was also made on the sale of the records. The plaintiffs sued the defendants for breach of copyright, relying on s. 8 of the Copyright Act 1956 which provided that a person can make a record of a musical work provided it is designed for retail sale and royalties of 6¼ per cent 'of the ordinary retail selling price' were paid to the owner of the copyright. The defendants based their royalty fee on 1s. 6d. and the plaintiffs refused this on the basis that the money consideration was only part of the price and that the wrappers should also be taken into account in assessing the royalty fee. It was held that judgment should be given to the plaintiffs since the wrappers were certainly part of the consideration in that they represented an economic value, albeit one that might be very small. Lord Somervill stated:

> A contracting party can stipulate for what consideration he chooses. A peppercorn does not cease to be good consideration if it is established that the promisee does not like pepper and will throw away the corn.

A modern application of the rule can be seen in the case of *Midland Bank Trust Co Ltd* v *Green* [1981] AC 513 where a father, to avoid an option granted to his son, sold a farm to his wife for £500 even though it was valued at more than £40,000. In the Court of Appeal it was held that a sale at such an undervalued price could not amount to a sale for 'money or money's worth'. The House of Lords reversed the decision, stating that the court would not enquire into the adequacy as long as the consideration was real. There was thus a good contract between the parties.

The fact that the consideration must have an economic value means that simple love and affection cannot amount to adequate consideration. Similarly in *White* v *Bluett* (1853) 23 LJ Ex 36 the court held that a son's promise to stop boring his father by constantly complaining in return for his father's promise not to sue him on a promissory note was not good consideration.

Sufficiency of consideration

In discussing sufficiency of consideration we are analysing situations where a contract has been formed on the basis of a promise by one of the parties which, while being adequate in that it has an economic value, is not recognised by the law as amounting to consideration sufficient to support a simple contract. The consideration, in addition to amounting to an economic value, must be of a type recognised by law. Where a person promises to do something which he is already bound to do because the law has imposed that obligation on him, then that promise does not furnish sufficient consideration to support a simple contract. Merely repeating an obligation already imposed on a promisee amounts to a promise to do nothing at all.

The situations where the law finds the consideration to be insufficient fall into two principal categories:

(a) where there is a performance of an existing obligation, and
(b) where there is a promise to pay part of a debt.

Performance of existing obligations

This category may be further subdivided as follows:

(a) *Where a public duty is imposed by law.* Very often certain persons, by their official status, or because of obligations imposed on them by the law, are obliged to carry out or do things in a certain way in order to discharge the public duties required of them. The carrying out of the public duties imposed on them by the law is not recognised by the law when it is used to support a simple contract. The leading case in this field is *Collins* v *Godefroy* (1831) 1 B & Ad 950, where the plaintiff attended and gave evidence at a civil trial by reason of a subpoena issued by the defendant. Afterwards the defendant promised to pay him a fee of six guineas. It was held that the plaintiff could not recover the monies owed since he had furnished no consideration for the promise since he was already legally obliged to attend the trial. His consideration, in other words, was insufficient to support the promise of the defendant.

The issue of existing public duties has proved a particular problem in respect to public authorities, particularly the police, over the years.

In *Glassbrook Bros* v *Glamorgan County Council* [1925] AC 270, a colliery manager applied for police protection for his mine during a strike. He insisted that the mine could only be protected by having police officers actually billeted on the colliery premises. The police authorities considered that the colliery could be adequately protected by units of policemen patrolling the area in the vicinity of the mine, but nevertheless agreed to billet police officers at the premises provided the manager agreed to pay the specified rate. The bill for the protection amounted to £2,300, which the manager refused to pay, indicating that the police protection amounted to insufficient consideration since the police were already under an existing public duty to protect the premises. The House of Lords held that whilst it was true that the police were under a public duty to protect the premises, they were entitled to exercise their discretion as to the level of protection required. If the police considered that the premises would be adequately protected by an external mobile force then any level of security over and above that, as insisted on by the manager, amounted to good and sufficient consideration to support the promise of the mine manager to pay the £2,300.

The House of Lords in the above case relied heavily on the earlier case of *England* v *Davidson* (1840) 11 Ad and El 856, where the defendant offered a reward to anyone who gave information that would lead to the conviction of a certain felon. The plaintiff, a police constable, supplied the information and claimed the reward. The defendant refused to pay and alleged in his defence that the plaintiff had done no more than the public duty imposed on him by the law to supply such information. The defendant also stated that such a contract was contrary to public policy. The basis for this is that to allow officials such as policemen to claim in circumstances where they were already under an existing public duty to act would be to risk the promotion of corruption and extortion. Both these defences were rejected by the court, the first on the ground that there were certain services a policeman was not required to render and clearly these services can amount to sufficient consideration in the proper circumstances. The second defence was rejected on the basis that to hold a contract void as being contrary to public policy requires very clear grounds for doing so and the courts do not readily accede to such a finding, particularly in cases of reward since the effect here is to encourage and promote the interests of justice.

The principles and decisions in the above two cases have also been seen in the recent case of *Harris* v *Sheffield United Football Club Ltd* [1987] 2 All ER 838 where police officers were required to be on duty within the grounds of the club when matches were being played there. The club was required to pay for 'special police services' when these were provided at the request of the club. The club refused to pay for these services on the basis that the police were merely carrying out their normal public duties in ensuring the maintenance of law and order and thus provided insufficient consideration for the promise of the club to pay for those services. The court held that the police provided more than their public duty required of them and therefore they were entitled to charge and claim for the monies owed to them in respect of the 'special police services'.

It can be seen in the above cases that the courts will very often find on a matter of public policy, rather than the presence of consideration, in deciding that there is sufficient consideration to support the promisor's promise. In some circumstances, however, the finding of good consideration on a matter of policy is not possible and, in these circumstances, the courts can go to extraordinary lengths to find for the existence of sufficient consideration. Such an instance may be seen in the case of *Ward* v *Byham* [1956] 2 All ER 318, where an unmarried couple lived together from 1949 to 1954. In 1950 they had a child. However, in 1954 the man turned the woman out of their house, helping and looking after the child. A few months later the woman, the plaintiff, requested that the child be returned to live with her. The defendant replied offering her the child, together with £1 per week maintenance, on condition first, that the child could decide for itself whether or not it wanted to live with its mother and, secondly, that the plaintiff could 'prove that she would be well looked after and happy'. The child decided that it did want to live with its mother and the defendant relinquished it to the mother for some seven months, paying the agreed £1 per week maintenance. The plaintiff then married another man and the defendant promptly ceased to make any further payments. The plaintiff sued for breach of contract and the defendant pleaded s. 42 of the National Assistance Act 1948. The provision stated that the mother of an illegitimate child was bound to maintain that child. The defendant alleged that the mother had done no more than fulfil a duty imposed on her by law in return for the promise of the £1 per week maintenance, and that therefore her consideration was insufficient to support the defendant's promise of maintenance.

The Court of Appeal held that the plaintiff had exceeded the duty imposed on her by s. 42 since, whilst the mother of an illegitimate child is bound to maintain the child she is not necessarily bound to 'look after the child well' nor make it 'happy'. The plaintiff therefore had provided sufficient consideration for the promise of the defendant and was successful in her action. Denning LJ significantly went further than this and stated that the defendant would be bound even if the plaintiff had done no more than the duty imposed on her by law since 'a promise to perform an existing duty, or the performance of it, should be regarded as good consideration, because it is a benefit to the person to whom it is given'. This view was not shared by other members of the court. He qualified this statement however in *Williams* v *Williams* [1957] 1 All ER 305, adding, 'so long as there is nothing in the transaction which is contrary to the public interest'.

(b) Where the plaintiff is bound by the provisions of an existing contractual obligation owed to the defendant. A plaintiff provides insufficient consideration to support a promise made by the defendant if the plaintiff merely performs, or promises to perform, an obligation already owed by the plaintiff to the defendant by virtue of a previous contract made between them. Thus in *Stilk* v *Myrick* (1809) 2 Camp 317, the plaintiff entered into a contract to sail a ship from London to the Baltic and back. During the voyage two crew members jumped ship and subsequently the captain promised to divide the wages due to these two men between the rest of the crew since the ship was now short-handed as he had been unable to find replacements. On returning to London the captain refused to pay the extra wages and, when sued, alleged that the plaintiff had done no more than that which he was already contractually obliged to do, and that this could not therefore amount to sufficient consideration for the extra wages. The court agreed with this reasoning and found for the defendant.

The basis of the court's decision ignored the reasoning in an earlier decision contained in *Harris* v *Watson* (1791) Peake 102. The facts of this case were very similar to *Stilk* v *Myrick* but here the decision was based on what is known today as economic duress (which will be dealt with below, in Chapter 11). In other words, the reason the claim was disallowed was that if an emergency arose, such as a ship being short-handed, it would otherwise be possible for the rest of the crew to 'hold a gun to the head' of the captain and demand extra money. Lord Kenyon in the *Harris* case thought that the rule was founded on the ground of public policy, whilst in *Stilk* Lord Ellenborough denied this and stated that the proper reasoning was that the contract was void for lack of sufficient consideration, the seaman being under an existing contractual duty. A better view may be that the rule relating to existing duties not amounting to sufficient consideration is based on the possibility of the occurrence of economic duress.

The decision in *Stilk* v *Myrick* might have been different if the plaintiff could have shown that he did something over and above his pre-existing contractual obligations. In the case of *Hartley* v *Ponsonby* (1857) 7 E & B 872, where the facts were similar to those in *Stilk* v *Myrick*, the plaintiff was successful in his claim. The court, however, found that so many of the crew had deserted the ship in this case that the nature of the voyage had changed. The ship had become so short-handed that it had now become hazardous to proceed. The remaining crew had not contracted for such a voyage, and therefore they were held to be discharged from their existing contractual duties and free to make a new contract.

Both the principle in *Stilk* v *Myrick* and the exception propounded in *Hartley* v *Ponsonby* have been affirmed in *North Ocean Shipping Co Ltd* v *Hyundai Construction Co Ltd* [1979] QB 705. Recently, however, the principle and the qualification to it have been subject to further discussion and analysis in *Williams* v *Roffey Bros & Nicholls (Contractors) Ltd* [1990] 1 All ER 512. The case requires very careful consideration since the ramifications of the decision could potentially go far beyond the boundaries of sufficiency of consideration and, indeed, raise questions about the doctrine of consideration generally.

The facts of *Williams* v *Roffrey Bros* were that the defendant building contractors entered into a contract to refurbish a block of 27 flats. They subcontracted the joinery work to the plaintiff for a price of £20,000. It was an implied term of the subcontract that the plaintiff would receive interim payments for completed work. The plaintiff received £16,000 for completing work on the roof, nine flats and preliminary work on the remaining flats. This sum represented 80 per cent of the contract price though in fact the plaintiff still had far more than 20 per cent of the work to complete. The plaintiff thus found himself in financial difficulties because his initial price was too low and he had failed to supervise his workforce adequately. The defendants, who were under a penalty clause in the main contract if the work was not completed on time, became aware of the plaintiff's difficulties. The defendants agreed to pay the plaintiff an extra £10,300 based on a sum of £575 per flat on completion to ensure that he continued the work and completed the work on time. The plaintiff completed a further eight flats and the defendants made one further payment of £1,500. The plaintiff stopped work and brought an action for £10,847. The defendants denied their liability and, in particular, denied they were liable to pay any part of the £10,300 since the promise to pay these monies was not supported by sufficient consideration from the plaintiff. The plaintiff was already under an existing contractual duty to complete the flats and as a result this could not amount to sufficient consideration to support the promise to pay the extra £10,300. Further, the defendants argued that the additional sums were only payable when the work was completed and that, as the plaintiff had left the site before this was done, he was not entitled to the extra monies. However, both at first instance and in the Court of Appeal, it was held that the subcontractor was entitled to the contract price, less a deduction for defects.

The main argument in the case surrounded the problem of sufficiency of consideration and whether it existed to support the promise to pay the additional price of £575 per flat completed. At first instance the judge found that the contractors, the defendants, had agreed too low a price with the subcontractor and that this was clearly contrary to their interests – they would never get the job done unless they paid more money. The judge concluded that the agreement to pay the additional monies was in both the parties' interests and that the agreement did not fail for lack of consideration. On the face of things the decision appears to be wrong since clearly on orthodox theory the subcontractor was already under an existing contractual duty to the defendants and this could not therefore amount to 'good' consideration. It may well be the case that the subcontractor had put in too low a price in his bid for the work, but it is not for the court to rewrite the contract simply because the plaintiff had made a bad bargain. It is always possible for the parties to abandon the contract by agreement and enter into a new one if they so wish. No evidence of this was forthcoming in the facts of the case.

On appeal to the Court of Appeal the defendants indicated that they hoped to obtain three principal benefits from the agreement, namely, getting the job finished, avoiding any penalties and avoiding the trouble of engaging new carpenters. The defendants nevertheless maintained that these benefits were not benefits of law since the plaintiff was already bound by his contractual duties to carry out the contract. The Court of Appeal held that the defendants were obliged to pay the extra monies due and that the plaintiff had provided sufficient consideration to support the promise of the defendants.

In the Court of Appeal Glidewell LJ expressed the law in the following terms:

> (i) if A has entered into a contract with B to do work for, or to supply goods or services to, B in return for payment by B and (ii) at some stage before A has completely performed his obligations under the contract, B has reason to doubt whether A will, or will be able to, complete his side of the bargain, and (iii) B thereupon promises A an additional payment in return for A's promise to perform his contractual obligations on time and (iv) as a result of giving his promise B obtains in practice a benefit, or obviates a disbenefit, and (v) B's promise is not given as a result of economic duress or fraud on the part of A, then (vi) the benefit to B is capable of being consideration for B's promise, so that the promise will be legally binding.

On the face of things, the decision seems to go completely contrary to *Stilk* v *Myrick*, though Glidewell LJ was at pains to affirm the decision in that case and stated that his decision in *Williams* v *Roffey Bros* was merely a refinement of *Stilk* v *Myrick*. It will be recalled that in *Stilk* v *Myrick* Lord Ellenborough approved of the decision in *Harris* v *Watson* but not on the basis of the decision, that is, the application of public policy; instead he relied on the lack of consideration. It might be said then that the rule relating to sufficiency of consideration was a means of applying a crude notion of economic duress, which was unknown in a substantive form until recent times. If this is the case then it may be possible to extrapolate a principle that an existing duty may be good consideration in the absence of economic duress or fraud on the part of the plaintiff provided the defendant obtains a benefit in fact from the existing duty being executed. Such a proposition would also give credibility to Denning's comments in *Ward* v *Byham* and *Williams* v *Williams* above, and which appeared to be tacitly approved of in Glidewell's judgment. Further, the proposition would also support and explain the existence of the exception to the rule in *Stilk* v *Myrick* where a promise to perform, or the performance of, a pre-existing contractual obligation to a *third party* can be valid consideration, as expressed in *Pao On* v *Lao Yiu Long* and *New Zealand Shipping Co Ltd* v *A. M. Satterthwaite & Co Ltd* [1975] AC 154 (see below).

It should be noted that promissory estoppel could not be pleaded by the plaintiff in the case since this cannot be used as a means of bringing an action. Clearly the case could give rise to a great deal of discussion, not least an argument that the stance taken by the Court of Appeal is a move towards an adoption of a law of obligations, which is not based on the doctrine of consideration. Indeed, the role played by promissory estoppel itself, as we shall see later, takes us somewhat nearer this result. In any event the emergence of a formal substantive doctrine of economic duress may well sound the death-knell of *Stilk* v *Myrick*.

From a practical point of view, it is somewhat perverse that, if the defendants had not taken the trouble to increase the fees owed to the plaintiff, they could merely have allowed him to carry on with the contract and could then have sued him for their losses under the penalty clause when the plaintiff inevitably failed to complete the work and was in breach of contract.

(c) Existing contractual duties owed to third parties. An existing contractual duty owed to a third party may amount to sufficient consideration in return for a promise given by the promisee. This exception is usually expressed in the context of existing contractual duties, though there appears to be no reason why it could not equally apply to existing public distress. However such instances would be rare since such duties are largely imposed by statute.

A typical example of this exception can be seen in the case of *Shadwell* v *Shadwell* (1860) 9 CBNS 159, where the plaintiff's uncle wrote congratulating him on his engagement and promised to pay him £150 per annum until such time as he was earning £600 per annum as a chancery barrister. The plaintiff married and sued his uncle's executors on the promise. It was held that, even though the plaintiff was already contractually bound to marry, this was nevertheless good consideration for the uncle's promise.

Whilst *Shadwell* v *Shadwell* illustrates the point, it is of dubious authority not least because, as a family arrangement, it is questionable whether an intention to create a legal relationship existed or not. Further, it is doubtful whether the uncle intended the marriage to amount to consideration and, if he did not, where does the consideration lie?

The decision in *Shadwell* v *Shadwell* was followed in the case of *Chichester* v *Cobb* (1866) 14 LT 433 where the facts were somewhat, though not altogether, similar. The case which firmly establishes the principle contained in the exception is *Scotson* v *Pegg* (1861) 6 H & N 295, where the plaintiffs contracted with a third party, A, to deliver coal to A, or to the order of A. A then sold the coal to the defendant and directed the plaintiffs to deliver it to the defendant. The defendant entered into an agreement with the plaintiffs whereby, 'in consideration that the plaintiffs, at the request of the defendant, would deliver [the coal] to the defendant', the defendant promised to unload the coal at a fixed rate per day. The defendant failed to keep to his promise and, when sued for breach of contract, pleaded lack of sufficient consideration to support his promise. It was held that the defendant was liable and that the performance of an existing contractual duty could be consideration for a promise given by a third party. Whilst the decision in the case would probably be correct today it is deficient in that there is no definite statement as to where the consideration lies.

All three cases which tend to establish the principle have question marks hanging over them, though despite this they all positively direct us towards the principle. The question marks however are largely academic today and any doubts as to the probity of the principle has to be put on one side following the decision of the Privy Council in *New Zealand Shipping Co Ltd* v *A. M. Satterthwaite & Co Ltd, The Eurymedon* [1975] AC 154.

The facts of the case put simply were that the plaintiff made an offer to the defendant that if the defendant unloaded the plaintiff's goods, which the defendant was already obliged to do by virtue of a contract with a third party, the plaintiff would not hold the defendant liable for any damage to the goods. The question arose as to whether the existing contractual duty owed by the defendant to the third party could amount to consideration for the promise of the plaintiff. The majority decision of the court is best summed up in the words of Lord Wilberforce, who stated:

> An agreement to do an act which the promisor is under an existing obligation to a third party to do, may quite well amount to valid consideration and does so in the present case: the promisee obtains the benefit of a direct obligation which he can enforce. This proposition is illustrated and supported by *Scotson* v *Pegg* . . . which their Lordships consider to be good law.

It is of further significance that the decision in *The Eurymedon* was also supported in *Pao On* v *Lau Yiu Long*.

Part-payment of debt

(a) The common law rule. We now need to consider the second area where the law considers the consideration to be insufficient. It should be said immediately that some authors treat this as part of the rules relating to existing contractual duties owed to the promisor. There is nothing wrong with this approach since here the debtor is attempting to show consideration by performing only part of what he is already contractually bound to do. It is, however, possible to distinguish this category in that what is in question here is whether some previous obligation owed has been discharged by only part of it being performed. By contrast, in the category already discussed we examined whether some new obligation could be supported by an existing contractual obligation. This difference is significant since in the previous category we were examining how the promisee could enforce the new obligations against the promisor. In the present category we are examining how to prevent the promisor from enforcing obligations against the promisee which he, the promisor, had agreed not to so enforce. It is for this reason that promissory or equitable estoppel is so applicable to this category since, as we shall see, it can only be used as a defence to a course of action, not as a course of action itself.

The problem arising here occurs where X owes Y a sum of money and pays, or promises to pay, part of the amount owed, provided Y agrees to forgo the balance. The question now arises as to whether Y is bound by his promise. The general common law rule in English law is that all debts are payable in full and that any creditor is not bound to accept part of a debt in satisfaction of the whole amount owed.

The rule enunciated above is known as the rule in *Pinnel's* case (1602) 5 Co Rep 117a, in which it was stated:

> Payment of a lesser sum on the day in satisfaction of a greater cannot be any satisfaction for the whole, because it appears to the Judges that by no possibility a lesser sum can be a satisfaction to the plaintiff for a greater sum. But the gift of a horse, hawk or robe, etc in satisfaction is good. For it shall be intended that a horse, hawk or robe, etc might be more beneficial to the plaintiff than the money in respect of some circumstance, or otherwise the plaintiff would not have accepted it in satisfaction . . . The payment and acceptance of parcel before the day in satisfaction of the whole would be a good satisfaction in regard to circumstance of time, for peradventure parcel of it before the

day would be more beneficial to him than the whole at the day, and the value of satisfaction is not material.

Thus whilst part-payment of debt is not sufficient consideration, such part-payment would be sufficient if some new element is included. The new element might be a different place of payment, or a different time, or some change in the nature of the consideration offered for satisfaction of the whole debt.

The introduction of the new element as amounting to full satisfaction of a debt is, however, subject to one qualification: the new element must be introduced at the request of the creditor not the debtor. This factor is required to protect the creditor against a debtor who attempts to use some financial weakness of the creditor for his own purposes, or who attempts to use the threat of potential litigation on the part of the creditor as a means of reducing the amount payable.

Such a case is *D. & C. Builders Ltd* v *Rees* [1966] 2 QB 617, where the plaintiffs had done building work for the defendant for which they were owed £482. The plaintiffs pressed for payment for some six months and in fact were in dire financial straits. The defendant's wife, knowing of the financial difficulties, offered them £300 in full settlement, adding that if this was not accepted they would get nothing. The plaintiffs reluctantly agreed to this arrangement but once the cheque for £300 had cleared they sued for the balance. It was held that their claim would be successful, the Court of Appeal basing its decision on *Pinnel's* case.

On the facts the decision in *D. & C. Builders Ltd* v *Rees* is a correct application of *Pinnel's* case, though today, with the development of the concept of economic duress, the arrangement would no doubt be void anyway. Given the development of economic duress, it is questionable whether the rule in *Pinnel's* case continues to serve any useful purpose, especially when it can result in inordinately unfair decisions. Such a situation occurred in the case of *Foakes* v *Beer* (1884) 9 App Cas 605, where the rule in *Pinnel's* case was nevertheless affirmed.

In the case of *Foakes* v *Beer*, Mrs Beer had obtained judgment against Dr Foakes for £2,090 and some time later he asked for time to pay. The parties then entered a written agreement where Dr Foakes would pay £500 immediately and the balance by instalments. Mrs Beer agreed also that she would not 'take any proceedings whatever on the judgment'. The parties failed to take into account that a judgment debt carries interest from the date of the judgment. Some five years later Dr Foakes had paid the whole of the judgment debt; Mrs Beer claimed £360 for the interest on the debt. Dr Foakes refused to pay, relying on the agreement and the undertaking by Mrs Beer as a defence. It was held by the House of Lords that Mrs Beer could claim the £360, the court relying on the rule in *Pinnel's* case. Although the decision no doubt was correct in law it has been subject to criticism, in particular from Lord Blackburn, who only reluctantly accepted the decision when confronted with powerful authorities in support of the rule in *Pinnel's* case, and commented:

> all men of business . . . do every day recognise and act on the ground that prompt payment of a part of their demand may be more beneficial to them than it would be to insist on their rights and enforce payment of the whole. Even where the debtor is perfectly solvent, and sure to pay at last, this is often so. Where the credit of the debtor is doubtful it must be more so.

How can the case of *Foakes* v *Beer* be reconciled with *D. & C. Builders Ltd* v *Rees*? The question is important since both decisions rest on the rule in *Pinnel's* case, though the effects are very different. In *Foakes* v *Beer* it has been stated that the common law rule produces a harsh and unfair decision, whilst the application of the rule in *D. & C. Builders Ltd* v *Rees* is undoubtedly quite the opposite. The fact of the matter is that the circumstances of *Foakes* v *Beer* are somewhat exceptional, in that the rule in *Pinnel's* case was never formulated on the basis of the creditor acting in an unfair manner, but on the basis of an impecunious debtor attempting to wring an advantage out of the precarious financial position of the creditor by saying, 'Accept this or you won't get anything at all'. Dr Foakes was unfortunate enough to be caught by a rule which was never intended to apply to circumstances such as his own.

In the absence of an overturning of the rule in *Pinnel's* case, and with the concept of economic duress replacing this rule in cases like *D. & C. Builders Ltd* v *Rees*, a number of exceptions to the rule have developed. The most important of these can be found in the intervention of equity with the use of promissory estoppel.

(b) The exceptions to the rule in Pinnel's *case.* There are three exceptions to the rule in *Pinnel's* case:

(i)   the doctrine of promissory estoppel;
(ii) cheques;
(iii) compositions with creditors.

(i) **The doctrine of promissory estoppel.** The harshness of the application of the rule in *Pinnel's* case, as seen in *Foakes* v *Beer*, has been substantially mitigated by the modern development of the doctrine of equitable estoppel, now usually referred to as promissory estoppel in this context.

The modern doctrine is founded in the case of *Central London Property Trust Ltd* v *High Trees House Ltd* [1947] KB 130 where, in September 1939, the plaintiffs leased a block of flats to the defendants at a ground rent of £2,500 per annum. In January 1940 many of the flats became vacant because of the prevailing war conditions and the plaintiffs reduced the ground rent to £1,250 in recognition of these factors. No time limit was fixed for the arrangement and the defendants continued to pay the reduced rent until 1945. In 1945 the flats were again full and in 1946 the receiver of the defendant company sought to recover the back rent for the last two quarters of 1945 and for future years. It was held by Denning J (as he then was) that the arrangement as to the reduced rent was only intended to apply while war conditions affected the letting of the flats. The flats were again full in June 1945, therefore Denning allowed the receivers to recover the full rent for the last two quarters of 1945 and for future years.

In fact the plaintiffs were only testing their claim by suing for the last two quarters of 1945 and what they intended to do was to attempt to claim the arrears of the rent owed for the years from 1940 to June 1945, basing the claim on the rule in *Pinnel's* case. Whilst this action was not in issue in the case Denning nevertheless turned his attention to whether such a claim would succeed. Undoubtedly if the rule in *Pinnel's* case was applied to this problem the plaintiffs' claim would succeed. The plaintiffs during discussion had promised to accept a lesser sum as payment for a greater sum, no consideration having been given by the defendants to support this promise and the exceptions to the rule in *Pinnel's* case, above, did not apply. Denning concluded, *obiter dicta*, that the plaintiffs would fail in such an action, relying on the operation of the doctrine of equitable estoppel as expressed in the nineteenth-century case of *Hughes* v *Metropolitan Railway Co Ltd* (1877) 2 App Cas 439.

In the *Hughes* case the appellant landlord gave his respondent tenant six months' notice to repair the premises let. Before the notice expired negotiations began between the parties for the sale of the reversion. These negotiations broke down and when the six months' notice expired the appellants brought an action for ejectment. It was held by the House of Lords that the opening of the negotiations by the appellants amounted to a promise that whilst they were going on, no action would be taken to enforce the notice. The tenant had done nothing to the premises because of his reliance on this promise, and thus the six months' notice ran from the date of the failure of the negotiations and not from the original date of the service of the notice. The tenant was entitled to have relief from the action to forfeit his lease. Lord Cairns stated the principle of equitable estoppel in the following terms:

> It is the first principle upon which all Courts of Equity proceed, that if parties who have entered into definite and distinct terms involving certain legal results – certain penalties or legal forfeiture – afterwards by their own act or with their own consent enter upon a course of negotiations which has the effect of leading one of the parties to suppose that the strict legal rights arising under the contract will not be enforced or will be kept in suspense, or held in abeyance, the person who otherwise might have enforced those rights will not be allowed to enforce them where it would be inequitable having regard to the dealings which have thus taken place between the parties.

On examining the *Hughes* case Denning stated: 'I prefer to apply the principle that a promise intended to be binding, intended to be acted on and in fact acted on, is binding so far as its terms properly apply'. In *Combe* v *Combe* [1951] 2 KB 215, however, Denning stated the doctrine of promissory estoppel in more accurate terms as:

> where one party has, by his words or conduct, made to the other a promise or assurance which was intended to affect the legal relations between them and to be acted on accordingly, then, once the other party has taken him at his word and acted on it, the one who gave the promise or assurance cannot afterwards be allowed to revert to the previous legal relations as if no such promise or assurance had been made by him, but he must accept their legal relations as if no such promise or assurance had been made by him, but he must accept their legal relations subject to the qualification which he himself has so introduced, even though it is not supported in point of law by any consideration, but only by his word.

Applying the doctrine as expressed by Denning, the plaintiffs in the *High Trees* case would clearly be estopped in any attempt to claim the arrears of rent from 1940 onwards.

Whilst the doctrine of promissory estoppel as expressed above is fairly straightforward there are certain aspects which emanate from the basic notion of the doctrine and which themselves can give rise to specific problems. These aspects require detailed consideration and are as follows:

1   the nature of the promise;
2   the doctrine is 'a shield not a sword';
3   whether the doctrine is suspensory or extinctive;
4   whether the promisee must act to his prejudice.

(1) *The nature of the promise.* The nature of the promise as stated in *High Trees* is that it must be clear and unequivocal. However this alone is insufficient. Denning emphasised that there must be a clear and unequivocal promise by the promisor that he would not enforce his strict legal rights. Thus the promise must be intended to affect legal relations and not simply amount to a gratuitous privilege given to the promisee, as expressed in both *Woodhouse Israel Cocoa Ltd* v *Nigerian Produce Marketing Co Ltd* [1972] AC 741 and *Scandinavian Trading Tanker Co AB* v *Flota Petrolera Ecuatoriana, The Scaptrade* [1983] 2 All ER 763.

(2) *A shield not a sword* It is well settled that the doctrine of promissory estoppel may only be used as a defence and not as a course of action, that is, it may be used as 'a shield and not a sword'. This principle was established in the case of *Combe* v *Combe*, where after a divorce, a husband promised to pay the ex-wife £100 per annum maintenance, but he failed to make any payments. Whilst she pressed him for payment, she did not in fact make any application for maintenance to the divorce court. Nearly seven years after being awarded the decree absolute, the ex-wife brought an action for £675 representing arrears for six years nine months' maintenance. She alleged that her husband had made an unequivocal promise, intending that she would act on it and that she had in fact acted on that promise, and that the husband should therefore be estopped from going back on that promise. At first instance the court upheld her claim but this decision was reversed in the Court of Appeal which held that the use of estoppel as a cause of action was an illegitimate extension of the principle. The reason for this rule is that to allow estoppel to be used in this manner would be completely contrary to the whole principle of the need for consideration in the law of contract since it would allow promises to be enforceable without consideration being present. Lord Denning took the opportunity to restate the position in the following way:

> The principle stated in the *High Trees* case . . . does not create new causes of action where none existed before. It only prevents a party from insisting upon his strict legal rights when it would be unjust to allow him to enforce them, having regard to the dealings which have taken place between the parties.

The principle as stated is an easy one for students to recall but it is an inaccurate statement. The principle gives the impression that only defendants can make use of promissory estoppel, but this is not necessarily the case. A plaintiff can rely on estoppel provided it does not form the main part of his action. Cheshire and Fifoot refer back to the *Hughes* case and state that if the landlord had gone into possession, the tenant would have brought an action on the basis of the lease, but used estoppel as an answer to the landlord's possible defence that he had a right to forfeit the lease. Here the principal action is based on the lease, with estoppel forming a subsidiary line of argument. Similarly if a buyer of goods states to a seller that he would not insist on delivery of the goods according to the date stated in the contract, and subsequently refused to accept the goods delivered after this date because they were late, the seller could sue for breach of contract and use estoppel as a means of blocking the defence of lateness alleged by the buyer.

There have been attempts to reformulate the doctrine so as to allow actions to be based on it, principally by extending the principles found in the doctrine of proprietary estoppel, which does allow causes of action to be founded on such a doctrine. So far, however, these attempts have not been accepted in promissory estoppel and, in fact, were openly refuted in *Argy Trading Development Co Ltd* v *Lapid Developments Ltd* [1977] 1 WLR 444.

(3) Is the doctrine suspensory or extinctive?   In the *Hughes* case it was seen that the rights of the landlord were merely suspended until the six months' notice from the date of the end of the negotiations for the sale of the reversion had lapsed. In *High Trees*, however, whilst the right to the full rent was only suspended until the ending of war conditions meant that the flats were again full, the right to the arrears of the rent lost while those conditions prevailed was effectively extinguished.

The leading case in this area is the decision of the House of Lords in *Tool Metal Manufacturing Co Ltd* v *Tungsten Electric Co Ltd* [1955] 2 All ER 657. The appellants were the owners of a British patent and in April 1938 they contracted to give the respondents a licence to manufacture and sell certain alloys subject to the patent. The contract stipulated that if the respondent sold more than a certain quantity of the alloys, 'compensation' would be payable to the appellants. At the outbreak of the war the appellants agreed to suspend their compensation rights pending the negotiation of a new contract. The negotiations for the contract began in 1944 but soon afterwards broke down. In 1945 the respondents sued the appellants for breach of contract and they counter-claimed for the compensation payable as from 1 June 1945. The respondents' action was dismissed. In the Court of Appeal the counter-claim by the appellants also failed since it was held that the agreement reached in 1939 operated to prevent the appellants claiming compensation until they had given reasonable notice to the respondents of their intention to revert to the terms of the original contract and that they had not given such notice to the respondents.

In September 1950 the appellants began a second action in which they claimed compensation as from 1 January 1947. The appellants alleged that their counter-claim in the first action amounted to reasonable notice of their intention to claim compensation. The claim was upheld at first instance, reversed in the Court of Appeal, whose decision in turn was reversed by the House of Lords. It is apparent from the case that the appellants' rights to arrears of compensation that had already fallen due had been extinguished and that rights to future compensation had only been suspended until such time as the agreement of 1939 had been cancelled by the appellants on giving the respondents reasonable notice of such cancellation.

Generally the view of promissory estoppel is that it is only suspensory in operation, except in cases where 'the promisee cannot resume his position', as stated by the Privy Council in *Emmanuel Ayodeji Ajayi* v *R. T. Briscoe (Nigeria) Ltd* [1964] 3 All ER 556. This approach is certainly consistent with the *Hughes* case, where the landlord clearly did not intend to give up his right to forfeit the lease for all time. If this approach is applied to *Foakes* v *Beer* then the fact that Mrs Beer's right to the interest is merely suspended would be clearly offensive to equitable principles given her original undertaking. In order to reconcile this conflict the better view would seem to be that the doctrine is suspensory, except where the promisee cannot resume his position or where there is an express or implied intention on the part of the promisor that he is giving up his rights forever. Applying such an approach to *High Trees* produces the result that rights to future rent may be revived by the giving of reasonable notice, whilst until such notice is given any instalments of rent at the reduced rate rendered the balance of this and other previous instalments irrecoverable and to that extent extinguished. Of course this result in *High Trees* might have been different if the promisor had indicated that the intention was only to give the promisee time to pay.

Denning in *Brikom Investments Ltd* v *Carr* [1979] QB 467 considered that there were certain exceptional cases where it might be impossible for the promisor to go back to his strict legal rights even though he had given reasonable notice to the promisee of his intention to do so. It is doubtful whether the courts would ever go so far as to allow the complete extinction of a promisee's strict legal rights in these circumstances, though this situation has not yet been tested in a case.

It is clear that there are considerable difficulties with this area. As Treitel points out, it is an area which is ripe for review in the House of Lords, pointing to Lord Hailsham's comment in the *Woodhouse* case, above, that the *High Trees* principle 'may need to be reviewed and reduced to a coherent body of doctrine by the courts'.

(4) *Must the promisee act to his prejudice?* It is clear from the *High Trees, R. T. Briscoe* and *Tool Metal* cases that, to invoke the doctrine of promissory estoppel, the promisee must have either acted on the promise of the promisor, or at least altered his position in reliance on the promise. It has largely been assumed that the promisee must have been prejudiced by his reliance on the promise. Indeed, one might consider that the whole *raison d'être* of promissory estoppel is the notion that it is inequitable to allow the promisor to withdraw from his promise, because that would lead to the promisee incurring some detriment. Whilst the tenant suffered a detriment in the *Hughes* case, no such detriment or prejudice appears in the *High Trees* case.

In *W. J. Alan & Co Ltd* v *El Nasr Export and Import Co* [1972] 2 QB 189 Denning denied the need to prove that the promisee had suffered a detriment, and in fact, repeated such views in *Brikom Investments Ltd* v *Carr*, although in both cases the other members of the Court of Appeal left the question open.

In the New Zealand case of *P* v *P* [1957] NZLR 854, the judge thought that the test should be based not on the position of the promisee but on 'whether it would be inequitable to allow the party seeking so to do to enforce the strict rights which he had induced the other party to believe will not be enforced'. Such an approach was also thought correct by Goff J in *Société Italo-Belge pour le Commerce et l'Industrie SA v Palm and Vegetable Oils (Malaysia) Sdn Bhd, The Post Chaser* [1982] 1 All ER 19, who insisted that all that was required to be proved was that some inequity could be shown to result by the promisor attempting to resile from his promise. He stated:

> The fundamental principle is . . . that the representor will not be allowed to enforce his rights where it would be inequitable having regard to the dealings which have thus taken place between the parties. To establish such inequity, it is not necessary to show detriment; indeed, the representee may have benefited from the representation, and yet it may be inequitable, at least without reasonable notice, for the representor to enforce his legal rights. . . . But it does not follow that in every case in which the representee has acted, or failed to act, in reliance on the representation, it will be inequitable for the representor to enforce his rights for the nature of the action or inaction may be insufficient to give rise to the equity, in which event a necessary requirement . . . for the application of the doctrine would not have been fulfilled.

Clearly this whole area is in need of review by the House of Lords since the remarks of Goff J go very much towards a view expressed by Lord Denning extra-judicially that resiling from a promise is itself inequitable and should give rise to an application of the doctrine. Such a stance is far too radical since it strikes at the heart of consideration itself. A bargain must be supported by consideration and whilst promissory estoppel might, correctly, be allowed as an exception to the general principle, to allow it to develop to the point of enforcing gratuitous promises generally is unacceptable at the present time.

(ii) **Cheques.** It was stated earlier that a part-payment of debt may be good consideration if, at the creditor's request, it is made in a different form, or at a different place or time. The question that arises here is whether a cheque or other bill of exchange can amount to a different form of payment for the purposes of the exceptions to the rule in *Pinnel's* case. At one time cheques were regarded as a different form of payment and thus formed an exception to the rule in *Pinnel's* case. This is no longer the position as was made clear by Lord Denning in *D. & C. Builders Ltd v Rees*:

> No sensible distinction can be taken between payment of a lesser sum by cash and payment of it by cheque. The cheque, when given, is conditional payment. When honoured, it is actual payment. It is then just the same as cash. If a creditor is not bound when he receives a payment by cash, he should not be bound when he receives payment by cheque.

(iii) **Compositions with creditors** It is a common practice for a debtor who cannot pay his creditors in full to come to an arrangement with them that each will receive a percentage of the figure owed in full satisfaction of the whole of the original debts. It is clear from the rule in *Pinnel's* case that such an arrangement should not be binding on the parties to it, yet such arrangements are nevertheless upheld. The basis of their binding nature is somewhat elusive.

One theory is that the arrangements are binding since there is a contract between each and every creditor on the basis that each has promised to forgo his part of the debt. The theory is fundamentally flawed, however, since it is clear that the debtor would not be part of this contract since he himself has provided no consideration for the creditors' promises to him.

A second approach has been to justify composition arrangements on the basis that creditors will not be allowed to go behind the agreement and sue for the balance owed to them since such action amounts to a fraud on all the parties. Whilst such an approach can produce problems it has tended to be adopted on the basis that it is consistent with the position as regards part-payment of debt by third parties. Such part-payment, if accepted by the creditor in settlement of the whole debt, is regarded as a good defence to a later action by the creditor against the debtor for the balance, on the basis that otherwise the creditor would be committing a fraud against the third party. The fraud arises here since the creditor is inducing a payment from the third party on the basis that he agrees to discharge the debtor from the whole amount. This was the finding of the court in *Welby* v *Drake* (1825) 1 C & P 557, which finding has subsequently been affirmed in *Hirachand Punamchand* v *Temple* [1911] 2 KB 330.

(c) The effect of the decision in Williams *v* Roffey Bros *on* Pinnel's *case*. It has already been seen that the decision in *Williams* v *Roffey Bros and Nicholls (Contractors) Ltd* seems to withdraw from the authority laid down in *Stilk* v *Myrick* that the performance, or promise to perform, an existing contractual duty owed by the party to another is no consideration for a promise from that other party and that this principle may also be applied to part payment of debt. For example, if A is owed £500 by B and agrees to take £400 in full and final settlement, this agreement is unenforceable by B since he has provided no consideration for A's promise to accept the lower sum. B is under an existing contractual duty to pay the full amount and, in law at least, A has received no consideration or benefit in accepting less. In relation to part payment of debt the authority for this principle is found in *Pinnel's* case and *Foakes* v *Beer*. The reason for the existence of this principle in these cases is, just as in *Stilk* v *Myrick*, founded on the need to prevent the debtor extracting an advantage by extortion or economic duress of the type seen in *D & C Builders Ltd* v *Rees*. It is for this reason that the exception to the rule in *Pinnel's* case, whereby some new element is introduced, can only be brought about at the instance of the creditor. With the onset of the development of a doctrine of economic duress there would seem to be little need for the continuation of this approach.

The reasoning set out above was at least partly behind the decision in *Williams* v *Roffey Bros and Nicholls (Contractors) Ltd*. It will be recalled that the arguments advanced by Roffey Bros in their defence was that their promise to pay the additional monies was unenforceable because Williams had provided no consideration for it, merely carrying out their existing contractual duties which, as stated in *Stilk* v *Myrick*, would be insufficient consideration for the later promise. Roffey Bros admitted that they enjoyed certain benefits from their promise to pay the extra monies in that the work would have been completed on time and that, as a result, they would have avoided the disbenefit of having to pay penalties. Roffey Bros thus gained a *factual* benefit, though one which was not recognised in *law* in terms of the rule as stated in *Stilk* v *Myrick*. The Court of Appeal rejected the defence of Roffey Bros based on *Stilk* v *Myrick* and found for Williams, ruling that, in the absence of economic duress for fraud, where one party to a contract agrees to make a payment or convey an advantage to the other over and above his contractual obligations in order to ensure that the contract is completed on time, and that as a result obtains a benefit or avoids a disbenefit, the obtaining of that benefit could amount to consideration for his own promise to pay the extra monies or convey the extra advantage to the other party.

The case of *Williams* v *Roffey Bros* was confined to a contract for goods and services but, if one accepts that the rule in *Pinnel's* case no longer serves a useful purpose in the light of the development of economic duress, this raises the question of the extent to which the decision in *Roffey Bros* could be applied to cases of part-payment of debt. Acceptance of part-payment of debt, in the absence of economic duress and fraud, may be a perfectly reasonable transaction for the creditor to enter into. The reasoning bears a close analogy to *Williams* v *Roffey Bros* since, whilst the creditor only receives a proportion of his monies (or as in *Foakes* v *Beer* only receives them by instalments instead of in one lump sum), he also receives the benefit of avoiding having to take legal action to claim the full amount, with the possibility in the event of the bankruptcy of the debtor of only receiving a proportion of his monies, which may be less than the amount offered by the debtor. The benefit obtained by the creditor here is clearly only a *factual* benefit since the rule in *Pinnel's* case and *Stilk* v *Myrick* prevents the benefit from being recognised in *law*, just as in *Williams* v *Roffey Bros*.

The application of the decision in *Williams* v *Roffey Bros* to debt situations was attempted in *Re Selectmove Ltd* ((1994) *The Times*, 13 January, p 28) where the company entered into negotiations with the Inland Revenue concerning the payment of taxes owed. During the negotiations the company offered to pay its tax debts by instalments, the Collector of Taxes stating that he would come back to the company if the arrangement was found to be unsatisfactory. As a result, the company commenced paying the taxes owed by instalments but was then contacted by the Inland Revenue, who insisted that all the arrears of taxes should be paid immediately, otherwise it would commence winding-up proceedings against the company.

In order to avoid the winding-up petition the company argued that the case of *Williams* v *Roffey Bros* was authority for the proposition that promising to perform an existing obligation could amount to good consideration, provided that the promisee obtained a practical or factual benefit. They agreed that, whilst they were under an existing obligation to pay their arrears in taxes in full, the Inland Revenue, by accepting payment by instalments, recovered the full amount without including the cost of recovering the debt by way of legal action. The company therefore argued that this benefit was analogous to that obtained by Roffey Bros.

It was held in the Court of Appeal that the agreement to accept payment of the debt by instalments was not binding on the Inland Revenue. Their Lordships distinguished the case from that of *Williams* v *Roffey Bros* on the basis that the present case was concerned with an existing obligation to pay a debt, whilst the *Roffey* case was concerned with a contract for goods and services, and as such the court was bound by the House of Lords' decision in *Foakes* v *Beer*. On this basis the decision is correct though it is clearly inconsistent with the decision in *Williams* v *Roffey Bros*.

The problem here is that the decision in *Foakes* v *Beer* itself ignores the realities of commercial life. Indeed, in the case itself, Lord Blackburn criticised the rule stating that part-payment of a debt was sometimes more beneficial to the creditor than strictly insisting on compliance with his legal rights. An example of this can clearly be seen in compositions with creditors and can be seen in the facts of *Re Selectmove* itself. Surely it was better for the Inland Revenue to receive the full amount, albeit by instalments, than to take immediate action for the whole sum, with the possibility of only receiving a proportion of the monies owed?

Until the rule in *Foakes* v *Beer* is overturned in the House of Lords the present inconsistent position will remain. It should, of course, be remembered that the rule in *Foakes* v *Beer* will continue to be tempered by the doctrine of promissory estoppel. Two further points should be noted: firstly, if the rule in *Pinnel's* case as stated in *Foakes* v *Beer* is eventually overruled, agreements in relation to part payment of debt will only be enforceable in the absence of economic duress or fraud as in *Williams* v *Roffey*; secondly, the doctrine of promissory estoppel will be of significantly less importance in this situation.

A further aspect to the decision is that it is surprising that the House of Lords did not attempt to distinguish the case on the basis that in *Selectmove* the company, i.e. the debtor, had approached the Inland Revenue. The exceptions to the rule in *Pinnel's* case are all based on the fact that it is the creditor, i.e. the person receiving the factual benefit, who should make the approach to the debtor, in order to avoid the possibility of economic duress arising from the debtor. Similarly in *Williams* v *Roffey Bros* the approach was made by Roffey Bros, again the party obtaining the factual benefit. It should also be noted that there was no indication that the Inland Revenue had accepted the arrangement. The fact that the creditor was the Inland Revenue may also have had some influence on the decision.

Further reading

Atiyah, 'Consideration: A Restatement', *Essays on Contract*, 1990, Oxford University Press

Beale, Bishop and Furmston, *Contract – Cases and Materials* 2nd ed. 1990, Butterworths

Brinkworth and Powell, 'Contract and Consideration: A New Commercial Reality?', 12 *Business Law Review* 5, 1991

Cheshire, Fifoot and Furmston, *The Law of Contract* 12th ed. 1991, Butterworths

Denning, 'Recent Developments in the Doctrine of Consideration', 15 *Modern Law Review* 1, 1952

Guest, *Anson's Law of Contract* 26th ed. 1984, Oxford University Press

Hooley, 'Consideration and Existing Duty', *Journal of Business Law* 19, 1991

Jackson, 'How Many Kinds of Estoppel?', *The Conveyancer and Property Lawyer* 450, 1982

Kee, 'Pragmatic Approach Towards Consideration: *Williams* v *Roffey Bros and Nicholls (Contractors)*', 1 *Modern Law Review*, 1991

Noble, 'For your consideration', 141 *New Law Journal* 1529, 1991

Peel, 'Part Payment of Debt is no Consideration', 110 *Law Quarterly Review* 353, 1994

Pollock, *Principles of Contract*, 13th ed. 1950, Stevens

Treitel, *The Law of Contract* 8th ed. 1991, Sweet & Maxwell

4 | Intention to create legal relations

INTRODUCTION

So far it has been seen that a contract must contain an element of agreement supported by consideration. The mere presence, however, of these elements does not necessarily mean that a legally binding contract has come into existence.

The modern law of contract has an underlying philosophy based on the will of the participants, and if they do not consent to the creation of a legal relationship then no contract that is legally enforceable will emanate from the relationship of the parties. As Lord Justice Atkin expressed it in the case of *Balfour* v *Balfour* [1919] 2 KB 571: 'In respect of these promises each house is a domain into which the King's writ does not seek to run.'

On the face of things then the rule appears very simple and straightforward but, as every student of the law of contract should now be starting to realise, this is rarely the case in this subject. It is clear that serious legal, administrative and economic problems could result if, in every dispute concerning a contract, an intention to create a legal relationship had to be proven. The courts have thus assumed a more restrictive and pragmatic approach to this problem based on the presumed intentions of the parties. In commercial matters the courts presume that the parties intend to create a legal relationship, whilst in agreements of a social or domestic nature no such presumption is made. In either case, however, the presumption may be overturned by actual evidence to the contrary. Usually the burden of rebutting this presumption is very high; indeed, one is not just attempting to overturn a straightforward legal rule, but a legal rule with judicial policy at its foundation, the policy being that the law should not interfere in respect of such transactions.

SOCIAL AND DOMESTIC ARRANGEMENTS

Most social and domestic arrangements do not amount to binding contracts since they are not intended to be such. To agree to take a friend out for a meal or a drink is clearly not intended to confer on the friend a right of action before the courts should one fail to carry out one's commitment. Cases that amount to social/domestic arrangements tend to fall into two broad areas:

Family arrangements

The case of *Balfour* v *Balfour*, above, forms a leading authority in this area. In the case a husband, who was a civil servant based in Sri Lanka, brought his wife to England. Eventually he had to return but his wife had to stay in England for medical reasons. He agreed to pay her £30 per month maintenance during his absence. When he failed to pay the allowance she sued. Her action failed on two grounds: firstly, she had not provided any consideration for the £30 per month and, secondly, the parties had no intention of creating a legally binding agreement. The court stated that where the parties were husband and wife the burden was on the plaintiff, the wife, to rebut the presumption that there was no intention to create a contract.

It should be noted that agreements between husband and wife can, from time to time, produce legally binding consequences.

In *Merritt* v *Merritt* [1970] 1 WLR 1121, the husband left the matrimonial home to live with another woman. At a meeting with his wife he agreed in writing to pay her £40 per month maintenance from which she had to repay the mortgage and, when the repayment was completed, to transfer the house into her sole ownership. The wife did in fact pay off the mortgage but the husband then refused to transfer the house to her. The Court of Appeal held that there was an intention to create a legal relationship and therefore held the husband to his agreement. The reasoning enunciated in the Court of Appeal was based largely on the fact that the agreement took place in response to a marital breakdown. In *Balfour*, on the other hand, the arrangements were made on the basis of an amicable agreement. The *Merritt* case illustrates the point that the courts will take all factors into account in deciding the existence or non-existence of the intention to create a legal relationship.

Further, the case of *Pettit* v *Pettit* [1970] AC 777 also serves as a warning to those who read too much into the principles in the *Balfour* case, where Lord Diplock stated:

> It would in my view, be erroneous to extend the presumption accepted in *Balfour* v *Balfour* that mutual promises between a man and wife in relation to their domestic arrangements are prima facie not intended by either to be legally enforceable to a presumption that NO legal consequences should flow from acts done by them in performance of mutual promises with respect to the acquisition, improvement or addition to real or personal property – for this would be to intend what is impossible in Law.

Similar problems of intention also occur in relations between parents and children.

In the case of *Jones* v *Padavatton* [1969] 1 WLR 328 a mother agreed with her daughter that if the latter gave up her job in the USA and read for the Bar in England, the mother would pay her an allowance of $200 a month. On this basis the daughter came to England and began her legal studies in November 1962. In 1964 the mother bought a house for £6,000, whereupon the earlier agreement was now varied so that the daughter, instead of receiving her allowance, would live in part of the house and let the rest, using the rent to cover expenses and her maintenance. In 1967 the parties had an argument and as a consequence the mother brought an action for the possession of the house. The mother based her claim on the allegation that the agreement was not made with the intention of creating a legal relationship. A majority of the Court of Appeal held that there was no intention to create a legal relationship between the parties and gave the mother possession of the house. Lord Salmon agreed with the decision but arrived at it on different grounds. He considered that the first agreement was a binding contract that was intended to last for a reasonable time in order to allow the daughter to pass her Bar Finals. When five years had gone by and she had still not passed them he considered that the contract had lapsed. The second agreement concerning the possession of the house he considered to be so ambiguous and uncertain as to be incapable of being described as a contract. Lord Salmon based his decision regarding the first agreement on the basis that he thought it inconceivable for the daughter to give up a lucrative job without there existing an enforceable promise of financial support.

Other social arrangements

Questions such as those discussed above may also occur in agreements other than those between husband and wife and parent and child, that is in everyday social arrangements. Similarly the presumption is against a finding of an intention to create a legal relationship, though this may also be rebutted by evidence to the contrary. A factor that can be very influential here is the notion of mutuality. In *Simpkins* v *Pays* [1955] 3 All ER 10 the defendant owned a house in which she lived with her granddaughter, and the plaintiff, a paying lodger. The three regularly took part in a competition in a Sunday newspaper. Whilst the entries were entered under the defendant's name, all of them contributed to the competition, though there was no regular arrangement as to the payment of postage and other expenses. One week the entry was successful but the defendant refused to pay the plaintiff his share of the prize and claimed that there was no intention to create a legally binding relationship. It was held that the plaintiff was entitled to his share, the judge stating that there was sufficient 'mutuality in the arrangements between the parties' to establish a legally binding agreement to share any prize that might be won.

COMMERCIAL AGREEMENTS

In these types of agreements there is a strong presumption that there is an intention to create a legally binding relationship. This presumption can, of course, be rebutted, but in fact very strong evidence is required to do this. One way of rebutting the presumption is by inserting an express statement to this effect in a written statement. In *Appleson v H. Littlewood Ltd* [1939] 1 All ER 464 and in *Jones v Vernon's Pools Ltd* [1938] 2 All ER 626 the plaintiffs in both cases attempted to claim monies which they had alleged had been won in a football pool. The words 'Binding in honour only' were contained on each coupon. It was held that the words were sufficient to rebut the presumption and the plaintiffs thus failed in their action.

The decisions in the *Littlewoods* and *Vernon's* cases are not difficult to understand given the nature of the transactions, which could hardly be said to arise from the harsh world of commercial bargaining. A remarkable case that does however so emanate is that of *Rose and Frank Co v J. R. Crompton and Bros* [1925] AC 445.

In the case an English company agreed to sell certain carbon copy materials in the USA through a New York based firm. The transaction, which was made in writing, gave the plaintiffs the sole rights to market and sell the products in the USA and Canada for a period of three years with an option to extend the period. The document contained a clause, which was described as an 'Honourable Pledge Clause', and which provided: 'This arrangement is not entered into . . . as a formal or legal agreement and shall not be subject to legal jurisdiction to the law courts either of the United States or England'. The original agreement began in July 1913 but at the end of the three-year period the option to extend was exercised; as a result the agreement was to last until March 1920. In 1919 the English defendants terminated the agreement and failed to give appropriate notice as required by the agreement, and also refused to fulfil orders received by them prior to their decision to terminate the agreement.

The Court of Appeal decided that with regard to the orders already received there arose a separate and binding contract which the defendants were bound to fulfil. With respect to the grant of the selling rights, the court found that as the parties had specifically declared that the document was not to bring about legally binding consequences then none could exist; as a result there was no obligation to give orders or to receive them, though once they were given and accepted the defendants were bound to execute the order.

Whilst the case gives effect to the intentions of the parties as expressed in the written memorandum and no doubt produces a fair result as regards the orders already received, the decision in the Court of Appeal fails to address satisfactorily two problems, both of which were raised at first instance. First, how can the clause bind the parties if there is no binding contract as alleged by the clause itself? This is obviously illogical and whilst the end result may be said to be justifiable where the contract is entered into by businessmen negotiating at arm's length, serious problems might result if such clauses were to become part and parcel of a standard-form contract imposed on an unwary or weaker party. Secondly, the clause would appear to be void in any event as being contrary to public policy in that it purports to oust the jurisdiction of the courts. This principle is a fundamental element of the common law and seems to have been side-stepped by the argument that it only operates where the contract was intended to be legally binding in the first place. As Atiyah points out in *Introduction to the Law of Contract*, such a distinction appears to be highly artificial.

Despite the decision in the *Rose and Frank* case, it still remains a strong presumption in commercial agreements that there is an intention to create a legally binding contract. This is particularly true where a party attempts to overturn the presumption but does so in a clause that is ambiguous. The burden of proving this assertion falls on that individual.

This was the case in *Edwards* v *Skyways Ltd* [1964] 1 All ER 494, where the plaintiff was employed as an airline pilot when the defendants, his employers, informed him that they were making him redundant and gave him three months' notice. By virtue of his contract the plaintiff was a member of the defendants' contributory pension fund which entitled him to one of two options on leaving their service. He could either take his contributions out of the fund or receive a paid-up pension which would take effect when he was 50 years of age. The plaintiff's professional association, negotiating on his behalf, agreed with the defendants that if the plaintiff chose the first option the defendants would make him an *ex gratia* payment equal to the defendants' contribution to the fund. The plaintiff accepted the agreement and chose to withdraw his contributions. The defendants then paid him his total contributions but refused to make the *ex gratia* payment. The plaintiff sued for breach of contract and won. The judge stated that the words *ex gratia* did not give rise to a negative contract agreement but simply meant that the employers did not admit to any pre-existing legal liability on their part. They failed to discharge the burden of overturning the presumption that there was an intention to create a legal relationship and were thus liable to make the payment.

A recent development in this area has been the emergence of so-called 'letters of comfort'. A letter of comfort is a letter or memorandum usually written by a holding company to a lender about to lend money to a subsidiary of the holding company so as to reassure the lender of the financial viability of the subsidiary. Such letters are not guarantees in that the holding company is not willing to enter into a legally binding financial commitment. The possible reasons for adopting such a stance could be that the amount of the guarantee exceeds the financial commitments embodied in the articles of association of the holding company or the presence of such a financial commitment in the accounts of the holding company would have an adverse effect on its own affairs.

The leading case in this area is that of *Kleinwort Benson Ltd* v *Malaysia Mining Corporation Bhd* [1989] 1 All ER 785 where the plaintiff bank agreed a loan facility to the wholly owned subsidiary of MMC, MMC Metals Ltd, which was trading in tin on the London Metal Exchange. The bank was not willing to lend the money simply on the basis of MMC Metals' creditworthiness and called on MMC itself to guarantee the loan. MMC replied to this proposal that it was not its policy to guarantee the loans of its subsidiaries. After considerable negotiations MMC agreed to issue a letter of comfort in which it stated, *inter alia*, 'It is our policy to ensure that the business of MMC Metals Ltd is at all times in a position to meet its liabilities to you'. KB agreed to accept the letter of comfort but on the basis that a higher rate of interest would be charged. Eventually the world tin market collapsed, leaving MMC Metals insolvent. The plaintiffs claimed the balance of the monies owed from the parent company, the defendants.

At first instance the case was treated as one dealing with an intention to create a legal relationship, the judge finding that since this was a highly commercial agreement, a contractual obligation existed on the part of the defendants. The judge relied heavily on the decision in the *Skyways* case, stating that in a business context an intention to create a legal relationship was presumed and that the onus of proving a contrary assertion lay on the party making it, in this case MMC. He found that MMC had not discharged this burden and they were therefore bound to meet the liabilities of MMC Metals.

The Court of Appeal disagreed with the judge at first instance and stated that the *Skyways* case concerned a promise supported by consideration and therefore had no application to the present case. The question that had to be asked was whether the clause conveyed an express intention to create a legal relationship in that it contained within it a contractual promise. The court found that it merely conveyed a statement as to present intention and was carefully drafted so as not to contain a statement as to future conduct. The appeal of MMC was thus allowed. Nevertheless some care has to be exercised with the case in two respects: firstly, the case turns very much on the court's interpretation of the clause in question, and the absence of express words indicating a promise does not necessarily prevent a statement from amounting to a contractual promise. Secondly, the clause in question would not be devoid of all legal effect if in fact it amounted to a fraudulent misrepresentation of the existing position.

A further exception to the presumption of an intention to create a legal relationship in commercial agreements lies in the case of advertisements. In order to protect advertisers who make flamboyant claims regarding the products advertised, the law assumes that there is no intention to create a legal relationship, thus preventing some disappointed individual who finds the claims exaggerated from taking any action. Such exaggerated claims are referred to as mere 'puffs', in that they 'puff' the product up in order to make it more attractive and thereby induce consumers to purchase it. Very often such claims are gross exaggerations and no one really expects the products to produce the effects envisaged by the advertiser. Contemporary examples are very often visual and would appear to hope, for instance, to persuade the public to buy a certain brand of coffee to experience some unlikely romantic liaison for which a beer that reaches the parts the others cannot reach would also be required at some stage of the evening. In the past, slogans were very much the forte of the advertising agency, for example: 'Daz washes whiter than white!' Probably the more exaggerated the claim the safer the advertiser is since if the claim appears to have some semblance of credibility the more likely it is to have a contractual effect that is legally enforceable. The case of *Carlill* v *Carbolic Smoke Ball Co*, already discussed, provides a classic example of such a case.

Further reading

Beale, Bishop and Furmston, *Contract – Cases and Materials* 2nd ed. 1990, Butterworths

Cheshire, Fifoot and Furmston, *The Law of Contract* 12th ed. 1991, Butterworths

Guest, *Anson's Law of Contract* 26th ed. 1984, Oxford University Press

Hedley, 'Keeping Contract in its Place: *Balfour* v *Balfour* and the Enforceability of Informal Agreements', 5 *Oxford Journal of Legal Studies* 391, 1985.

Treitel, *The Law of Contract* 8th ed. 1991, Sweet & Maxwell

5 | Capacity

Prima facie the law assumes that all parties to a contract have the power to enter into that contract. However the law places restrictions on the ability of a number of groups of persons to enter into contractual relations. The idea of restrictions on contractual capacity belies the underlying reasoning behind the notion of capacity to contract since the aim of the law is to protect rather than to restrict. The approach taken by the law depends on whether the person is a natural person or an artificial person, that is, a corporation.

THE CAPACITY OF NATURAL PERSONS

Introduction

The traditional role model of the natural person entering into contractual relations is that of the sane, sober and adult male individual. Deviation from this model immediately raises questions as to the ability of the individual to negotiate the responsibilities thrust upon him or her. Thankfully the incapacity of females, in particular married women, to enter into contracts has disappeared in law despite the persistence of social prejudice, though protection is still imposed on drunks or those suffering from mental impairment or disability due to age.

Drunks

A contract is voidable if drunkenness prevents an individual from understanding the transaction he has entered into and the other party is aware of his level of intoxication, though this latter situation rarely arises since it must be virtually impossible for a person to be so drunk as not to know what he is doing without this factor being obvious to the other party. It should be noted that a drunk will be liable to pay a reasonable price for items considered necessaries (see below for the meaning of this term) and in any event will be liable on the contract should he ratify it on becoming sober.

Mentally disordered persons

Such individuals are bound by the contract unless they fall into two categories:

Those certified insane

By virtue of Part VII of the Mental Health Act 1983 a person may be certified as being insane by two medical practitioners where they are both of the opinion that the person in question is incapable of managing his own affairs and property because of his mental state. In these circumstances the property of the insane person falls under the control of the court, so that any attempt by the individual to dispose of the property does not bind him. It does not seem to be settled whether contracts other than those to dispose of the property will bind the individual involved. Treitel suggests not, since all contracts are a potential interference with a person's property.

Those not certified as insane

Where the person is not certified as insane, the contract will be voidable if the other party is aware of the person's disorder and the mentally disordered person did not understand the transaction in question. The burden of proving these two factors is on the mentally disordered person. Further, if the disordered person ratifies the contract on being cured of his condition then he will become absolutely bound by the contract.

Necessaries

The Sale of Goods Act 1979, s. 3(2), provides:

> Where necessaries are sold and delivered to a person who by reason of mental incapacity or drunkenness is incompetent to contract, he must pay a reasonable price for them.

It should be noted that s. 3(2) does not apply where a mentally disordered person purchases necessaries which are delivered to him by a seller who is not aware of the disability. Here the seller may recover the full price and is not restricted to a claim for a reasonable price.

Minors

Introduction

The Family Law Reform Act 1969, s. 1, provides that any person below the age of 18 is classed as a minor (very often referred to as an 'infant' in older cases). As already stated, despite the petulant views of youth, the aim of the law here is to protect rather than restrict, and this includes not only protecting minors from entering into unfair contracts, but also protecting adults in their dealings with minors, provided they act in a fair and reasonable manner. The result is that minors' contracts are regarded as binding or voidable, depending on the circumstances.

Contracts regarded as binding on minors

(a) Contracts for necessaries.   From the earliest times of the common law minors have been obliged to pay for goods or services necessary to maintain them in their particular station of life. It is important to note that necessary goods are not the same as necessities. A silk blouse may be necessary for the daughter of a millionaire, but this is hardly a necessity since one made of a cheaper material would do equally as well, as of course it must for the daughter of a process worker, for instance.

The rules relating to necessary goods are contained in s. 3(3) of the Sale of Goods Act 1979, which provides that an infant must pay a reasonable price for 'necessaries'. Necessaries are defined as goods 'suitable to the condition in life of the minor and to his actual requirements at the time of the sale and delivery'. The effect is that a plaintiff wishing to enforce such a contract has to establish three points:

(a) that the goods are capable of being necessaries;
(b) that the minor has not already been adequately supplied with such items at the time of their delivery;
(c) the supplier must show that the goods have been sold and delivered.

Whether the goods are **capable of being necessaries** is a question of law. Thus in *Ryder* v *Wombwell* (1868) LR 4 Exch 32 it was held by the jury that a pair of cuff-links worth £25 and an antique goblet worth £15 could amount to necessaries for an infant with an income of £500 per year. The court, however, set the verdict aside on the fact that the evidence could not properly justify such a finding.

The second point which must be established is whether the minor has not been already *adequately supplied with such items* at the time of their delivery. In other words, the supplier must show that the items are *de facto* necessary to the minor. In *Nash* v *Inman* [1908] 2 KB 1, for instance, a Savile Row tailor attempted to recover £122 16s 6d. for items (which included 11 fancy waistcoats at £2 2s. each), supplied to an undergraduate. The action failed as it was shown that the minor was already adequately supplied with clothes and therefore those supplied by the tailor could not amount to necessaries.

The third matter required for the enforcement of such a contract is that the supplier must show that the **goods have been sold and delivered**. An executory contract would thus appear to be unenforceable; in other words can an infant who has agreed to buy goods which have yet to be delivered to him repudiate the contract? The answer is inconclusive since, whilst s. 3(3) talks in terms of the goods having been delivered, that is, executed, and indeed in *Nash* v *Inman* it was thought that the minor was liable because he had been supplied with the goods, in *Roberts* v *Gray* [1913] 1 KB 520 an executory contract was held to be binding. This case was concerned with a contract for education, but it is difficult to comprehend why such a contract should be treated differently and Treitel indicates that there should be no distinction between the two categories of contract. In any event the 1979 Act seems to be quite definite that the contract must be executed.

Even if the supplier should satisfy the above requirements, a contract may still be void if its terms are harsh and onerous to the infant. In *Fawcett* v *Smethurst* [1914] 84 LJ KB 473, where a minor hired a car in order to transport some luggage, prima facie the contract of hire was a necessary but nevertheless it was held to be void since it was considered that a term rendering the minor absolutely liable for any damage to the car whether or not caused by his neglect was harsh and onerous.

(b) Beneficial contracts of service. The rules here again have their foundations in the common law and are essentially the same as for goods, though here executory contracts may be enforceable.

It should be noted before we proceed any further that the minor need only pay a reasonable price, not necessarily the contract price, for goods or services found to be necessaries. A beneficial contract of service, such as a contract of apprenticeship, education or of employment are prima facie binding on a minor provided they are substantially for the minor's benefit. The *whole* contract must be assessed because, even though one or more stipulations may be regarded as prejudicial, this does not invalidate the contract. Adverse terms have to be expected in service agreements to a certain extent. The question to be considered is whether, in the light of an assessment of the surrounding circumstances, the contract can be said to favour the minor. In *Clements* v *LNWR* [1894] 2 QB 482 the minor joined the railway as a porter and agreed to join the company's own insurance scheme, which meant that he relinquished his rights to sue under the Employers' Liability Act 1880 should he ever suffer personal injury whilst so employed. The insurance scheme was more favourable than the Act in that it provided for compensation for more types of accidents, though the level of compensation was lower than was provided in the Act. It was held that the agreement was on balance of benefit to the infant and therefore valid and binding. In *De Francesco* v *Barnum* (1890) 45 Ch D 430, on the other hand, a 14-year-old girl was apprenticed to the plaintiff for seven years in order to be taught stage dancing. The deed signed stated that she was to be at the total disposal of the plaintiff; she would not be paid unless he employed her, which he was not bound to do, nor was he bound to maintain her. It was agreed that she would be paid 9d. per evening performance and 6d. per matinee for the first three years, after which her pay rose to 1s. 0d. per evening performance and 6d. per matinee. It was further agreed that she could not accept any professional engagement without his consent, and that she was also required to obtain his consent if she wished to marry. Not least, the plaintiff could terminate her contract without notice when he wished. It should come as no surprise that the court held that the contract was unduly harsh and onerous and as a result was unenforceable.

A progressively wider notion of a beneficial contract of service has emerged in recent times. Thus in *Doyle* v *White City Stadium* [1935] 1 KB 110 it was held that a contract between a minor professional boxer and the British Boxing Board of Control which stated that he would lose his purse if he was disqualified was valid in that it not only encouraged clean fighting but encouraged the proficiency of the infant in the art of boxing. The case was thus decided on similar principles to the *De Francesco* case even though it was not strictly speaking a contract of employment. A further widening of the types of contracts covered by the term 'beneficial contract of service' can be seen in *Chaplin* v *Leslie Frewin (Publishers) Ltd* [1966] Ch 71 where the minor agreed, in return for royalties on the book which would be published, to tell his life story to a publishing company. It was held that the contract was analogous to a contract of service and binding on the minor.

Voidable contracts

Two classes of contract are described as voidable at common law, those by which the minor acquires an interest in some subject matter of a permanent nature (such as contracts to take a lease, to buy shares or to enter a partnership) and a residual class of contracts, which will be described below.

Contracts of the first type are valid and binding on the minor unless he chooses to repudiate the contract within his minority or within a reasonable time of his acquiring majority. Until the minor decides to repudiate the contract he will be liable on the terms of the contract. In a lease, for instance, he will be liable for breach of any covenants, whilst in a contract for the purchase of shares the minor will continue to be liable for any calls made on him for any amounts outstanding on the shares.

Since the minor is free to repudiate these contracts during infancy or within a reasonable time thereafter, the question arises as to what constitutes a reasonable time. The answer here largely depends on the facts of the particular case. In *Edwards* v *Carter* [1893] AC 360 it was held that a minor who purported to repudiate an agreement to pay £1,500 to trustees under a marriage settlement some four years after attaining majority would not be allowed to do so.

Whilst a minor who repudiates a voidable contract is no longer liable to honour any obligations arising in the future, it is not settled whether he will be free from those that have already accrued at the time of his repudiation. The authorities support two viewpoints; firstly, that the repudiation is the equivalent of rescission and is therefore retrospective in operation; and secondly, that repudiation does not have a retrospective operation and that the minor remains liable on such obligations. Cheshire and Fifoot tend to suggest that the better view is that the second should prevail although the position is unclear.

Looking at the other side of the coin, we find that a minor who attempts to recover any monies, having repudiated the contract, has to show that he has suffered a total failure of consideration. In *Steinberg v Scala* [1923] 2 Ch 452 the plaintiff, a minor, had applied for shares in a company and had paid the amounts due on allotment and on a subsequent first call. She was not paid any dividends, nor did she attend any meetings. The shares never increased in value. Some 18 months after the shares had been allotted to her, she sought to repudiate the contract and reclaim all that she had paid for the shares. Her action failed since the company had fulfilled its side of the bargain in that it had allotted her shares on the basis of the payments made to them, and there was, therefore, no total failure of consideration.

The second class of voidable contracts is really a residual class of contracts that fail to come within the heads already discussed. The major example of such a contract is a trading contract, that is, a contract entered into by an infant during the course of his trade or profession. In reality such contracts will now be quite rare, given the reduction of the age of majority. At common law such contracts only became binding if the minor ratified the contract on his attaining majority. Whilst this position was altered by the Infants Relief Act 1874, this Act has now itself been repealed by the Minors' Contracts Act 1987. The position now is that the common law rules have become re-established. Thus a minor, after attaining majority, can ratify contracts that are unenforceable against him or voidable at his option.

To ratify the contract, the minor may simply make a unilateral confirmation of an earlier promise made during his minority. Previously, by s. 2 of the Infants Relief Act, in order to be bound, the former minor had to make a new contract relating to the subject matter of the old contract on attaining majority.

Section 5 of the Betting and Loans (Infants) Act 1892 provided that a new contract entered into by a minor, after attaining majority, to pay a debt due under a void loan contracted in infancy, was itself void. This provision is now repealed by s. 1 of the 1987 Act, with the result that any new agreement to repay a loan advanced during minority is now effective and binding.

The tortious liability of minors

It is possible for a tortious act to be at the same time a breach of contract. For instance, a person may induce another to enter a contract with him by making a fraudulent statement of fact, i.e., the tort of deceit. The law therefore seeks to prevent an adult from evading a minor's immunity from contractual liability by expressing his action in tortious terms on the basis that this amounts to an indirect enforcement of an invalid contract. However, an action in tort will only be barred if the wrongful act committed by the infant is of a type that is contemplated by the contract.

The point is illustrated in the following cases. In *Jennings v Rundall* (1799) 8 Term Rep 335 a minor who hired a horse for riding but injured it by excessive and improper use was held not to be liable in negligence. In *Burnard v Haggis* (1863) 14

CBNS 45 a minor who was specifically barred from jumping his hired horse was held to be liable for injuries caused when he ignored the restriction. A more modern application of the rule can be seen in *Ballett* v *Mingay* [1943] KB 281, where an infant who had borrowed audio equipment and without authority had lent it to a friend was held liable in the tort of detinue when he failed to return it.

The rule that a minor is not generally liable in tort where the tortious act was within the contemplation of a void contract also applies where the infant commits a tort in procuring the contract. Thus in *A. Leslie Ltd* v *Sheill* [1914] 3 KB 607, a minor could not be sued in deceit by inducing an adult to lend him money whilst fraudulently misrepresenting his age.

Restitution

It can be seen in cases like *Leslie* v *Sheill* that an adult could conceivably be left without a remedy if the strict letter of the common law was adhered to. To offset this unfairness equity has developed a doctrine of restitution which applied the principle that an infant should not be allowed to be enriched by his own fraud. Three situations need to be considered:

(a) The minor has obtained goods by fraud and still remains in possession of them. Restitution will be ordered in such cases.
(b) The minor has obtained goods by fraud but has sold or exchanged them. The position here is unsettled and whilst the case of *Stocks* v *Wilson* [1913] 2 KB 235 takes the view that the infant is accountable for the proceeds, *Leslie* v *Sheill* supports the contrary view.
(c) The minor has obtained a loan by fraud. It is clear here that the minor will be liable to account for any of the actual banknotes still in his possession, though it is unsettled whether any items purchased with the monies lent are recoverable. It seems probable that relief would be granted to the adult provided this does not diminish the minor's resources below what they were prior to the transaction obtained by fraud.

Apart from, and in addition to, the equitable remedy of restitution it is possible for relief to be obtained under the Minors' Contracts Act 1987. By s. 3(1), where the contract is unenforceable against a person because he was a minor at that time, or where the minor repudiates the contract, the court has the power where it thinks it is 'just and equitable to do so' to require the minor to return the property, or property representing that which he has acquired, to the plaintiff.

It is envisaged that the courts, rather than rely on the equitable doctrine of restitution, will choose s. 3(1) as the main remedy in these circumstances and, indeed, there are good reasons for their doing so. Firstly, there is no requirement as to fraud; and secondly, s. 3(1) extends to property representing that acquired under the contract, an aspect which was open to doubt in the equitable remedy of restitution. The discretion given to the courts in s. 3(1) will present few problems where the 'property acquired . . . under the contract' is still in the minor's possession. In relation, however, to exercising discretion over 'property representing it' there may still be some problems in certain circumstances, as, for example, if the 'property acquired' is sold and the proceeds paid into a bank account from which a further item is bought (also possibly under an unenforceable contract). Despite the changes wrought by the 1987 Act, if the minor has consumed or disposed of the goods or the proceeds he cannot be required to compensate the other party.

Like the remedy of restitution, the new remedy is also discretionary, and in the appropriate circumstances it may still be wiser for the plaintiff to rely on his remedies in quasi-contract, which have been specifically preserved in s. 3(2) of the Act. This remedy has the advantage of being a common law remedy and therefore available as of right.

Guarantees

The Infants Relief Act 1874 rendered guarantees invalid because the main contract itself was absolutely void. Section 2 of the 1987 Act repealed this provision so that a guarantor will now be liable for the infant's contractual obligation even though it is unenforceable or the infant has repudiated his contractual obligation. This provision does not apply to necessaries because the minor is obliged to pay a reasonable price for these in any event.

Section 2 does not affect the entitlement of the guarantor to recover his losses against the minor and here he is in exactly the same position as any other creditor of the minor.

The effect of an actual guarantee of a contractual obligation very largely depends on the terms of the guarantee. It may still be possible for the guarantee itself to be rendered unenforceable, but not on the ground that the contractual obligation was unenforceable or repudiated by the minor.

THE CAPACITY OF CORPORATIONS

Types of corporation

There are two broad categories of corporation:

Chartered corporations

Such corporations, which are a creature of the common law, can only be created by royal charter. Generally they have the same capacity as a private individual, though if a chartered corporation makes a contract that it is not authorised to do by virtue of its charter, the charter itself may be revoked. Any unauthorised contract will remain valid.

Statutory corporations

Most corporations today are created either by statute or under the authority of a statute. Of these the vast majority are commercial corporations created by incorporation under the Companies Act 1985, and they may take the form of either public or private companies, limited by shares or by guarantee.

The doctrine of *ultra vires*

The doctrine of *ultra vires* limits the capacity of the company to enter into certain contracts in that if a company enters into a contract which it is beyond the company's power to enter, then that contract is deemed to be void. If the corporation is created by statute then the limits of the corporation's powers are set out in the relevant Act of Parliament. If the corporation is created under the 1985 Act then the limitations on the company's powers are set out in the objects clause in the memorandum of association, which is a public document that has to be filed with the Registrar of Companies when the company is registered on its creation.

Central to the doctrine of *ultra vires* is the need to protect three groups of people: investors, creditors and third parties dealing with the company. The nature of this protection arises by means of informing interested persons of the purpose or purposes for which the company was formed, by allowing them to investigate the objects clause of the memorandum of association and as a result having actual notice of the objects of the company. On the face of things this concept is sound, although closer examination reveals the protection afforded to be illusory since anyone dealing with the company was deemed to have constructive notice of the contents of the objects clause. In other words, a person would be deemed to have read the objects clause even if he had never heard of the existence of such a document as the memorandum of association! The effect of this is that if the company was acting beyond the purposes afforded to it by the objects clause, any person dealing with the company would be deemed to know that the actions of the company were *ultra vires*, whether they had read the objects clause or not. The only way to ensure that the company was acting within its powers was to obtain a copy of the memorandum but, of course, it is totally unrealistic to expect a person to obtain the memoranda of every company he may do business with from the Registrar of Companies. It is at this point that the trap is sprung on the unsuspecting, since if it transpired that the company was acting outside its powers, then the contract would be void and neither could enforce the contract against the other. The reason for this, as far as investors, creditors and third parties are concerned, is that they are deemed to know the objects of the company and, as a result, to know that the company is acting outside those objects. In *Ashbury Railway Carriage Co Ltd* v *Riche* (1875) LR 7 HL 653, the company was formed with the object of carrying on business as mechanical engineers and to make and sell all kinds of railway plant and rolling stock. The directors contracted to assign a concession they had bought for the construction of a railway in Belgium to a Belgian company. The company, however, was not formed for the purpose of constructing railways by virtue of the objects clause and thus the contract was void on the grounds that the contract was *ultra vires* the company. Furthermore, the situation could not even be saved by the majority of members passing a resolution ratifying the contract. Thus the action by the Belgian company for breach of contract failed since it was deemed to have constructive notice of the objects of the company and, as a result, should have known that the company was not entitled to be involved in such a transaction.

An *ultra vires* act prior to the Companies Act 1989 (see below) could never be ratified by the shareholders, nor could such an act be enforced by a third party even if he could prove that he was unaware of the *ultra vires* nature of the company's transaction. The point is well illustrated by the case of *Re Jon Beauforte Ltd* [1953] Ch 131, where the objects clause of the company authorised it to make clothing, yet it decided to start a new venture manufacturing veneered panels instead. The company ordered coke for use in the manufacturing process of the new business on headed notepaper which described the company as veneered panel manufacturers. The new business venture was not a success and the company went into liquidation. The coke suppliers failed in their action to recover the monies owed to them. Clearly the letterhead *per se* did not give evidence of the fact that the company was involved in an *ultra vires* activity, but it did inform the supplier of the actual use to which the coke was to be put. Coupled with this was the fact that the supplier had constructive notice of the objects clause in the memorandum and the two factors when considered together gave a clear indication that the coke was being used for an illegitimate purpose. This resulted in the contract being rendered *ultra vires* and void, so that the supplier was unable to recover the debt owed to him. The result might have been different if the letterhead had not given any indication of the use to which the coke would be put, since the supplier could have claimed that the coke might have been put to a legitimate use.

Items which can have a general use within a company also give rise to problems in the context of the doctrine of *ultra vires*, since they may be put to both legitimate and illegitimate uses. Loans of money especially fall into this category, though it should be noted that a loan can never amount to an object of a company. Whilst the power to raise loans may be given in the objects clause, that is all it is, a power – a means for the company to achieve its objects and nothing more. In *Re Introductions Ltd* v *National Provincial Bank Ltd* [1970] Ch 199, the company was formed to provide entertainment and accommodation during the Festival of Britain. The company then decided to go into pig breeding and obtained a loan from the bank for that purpose. The bank's contention that the borrowing of money could be an object of the company was rejected by the Court of Appeal. The court stated that the power to borrow was merely a means by which a company achieved its objects and that therefore it had to be used for the furtherance of a lawful object, which of course pig breeding was not, thus the loan was *ultra vires* and void.

The decision in the *Introductions* case has been challenged in the case of *Rolled Steel Products (Holdings) Ltd* v *British Steel Corporation* [1985] 3 All ER 1016, where it was held that the borrowing of money in such circumstances was *intra vires* the company but *ultra vires* the powers of the directors, who could then be rendered liable to the company for borrowing money for an improper purpose. If the

Introductions case was decided on this basis the bank would have been able to recover the money from the company (that is, the loan would have been *intra vires* the company), though the company would have been entitled to claim an indemnity from the directors for any losses sustained. It should be noted that the decision in the *Rolled Steel* case has been the subject of serious criticism. However further consideration of the case is beyond the scope of this work.

Avoiding the effects of the doctrine of *ultra vires*

It can be seen from the discussions above that the doctrine of *ultra vires* fails to protect the very people it was designed to give protection to. The doctrine also has a further negative effect in that it stultifies the ability of companies to expand their operations into areas which are not within the ambit of their objects clauses. The effect of this was to motivate businessmen and their legal advisers to devise methods of avoiding the effects of the *ultra vires* doctrine. These methods were eventually so effective that the doctrine started to have little significance in the operational management of companies. Whilst these devices aided companies, third parties were still very much at risk but this was remedied by the passing of the European Communities Act 1972, s. 9(1). This provision was later re-enacted in s. 35 of the Companies Act 1985, which provided:

> (1) In favour of a person dealing with a company in good faith, any transaction decided on by the directors shall be deemed to be one which it is within the capacity of the company to enter into, and the power of the directors to bind the company shall be deemed to be free of any limitations under the memorandum of articles.
> (2) A party to a transaction so decided on is not bound to enquire as to the capacity of the company to enter into it or as to any such limitation on the powers of the directors and is presumed to have acted in good faith unless the contrary is proved.

The above provision has now been replaced by a new s. 35 enacted by s. 108 of the Companies Act 1989 and therefore it must be stressed that any consideration of the old s. 35 is largely historical. Nevertheless it is of interest to see how it applied, since this gives some insight into the workings of the new provision.

The above provision had two principal effects; firstly, if the conditions in the section were satisfied, a company could not raise *ultra vires* as a defence against an outsider and, secondly, registration of the memorandum of association no longer amounted to constructive notice of its contents to the whole world. It was the actual notice of the third party that became important. Had this provision been in force at the time of the decision in *Re Jon Beauforte* its effect would have been to allow the coke supplier to recover the sums owed to him.

The old s. 35 nevertheless had its limitations, for it did not aid the company, only third parties, and therefore companies were not able to enforce their own *ultra vires* contracts. The provision did not prevent a shareholder from obtaining an injunction to restrain the directors from making an *ultra vires* contract, nor did it absolve directors from liability for losses caused to the company by the entering into of an *ultra vires* contract.

It will also be noted that the third party must have acted in good faith and that the provision excluded anyone who knew, or ought to have known, that the transaction was *ultra vires*. In *International Sales and Agencies Ltd* v *Marcus* [1982] 3 All ER 551, however, it was suggested that a person, acting reasonably and honestly, who knew the contents of the objects clause but had failed to realise that it had the effect of prohibiting the company from making the contract, could nevertheless be regarded as acting in good faith.

Section 35 only applied where the transaction had been decided on by the directors, or a single director who had been given actual authority by his co-directors to act.

The Companies Act 1989

This Act has made substantial changes to the scope of the lawful actions of a company, the degree of protection offered to third parties, the duties of directors and the rights of shareholders with respect to *ultra vires* transactions. Despite recommendations going back to the report of the Cohen Committee in 1945 and the report of the Jenkins Committee in 1962, both of which called for the abolition of the *ultra vires* rule, the Act at the end of the day fails to go quite as far as that. For all intents and purposes, however, this is the effect of the Act except in certain very limited circumstances.

Section 35, as amended by s. 108 of the 1989 Act, deals with three aspects of the doctrine of *ultra vires*:

The capacity of the company – s. 35

This provides that the validity of an act done by a company cannot be called into question on the basis that it is beyond the capacity of the company. The result is that a company will no longer be limited by the contents of its memorandum and therefore third parties will be protected from the effects of the doctrine of *ultra vires* and will be able to enforce such transactions against the company. Whilst the company may also enforce a transaction entered into against a third party, a shareholder will still be able to restrain a company from entering into an *ultra vires* contract by way of an injunction (s. 35(2)). By virtue of s. 35(3) it still remains the duty of the directors to comply with any limitations on their powers contained in the memorandum or articles of association. Any actions by the directors which, but for the operation of s. 35(1) above, would be *ultra vires* the company, can now be ratified by the members by way of a special resolution.

The Act also relaxed the general approach to the construction of objects clauses. It has been seen that a company's objects are restricted to those which are listed in the memorandum. However, s. 110 provides that it is now possible for a company's objects clause to state simply that it 'is to carry on business as a general commercial company'. Such a clause would have the effect of creating a general commercial company which would find it virtually impossible to fall foul of the *ultra vires* doctrine. It is now also easier for a company to alter its objects to incorporate such a general objects clause, though a special resolution is still required. Minorities opposed to such a change are offered some protection, in that they have the right to apply to the court to have the alteration cancelled. In such a case the alteration would not take effect without the confirmation of the court.

The capacity of directors – s. 35A

Whilst the provisions contained in s. 35A are largely outside the ambit of this chapter in that they relate to the powers of the directors to bind the company, the provision has some relevance since its effect is to extend and clarify the protection contained in the old s. 35 as enacted by the 1985 Act. The effect is that a third party's position will not be prejudiced by his knowing that the directors are acting beyond their powers. Thus mere knowledge that the directors are so acting will not amount to bad faith. The Act, however, is very imprecise here since there is no definition of bad faith, though it is thought that it amounts to a fraudulent act or possibly assisting the directors in the abuse of their powers.

Shareholders will still be able to restrain directors from committing any act which is beyond their powers, though it will not be possible to take such proceedings where the directors act in order to carry out some pre-existing legal obligation. The section does not have any effect on any liability incurred by the directors, or any other person, by reason of the directors exceeding their powers.

The capacity of the company and third parties – s. 35B

By virtue of s. 35B a party to a transaction with a company is no longer obliged to make enquiries as to whether the transaction entered into by the company is one which is permitted by the memorandum. This is also the case with regard to any limitations on the powers of the board of directors to bind the company or authorise others to do so. It should also be noted that s. 143 abolishes the doctrine of constructive notice in this context, except in certain limited instances.

As already indicated the changes wrought on the doctrine of *ultra vires* by the 1989 Act are not universal. With regard to charitable companies the changes have been restricted, the reason being that their specialised purpose should preclude them from enjoying the same freedom from the effects of the doctrine of *ultra vires* as that afforded to other types of companies.

Further reading

Beale, Bishop and Furmston, *Contract – Cases and Materials* 2nd ed. 1990, Butterworths
Cheshire, Fifoot and Furmston, *The Law of Contract* 12th ed. 1991, Butterworths
Guest, *Anson's Law of Contract* 26th ed. 1984, Oxford University Press
Hudson, 'Mental Incapacity Revisited', *The Conveyancer and Property Lawyer* 178, 1986
Treitel, *The Law of Contract* 8th ed. 1991, Sweet & Maxwell

6 | Formalities

INTRODUCTION

The general requirements for a simple contract have now been assessed. One of the popular misconceptions of the layman is that for there to be a legally binding contract there must be a properly drafted document full of incomprehensible language, sealed with red molten wax into which the long-suffering parties have, somewhat painfully, plunged their fingers or, if they are lucky enough to have one, a seal ring. Nothing is of course further from the truth since the vast majority of contracts are made informally, either orally or by conduct or sometimes in writing. Obviously in commercial contracts, where the terms may be very extensive, it is highly desirable to have those terms set down in writing in a formal document in case any dispute should occur. The same is also true where the contract involves very large amounts of money and thereby carries an inordinate degree of risk. There are many reasons why the parties to a contract want to have the terms set out in a formal document, though the important fact to remember is that there is no legal requirement on them to do so, subject of course to a number of exceptions.

The exceptions occur where the law considers that the nature of the contract requires it to be certain, or where the transaction is such that the parties to it are in need of protection, as in hire purchase agreements. The degree of formality required generally reflects the relative importance of the contract. Three categories of contract may be discerned:

(a) contracts required to be made by deed;
(b) contracts required to be in writing;
(c) contracts required to be evidenced in writing.

CONTRACTS REQUIRED TO BE MADE BY DEED

Nowadays the dramatic, almost ceremonial procedure of sealing a document with molten wax has, for the most part, been replaced by the more practical, though less impressive, fixing of a self-adhesive wafer of red paper. The requirement that a certain transaction must be made under seal is for the most part a euphemism for the requirement that it must be contained in a deed. All deeds must be 'signed, sealed and delivered', but it is not the sealing of the document that makes the deed binding, rather it is the signature of the party making the deed, by virtue of s. 73 of the Law of Property Act 1925. Recently this provision has been indirectly reinforced by the Law of Property (Miscellaneous Provisions) Act 1989, s. 1(1)b, which provided that, 'Any rule of law which . . . requires a seal for the valid execution of an instrument as a deed by an individual . . . is abolished'. Given the abolition of the need for a seal, how does one know whether the document is a deed or not? The answer to this question lies in s. 1(2) and (3). Section 1(2) states:

An instrument shall not be a deed unless –

(a) it makes it clear on its face that it is intended to be a deed by the party making it or, as the case may be, by the parties to it (whether by describing itself as a deed or expressing itself to be executed or signed as a deed or otherwise); and

(b) it is validly executed as a deed by that person or, as the case may be, one or more of those parties.

Any instrument that is expressed to be by deed is sufficient for s. 1(2)a. Very often instruments begin, not by expressing themselves to be by deed, but by expressing the purpose or nature of the instrument itself, as, for example, 'This Conveyance . . .' or 'This Underlease . . .'. If this practice is to continue then the intention that the document is to be a deed must be indicated somewhere else within the document. For the most part this intention will be shown by the document being signed and witnessed 'as a deed'.

Section 1(3) states:

An instrument is validly executed as a deed by an individual if, and only if

(a) it is signed –

    (i) by him in the presence of a witness who attests the signature; or

    (ii) at his direction and in his presence and the presence of two witnesses who each attest the signature; and

    (iii) it is delivered as a deed by him or a person authorised to do so on his behalf.

Quite clearly if the provisions of s. 1(3) are not complied with then the purported deed will be void.

The most common type of transaction that requires a deed is the conveyance of a legal estate in land by virtue of s. 52(1) of the Law of Property Act 1925. Further, by s. 54(2) a deed is required to create a legal lease of more than three years. A deed can also be used to turn a bare or gratuitous promise into a legally binding enforceable obligation, its use in this respect evolving separately from the doctrine of consideration.

CONTRACTS REQUIRED TO BE IN WRITING

Generally

Apart from some contracts requiring to be by deed, some contracts are required to be set out in writing in order to be enforceable. There are many examples of such contracts but by far the most important until recently are contracts governed by the Consumer Credit Act 1974, which requires that certain regulated agreements, such as hire purchase and credit sales agreements, are 'not properly executed' unless in the form prescribed by regulation under the Act.

Failure to comply with the requirement of being in writing has the general effect of rendering the contract unenforceable. In the case of the Consumer Credit Act 1974, however, an agreement that is not properly executed can nevertheless be enforced against a debtor on an order of the court. No such order can be made if the agreement has not been signed by the debtor, or if he has not been given a copy of the agreement or notice of his right to cancel.

Contracts for the sale or other disposition of an interest in land

The Law of Property (Miscellaneous Provisions) Act 1989 now presents probably the most important category of contracts that are required to be in writing. Prior to this Act, s. 40 of the Law of Property Act 1925 provided:

> (1) No action may be brought upon any contract for the sale or other disposition of any interest in land, unless the agreement upon which such action is brought, or some memorandum or note thereof is in writing, and signed by the party to be charged or by some other person thereunto by him lawfully authorised.
> (2) This section applies to contracts whether made before or after the commencement of this Act and does not affect the law relating to part performance, or sale by the court.

The result of this provision was that the contract had to be evidenced by some note or memorandum in which there had to be an adequate identification of the parties to the contract, together with a description of the subject matter. Further, the nature of the consideration had to be indicated and the memorandum had to include any other terms deemed material by the parties. The memorandum was required to be signed by the party to be charged, that is, the party against whom it was sought to enforce the contract.

It was possible for the memorandum to be made up from two or more documents, provided that a document signed by the plaintiff existed, that there was sufficient reference in that document to a second document, and that the two, when read together, formed a complete memorandum. One further feature, and one that could and did cause substantial problems, as seen in *Law v Jones* [1974] Ch 112 and *Tiverton Estates Ltd* v *Wearwell Ltd* [1975] Ch 146, was the fact that the memorandum need not have been deliberately prepared as a memorandum and indeed may have been made inadvertently.

Section 40 did not provide that contracts for the sale or other disposition of an interest in land could not be created orally, but merely that such a contract was unenforceable by action unless there was a memorandum containing the information required by s. 40(1). The only way to save a contract not just evidenced in writing was to bring the contract within the doctrine of part-performance as contained in s. 40(2), and this was not always easy to do.

Section 2(1) of the new Act now provides:

> A contract for the sale or other disposition of an interest in land can only be made in writing and only by incorporating all the terms which the parties have expressly agreed in one document or, where contracts are exchanged, in each.

The requirements of s. 2(1) are far more formal and the problems that arose in *Law v Jones* and *Tiverton Estates Ltd* v *Wearwell Ltd* will no longer arise, since the contract for the sale or other disposition of an interest in land can only be made in writing, not just evidenced in writing. The change in effect is dramatic; no longer would a contract be merely unenforceable unless it was in writing, now it would be void for non-compliance. Further, there is no longer the possibility of the agreement being saved by the doctrine of part-performance since the whole of s. 40, which includes that doctrine, is repealed.

The requirements as to the actual content of s. 2 contracts or other dispositions are also more formal. All the terms which the parties have expressly agreed must be incorporated in one document or, where contracts are exchanged, in each (s. 2(1)). It is, however, possible to incorporate the terms in a document either by having them set out in that document or by reference to some other document (s. 2(2)), thus allowing for the possibility of joinder. Further the document incorporating the terms or, where contracts are exchanged, one of the documents incorporating them (but not necessarily the same one) must be signed by or on behalf of each party to the contract (s. 2(3)). There is an obviously important difference here between s. 2 and s. 40(1) in that s. 40(1) only required the contract to be signed by one party – 'the party to be charged' – whilst s. 2 requires the contract to be signed by each party. The aim here is to redress the somewhat unfair situation which existed previously whereby, prior to the enactment of s. 2, a party, once he had received a s. 40(1) memorandum signed by the other party, could enforce the contract even though he himself had not signed any written evidence of the contract and thus could not have it enforced against himself.

As has already been stated, it is clear that a contract under s. 2 must contain all the terms which the parties have expressly agreed and thus the omission of such a term will be prima facie fatal. A similar problem also existed in relation to s. 40(1), as pointed out by Professor Pettit in 'Farewell Section 40' (*The Conveyancer*, 1990, p. 435), in that a defendant could defeat a claim simply by producing evidence of a term that had been omitted. In *Farrell* v *Green* (1974) EG 587, Pennycuick V-C qualified this by stating *obiter* that if the omitted term expressly agreed between the parties is one which would have been implied by the court in any event, then the omission of the term would not be fatal to the enforceability of the contract. Possibly this exception would not apply in the case of s. 2 contracts since the requirements of the section are strict – all the express terms must be in writing. Any parol (oral) variations of a written contract would also not be valid and would be ineffective.

Having examined some of the issues surrounding the construction of s. 2 we must now assess the effects of the repeal of s. 40 and its replacement by s. 2 on the exercise of equitable jurisdiction. Such jurisdiction was previously exercised where there had been an informal contract for the sale or other disposition of an interest in land. It is a well-recognised equitable principle that 'equity looks to the intention and not to the form', and thus it is clear that s. 2 is likely to have a significant effect on this concept.

The role adopted by equity is that where there has been a failure to use a deed in the creation of a legal interest as required by s. 52(1) of the Law of Property Act 1925, equity regarded this as a contract to create such an interest, which it would then enforce by way of a decree of specific performance. Presumably such contracts must now be in writing to comply with s. 2(1). The possible effects of such a conclusion could be extensive when analysed in the context of transactions, such as leases and options.

Leases

In order to create a legal lease, a deed is required; however where the deed was imperfect, equity would treat the lease as a contract to grant a lease, provided the requirements of s. 40 were complied with. Similarly, if the lease was granted orally, equity would treat this as a contract to grant a lease, though here a sufficient act of part-performance was required. Such was the doctrine in *Parker* v *Taswell* (1858) 2 De G & J 559. Since part-performance under s. 40(2) has been repealed it is clear that there must be a s. 2 contract in order to establish an equitable lease under the doctrine in *Walsh* v *Lonsdale* (1882) 21 Ch D 9. At best, even if the imperfect grant of a lease could be interpreted as complying with s. 2, the establishment of equitable leases by this method must inevitably be restricted.

The problems indicated in the application of *Walsh* v *Lonsdale* do not, however, stop at leases since over the years the principles contained in the doctrine have been applied by analogy to other interests such as easements and mortgages.

A further problem that can occur with leases revolves around the exceptions to the requirements of s. 2(1) which are set out in s. 2(5). Section 2(5)a provides that s. 2 does not apply to 'a contract to grant such a lease as is mentioned in s. 54(2) of the Law of Property Act 1925'. Section 54(2) in turn provides that:

Nothing in the foregoing provisions of this part of this Act shall affect the creation by parol of leases taking effect in possession for a term not exceeding three years (whether or not the lessee is given power to extend the term) at the best rent which can be reasonably obtained without taking a fine.

The effect of the provision is that a grant of a lease for not more than three years would take effect as a legal lease despite the absence of a deed, provided the lease took effect immediately.

Such a lease would result even if there was a complete lack of formality and it was created orally. If, however, the lease did not take effect immediately then it would take effect as a contract to create a lease and it had to comply with s. 40(1) and (2), be evidenced in writing or be supported by a sufficient act of part-performance. Since s. 2 has now repealed s. 40 parties negotiating such short leases should be warned of the possible danger that any agreement reached might be legally binding although they are made orally. Clearly such agreements should be qualified by words such as 'subject to a written contract being drawn up'. Time-honoured words such as 'subject to contract' are probably not sufficient because the oral agreement will be binding as a contract in any event.

Options

An option to purchase is described in *Beesly* v *Hallwood Estates Ltd* [1960] 1 WLR 549 as an offer to sell which 'the grantor is contractually precluded from withdrawing so long as the option remains exercisable'. The contract to purchase then takes place when the grantor is given notice of the exercise of the option. As indicated in Cheshire and Burns (1988) *Modern Law of Real Property* at p. 121 and in *Pritchard* v *Briggs* [1980] Ch 339, the option itself does not form a contract, though it does create an immediate equitable interest in favour of the grantee as soon as the option is granted, since the grantee has a right to call for the conveyance of the land to himself, whether the grantor consents or not. Since the right of the grantee is an equitable interest in the land then surely the notice exercising this right must comply with the s. 2 requirements?

In the recent case of *Spiro* v *Glencrown Properties Ltd and Another* [1991] All ER 600 it was held that whilst the grant of an option depended on contractual agreement and required compliance with s. 2, the exercise of the power was a unilateral act and did not require such compliance. An option was described as 'a conditional contract . . . which the grantee is entitled to convert into a concluded contract of purchase'. Since the **grant** of the option did comply with s. 2 it was held that there was no need for the **exercise** of the option to comply since 'it would destroy the very purpose of the option if the purchaser had to obtain the vendor's countersignature to the notice by which it was exercised'. It was also stated that 'the purpose of s. 2 was to prescribe the formalities for recording the parties' consent. It followed that the grant of the option was the only "contract for the sale . . . of an interest or other disposition of an interest in land" '.

The decision would seem to be dubious since, whilst it may be correct in its explanation of the legal effects of the granting and exercise of options, it is wrong in principle when read in the context of the Act. The authorities are clear that the right of the grantee to exercise his right of option is an equitable interest in the land, and whilst the exercise of this right is not a contract of sale it does fall within the ambit of the expression 'other disposition' for the purpose of s. 2.

The new Act is based on the recommendation of the Law Commission Report No 164, in which the Law Commission indicated that, whilst non-compliance with s. 2 would render the 'contract of sale or other disposition' void, the parties would not be without a remedy; it saw no cause to fear that the repeal of s. 40 and its replacement by s. 2 should inhibit the courts in the exercise of equitable jurisdiction in order to do justice between individuals in 'otherwise hard cases'. Remarkably the Law Commission, whilst indicating the importance of complying with the s. 2 formalities, appeared to be recommending that the courts exercise equitable discretion in avoiding the worst effects of s. 2. The provision thus takes on the mantle of a latter-day Statute of Frauds (see below), with the Law Commission advocating the use of equitable discretion to prevent it from being used as 'an engine of fraud'.

Among the possible remedies advocated in the report are remedies in tort (for example, negligence or deceit), actions for restitution or in quasi-contract, on a *quantum meruit* or total failure of consideration basis, and also actions based on the concept of collateral contract. The Law Commission seemed strongly to advocate the use of promissory or proprietary estoppel as an equitable remedy, whilst the Act itself in s. 2(5) protected the creation and operation of resulting, implied and constructive trusts.

A further equitable remedy specifically preserved in the Act is rectification. This provision is found in s. 2(4):

> Where a contract for the sale or other disposition of an interest in land satisfies the conditions of this section by reason only of rectification of one or more documents in pursuance of an order of a court, the contract shall come into being, or be deemed to have become into being, at such time as may be specified in the order.

At one time it was thought that for rectification to apply there had to be a valid concluded contract; since this would not be the case if a term was omitted by virtue of s. 2, the document could not, of course, be rectified. This principle, however, would seem to have been overturned in *Joscelyne v Nissen* [1970] 2 QB 86 which, as was pointed out in the Law Commission report, established that there does not have to be a prior valid contract, but merely a prior agreement or a common intention to contract coupled with convincing proof that the written agreement does not adequately reflect the terms of the agreement.

One problem with rectification, as identified by the Law Commission, was the fact that it was retrospective in operation. The effect of this could be that third-party rights occurring between the time of contracting and rectification could be either validated or invalidated as a consequence of rectification. The Act thus reflects the Law Commission's concern and gives discretion to the court as to the effective date of rectification.

With such equitable remedies being suggested it is difficult to understand why the doctrine of part-performance has been repealed. It would seem that there is an attempt to remove the ability of equity to intervene on the basis of a contractual analysis of informality. Further, the Law Commission is assuming that a court would be willing to exercise its equitable jurisdiction. The exercise of such jurisdiction was not forthcoming in *Midland Bank Trust Co Ltd* v *Green* [1981] AC 513 where the court applied only the strict wording of the Land Charges Act 1972. A similar approach might well be taken with the Law of Property (Miscellaneous Provisions) Act 1989, with the adoption of an attitude that the Act requires the contract to be in writing and therefore in writing it must be, and if Parliament had intended that equity would have some part to play then express provision should have been made for it within the body of the Act.

Clearly it is difficult to predict how the courts will apply the Act and all one can do at the moment is to wait for cases to come before the courts.

CONTRACTS REQUIRED TO BE EVIDENCED IN WRITING

Introduction

With the repeal of s. 40 of the Law of Property Act 1925, the only type of contract now required to be evidenced in writing are contracts of guarantee. A guarantee may be defined as a promise made by one individual to another whereby the first agrees to meet the liabilities/debts owed by a third party to the second, should the third party be unable to meet those liabilities/debts.

Contracts of guarantee are governed by s. 4 of the Statute of Frauds 1677, an Act that tended to promote fraud rather than prevent it because it was so badly drafted. Indeed, such was its notoriety that it was described by Lord Wright as an 'extemporaneous excrescence on the common law'. Originally the Act governed some six classes of contract but four classes were repealed by the Law Reform (Enforcement of Contracts) Act 1954 and contracts for the sale or other dispositions of an interest in land have met the fate already detailed above.

Section 4 of the Statute of Frauds

Section 4 provides:

> No action shall be brought . . . whereby to charge the defendant upon any special promise to answer for the debt, default or miscarriage of another person, unless there is written evidence of the agreement.

The formal requirements of contracts of guarantee falling within s. 4 are very similar to those formerly required by s. 40(1) of the Law of Property Act 1925, in that they must be evidenced by some note or memorandum in writing and signed by the party to be charged, that is, the person against whom the contract is being enforced. The note or memorandum must contain all the material terms, that is, identify the parties and describe the subject matter and the nature of the consideration, and any other terms deemed material by the parties. The doctrine of part-performance has no application in such contracts. Failure to comply with the requirements of s. 4 renders the contract unenforceable.

At one time it was considered that the provision was confined to contractual liability, in particular guarantees arising out of a pre-existing debt, since it was considered that the terms 'debt, default or miscarriage' were synonymous. In *Kirkham* v *Marter* (1819) 2 B & Ald 613, the scope of guarantees required to be evidenced in writing was extended to cover tortious liability. In the case the defendant's son rode the plaintiff's horse, with his permission, so aggressively that he killed the horse. As a result of this action he was liable in tort to the plaintiff, who then threatened to sue him. At this point the defendant promised the plaintiff that he would compensate the plaintiff if he promised not to pursue the claim against his son. This was accepted by the plaintiff, but in fact the defendant failed to pay. The defendant pleaded the Statute of Frauds as a defence, stating that his promise, to be binding, had to be evidenced in writing as required by the Act. The plaintiff argued that the Act did not apply to guarantees regarding tortious liability, that it only applied to pre-existing debts, and these were not required to be evidenced in writing. It was held that the statute was not confined to cases of contract since the father had promised 'to answer for the *miscarriage* of another' (emphasis added). For the father to be liable on his promise the guarantee had to be evidenced in writing, and as it was not, the defendant escaped liability. The court considered that the term 'miscarriage' meant a wrongful act, and this interpretation brought guarantees in relation to tortious acts within the reach of the provision.

There are certain circumstances in which there is no requirement for the contract to be in writing within s. 4.

Promises made to third-party debtors

No requirement of evidence in writing arises where the promise to pay the debt is made to the third-party debtor. The promise of the guarantor must be made to the creditor as stated in *Eastwood* v *Kenyon* (1840) 11 A & E 438.

Indemnities

Section 4 only applies where the guarantor assumes secondary liability, in other words, the guarantee is not to pay the debts of the debtor in any event, but only where the debtor fails to meet his obligations. In situations where the guarantor assumes primary liability, this is not a guarantee but an indemnity, arising out of a promise to meet the losses of the creditor from the principal contract.

The practical difference between indemnities and guarantees can be seen in the case of *Birkmyr* v *Darnell* (1704) 1 Salk 27. In the case it was stated that should two persons go into a shop and one of them decides to buy something, at which point the other says to the shopkeeper, 'Let him have the goods; if he does not pay you, I will', this will amount to a guarantee. However, if he says: 'Let him have the goods, I will be your paymaster' or 'I will see you paid', this is an undertaking for himself and he shall be intended to be the very buyer and the other to act but as his servant', this is an indemnity. It is not always possible to have such a clear-cut situation and the court must decide whether primary or secondary liability has been assumed by the defendant.

A further application of the principles can be seen in *Mountstephen* v *Lakeman* (1871) LR7 AB 196 where the defendant was chairman of the Brixham Local Board of Health. A surveyor to the Board proposed to the plaintiff, a builder, that he should make the connections between the drains of certain houses and the main sewer. The plaintiff then asked what arrangements were being made to pay him, at which point the defendant asked him what his objections were to doing the work, to which the plaintiff replied, 'I have none, if you or the Board will order the work or become responsible for the payment'. The defendant replied to this by saying, 'Go on Mountstephen, and do the work, and I will see you paid'. The plaintiff completed the work but the Board refused to pay him on the basis that it had not made any agreement with him. The plaintiff then sued the defendant chairman, who alleged that his statement amounted to a guarantee which had to comply with s. 4 of the Statute of Frauds and that since this had not been complied with, he assumed no liability for the debt. It was held that because the Board had not contracted for the work there was no debt of another person to answer for. As a result, the defendant was the only debtor. His promise amounted to an assumption of primary liability which fell outside the statute and he was thus liable on the debt.

The guarantee is part of a larger transaction

Section 4 has no application where the guarantee forms part of a larger transaction. The guarantee must therefore stand alone. The courts have developed this exception to s. 4 in two ways:

(a) *Del credere agents.* A del credere agent guarantees, usually in exchange for extra commission, the solvency of any customers or clients whom he introduces to the principal and with whom the principal enters into a contract. The agent promises to pay his principal should the client fail to do so. The object behind such a relationship is to aid the principal to sell and promote his products, whilst at the same time allowing the agent to make a more substantial commission. The result of such a relationship is that the courts regard this undoubted guarantee as part of a wider transaction and thereby free from the requirements of s. 4, though the reasoning is hard to justify.

(b) *Protection of property.* A further exception has been developed in cases where a defendant offers a guarantee in order to protect a proprietary interest which he has in certain goods or property held by a third party. The type of situation that might arise is where the guarantor buys certain items from a seller, though the items are, in fact, held by a third party as security for an outstanding debt owed by the seller to that third party. The guarantor in these circumstances might approach the third party and negotiate the release of the goods to himself, provided he guarantees the debt of the seller. In these circumstances the guarantee is regarded as being outside the reach of the Statute of Frauds and will be binding despite the lack of evidence in writing. An example of such a situation may be seen in the case of *Fitzgerald* v *Dressler* (1859) 7 CBNS 374.

Further reading

Beale, Bishop and Furmston, *Contract – Cases and Materials* 2nd ed. 1990, Butterworths
Cheshire, Fifoot and Furmston, *The Law of Contract* 12th ed. 1991, Butterworths
Dumbill, 'Spiro: The Easy Option', 141 *New Law Journal* 124, 1991
Guest, *Anson's Law of Contract* 26th ed. 1984, Oxford University Press
Howell, 'Informal Conveyances and Section 2 of the Law of Property (Miscellaneous Provisions) Act 1989', *The Conveyancer and Property Lawyer* 441, 1990
Law Commission, *Contracts for Sale etc. of Land* Law Commission Report No. 164
Petitt, 'Farewell Section 40', *The Conveyancer and Property Lawyer* 431, 1989
Treitel, *The Law of Contract* 8th ed. 1991, Sweet & Maxwell

Part II

THE CONTENTS OF THE CONTRACT

7 | The terms of the contract

INTRODUCTION

Having analysed the basic requirements for a simple contract, we must of course examine what the parties have actually agreed to undertake in the contract. In commercial contracts the obligations agreed to by the parties are reduced to a formal written document, whilst for most of the public a mere oral agreement is sufficient. The terms in these contracts have then been expressly agreed by the parties, but this is not the whole story since the law, either by statute or by trade usage, may imply further terms into such contracts. In addition, a court may imply into any contract any terms which the court thinks necessary to give commercial efficacy to the contract, or where the court considers that a particular term would have been included in the contract but for an oversight on the part of the parties to it.

In addition to the contents of a contract one has also to assess what effect a breach of a particular term will have on the ability of the parties to terminate the contract or to claim damages. The effect of the breach largely revolves around the importance attached to a particular term, since it is clear that not all terms are of equal importance.

The final consideration in this aspect of the law of contract concerns the ability of the parties to limit or exclude their liability for breach of contract. This aspect of the contents of a contract will be discussed in Chapter 8.

EXPRESS TERMS

A contract may be agreed upon either orally or in writing, or both. If a dispute arises out of an oral contract the role of the judge is to discern what the parties have agreed upon from the evidence put before him. The finding of the judge here is clearly one of fact.

Where the contract has been reduced to writing the actual contents of the contract present little difficulty for the judge since they are apparent from the document or documents submitted. The role of the judge here is to decide issues concerning the interpretation of a particular term or terms *within the contractual document*. It is this last aspect that is important since the courts confine the agreement reached by the parties to the written document and, in the main, refuse to allow evidence by one of the parties that he did not agree to a particular term or that the document misinterprets his original intentions, especially if he has signed the document.

From the above it can be seen that the problems confronting the courts with regard to express terms can be reduced to two. Firstly, to what extent are any statements made by the parties terms of the contract and, secondly, to what extent may the parties adduce evidence other than that contained in the document in order to prove that the document misstates their original intentions?

Incorporation of statements as terms of the contract

Simply because the parties have entered into discussions, either orally or in writing, it does not necessarily mean that any conclusions reached from those discussions are automatically terms of the contract. A distinction has to be made between statements which merely amount to representations and those that amount to terms of the contract. A term of a contract is an expression of a willingness by the parties to agree to abide by that obligation and breach of it will enable the parties to sue for breach of contract. A representation, often referred to as a 'mere representation', is only an inducement to persuade the other party to enter into the contract, but it is not a term of the agreement and no action lies for breach of contract if it is not complied with. This is not to say a representation is devoid of legal effect, since clearly one could not allow an individual to make all sorts of untrue statements simply to induce the other party to enter into a legally binding contract and yet not bear responsibility for the untruths. Thus where a person makes an untrue statement which induces the other party to enter into a contract he will be liable for misrepresentation, though here the action lies either in the tort of deceit or under the Misrepresentation Act 1967, or for innocent misrepresentation, depending on the degree of culpability of the representor. Further consideration of this aspect of the law will be analysed in Chapter 9.

The problem that thus confronts the courts is whether a statement is a term or a 'mere representation'. The distinction is not easy to make but the effect, as we have seen, is crucial. In order to make the distinction the courts adopt an objective analysis of the intentions of the parties, that is, what would a reasonable man consider to be the intentions of the parties in relation to a particular statement given the circumstances present in the case? Whilst this test appears simple enough it is not so easy to apply and substantial numbers of cases have resulted from attempts to apply it. A result of this is that the courts have developed several aids to help determine the outcome of the test and to attempt to produce a degree of coherence within the law, though not always successfully. The aids adopted may be broken down as follows:

Timing

The lapse of time between the making of the statement and the entering into the contract may be relevant in determining whether the statement is a term or a representation. In *Bannerman* v *White* (1861) 10 CBNS 844, the parties negotiated for the sale of hops. Prior to the negotiations the defendants had indicated that they did not wish to purchase hops which had been treated with sulphur. When the plaintiff produced samples, the defendants again enquired whether sulphur had been used and they were assured that it had not. It then transpired that five acres out of a total of some 300 acres had been so treated. The defendants then repudiated the contract. The defendants argued that they had stressed the importance of their need for untreated hops and that since the seller must have known about the treatment of the five acres this was a term of the contract which allowed them to repudiate the contract should it be broken. The plaintiff, however, contended that the question regarding this non-use of sulphur had arisen in preliminary negotiations and was not therefore a term of the contract. The jury, however, found that the seller's statement was understood by both the parties to be part of the contract and that the defendants were entitled to repudiate it. This conclusion was then affirmed on appeal.

A more modern application of the principle can be seen in *Routledge* v *McKay* [1954] 1 All ER 855 where a motor cycle was first registered in 1930 but when a new registration book was issued the date of the original registration was given as 9 September 1941. In 1949 the seller, who was not responsible for the incorrect entry, stated, in response to a question by the buyer, that it was a late 1941 or early 1942 model. One week later the buyer and seller entered into a contract of sale. The note of the contract made no mention of the date of the motor cycle. The buyer claimed damages for breach of warranty. It was held that the interval between the negotiations and the entering into of the contract was too wide for a relationship between the two to be established. Consequently the incorrect statement was a representation and not a term of the contract and the claim for breach of warranty failed.

Reduction of the contract into writing

It may be that there has been an oral agreement but that this is later reduced into a written document. If a statement made orally between the parties is not included in the written document the inference drawn by the courts is that the statement was not intended to be a term of the contract but a mere representation. The case of *Routledge* v *McKay* above is a clear illustration of the principle since the note of the agreement made no mention of the date of the machine, the assumption being that if this was regarded as a significant factor in the sale the parties would have ensured its inclusion in the note. This position is also consistent with the attitude of the courts to bind the parties within the four corners of a written agreement, and to disallow the adducing of evidence of further terms outside the written agreement into the contract. In *Birch* v *Paramount Estates Ltd* (1956) 16 EG 396, however, the defendants made a statement regarding the quality of a house that was being sold. The written contract made no reference to the statement. The Court of Appeal nevertheless regarded this statement as a contractual term, though in this case the defendants were held to have special knowledge, which is a separate factor in itself in determining the status of a particular term (see below).

The importance of the statement

A statement may be regarded as a term of the contract if such importance is attached to it that the injured party would not have entered into the contract but for this statement. An example of the application of this guideline has already been seen in *Bannerman* v *White* above, since there was no question of the defendants entering into the contract if the hops had been treated with sulphur. Indeed, the defendants stated that they would not even have bothered to ask the price if they had known that sulphur had been used in cultivating the hops.

A similar approach can also be seen in *Couchman* v *Hill* [1947] 1 All ER 103 where the plaintiff bought a heifer at an auction. The catalogue described the heifer as being 'unserved'. The conditions of sale provided that the auctioneers did not warrant the condition or description of any animal auctioned. Prior to the sale, whilst the heifer was in the ring, the plaintiff asked the auctioneer to confirm that the animal was unserved, and this he did. Eight weeks after the sale the heifer died as a result of carrying a calf at too young an age. It was held that the statement that the heifer was 'unserved' amounted to a warranty, that is, a term of the contract, which overrode the auctioneers' conditions of sale. It was clear that the plaintiff placed such importance on the statement that he would not have bid for the animal had he known the truth of its condition. He could therefore claim damages.

The two cases stated above have, however, to be contrasted with the case of *Oscar Chess Ltd* v *Williams* [1957] 1 All ER 325.

Here the defendants sold a car to the plaintiffs, who were motor dealers, for £290. They described the car as a 1948 Morris 10, which they honestly believed to be the case since this fact was also confirmed by the registration book. Some six months later the plaintiffs discovered that the car was in fact a 1939 model and therefore sued for damages on the basis of a breach of warranty. It was held that their action should fail since the court, after considering all the facts, came to the conclusion and found that the defendants had no intention of binding themselves by way of a contractual obligation as to the veracity of the date of registration of the vehicle. The defendants, the court decided, had made an innocent misrepresentation as to the date when the vehicle was first registered.

Special knowledge or skill

The court is more willing to regard a statement as amounting to a term of the contract where a representor has some special knowledge or skill that places him in a stronger position of discovering the truth of the matter. The principle has already been seen in *Birch* v *Paramount Estates* (above), where the defendants were regarded as holding out to the plaintiffs that they had particular knowledge to the extent that the plaintiff considered that there was no need to make a check on the information supplied by the defendants. A further example can be seen in *Schawel* v *Read* [1913] 2 IR 81 in which the plaintiff, who was seeking a stallion for stud purposes, examined a horse which was potentially suitable. Soon after the plaintiff commenced the examination the defendant interrupted, saying, 'You need not look for anything: the horse is perfectly sound', whereupon the plaintiff stopped his examination. A few days after this incident a price was agreed and three weeks later the purchase was completed. The horse proved to be unfit for stud purposes and the plaintiff sued for breach of contract, the defendant arguing that he had made a mere representation. The statement was held to be a term of the contract since the court not only considered that the representation had taken place at the time of the sale but that the defendant, who was the owner of the horse, clearly had special knowledge as to its condition.

The application of the special knowledge or skill criterion by the courts is best illustrated by a comparison of the cases of *Oscar Chess Ltd* v *Williams* and *Dick Bentley Productions Ltd* v *Harold Smith (Motors) Ltd* [1965] 2 All ER 65. The facts of *Oscar Chess* have already been discussed above, but it is necessary to recall that the statement regarding the age of the vehicle was held not to be a term of the contract. That decision continues to represent something of an absurdity in that a statement of such importance was not regarded as a term of the contract. Two of the criteria already discussed pointed to such a fact, in that the statement was made at the time of the contract and that the contract had not been reduced to writing and, therefore, no question arose in relation to the possibility of an oral statement being overridden by a written document. Both these factors weighed in favour of the plaintiff. However the Court of Appeal was swayed by the argument that whilst the defendant seller had no actual knowledge of the first year of registration of the vehicle, the plaintiff buyers were experienced car dealers and, as such, possessed the knowledge, experience and means of determining the true age of the vehicle. Put another way, the plaintiffs, knowing that the seller was not well versed in such matters, coupled with the fact that he had not acted negligently in relation to the date of first registration, were not entitled to assume that the defendant seller had assumed responsibility for the accuracy of the date.

In the *Dick Bentley* case, a motor dealer made an untrue statement to a private purchaser that a car had done only 20,000 miles since being fitted with a new engine and gearbox. In fact the car had done nearly 100,000 miles. The purchaser eventually found the car to be unsuitable and the mileage untrue. The purchaser sued for breach of contract. The Court of Appeal held that the statement was a term of the contract since the defendants were clearly better placed to know the truth of the statement than the plaintiff, who thus was successful in his claim for damages.

The problem that now arises is how to reconcile the decisions in the two cases.

Lord Denning was of the opinion in *Dick Bentley* that the final decision as to whether the statement was a term or a mere representation was based on the presence or absence of fault in relation to the accuracy of the statement. In *Dick Bentley* the defendants were at fault in relation to the number of miles since they were in a position to know the true position or at least to find out, and thus the statement was a term of the contract. In *Oscar Chess* negligence was not present as to the truth of the statement, but also the defendant seller, not being involved in the motor trade, was not in a position to confirm the date of first registration. It is, however, naive to reduce the comparison to the presence or absence of negligence, and in any event why should this be a decisive factor in determining whether a statement is a term or a representation? The answer may well lie in Lord Denning's view in *Dick Bentley* that prima facie a statement that induces a contract should be considered a warranty. If, however, the entering into of a contract is induced by an untrue statement made either fraudulently or negligently, then the statement amounts to either a negligent or a fraudulent misrepresentation. The effect of such a finding would be to allow the innocent party not only to claim damages but also to rescind the contract. If, on the other hand, the statement is made innocently and not negligently then in practical terms it is important for the statement to be incorporated into the contract as a term of it, since the innocent party would be able to sue for breach of contract and, at the very least, claim damages. Such a remedy would not be available to the innocent party if the statement was held to be a mere representation since here he would have to sue for innocent misrepresentation, which only gives rise to the remedy of rescission – and this may be barred in certain circumstances (see Chapter 9 below), such as an undue delay in claiming for it, as in *Oscar Chess*. Whilst the courts may award damages in lieu of rescission under s. 2(2) of the Misrepresentation Act 1967, they cannot do so where the remedy of rescission is itself lost. Although it seems likely that the taking of fault into account when assessing whether an inaccurate statement amounts to a breach of a term or a misrepresentation will produce what appear to be inconsistent decisions, as seen above, this method of assessment nevertheless produces an equitable solution if the reasoning above is applied.

The parol evidence rule

Having discussed the extent to which statements made by the parties have become either mere representations or terms of a contract, we must now see to what degree the parties may adduce evidence other than that agreed in the document. The basic rule here is known as the 'parol evidence rule' which provides that generally evidence will not be admitted which seeks to add, vary or contradict the terms of a written contract. The use of the word 'parol' is somewhat deceptive since it applies not only to oral evidence but also to any other extrinsic evidence that seeks to have the above effect. The rule, in fact, reinforces the objective nature of the modern contract in that the law is not so much concerned with the actual intentions of the parties as with their manifest intentions as expressed within the four corners of the contractual document. The result of such an approach was to prevent a party from adducing evidence that the signed and written agreement did not contain the whole agreement. Thus in *Jacobs* v *Batavia and General Plantations Trust* [1924] 1 Ch 287 it was stated that:

> parol evidence will not be admitted to prove that some particular term, which had been verbally agreed upon, had been omitted (by design or otherwise) from a written instrument constituting a valid and operative contract between the parties.

Two principal reasons can be seen for this approach. Firstly, one might argue that if the parties have gone to considerable lengths to negotiate and reduce a contract into writing, then why has the term in question been omitted? The only answer might be that the omitted part was never intended to be a term of the contract. Secondly, if one is going to allow terms to be added to the written contract, the effect will be to introduce uncertainty in the agreement and into the law itself, since it would not then be possible for the courts, the parties or other third parties thereby to rely on the written contract.

The parol evidence rule was originally applied by the courts as a strict rule and, indeed, as we have already seen in Chapter 6, certain types of contract in relation to land had to be contained within some sort of writing. The rule, however, began to be undermined by the fact that it did not apply to partly written and partly oral contracts and the fact that it began to be regarded as a presumption rather than a strict rule of law. Thus in *Gillespie Bros & Co* v *Cheney, Eggar and Co* [1896] 2 QB 59 Lord Russell stated:

> Although when the parties arrive at a definite written contract the implication or presumption is very strong that such contract is intended to contain all the terms of their bargain, it is a presumption only, and it is open to either of the parties to allege that there was, in addition to what appears in the written agreement, an antecedent express stipulation not intended by the parties to be excluded, but intended to continue in force with the express written agreement.

As a result of this change of attitude, the number of exceptions to the rule continued to grow, to the extent that in 1976 the Law Commission (Working Paper No 70) proposed that what was left of the rule should be abolished. This legislation has not been forthcoming. In any event in 1986 the Law Commission in its report, 'Law of Contract: The Parol Evidence Rule', Working Paper No 154, stated that legislation was no longer necessary since the rule no longer existed. It is nevertheless important to know the exceptions which have caused the demise of the 'rule', though collateral contracts will be considered separately.

Custom

The parol evidence rule does not prevent the parties adducing evidence of a custom or trade usage, which will result in terms being added to the contract.

Non-operation

There is no objection to extrinsic evidence being offered that indicates that the parties had agreed that the contract would not operate until some specific event occurs, despite the fact that prima facie a valid enforceable contract had been entered into. The basis behind this exception, if that is the correct expression, is that the written contract is not varied or supplemented in any way, but simply that its operation is suspended. In *Pym* v *Campbell* (1856) 6 E & B 370 the parties negotiated for the sale of a share of a patent. The contract was in writing but the parties agreed orally that the contract would not operate until the patent had been examined and verified by a third party. It was held that parol evidence as to the oral arrangement would be admitted.

Invalidity

The parol evidence rule does not forbid the adducing of evidence that calls into question the validity of the written agreement, such as lack of capacity, mistake or misrepresentation.

Rectification

Whilst the written agreement is intended to reflect the intentions of the parties, it may be that the written document has done this inaccurately. Clearly this is more of a problem where the individuals themselves have attempted to draft the document, though this situation may also arise where a professional adviser or lawyer has been given inaccurate information or where that professional lacks competence. In such an instance one of the parties may apply to the court to have the document rectified in order to reflect the true intentions of the parties or the true state of affairs. The effect of the order is to amend the document retrospectively so that it states what it should have stated all along. Parol evidence is admissible here to support the application to rectify.

Incompleteness

A further exception to the rule occurs where the court finds that the written contract was not intended to amount to a complete reflection of the agreement entered into by the parties. Where the court comes to such a finding then it will permit extrinsic evidence of the rest of the contract to be adduced by the parties. In coming to such a finding the court has reference to the intentions of the parties. The courts nowadays generally infer that the parties did not intend that the written contract was to be final and conclusive, but that it was to be read alongside any oral arrangements made between the parties. An example is the case of *Couchman* v *Hill* above, where it was held that the oral assurance given by the auctioneer that the heifer was unserved was part and parcel of the written conditions of sale.

A somewhat more modern case illustrating the principle is that of *J. Evans and Son (Portsmouth) Ltd* v *Andrea Merzario Ltd* [1976] 2 All ER 930 where the plaintiffs were in business shipping machinery from Italy, using the defendant carriers for this purpose, conducting the business on the standard conditions used by the forwarding trade. Prior to 1967 the machinery was shipped on trailers and because of the risk of corrosion it was agreed that both the machinery and the trailers would always be carried below deck. In 1967 the defendants changed over to containers and, during discussions, they assured the plaintiffs that their goods would continue to be stowed below deck. On this basis the plaintiffs continued to use the defendants as their carriers on the written standard conditions, but these standard conditions permitted the defendants to have the goods stowed on deck. Some time later a container with goods belonging to the plaintiffs was washed overboard in heavy seas after being stowed on deck. In an action for breach of contract the Court of Appeal held that the defendants could not rely solely on the written standard conditions and permitted the plaintiffs to raise evidence as regards the oral discussions and subsequent assurance. It was clear that the parties did not intend that the written standard conditions would form the complete basis of the ensuing contracts.

The actual reasons behind this decision in the Court of Appeal are interesting in that two approaches were adopted in arriving at the decision. Roskill and Lane LJJ considered that the contract was one which was both written and oral and therefore free from the influence of the parol evidence rule. Lord Denning, however, considered that the oral agreement amounted to a second contract, a collateral contract. With respect to the arguments of Lord Denning supporting the collateral contract approach, Roskill LJ stated:

> That phrase is normally only applicable where the original promise was external to the main contract, the main contract being a contract in writing, so that usually parol evidence cannot be given to contradict the terms of the written contract . . . But the doctrine, as it seems to me, has little or no application where one is not concerned with a contract in writing (with respect I cannot accept counsel for the defendants' argument that there was here a contract in writing) but with a contract which, as I think, was partly oral, partly by writing and partly by conduct. In such a case the court does not require to have recourse to lawyers' devices such as collateral oral warranty in order to seek to adduce evidence which would not otherwise be admissible. The Court is entitled to look at and should look at all the evidence from start to finish in order to see what the bargain was that was struck between the parties.

At the end of the day the two approaches made no difference to the result, but the fact that Denning's approach produces two contracts rather than a single partly written and partly oral one, as in Roskill and Lane's reasoning, may be significant in other cases. In contracts for the sale of land which, under the Law of Property (Miscellaneous Provisions) Act 1989, s. 2, are required to be in writing, the oral collateral contract of Denning could not be included in the sale. It is, however, important to note that this Act specifically preserves the equitable remedy of rectification, which could be used to incorporate terms from an oral contract. It should also be noted that the contract could also contain a merger clause, the effect of which would be to provide that the written contract was intended to contain the entire terms of the agreement specifically excluding the inference of a single partly written and partly oral contract.

Collateral contracts

The device of the collateral contract has been known to the law for well over 100 years, yet its rise to importance in recent times means that a student of the law of contract who ignores it does so at his peril. The collateral contract has particular significance in relation to the status of terms and has provided a substantial exception to the parol evidence rule. Its use also arises in relation to exemption clauses and privity of contract.

The concept was summed up by Lord Moulton in *Heilbut, Symons & Co v Buckleton* [1913] AC 30 when he stated:

> It is evident, both on principle and on authority, that there may be a contract the consideration for which is the making of some other contract, 'If you will make such and such a contract, I will give you one hundred pounds', is in every sense of the word a complete legal contract. It is collateral to the main contract, but each has an independent existence, and they do not differ in respect of their possessing to the full the character and status of a contract.

It remains to examine its use in relation to terms and the parol evidence rule.

Terms or mere representations

If a court considers that a statement does not amount to a term but a mere representation in the principal contract, it may find that it nevertheless amounts to a term of a collateral contract, that is, that there is an implied secondary contract running alongside the principal one. The approach is supported by a number of cases, for example, *City and Westminster Properties (1934) Ltd v Mudd* [1958] 2 All ER 733, where the defendant had rented the plaintiffs' shop for some six years. Annexed to the shop was a room in which the defendant used to sleep, as the plaintiffs knew well. The lease came up for renewal and the plaintiffs inserted a new clause that restricted the use of the shop to 'showrooms, workrooms and offices only'. Such a clause would obviously prevent the defendant from sleeping on the premises so he asked whether he could continue the practice, to which the plaintiffs agreed. On this understanding the defendant signed the lease, though when he did sleep on the premises the plaintiffs brought an action seeking forfeiture of the lease for breach of covenant. It was held that the promise not to enforce the clause against him was a collateral contract which he could claim as a defence to the action for breach of covenant.

The use of the collateral contract to incorporate a statement as a term of a contract, as seen in the *Mudd* case above, has a useful spin-off in that it does away with the need for the plaintiff to frame his claim in an action for misrepresentation which might be complex. It is primarily for this reason that the use of the collateral contract device has increased in recent years despite the fact that Lord Moulton and the rest of the House of Lords in the *Heilbut* case considered it should be used very sparingly. This trend towards its use can be seen in *Esso Petroleum Co Ltd v Mardon* [1976] 2 All ER 5, where the Court of Appeal not only found for the existence of negligent misrepresentation but also for the presence of a collateral warranty as to the accuracy and reliability of an estimate for the annual sales of petrol at a garage.

The parol evidence rule

It has already been noted that the collateral contract device may be used to avoid the parol evidence rule. Originally the parol evidence contained in the collateral contract had to be independent of the principal contract, that is, the collateral contract could not alter or add terms to the original contract, nor was it supposed to contradict the terms of that contract. It has been seen in the *Mudd* case that the courts will now allow the collateral contract device to be used to give effect to such changes. It may be that the original limitations as described above were formed on a false assumption, but if one takes the idea of the collateral contract giving effect to an agreement independent of the principal contract, there does not appear to be any compelling reason why the collateral contract should not add to, vary or contradict the principal one. If anything, the limitations placed on the collateral contract should revolve around the need to prove the existence of a legally binding agreement supported by consideration.

IMPLIED TERMS

The vast majority of the primary obligations of the parties to a contract will normally be expressed within the contract itself, but it is of course possible for the parties to overlook certain primary obligations or, in fact, to fail to recognise all the eventualities that might flow from the execution of the contract. In these circumstances terms may be implied into the contract in order to make up for the omissions of the parties. The role of the courts in this process clearly contradicts the classical theory of contract which was based on the concept of the contract as a reflection of the will of the parties, independently and freely entered into. In order to avoid this contradictory stance the courts proceeded by way of fiction, in that when they implied terms into the contract they were merely giving effect to the unexpressed will of the parties by making up for their omissions within the contract. Eventually the courts began to go beyond this fiction by implying terms irrespective of the presumed intentions of the parties. At this point there is a profound separation of the nature of the implied term since, whilst the earlier fiction used by the courts implied terms as a matter of fact into a particular contract, the latter role of the courts was to imply certain terms into all contracts of a particular nature, the result being that the term is now implied as a matter of law.

Whether the term is implied as a matter of fact or law, the role of the courts is subject to two reservations. Firstly, as we have already seen in Chapter 2, the contract must be certain and the court will not attempt to write the contract for the parties. Thus if there are a substantial number of omissions the courts may well find that the contract in question is void for uncertainty. Secondly, if the parties have produced a written contract which is very detailed the courts may also be reluctant to interfere, regarding the contract as being definitive as to the intentions of the parties, though the courts may be persuaded to imply a term into the contract where the term in question is one imposed generally by the law in the situation occurring in the case in question.

So far we have considered the case where the courts have implied terms into the contract, but one must not ignore the fact that Parliament itself, by means of a statute, imposes terms into certain types of contracts. Very often the role undertaken by Parliament is to protect certain types of parties to a contract and is a recognition of the fact that the classical idea of freedom of contract is very often a nonsense. Uppermost in the mind of Parliament here is the consumer, the lone individual, who quite clearly has little protection from the vagaries of the businessman. Parliament will thus impose certain terms, thereby giving the individual consumer certain rights within the contract which would otherwise no doubt be omitted by the businessman, given his superior bargaining position.

Terms implied on a matter of fact

Terms which are implied as fact are those which are imputed from the intentions of the parties. In order for a term to be implied it must be obvious and necessary to give business efficacy to the agreement, and thus only those the absence of which would render the contract incomplete will be implied. An attempt was made by Lord Denning in *Liverpool City Council v Irwin* [1976] 2 All ER 39 to extend the circumstances in which terms could be implied into a contract. He considered that a term could be implied into a contract merely on the grounds that it would be reasonable to do so in that the contract would be better for its inclusion. The House of Lords rejected Denning's approach, Lord Cross stating:

> it is not enough for the court to say that the suggested term is a reasonable one the presence of which would make the contract a better or fairer one; it must be able to say that the insertion of the terms is necessary to give – as it is put – 'business efficacy' to the contract and that if its absence had been pointed out at the time both parties – assuming them to have been reasonable men – would have agreed without hesitation to its insertion.

The classic test used to decide whether a term falls within the criteria set out in the statement of Lord Cross is the 'officious bystander test'. There have been many attempts at defining the test but the one that has survived the test of time and is often quoted is that of MacKinnon LJ in *Shirlaw v Southern Foundries (1926) Ltd* [1939] 2 KB 206 where he stated:

> Prima facie that which in any contract is left to be implied and need not be expressed is something so obvious that it goes without saying; so that if, while the parties were making their bargain an officious bystander were to suggest some express provision for it in their agreement, they would testily suppress him with a common 'Oh, of course'.

An application of the officious bystander test can be seen in the case of *The Moorcock* (1889) 14 PD 64 where the defendant owners of a wharf contracted to allow the plaintiff owner of a ship, *The Moorcock*, to discharge it at their jetty provided he paid landing charges. The jetty extended into the Thames and both parties were aware that the ship would be grounded at low tide. While the ship was unloading the tide went out and the ship settled on to a ridge of rock beneath the mud, breaking its back. The plaintiff sued for the damage sustained by the ship. The defendants argued that they had not guaranteed the safety of the anchorage and further the river bed by the jetty was not vested in them. The Court of Appeal nevertheless found the defendants to be liable on the basis that there was an implied undertaking given to the plaintiff at the time of contracting that the anchorage would, so far as reasonable care could provide, be in such a condition as not to endanger the vessel.

Whilst the concept of the officious bystander test is still very much alive and kicking, as seen in *Finchbourne Ltd* v *Rodrigues* [1976] 3 All ER 581 or *Gardner* v *Coutts & Co* [1967] 3 All ER 1064 it has to be applied rather cautiously. In many respects it is too easy to make use of the test simply to correct some oversight of the parties. It should be borne in mind that the test cannot be utilised in two situations.

The first situation arises where one of the parties is unaware of the term that it is sought to imply into the contract.

In *Spring* v *National Amalgamated Stevedores and Dockers Society* [1956] 2 All ER 221, the defendants and the union had agreed in 1939 on certain rules which governed the transfer of members from one union to another. This agreement had become known as the 'Bridlington Agreement'. In 1955 the defendants admitted the plaintiff to their union in breach of the agreement, although the plaintiff was completely unaware of the rules contained in the Bridlington Agreement. The breach of the rules was reported to a committee of the Trades Union Congress (TUC), who ordered the union to expel the plaintiff from its membership. When the union attempted to do this the plaintiff sued them for breach of contract, seeking an injunction restraining the expulsion. The union argued that a term should be included in the contract that the terms of the Bridlington Agreement had to be complied with. The court rejected this suggestion and granted the injunction. The reason for the rejection of the argument of the defendants was based on the reply the plaintiff would have given had a bystander asked whether the Bridlington Agreement had been included in the contract. In this case the plaintiff would have replied 'What's that?' rather than the 'Of course' as required by the officious bystander test enunciated by MacKinnon LJ. A term cannot be implied if an individual is unaware of the term it is sought to imply into the contract.

The second reason for the failure of the officious bystander test arises where there is uncertainty as to whether both the parties would have agreed to the term which has been omitted from the contract.

In *Shell (UK) Ltd* v *Lostock Garages Ltd* [1976] 1 WLR 1187, a written contract provided that Shell should supply petrol and oil to the defendants, who reciprocally agreed to buy such products only from Shell. A price-war subsequently developed during which Shell reduced the price of petrol to other neighbouring garages, and this resulted in the plaintiff having to trade at a loss. The plaintiff attempted to have a term implied into the contract that Shell would not 'abnormally discriminate' against the plaintiff. The Court of Appeal refused the plaintiff's application on the basis that Shell would never have agreed to the insertion of such a term and, anyway, the term was too vague and uncertain.

Terms implied as a matter of law

By the courts

So far we have seen that terms implied as a matter of fact are based on the idea that such a term emanates from the common implied intention of the parties to the contract. Terms implied by law are obligations that arise within the contract irrespective of the intentions of the parties or the facts of a particular case. Once a term is implied by law and the courts find for its existence in the particular circumstances of a case, then that case becomes the authority for the inclusion of the term in all subsequent similar cases.

An important example of this process arose in the case of *Liverpool City Council* v *Irwin* [1976] 2 All ER 39 where the Council had let flats in a tower block to the tenants. Whilst the tenancy agreements imposed obligations on the tenants, they were silent as to the obligations of the Council as regards the maintenance of the building. Lifts regularly broke down and rubbish chutes blocked with the result that the appellant decided to withhold his rent as a protest against the Council's failure properly to maintain the building. The Council brought an action to seek possession of the appellant's flat, and he counter-claimed that the Council were acting in breach of an implied obligation properly to maintain the building. The term could not be implied as a matter of fact since it did not satisfy the officious bystander test nor was it reasonably necessary to give business efficacy to the contract. However, the House of Lords implied the term as a matter of law. There was a duty on a landlord 'to take reasonable care to keep in reasonable repair and usability' the common areas of the building, such as lifts, stairways, corridors and rubbish chutes, and so on. Lord Cross thought that the test to be applied in making a decision to imply a particular term into all contracts of a specific type was whether in the general run of such cases the term in question would be one which it would be reasonable to insert.

By statute

Over the years obligations which have been formally implied into contracts by the courts have very often been given statutory authority. It is, of course, impossible to trace all such instances and therefore our discussion of terms implied by statute has been limited to what is debatably the most important area, that of contracts for the sale of goods and the standard of care in relation to contracts for services. These areas are governed by the Sale of Goods Act 1979 and the Supply of Goods and Services Act 1982. Both Acts have been subject to amendment by the Sale and Supply of Goods Act 1994, the main effect of which has been to substitute a new s. 14(2) into the 1979 Act and a new s. 4(2) into the 1982 Act implying a condition that goods must be of a satisfactory quality instead of being of merchantable quality.

The following terms are implied under the Sale of Goods Act 1979.

(a) *Implied terms as to title – s. 12.* In every contract for the sale of goods there is an implied condition on the part of the seller that in the case of a sale he has a right to sell the goods, and in the case of an agreement to sell he will have such a right at the time the property is to pass' (s. 12(1)).

Apart from the above implied condition the provision also contains two implied warranties that the buyer will enjoy the right to enjoy quiet possession of the goods and that the goods will be free from any undisclosed encumbrances, such as a lien over the goods (s. 12(2)).

In *Rowland v Divall* [1923] 2 KB 500 a buyer of a car found out that it had in fact been stolen and as a result he had to return it to the true owner. He sued on the implied condition and it was held that he was entitled to recover the full price he had paid for the car, despite the fact that he had used the car for some four months and as a result the car was worth less than he had paid for it. The logic is simple, in that he had paid to become the full owner of the vehicle and since he had not acquired this ownership he was entitled to recover his full purchase price, despite the depreciation of the car during the period that it was in his possession.

(b) *Implied condition as to description – s. 13.* In contracts for the sale of goods by description there is an implied condition that the goods shall correspond with the description.

In *Beale v Taylor* [1967] 1 WLR 1193 a private motorist advertised his car for sale as a 'Herald convertible, white, 1961, twin carbs'. The buyer, another private motorist, later discovered that the car was in fact a composite of two cars and that only the rear half corresponded with the description given by the seller, who was unaware of the true situation. It was held that even though the buyer had inspected the car, he had nevertheless at least partly relied on the description, so that it was a sale by description and that the seller was liable under s. 13.

Before a breach of s. 13 can arise, the Court of Appeal has stressed in *Harlingdon & Leinster Enterprises Ltd* v *Christopher Hull Fine Art Ltd* [1990] 1 All ER 737 that there must be reliance on the description of the goods. Slade LJ stated:

> . . . where a question arises whether a sale of goods was one by description, the presence or absence of reliance on the description may be very relevant in so far as it throws light on the intentions of the parties at the time of the contract. If there was no such reliance by the purchaser, this may be powerful evidence that the parties did not contemplate that the authenticity of the description should constitute a term of the contract; in other words, that they contemplated that the purchaser would be buying the goods *as they were*. If, on the other hand, there was such reliance (as in *Varley* v *Whipp* [1900] 1 QB 513, where the purchaser had never seen the goods) this may be equally powerful evidence that it was contemplated by both parties that the correctness of the description would be a term of the contract (so as to bring it within s. 13(1)).

It should be noted that, like s. 12, s. 13 is not limited to consumer sales but is equally applicable to private sales. It should also be noted that a sale of unascertained goods will always be a sale by description.

(c) *Implied condition as to satisfactory quality – s. 14(2).* Prior to the Sale and Supply of Goods Act 1994, the Sale of Goods Act 1979, s. 14(2) provided that, where the seller sells goods in the course of a business, there is an implied condition that the goods supplied under the contract are of merchantable quality. No such implied condition arose where the defects were specifically drawn to the buyer's attention before the contract was made, or where the buyer examined the goods before the contract was made and that inspection should have revealed the defect.

It should be noted that the provision only applied to sales in the course of a business, not to private sales, and that the provision not only caught the goods themselves but also the packaging or anything else supplied with the goods, as illustrated in the case of *Wilson v Rickett Cockerell & Co Ltd* [1954] 1 QB 598.

The term 'merchantable quality' was defined in s. 14(6) as follows:

> Goods of any kind are of merchantable quality within the meaning of subsection (2) above if they are fit for the purpose or purposes for which goods of that kind are commonly bought as it is reasonable to expect having regard to any description applied to them, the price (if relevant) and all other relevant circumstances.

It was originally intended that the above statutory definition of merchantable quality would encompass two different common law definitions based on usability and acceptability. The test of usability provides that the goods should be usable for at least one of the purposes for which goods of that description are commonly bought; that is, 'do the goods work?' The test of acceptability requires the goods to be in such a state that the buyer, with knowledge of any defect in them, would buy them without any substantial reduction in the price obtainable for such goods when in a reasonable and sound condition and without special terms. It can be seen, however, that s. 14(6) placed more emphasis on the usability of the goods rather than their acceptability.

It should also be noted that s. 14(6) referred to the fact that the goods only had to be as fit for their purpose as one may 'reasonably expect'. This proviso effectively allowed a seller to reduce the standard of merchantable quality by showing, for instance, that one must not expect secondhand cars to be as good as new cars.

The case of *Bartlett v Sidney Marcus Ltd* [1965] 1 WLR 1013 illustrated the problems that could arise by virtue of the definition of merchantable quality in s. 14(6). The facts of the case were that a purchaser of a car was informed that the clutch of the car he was considering purchasing was defective. The sellers offered to either repair the clutch or reduce the price of the car by £25, the buyer opting for the latter. After driving 300 miles the purchaser had to replace the clutch at a cost of £45 more than was initially anticipated. It was held that the car was of merchantable quality since the car was not unfit for its purpose merely because the defect proved to be more serious than was originally thought. Lord Denning considered that the car was usable though not perfect. Denning's opinion was that one must expect a secondhand car to be less than perfect.

The usability test presented significant problems for the consumer in relation to minor or cosmetic defects in goods since such defects whilst not rendering the goods unusable could nevertheless render them unmerchantable in certain circumstances. Here a consumer could, because there was a breach of condition, reject the goods and claim damages where that was appropriate. In some cases, however, the courts were reluctant to find the goods unmerchantable in such circumstances because the goods remained usable. A typical example of such a situation might arise where a consumer took delivery of a new car, only to find when he got it home that there was a dent on the bodywork. Not surprisingly, the consumer would have wanted to reject the vehicle for a new one because he expected to get a car in pristine condition and he had not received that. Nevertheless, it may have been the case that all he could do was to accept a repair by the supplier since, despite the fact that the vehicle was not acceptable to the consumer, the car was merchantable in that it remained usable as a means of transportation. Furthermore, if the car was from a manufacturer who had a reputation for producing cheap and shoddy goods, it may have been the case that a court would have found that the purchaser should have had a 'reasonable expectation' of receiving a car in such a condition.

So, when would the courts have found that the goods were not of merchantable quality? The answer to this question would have depended largely upon the circumstances of a particular case. Very often the physical characteristics of the goods would determine whether the goods were of merchantable quality, although this was not always the case. As s. 14(6) itself stated, the price and the description applied to the goods may have been significant. A low-priced product described as 'seconds', 'shop-soiled' or 'secondhand' may have indicated a lower quality and therefore a finding that they were of merchantable quality, as in *Bartlett* v *Sidney Marcus Ltd* above. On the other hand, higher-priced goods variously described as 'luxury', 'deluxe' or 'premier' would have given an expectation of a higher quality and produced a finding of unmerchantability even though there was only the slightest blemish on the product. In *Rogers* v *Parish (Scarborough) Ltd* [1987] 2 All ER 232, for instance, the plaintiff bought a new Range Rover that suffered from a number of minor defects such as a misfiring engine, an oil leak, scratches to the paintwork, and a noisy gearbox. The Court of Appeal held that the vehicle was not of merchantable quality despite the fact that the defects were capable of being repaired. Similarly in *Shine* v *General Guarantee Corporation* [1988] 1 All ER 911, where the plaintiff bought a secondhand sports car, a Fiat X-19, which at some point had been submerged in water so that the manufacturer's anti-corrosion warranty was invalid. It was held that the vehicle was not of merchantable quality. Here the Court of Appeal placed particular emphasis on the description of the vehicle, stating that the buyer considered that: 'he was buying an enthusiast's car, a car of the mileage shown and at the sort of price cars of that age and condition could be expected to fetch, a car described as "a nice car, good runner, no problems . . .".'. What he in fact was buying for the same price was . . . potentially a "rogue car" and irrespective of its condition it was one which no member of the public, knowing the facts, would touch with a barge pole unless they could get it at a substantially reduced price.'

Apart from the description and price, the consequences of a defect could also be a relevant factor in determining whether a product was of merchantable quality or not. Thus in *Bernstein* v *Pamsons Motors (Golders Green) Ltd* [1987] 2 All ER 220 the plaintiff bought a new car which, within three weeks of delivery and having only travelled 140 miles, suffered from a seized-up engine. This was caused by a drop of sealant blocking up the lubrication system. Repairs were carried out free of charge but the plaintiff refused to take the car back and asked for the return of his money. The defendants argued on the basis of *Bartlett* v *Sidney Marcus Ltd* that the car was still usable and therefore of merchantable quality. Rougier J stated that the *Bartlett* case applied to secondhand cars and that the purchaser of a new car was entitled to expect more, though how much more depended on a number of factors. One was the intractability of a defect which was difficult to find and rectify, since here the person acquired not so much a car as a running battle with a defective machine. Another factor was the time it took to repair the defect and it was not relevant that the repair was done free of charge to the purchaser under the vendor's warranty. Another factor was the price and in that respect he considered that a mere blemish on a Rolls Royce might render it unmerchantable, while on a more modest car it would not have this effect. He stated finally that, whilst the car had been repaired, there was a possibility that the effect of the engine seizure could have transmitted stress to other parts of the engine and created some 'knock-on damage'. While a buyer of a new car had to put up with some teething problems and have them repaired, a defect of the type that occurred in this case went far beyond what a buyer has to accept, and therefore the car was not of merchantable quality. Rougier J also stated that a relevant factor in arriving at his decision was that the car, though driveable prior to the engine seizure, was not safe since the seizure could have occurred in the fast lane of a motorway with devastating consequences.

Two other contentious issues arose out of s. 14(6). Firstly, the provision made reference that goods had to be fit for the purpose or purposes for which goods of that kind were commonly bought. It was considered that this reversed the previous position as set out in *Kendall & Sons* v *Lillico & Sons Ltd* [1969] 2 AC 31 that, if goods were commonly bought for a range of purposes, then they would be of merchantable quality provided that they were fit for at least one of their purposes. Thus s. 14(6) gave the impression that if goods had more than one purpose then they had to be fit for all those purposes. In fact this position was dismissed in *Aswan Engineering Establishment Co* v *Lupdine Ltd* [1987] 1 All ER 135 where the Court of Appeal decided that the previous position had not been changed by s. 14(6). It should be noted that s. 14(2) in the 1994 Act, as set out below, does in fact reverse the position and that now where goods have several purposes they must be fit for all the purposes that those goods are commonly supplied for. The new provision will not be without difficulties. For instance, is it conceivable that a buyer could reject goods that are fit for his particular purpose but nevertheless unfit for some other purpose for which those goods are commonly supplied?

Secondly, the condition of merchantable quality only had to be satisfied at the time the goods were delivered, though this did not leave a buyer unprotected if a defect manifested itself after delivery. The reason for this is that merchantable quality was regarded as a continuing term so that, if any defects revealed themselves within a reasonable time after delivery, the goods were still capable of being deemed unmerchantable. The basis of this position lies in the idea that if goods fail or wear out sooner than expected this is evidence of the fact that the goods were not of merchantable quality at the time of delivery. The problem here, however, is one of proof since the onus is on the buyer to show that the goods proved defective or wore out because of some defect rendering them unmerchantable at the time of delivery. The result of this is that there is no notion, or at best a very limited notion, of a requirement of durability in s. 14 as presented in the 1979 Act. The new s. 14(2) attempts to resolve this position by including durability in the list of factors to be taken into account when assessing whether the goods are satisfactory or not. Again it may be questioned whether this will in fact benefit a buyer to any great degree since it is likely that his remedy will be confined to damages only, unless he discovers the defect fairly quickly. Otherwise he may be deemed to have accepted the goods and therefore have lost his right to rejection.

The problems associated with attempting to find that a product was not of merchantable quality have, as already indicated, led to the passing of the Sale and Supply of Goods Act 1994, s. 1 of which substitutes for s. 14(2) in the 1979 Act the following provision:

> **1.**–(1) In Section 14 of the Sale of Goods Act 1979 (implied terms about quality or fitness) for subsection (2) there is substituted—
>
> "(2) Where the seller sells goods in the course of a business, there is an implied term that the goods supplied under the contract are of satisfactory quality.
>
> (2A) For the purposes of this Act, goods are of satisfactory quality if they meet the standard that a reasonable person would regard as satisfactory, taking account of any description of the goods, the price (if relevant) and all the other relevant circumstances.
>
> (2B) For the purposes of this Act, the quality of goods includes their state and condition and the following (among others) are in appropriate cases aspects of the quality of goods—
>
> (a) fitness for all purposes for which goods of the kind in question are commonly supplied,
> (b) appearance and finish,
> (c) freedom from minor defects,
> (d) safety, and
> (e) durability.
>
> 2(C) The term implied by subsection (2) above does not extend to any matter making the quality of goods unsatisfactory—
>
> (a) which is specifically drawn to the buyer's attention before the contract is made,
> (b) where the buyer examines the goods before the contract is made, which that examination ought to reveal, or
> (c) in the case of a contract for sale by sample, which would have been apparent on a reasonable examination of the sample."

The new provision imposes an objective test and reforms the previous law regarding merchantable quality in such a way as to make it more appropriate to modern commercial conditions. The Act thus attempts to address the various issues that have arisen out of the cases discussed above.

(*d*) *Implied condition as to fitness for purpose – s. 14(3).* Where the seller sells goods in the course of a business and the buyer either expressly or impliedly makes known to the seller any particular purpose for which the goods are being bought, there is an implied condition that the goods supplied under the contract are reasonably fit for that purpose, whether or not that is a purpose for which goods of that type are commonly supplied. The implied condition does not operate where the buyer does not rely, or it is unreasonable for him to rely on the skill or judgment of the seller. It follows that if one is going to use the goods for an abnormal purpose then to gain the protection of the provision one should make known to the seller what that purpose is.

An example of an application of the provision can be seen in the case of *Godley* v *Perry* [1960] 1 WLR 9 where the defendant sold a plastic catapult to the plaintiff, who was a boy of six years of age. When the boy used the catapult it broke, blinding him in his left eye. It was held that the defendant was liable both under s. 14(2) – merchantable quality – and s. 14(3) – that the catapult was not fit for the purpose for which it was sold.

(*e*) *Implied condition as to sample – s. 15.* Where a sale is agreed to be by sample three conditions are implied into the contract. Firstly, the bulk must, with regard to quality, correspond with the sample. Secondly, the buyer must have a reasonable opportunity of comparing the bulk with the sample. Finally, the goods must be free of any defect rendering them unmerchantable, which a reasonable examination of the sample would not reveal. This latter implied condition was of particular relevance in the case of *Godley* v *Perry*, above, since the retailer sued the wholesaler under this provision. When buying the goods from the wholesaler, the retailer had tested the catapults by pulling back the elastic but no defect was revealed by this examination and as a result the retailer's claim was successful.

The following terms implied under the Supply of Goods and Services Act 1982 will be considered:

(*a*) *Contracts for the supply of goods.* The 1982 Act applies to contracts for the transfer of ownership of goods. Such transfer amounts neither to contracts for the sale of goods nor to hire purchase agreements. The Act thus applies to contracts for the exchange of goods, such contracts not amounting to contracts for the sale of goods because of the lack of a money consideration. Similarly the Act will apply to a contract of service where, though goods are transferred, the main element is the purchase of a service. An example may be where a painter is employed to paint one's portrait; here the main element of the contract amounts to the purchase of a skill or service but nevertheless goods are transferred within the contract.

The implied terms applied to the goods transferred under the contracts described above are exactly the same as those found in the Sale of Goods Act 1979, as amended by the Sale and Supply of Goods Act 1994, in that they cover title (s. 2), description (s. 3), satisfactory quality and fitness for purpose (s. 4) and sample (s. 5).

(*b*) *Contracts for the supply of services.* Further terms are implied in the 1982 Act where a supplier has agreed to carry out a service, with the exception of contracts of employment or apprenticeship. In such contracts, which may arise in relation to contracts for the sale of goods or hire purchase agreements, there is an implied term that the supplier, acting in the course of a business, will carry out the service with reasonable care and skill (s. 13).

An application of s.13 can be seen in *Wilson* v *Best Travel* [1993] 1 All ER 353, where the plaintiff went on holiday to Greece and stayed in a hotel booked through the defendant tour operator. Whilst on holiday, the plaintiff fell through a glass door and suffered severe injuries. In their holiday brochure there was a statement that the defendants would not accept liability in respect of any loss, damage or inconvenience, unless that was caused by the negligence of their own employees. The defendants further undertook to 'keep an eye' on the accommodation contained in the brochure, though they would not always be able to maintain day-to-day control of the holiday arrangements.

The glass doors were only fitted with ordinary 5mm glass, which complied with Greek safety requirements, though not with British standards. The plaintiff contended that the type of glass fitted meant that the hotel was not reasonably safe and that the defendants were in breach of the duties imposed on them by the Supply of Goods and Services Act 1982 s. 13, in that as a supplier of a service they had not carried out that service with reasonable care and skill.

The court held that the duty of care imposed on holiday companies by s. 13 was such that they should take reasonable care not to offer holiday accommodation of such a nature that clients could not spend a holiday there in reasonable safety. The duty to ensure that the holiday accommodation was safe would be discharged if the tour company checked that the local safety regulations had been complied with. The duty did not extend to ensuring that the safety standards complied with those in operation in the United Kingdom, provided the absence of a safety feature was not such that a reasonable holidaymaker would decline to take a holiday there. The court decided that the tour operator was not in breach of its duty of care under s. 13 since it had inspected the premises, the glass doors complied with Greek safety regulations and the danger posed by the doors was not one which would cause a reasonable holidaymaker to decline to stay in the accommodation.

There is also an implied term that the supplier acting in the course of a business will carry out the service within a reasonable time, this being based on a question of fact, unless the contract fixes a time or the time for the carrying out of the service is determinable by some arrangement within the contract itself or some previous course of dealing (s. 14). Finally, where the consideration due under the contract is not determined by the contract, or by some arrangement within the contract, or some previous course of dealing, the person supplied with the service will have to pay a reasonable charge, this being based on a question of fact (s. 15).

It must be pointed out, however, that the terms implied by the above Acts do not necessarily apply to all contracts for the sale of goods or the supply of goods and services. With regard to contracts for the sale and supply of goods, the implied condition as to title in s. 12 cannot be excluded in any type of contract, any attempt to do so being void. The other implied conditions in ss. 13–15 cannot be excluded in any consumer sale, which was originally defined in the Act as 'a sale of goods . . . by a seller in the course of a business where the goods – (a) are of a type ordinarily bought for private use or consumption, and (b) are sold to a person who does not buy or hold himself out as buying them in the course of a business'. This definition has been replaced by that in the Unfair Contract Terms Act 1977 which talks in terms of a contract entered into by a person 'dealing as a consumer', a concept which will be discussed more fully in the next chapter. It should also be noted that ss. 13–15 can be excluded in non-consumer sales. Here the exclusion clause is subject to a test of reasonableness – which is also imposed in the 1977 Act. Again this will be discussed more fully later.

In relation to contracts for the supply of services any attempt to exclude obligations arising out of the 1982 Act will normally be governed by the test of reasonableness under the Unfair Contract Terms Act 1977, though liability for death or personal injury sustained through negligence cannot be excluded at all. This aspect will be dealt with in Chapter 8.

Terms implied by custom

It is of course possible that terms may be implied into a contract by way of custom or trade usage. In *Hutton* v *Warren* (1836) 1 M & W 466 a tenant proved, by virtue of local custom, that on quitting in accordance with the notice issued by the landlord, he was entitled to an allowance for seeds and labour he had expended on the land.

THE CLASSIFICATION OF CONTRACTUAL TERMS

Warranties and conditions

It will have been seen in our analysis of terms implied by statute that terms may be divided into two types, warranties and conditions, which have differing degrees of importance. The same is also true of other terms, whether expressly agreed upon by the parties or implied by the courts. A condition is regarded as a major term of the contract, that is, one which goes to the very root of the contract. If a party to a contract breaks a condition the consequence is serious since it entitles the other party not only to sue for damages but also to terminate the contract. The injured party, however, does have the option of affirming the contract and simply claiming damages if he so wishes. A warranty is regarded as a minor term of a contract, that is, one which imposes a term that is merely ancillary to the main thrust of the contract. A word of warning is necessary here since, rather confusingly, a warranty in a contract of insurance is regarded as a major term, with all the rights appropriate to such a term should a breach occur. Ordinarily, however, a breach of warranty merely gives the injured party the right to sue for damages only.

In *Poussard* v *Spiers and Pond* (1876) 1 QBD 410 an actress was employed to play the leading role in an operetta for the season. In fact she was unable to take up her role until a week after the season had begun, with the result that the producers had to engage a substitute. When she eventually appeared they refused her services and purported to terminate the contract. The actress sued for breach of contract and lost her case. It was held that since the opening night of the operetta was regarded as of the utmost importance, her absence amounted to a breach of condition which entitled the producers to terminate the contract.

A contrasting illustration of the difference between conditions and warranties may be seen in the case of *Bettini* v *Gye* (1876) 1 QBD 183 where a singer was also engaged to perform for a whole season at various theatres. Part of the contract required him to appear six days before the start of the season for rehearsals, but in fact he arrived only three days in advance. The producers sought to treat the singer's absence as breach of a condition and thereby considered this gave them the right to terminate the contract. The singer sued for breach of contract and was successful. The court held that the terms regarding the rehearsals were merely ancillary to the main part of the contract and thus amounted to a warranty only. The producers, while being entitled to sue for damages, were not entitled to terminate the contract.

The right to terminate a contract for breach of condition is modified in relation to non-consumer contracts for the sale of goods by the Sale and Supply of Goods Act 1994, s. 4(1), which inserts a new section, s. 15A, into the Sale of Goods Act 1979. This states:

> 15A.—(1) Where in the case of a contract of sale—
>
> > (a) the buyer would, apart from this subsection, have the right to reject goods by reason of a breach on the part of the seller of a term implied by section 13, 14 or 15 above, but
> > (b) the breach is so slight that it would be unreasonable for him to reject them,
>
> then, if the buyer does not deal as consumer, the breach is not to be treated as a breach of condition but may be treated as a breach of warranty.

Section 15A(2) provides that s. 15A(1) will apply unless a contrary intention appears in, or is implied from, the contract. Section 15A(3) further provides that the burden of proof is on the seller to show that the breach falls within subsection (1)(b).

Innominate terms

The distinction between conditions and warranties arises out of the relative importance attached to the terms when considered against the total background of the contract. Very often the parties to a contract may expressly agree to designate a term as a condition or warranty as an indication of the emphasis they wish to place on the importance of the term within the contract. Similarly the law itself may give an indication of the importance of a term either by means of a statute, as in the case of the implied terms contained in the Sale of Goods Act 1979 for instance, or by means of a judicial decision as to the status of a particular term. In recent years, however, where no expression of the status of a particular term has arisen out of the agreement from whatever source, the courts have taken to classifying the term as an innominate term (referred to by some authorities as an intermediate term). The effects of a breach of an innominate term do not depend on the status of the term in the contract when it is entered into but on the effects of a breach of the term on the contract.

The concept of the innominate term first arose in the case of the *Hong Kong Fir Shipping Co Ltd* v *Kawasaki Kisen Kaisha Ltd* [1962] 1 All ER 474 where the defendants had chartered a ship from the plaintiffs for two years. The charterparty contained a term which required the plaintiffs to provide a ship which was 'in every way fitted for ordinary cargo service'. It transpired that the engine room crew were incompetent and that the ship was in a poor state of repair. In fact the plaintiffs openly admitted that the ship was unseaworthy. As a result of these factors some 20 weeks' use of the ship was lost and the defendants claimed to treat the contract as terminated for breach of condition. The plaintiffs claimed that the breach only entitled the defendants to sue for damages. The plaintiffs succeeded in their action against the defendants for wrongful termination. Lord Diplock stated:

> The problem in this case is, in my view, neither solved nor soluble by debating whether the shipowner's express or implied undertaking to tender a seaworthy ship is a 'condition' or a 'warranty' . . . There are many contractual undertakings of a more complex character which cannot be categorised as being 'conditions' or 'warranties' . . . Of such undertakings all that can be predicted is that some breaches will, and others will not, give rise to an event which will deprive the party not in default of substantially the whole benefit which it was intended that he should obtain from the contract; and the legal consequences of the breach of such an undertaking, unless provided for expressly in the contract, depend on the nature of the event to which the breach gives rise and do not follow automatically from a prior classification of the undertaking as a 'condition' or a 'warranty'.

Where a term is found by the court to be an innominate term the rights of an innocent party in the event of a breach are found by applying the test as to whether he has been substantially deprived of the whole of the benefit which it was intended he should obtain from the contract. If he has been so deprived then he will be entitled to terminate the contract and sue for damages; if not, he can claim damages only.

The decision in the *Hong Kong Fir* case does create a certain level of uncertainty since the parties will not know what their rights are in relation to a breach of contract until an action is brought before the court. Of course the parties can expressly state within the contract itself what the consequences of breaking a particular term would be and, indeed, it would be in their interests to do so. The absence of such express intentions nevertheless creates substantial problems, so much so that there have been attempts to limit the scope of the concept of the innominate term by the courts themselves. Such an attempt can be seen in the case of *The Mihalis Angelos* [1970] 3 All ER 125, where a charterparty was entered into on 25 May 1965 providing that the ship in question would be 'expected to be ready to load under this charter about 1st July 1965 at Haiphong'. The charter also provided that should the ship 'not be ready to load on or before 20th July 1965' the charterers would be able to cancel the contract. In fact the ship was unable to be at Haiphong at this date and it transpired that the owners knew the ship would not be available on this date when they entered into the charter. The charterers purported to terminate the contract and the owners sued for breach of contract. Although the court was pressed to adopt the approach taken in the *Hong Kong Fir* case it declined to do so. The opinion was formed that the classic approach of labelling a term as a condition or warranty was still valid and, in fact, desirable in order to establish a level of certainty in such cases. It is clearly undesirable on a matter of commercial exigency to expect a charterer of a ship to have to delay the transportation of a cargo because the owners have failed to comply with the date of expected readiness to load, especially when the owners knew full well on the signing of the charter that that date could not realistically be met. Furthermore it is unfair effectively to prevent a charterer from terminating the contract and chartering another ship on the basis of the possibility that the decision might be challenged by a legal action for breach of contract by the owners. The point is summed up well by Megaw LJ:

> One of the important elements of the law is predictability. At any rate in commercial law there are obvious and substantial advantages in having, where possible, a firm and definite rule for a particular class of legal relationship. . . It is surely much better both for shipowners and charterers (and incidentally for their advisers) when a contractual obligation of this nature is under consideration – and still more when they are faced with the necessity of an urgent decision as to the effects of a suspected breach of it – to be able to say categorically: 'If a breach is proved, then the charterer can put an end to the contract'.

The approach taken in *The Mihalis Angelos* was approved of and adopted by both the Court of Appeal and the House of Lords in *Bunge Corporation v Tradax Export SA* [1981] 2 All ER 513 where the status of an 'expected readiness to load' clause was again questioned. Both courts had no hesitation in stating that this was a condition and rejected attempts to persuade them to apply the *Hong Kong Fir* test. Lord Wilberforce stated that to find otherwise 'would fatally remove from a vital provision in the contract that certainty which is the most indispensable quality of mercantile contracts'.

The decision of a court to adopt the traditional or the *Hong Kong Fir* approach is driven by several considerations. The most important of these by far is the need for certainty and this takes on even more importance where a term is a fairly standard one, always found in particular types of contract. The 'expected readiness to load' clause in the above cases is a good example of such a term since it is common to all charterparties and one which is commonly broken. It is thus desirable to have a high level of certainty with regard to such a clause. The same considerations do not arise to the same degree where the contract is non-standard or a 'one-off' contract. Here the prime consideration may be one of doing what is just between the parties, and the innominate term concept usually achieves a greater level of fairness in such a situation. The reason for this is that parties to a contract may attempt to terminate the contract for breach of condition when they have no real justification other than purely economic or commercial motives. The choice open to the courts then is usually governed by a judicial impression of a need to achieve either certainty or fair play.

One must not assume from the above that the concept of the innominate term has been rejected by the courts. This is most certainly not so and the above cases merely qualify its use. The application of the concept can be seen in *Cehave NV v Bremer Handelsgesellschaft mbH, The Hansa Nord* [1975] 3 All ER 739, where a cargo of citrus pellets was sold to a buyer in Rotterdam. The contract provided for 'shipment to be made in good condition'. Part of the cargo was not transported and the buyer then purported to reject the whole cargo, even though there was nothing wrong with the pellets themselves. In fact the rejected cargo, when eventually sold by the Rotterdam

Court, was ultimately bought by the original buyers at a greatly reduced price, and this probably reflects the true reason for rejecting the cargo in the first place. The buyers attempted to persuade the court that the *Hong Kong Fir* approach was inappropriate since the Sale of Goods Act 1979 by implication envisaged that all terms in such contracts should be classified as conditions or warranties. The court rejected this contention and applied the *Hong Kong Fir* test, stating that the consequences of the breach were not so serious as to allow the buyer to reject the whole cargo; they had not been deprived of substantially what they had contracted for.

The reasoning in *The Hansa Nord* case was confirmed in *Reardon Smith Line Ltd* v *Hansen-Tangen* [1976] 3 All ER 570 by the House of Lords.

Conclusion

Having examined the relative importance of contractual terms and the different approaches used to assess an innocent party's rights where a breach of contract arises, we shall now take an overview of the choices and possibilities that might confront that individual.

Firstly, the parties can always expressly state what the effects of a breach of a particular term may be. If the contract specifically gives the innocent party the right to terminate the contract then the courts will allow that right to be exercised.

Secondly, if the contract does not expressly provide a right to terminate the contract it may be that such a right is implied. For example in *Schuler A G* v *Wickman Machine Tool Sales Ltd* [1974] AC 235 it was stated by the House of Lords that the use of the expression 'condition' would tend to indicate a right of the innocent party to terminate the contract, whilst the use of the expression 'warranty' would tend to indicate only a right to recover damages.

Thirdly, if the right to terminate is not implied from the description ascribed to a term then it may be implied from the operation of law. This may arise through statute, as in the case of the implied conditions and warranties contained in the Sale of Goods Act 1979. It may also arise from judicial impression as in the case *The Mihalis Angelos*, which established that all 'expected readiness to load' clauses contained in charterparties will be regarded by the courts as conditions, thus achieving considerable certainty as to the position of the innocent party.

Finally, where the status of a term is not ascribed from the operation of some rule of law then one must ask the *Hong Kong Fir* question, namely 'Has the innocent party been deprived substantially of what it was intended that he should receive under the contract?' If the answer to this question is in the affirmative he can terminate the contract; if not, he may only claim damages and has no right to terminate.

Further reading

Beale, Bishop and Furmston, *Contract – Cases and Materials* 2nd ed. 1990, Butterworths
Bojeczuk, 'When is a Condition not a Condition?', *Journal of Business Law* 353, 1987

Cheshire, Fifoot and Furmston, *The Law of Contract* 12th ed. 1991, Butterworths

Guest, *Anson's Law of Contract* 26th ed. 1984, Oxford University Press

Law Commission, *The Parol Evidence Rule* Working Paper No. 70 1976

Law Commission, *The Parol Evidence Rule* (Law Commission Report No. 154)

Macdonald, 'The Duty to Give Notice of Unusual Contract Terms', *Journal of Business Law* 375, 1988

Treitel, *The Law of Contract* 8th ed. 1991, Sweet & Maxwell

8 | Exemption clauses

INTRODUCTION

Exemption clauses are those which seek to enable one of the parties to a contract to exclude his liability. Limitation clauses, although governed by the same principles, seek to restrict the liability of a particular individual. These clauses are not by any means new since they arose from the development of the standard-form contract during the Industrial Revolution. Therein lies the great problem with exemption clauses in modern times since, while they developed during the golden age of the development of the law of contract when *laissez-faire* principles reigned, as did the notion of equality of bargaining power, the emphasis in the twentieth century has been upon the need to protect the consumer and the realisation that equality of bargaining power is, to a large degree, a myth.

In order to balance these two diametrically opposing positions the courts have attempted to limit the use of exemption clauses. First, just as with other clauses which the parties wish to form part of the contract, the party relying on the exemption clause will have to show that the clause amounts to a term of the contract. Secondly, the exemption clause, in order to protect the party relying on it, has to be constructed in such a way that it actually deals with the loss or damage that has occurred. Finally, in addition to this prescriptive approach, the law has introduced other measures designed to restrict or prevent the operation of exemption clauses in certain circumstances.

INCORPORATION OF THE EXCLUSION CLAUSE INTO THE CONTRACT

A party to a contract who seeks to rely on the protection of an exemption clause has to be able to show that it has become incorporated into the contract. There are three ways in which he may be able to do this.

Incorporation by signature

Should a party sign a contractual document he will be prima facie bound by the terms of that contract, even if he has failed to read that document, unless he has been induced to sign by virtue of some misrepresentation or fraudulent conduct. The general principle is well illustrated by the case of *L'Estrange* v *Graucob* [1934] 2 KB 394, where the plaintiff purchased an automatic vending machine. The purchase was made on terms set out in a document stated to be a 'Sales Agreement'. A number of the terms were set out in what was described by the court as 'legible, but regrettably small print'. The plaintiff signed the 'agreement' but did not bother to read it. It was held that the plaintiff was bound by the terms of the agreement, so that the exclusion clause contained in it meant that the defendants were not liable on the basis that the machine was not fit for the purpose for which it was sold.

Incorporation by notice

A party to a contract may be bound by its terms provided reasonable notice of those terms is brought to his attention, despite the fact that the contractual document has not been signed. What is reasonable here depends on a number of factors.

The document must be a contractual document

The exemption clauses contained in an unsigned document will fail to form part of a contract if it was never intended that the document was to have such an effect. If the person to whom the document was given knew that the document was to be a contractual one or the handing of the document to that individual could be regarded as having given him reasonable notice of the fact that it contained terms and conditions, he may be bound by any exemption clauses contained in the document.

The test of whether a document has contractual force or not depends on a reasonable man test, that is, an objective test. In other words, would a reasonable man have assumed that the document was to be a contractual document? The description thus given to the document is not necessarily equivocal as to its effect in law. A document described as a 'receipt', for instance, is not necessarily precluded from having contractual force if the objective test above is decided in the affirmative. In *Chapelton* v *Barry UDC* [1940] KB 532, however, the plaintiff was given a ticket, on hiring a deck-chair. He did not read the ticket, which stated on its back that the Council would not be liable for any damage or injuries suffered to the hirer whilst using the chair. The canvas on one of the chairs was defective and he claimed damages for injuries which resulted from the defect. It was held that the ticket was not a contractual document but a mere voucher or receipt which no reasonable man could regard as otherwise. The exemption clause did not thereby afford the local authority with a defence to the action.

What degree of notice is required?

If the unsigned document is to be regarded as being an integral part of the contract, reasonable notice of the exemption clause must be brought to the attention of the other party. This test was first formulated in the case of *Parker* v *South Eastern Railway Company* (1877) 2 CPD 416 where a bag was left at a left luggage office. The plaintiff paid the fee, for which he was given a ticket which contained a limitation clause on the back. When the plaintiff attempted to reclaim his bag it could not be found. He attempted to claim the value of the bag and contents which exceeded the limit stipulated on the ticket. The railway company attempted to rely on the clause which the plaintiff claimed to be ignorant of. The Court of Appeal held that for the company to be able to rely on the clause it had to show that reasonable steps had been taken to bring the notice of the clause to the plaintiff. Since the company could not show this it was held that it could not rely on the clause. It is clear that merely handing a ticket with an exclusion clause printed on it is insufficient since it may not be intended that the ticket will have a contractual force, as was also the case in *Chapelton* v *Barry UDC*.

The objective test formulated in the *Parker* case nevertheless has to be applied within the facts of the particular case. In *Thompson* v *L M & S Railway Company* [1930] 1 KB 41, the plaintiff, who was illiterate, was handed an excursion ticket which stated that the ticket was issued subject to the defendant's conditions as stated in the company's timetables, which excluded liability for injury. The plaintiff suffered injuries on her journey and claimed for damages. It was held that her claim must fail. The fact that she could not read did not alter the position that she was bound by the contract since it was held that reasonable notice of the exemption clause had been brought to her attention. Treitel suggests that the decision would have been different if the company had been aware of the plaintiff's disability since simply handing over the ticket would clearly not have been reasonable notice of the clause. He suggests that this would also be the case if the party relying on the clause knew that the other did not speak the language in which the clause is expressed. This situation has recently been affirmed judicially in *Harvey* v *Ventilatorenfabrik Oelde GmbH* (1988) Tr LR 138.

A further consideration when assessing if reasonable notice of an exemption clause has been given arises where the clause is particularly onerous or unusual. In these circumstances a higher degree of notice is required in order to satisfy the reasonableness test. Very often, in order to satisfy the test, the other party's attention has to be specifically drawn to the terms incorporating the exemption clauses, or at the very least due prominence has to be given to such clauses. In *Thornton* v *Shoe Lane Parking Ltd* [1971] QB 163 it was held that whilst a motorist could anticipate a clause purporting to exclude liability for loss or damage to his vehicle, this was not true of a clause which purported to exclude liability for personal injury. The consequence of this finding was that the owner of the car-park, in order to exclude liability for personal injury, would have to take special precautions to draw the term to the attention of customers using the car-park. Such a conclusion has also been affirmed by Lord Denning in *Spurling* v *Bradshaw* [1956] 2 All ER 121 where he stated: 'Some clauses I have seen would need to be printed in red ink on the face of the document with a red hand pointing to it before the notice could be held to be sufficient.'

The case of *Interfoto Picture Library* v *Stilletto Visual Programmes* [1988] 1 All ER 348, whilst not involving exemption or limitation clauses, but onerous penalty terms, is a further example. Here the court decided that it was not sufficient for such terms to be incorporated into the contract via the standard printed contract. The onerous terms should be given prominence within the document with bold or red type, or indeed by having a special note drawing the other party's attention to the clauses.

When was notice of the exemption clause given?

In order for the exemption clause to be a term of the contract the reasonable steps to bring notice of the clause to the other party must be brought before or at the time of contracting.

The classic case involving this requirement is that of *Olley* v *Marlborough Court Ltd* [1949] 1 All ER 127 where a husband and wife booked into a hotel and paid for one week's stay in advance. They went to the room allotted to them where they found a notice stating that 'the proprietors will not hold themselves responsible for articles lost or stolen unless handed to the manageress for safe custody'. The wife had a number of valuable fur coats which she left in the room and which were subsequently stolen. When sued in negligence the defendants sought to incorporate the exemption clause into the contract. The Court of Appeal decided that the contract had already been entered into before the notice of the exemption clause had been brought to the plaintiff's attention. It was therefore not contemporaneous with the making of the contract and thus not incorporated into it so that the defendants could not rely on it for protection.

Lord Denning, who also sat in *Olley* v *Marlborough Court Ltd*, applied similar reasoning in the case of *Thornton* v *Shoe Lane Parking Ltd* [1971] 1 All ER 686, where it was held that the owner of a ticket machine at an automatic car-park made an offer when he held the machine out as being ready to receive money and that this offer was accepted when a customer placed his money in the slot, the contract being formed at this point. Since the contract was already in existence when the ticket was issued, any terms and conditions expressed or referred to on the ticket came too late and were not part of the contract. The defendant proprietor of the car-park could not therefore rely on the protection of the exemption clause.

Incorporation by a previous course of dealing

The courts may infer notice of an exemption clause in a contract where there has been a previous course of dealings between the parties in which exclusion clauses have been part of a contract, either by virtue of the document being a signed document or by virtue of reasonable notice of the clause being brought to the parties' attention. The possibility of such an inference can be seen to operate in the case of *Spurling* v *Bradshaw* [1956] 2 All ER 121, where the defendant and plaintiffs had previously dealt with each other for a number of years. The defendant delivered eight barrels of orange juice to the plaintiffs for storage, later receiving an acknowledgement of the deposit of the goods which exempted the plaintiffs 'from any loss or damage occasioned by negligence, wrongful act or default' either of themselves or their servants. When some time later the defendant went to collect the barrels he found them empty and thus refused to pay the storage charges. When sued for the charges he counter-claimed for negligence, though the plaintiffs defended this action on the basis of the exemption clause. The defendant for his part attempted to maintain that the notice of the exemption clause was not contemporaneous with the making of the contract and as such could not form part of the contract. The defendant admitted that in his previous course of dealings with the plaintiffs he had been sent such a document though he had never bothered to read it. The terms and conditions were held to be part and parcel of the present agreement by virtue of the previous course of dealings that had taken place between the parties.

The notion of a previous course of dealing is relatively difficult to define, though it is certain that it must be a consistent course of dealings.

In *McCutcheon* v *David MacBrayne Ltd* [1964] 1 All ER 430, where the respondents operated ferries between the Scottish mainland and islands, the appellant asked a relative, a Mr McSporran, to have his car transported to the mainland. McSporran paid the freight charge and received a receipt. The ship sank due to the respondents' servants' negligence and the vehicle was a total write-off, for which the appellant sought compensation. The respondents' liability was excluded under the terms of their printed conditions, to which reference was made on the receipt, as well as being displayed in the respondents' offices. Neither the appellant nor McSporran had read the notices and McSporran had not bothered to read the receipt. The purser had also failed to ask McSporran to sign a risk note, which included the conditions, even though one had been prepared for him to sign. Such notes had been signed on previous occasions by the appellant and McSporran, but not on every occasion, and even then they had not read them, though they knew such notes contained conditions. It was held that the appellant would succeed since the receipt and the notices did not form part of the oral contract, in that the receipt had come after the contract had been entered into and the respondents had not done what was reasonably sufficient to bring the notices displayed in the office to the attention of the appellant or McSporran. There had not been a consistent course of dealings which would allow the conditions to be implied into the contract. Lord Hodson commented:

> The course of dealing on earlier occasions is often relevant in determining contractual relations, but does not assist when, as here, there was on the part of the respondents a departure from an

earlier course in that they omitted to ask the appellant's agent to sign the document by which they would have obtained protection.

It can be seen in the above case that a long consistent course of dealings did not apply because the usual steps taken to incorporate the conditions into the contract had not been taken or applied consistently. Terms and conditions may nevertheless be incorporated into a contract if the parties were aware of them even though, on the occasion in question, they had not formed part of the contract, as in *Hardwick Game Farm* v *Suffolk Agricultural Association* [1969] 2 AC 31. In that case a similar contract had been entered into three or four times a month before the contract in question. The usual steps taken to incorporate the terms into the contract were not carried out, but the court held it was sufficient to show that the parties knew and intended the terms to form part of the agreement.

Whatever a court's view regarding the need for consistency it is certain that there has to be a course of dealings and this cannot be established if the parties have only contracted with each other on a few occasions over a lengthy period of time. This is a matter for the court to decide as a question of fact. In *Hollier* v *Rambler Motors (AMC) Ltd* [1972] QB 71 three or four occasions in a period of five years was held to be insufficient to establish a course of dealing. One exception to the need for a course of dealing arises, however, where the exemption clause is implied into the contract by virtue of a general course of dealing amounting to trade usage. In *British Crane Hire Corporation Ltd* v *Ipswich Plant Hire Ltd* [1975] QB 303, for instance, it was held that an oral contract between the parties was subject to the standard terms and conditions of a trade association on which the parties normally contracted.

CONSTRUING EXEMPTION CLAUSES

As stated at the start of this chapter, one of the tasks confronting the courts over the past 150 years has been the need to balance the principle of the equality of bargaining power with the notion of consumer protection. One of the means by which this task has been accomplished may be seen in the way the courts have construed exemption clauses coming before them. The courts have approached this problem in three ways.

Exemption clauses are to be construed *contra proferentem*

The rule here is that exemption clauses are construed against the party relying on them. The result of this is that if the clause fails to deal with a particular matter then it is deemed not to cover that matter. The case of *Baldry* v *Marshall* [1925] 1 KB 260 provides an example of this process where the defendant car dealers were asked to supply a car 'suitable for touring purposes'. The dealer recommended a Bugatti which proved eminently unsuitable for the required use. The plaintiff rejected the car and claimed to recover the price. The contract contained a clause excluding 'guarantees or warranties, statutory or otherwise'. The court held that the stipulation as to the suitability of the car was a condition, not a guarantee or a warranty, and as such was not covered by the exemption clause.

The attitude of the court in the above case was clearly to construe the clause against the person seeking to rely on it. A further example can be seen in *Andrews Bros (Bournemouth) Ltd* v *Singer and Co* [1934] 1 KB 17 where there was a contract to purchase 'new Singer cars'. The contract contained a clause which excluded 'all conditions, warranties and liabilities implied by statute, common law or otherwise'. One of the cars delivered by the dealer was a used car and when sued for damages he attempted to rely on the exemption clause. The Court of Appeal held that the term regarding 'new Singer cars' was an express term and thus the exemption clause, which only excluded liability for implied terms, did not protect the dealer.

Exempting liability for fundamental breach of contract

The processes analysed here are really only particular applications of the *contra proferentem* rule discussed above. Even in the golden age of contract in the last century, when the notion of equality of bargaining power allowed the parties to exclude themselves from various aspects of their contractual liability, the courts were reluctant to allow a party to exclude himself from serious or fundamental breaches of the contract. The approach of the courts to this process of limiting the effect of exemption clauses took two distinct lines: first, an exemption clause which sought to exclude a serious breach of contract was to be construed narrowly in order to reduce the protection offered by the clause; secondly, the courts developed a substantive rule of law that exemption clauses that sought to exclude liability for fundamental breach would be ineffective.

An example of the first approach by the courts can be seen in the case of *Karsales (Harrow) Ltd* v *Wallis* [1956] 1 WLR 936 where the defendant, having inspected a secondhand car and found it to be in good order, decided to buy it on hire purchase terms. The hire purchase agreement contained a clause which stated that 'no condition or warranty that the vehicle is roadworthy or as to its condition or fitness for any purpose is given by the owner or implied therein'. The car was eventually delivered one night and whilst it appeared to be the car the defendant had inspected, daylight revealed the car to be a mere shell. The cylinder head and pistons were broken, valves were burnt out, in short it was incapable of propulsion. Not surprisingly the defendant refused to accept the car or pay the hire purchase instalments and when eventually sued, pointed to the condition of the car. The plaintiffs in turn attempted to rely on the clause. The Court of Appeal held that there had been a fundamental and substantial deviation between the thing contracted for and that which was actually delivered. In such circumstances the plaintiffs could not avail themselves of the clause and judgment was given to the defendant.

The position of the court may be seen in the statement of Lord Wilberforce in the later case of *Suisse Atlantique Société D'Armement Maritime SA* v *NV Rotterdamsche Kolen Centrale* [1966] 2 All ER 61:

Since the contracting parties could hardly have been supposed to contemplate such a misperformance or to have provided against it without destroying the whole contractual substratum, there is no difficulty here in holding exception clauses to be inapplicable.

This approach by the courts is very common in relation to the carriage of goods by sea where the route to be taken by a ship is usually regarded as fundamental. The result is that any deviation from the route will have the effect of preventing the shipowner from relying on the benefit of an exemption clause contained in the contract. An example of such a case may be seen in *Glyn v Margetson* [1893] AC 351 where there was a contract to ship oranges from Malaga to Liverpool. In fact the contract gave the carrier a wide discretion to deviate from his route, but this was held not to protect him when the ship first set a course east from Malaga, then returned to Malaga before making for Liverpool. It was held that the clause was limited to the 'main object and intent' of the contract, which was to sail from Malaga to Liverpool, though the contract permitted the carrier to deviate from this course, provided the deviation was *en route* for Liverpool. Sailing east was clearly not within such 'object and intent' and therefore the carrier was liable for the deterioration in the condition of the cargo.

The second approach of the courts to fundamental breaches of contract has been the development of a substantive rule that rendered exemption clauses invalid. There has been extensive debate as to whether such a rule exists as a substantive rule of law or merely as a rule of construction. It should be borne in mind that by a fundamental breach one means not a simple breach of condition but one that goes to the very core of the contract itself. Whether a particular breach is regarded as fundamental or not rests upon the facts of the particular case, the onus of proof lying on the party alleging the fundamental breach to prove it, as in *Hunt and Winterbotham (West of England) Ltd v BRS (Parcels) Ltd* [1962] 1 All ER 111.

If the court finds that a fundamental breach has occurred it has to decide whether the exemption clause is sufficiently specific to either exclude or limit a party's liability for the breach. A divergence of approach arises here between consumer and commercial contracts. In a consumer contract the courts apply the doctrine of fundamental breach as a substantive rule of law, so that an exemption clause could not exclude or limit liability for such a breach, whatever the intention of the parties. In a commercial contract, however, the doctrine was applied merely as a rule of construction, that is, an assessment was made of the intentions of the parties and if it was intended that the clause should exclude liability in the case of such a breach then the court would give effect to that intention. In the latter instance the parties were regarded as being of equal bargaining strength and having contracted at arm's length, and therefore it was correct to allow them to allocate their risks as they wished.

The above position regarding the doctrine of fundamental breach was sustained until the *Suisse Atlantique* case in 1966 when the House of Lords considered this divergence of approach to be incorrect and that the proper view was that the doctrine was a rule of construction only, whatever the status of the contract. Viscount Dilhorne stated:

> In my view, it is not right to say that the law prohibits and nullifies a clause exempting or limiting liability for a fundamental breach or breach of a fundamental term. Such a rule would involve a restriction on freedom of contract and in the older cases I can find no trace of it.

While the other members of the House of Lords concurred with Viscount Dilhorne's statement, all of these statements were only *obiter dicta*. This, together with the fact that it was questionable whether the case was one involving a fundamental breach at all considerably weakened the effect of the case on the doctrine. The Court of Appeal under Lord Denning did not take too kindly to this move by the House of Lords, their dislike of the decision revolving around the fact that it tended to weaken their ability to protect consumers. The result was that through a series of decisions they reworked the doctrine so that it once again existed as a substantive rule of law. The case of *Harbutt's 'Plasticine' Ltd* v *Wayne Tank Co Ltd* [1970] 1 QB 477 is an example of this.

The passing of the Unfair Contract Terms Act 1977 rendered the position of the Court of Appeal obsolete since consumers were now protected by the provisions of the Act. Where the Act did not apply in commercial contracts, the view that the parties should again be free to allocate their liabilities under the contract by way of exemption clauses again came into vogue. In 1980 the reversal to this position was confirmed by the House of Lords in *Photo Production Ltd* v *Securicor Transport Ltd* [1980] AC 827 where Lord Wilberforce stated:

> It is significant that Parliament refrained from legislating over the whole field of contract. After this Act, in commercial matters generally, when the parties are not of unequal bargaining power, and when risks are normally borne by insurance, not only is the case for judicial intervention undemonstrated, but there is everything to be said, and this seems to have been Parliament's intention, for leaving the parties free to apportion the risks as they think fit and for respecting their decisions.

The decision of the House of Lords in the *Photo Production* case has since been affirmed by the House of Lords in *George Mitchell (Chesterhall) Ltd* v *Finney Lock Seeds* [1983] 2 AC 803. The position at common law is that whether an exemption clause protects a party when a breach occurs depends on the construction of the clause, having regard to the degree of risk assumed by the parties to the contract and the possibility of the risk being offset by insurance.

Exempting liability for negligence

One aspect of the *contra proferentem* rule is that it regards exemption clauses as excluding liability in respect of contractual duties only. It is always possible that whilst a plaintiff may have contractual rights against a defendant he might also have rights in tort, usually negligence. The effect here is of course to give the plaintiff an additional remedy should an exemption clause operate to protect the defendant in respect of his contractual duties. The defendant for his part would, in these circumstances, be prudent to express the exemption clause in the widest possible terms, so that his liability in tort is also covered. Because of the operation of the *contra proferentem* rule, however, he must generally expressly refer to negligence within the exemption clause, although the rule will be satisfied if the clause is nevertheless wide enough to cover liability for negligence, for example, by exempting a party from 'all liability whatsoever'.

The main problem that occurs in this context is where the exemption clause is ambiguous, since here the defendant is prime facie liable in both contract and tort because the clause will be construed in such a way as to exclude contractual liability only, very specific language being required to exclude liability in tort. This is so in *White* v *John Warwick & Co Ltd* [1953] 2 All ER 1021 where the plaintiff hired a bicycle from the defendant but, while he was riding it, the seat tipped forward thereby injuring him. The hire contract stated, 'nothing in this agreement shall render the owners liable for any personal injury'. It was held that whilst the clause was sufficient to exclude liability in contract for the defendant supplying a defective bicycle, it was not sufficient to exclude liability in negligence. The plaintiff thus succeeded in his claim in tort.

The requirement for the clause to be explicit in the face of ambiguity is also important even if liability could not arise in any way but negligence. In *Hollier* v *Rambler Motors (AMC) Ltd* [1972] QB 71 the plaintiff agreed to have his car towed to the defendants' garage for repairs. The car was subsequently totally destroyed by a fire that broke out at the garage as a result of the defendants' negligence. The contract contained a term which stated that 'the company is not responsible for damage caused by fire to customers' cars on the premises'. The Court of Appeal concluded that the defendants would only be liable for fire if it was caused by their negligence, though it was possible for the exemption clause to be read as a warning that the defendants were not liable for loss caused by fire which was *not* due to their negligence. The Court concluded that there was a sufficient degree of ambiguity to disallow the defendants from relying on the clause.

OTHER FACTORS LIMITING THE EFFECTIVENESS OF EXEMPTION CLAUSES

So far we have seen how exemption clauses may be limited in their effectiveness because of the way they are constructed and interpreted. Even if an exemption clause when properly construed covers the losses or damages that have occurred there are further limitations on its effectiveness. The limitations divide into two groups, common law and statutory limitations.

Common law limitations on exemption clauses

Misrepresentation

An exemption clause will be held to be ineffective in affording protection to the person relying on it should that person or his agent, such as an employee, misrepresent the extent of the clause to the other party. In *Curtis* v *Chemical Cleaning and Dyeing Co Ltd* [1951] 1 KB 805 the plaintiff took a dress to the defendants for cleaning. She was given a receipt to sign and she asked what it was for. She was told that it was to exempt the defendants from certain types of damage, in particular damage to beads and sequins. On this basis she signed the receipt. In fact the clause was a general exemption in that it excluded liability for 'any damage, howsoever arising'. When the dress was returned it was found to be badly stained, whereupon the defendants claimed the protection of the clause. It was held that the plaintiff could succeed and that the defendants could not rely on the clause since the court found that the plaintiff had been induced to sign the document by the misrepresentation as to the extent of the clause.

Third parties

Where an exclusion clause is deemed to be effective, it is so only with regard to the actual parties to the contract. Any third parties to the contract cannot rely on the clause for protection. This rule is consistent with the doctrine of privity of contract which is discussed in Chapter 19.

The application of the doctrine in this context can be seen in the case of *Adler* v *Dickson* [1954] 3 All ER 397 where a sailing ticket issued to the plaintiff provided: Passengers . . . are carried at passengers' entire risk. . . . The Company will not be responsible for and shall be exempt from all liability in respect of any . . . injury . . . of any passenger . . . whether such injury . . . shall occur on land, on shipboard or elsewhere . . . and whether the same shall arise from or be occasioned by the negligence of the Company's servants . . . in the discharge of their duties, or whether by the negligence of other persons directly or indirectly . . . in the employment or service of the company . . . under any circumstances whatsoever . . .

The plaintiff was injured when a gangway was moved while she was walking up it to board the SS *Himalaya*. She brought an action for negligence, not against the shipping company, but against the captain and boatswain of the ship. It was held by the Court of Appeal that the clause only offered protection to the company and nobody else, and thus the plaintiff was successful in her claim against the two individuals.

A more modern example of the principle can be seen in *Scruttons Ltd* v *Midland Silicones Ltd* [1962] 1 All ER 1 where similar reasoning was employed by the judges in the House of Lords. In this case a drum containing chemicals was shipped in New York on a ship owned by United States Lines to the order of the plaintiffs. The bill of lading contained a limitation clause which restricted the carriers', the shipowners', liability to $500. The defendants were stevedores contracted to United States Lines in London on terms which purported to include the benefit of the limitation clause. The plaintiffs were unaware of the contract between the stevedore defendants and the carriers. The drum of chemicals was damaged because of the negligence of the stevedores, the damage amounting to $593 dollars. The plaintiffs sued in negligence but the defendants attempted to rely on the limitation clause in the bill of lading for protection. It was held by the House of Lords that the plaintiffs would succeed and that the stevedores could not rely on the clause since they were not parties to the bill of lading.

Not surprisingly, attempts have been made to avoid this effect of the doctrine of privity of contract. An elaborate attempt at achieving this can be found in the Privy Council case of *New Zealand Shipping Co Ltd* v *A. M. Satterthwaite & Co Ltd, The Eurymedon* [1975] AC 154, where it was held that the benefit of an exemption clause can be claimed by a stevedore provided the contract of carriage was explicit as to the fact that the stevedore was intended to be protected by the contract and that the shipowner/carrier made it clear that he was contracting as agent for the stevedore, as well as himself. In addition the carrier had to have the authority of the stevedore to contract on his behalf and there had to be some consideration moving from the stevedore. It was held that these factors were present and as a result judgment was given for the defendant stevedores. The case has, however, been subject to substantial criticism, which is dealt with more fully in Chapter 19.

Overriding oral undertaking

It is possible for an exemption clause contained in a written document to be overridden by an express inconsistent undertaking given before or at the time of contracting. An example of such an overriding undertaking can be seen in *J. Evans & Son (Portsmouth) Ltd* v *Andrea Merzario Ltd* [1976] 1 WLR 1078, already discussed in Chapter 7.

Collateral contracts

Such contracts may prevent a party seeking to rely on an exemption clause from doing so.

In *Webster* v *Higgin* [1948] 2 All ER 127 the defendant was considering purchasing a motor vehicle from the plaintiff garage proprietor on hire purchase. During the course of the negotiations the plaintiff's agent stated to the defendant: 'If you buy the Hillman we will guarantee that it is in good condition'. The defendant then decided to sign the hire purchase agreement which contained the following exemption clause: '. . . no warranty, condition, description or representation as to the state or quality of the vehicle is given or implied'. The car, when delivered, was later described by Lord Green as 'nothing but a mass of second-hand and dilapidated ironmongery'. Not surprisingly the defendant refused to accept the car or to pay the hire purchase instalments. The plaintiff sued to recover the vehicle and the instalments that had fallen due. If the exemption clause contained in the hire purchase agreement had stood alone then the defendant would have been precluded from pleading the state of the car as a defence to the action. He might have claimed that there had been a fundamental breach of contract, though this was not alleged in the case. Instead the defendant alleged that there had been two contracts entered into. He stated that the hire purchase agreement had been preceded by another contract whereby the condition of the vehicle had been guaranteed in return for the defendant promising to sign the hire purchase agreement. The Court of Appeal gave judgment to the defendant on the basis of the collateral contract that preceded the hire purchase agreement. The court found that the collateral contract had been broken and this entitled the defendant to treat the hire purchase agreement as at an end, enabling him to reclaim his deposit and the instalments already paid.

Statutory limitations on exemption clauses

Introduction

There have been many instances where Parliament has intervened to restrict or curtail the operation of exemption. For example, s. 151 of the Road Traffic Act 1960, now embodied in s. 29 of the Public Passenger Vehicles Act 1981, makes it void to negate or restrict the liability of a person in respect of the death or bodily injury to a passenger while being carried in, or alighting from, a vehicle. A similar provision also exists in the Road Traffic Act 1988 which renders ineffective any antecedent agreement or undertaking (whether this is intended to be legally binding or not) to restrict the liability of the user of a motor vehicle towards a passenger. Similarly Part II of the Fair Trading Act 1973 gives the Secretary of State the power to curtail certain types of business which he is advised by the Consumer Protection Advisory Committee are undesirable.

In the Misrepresentation Act 1967, s. 3, any provision in an agreement to exclude or restrict liability for a misrepresentation is only effective if the court considers the exemption or limitation clause to be fair and reasonable.

It can be seen that the different Acts have taken two broadly different approaches to exemption clauses, either to make them totally ineffective or to subject them to a test of reasonableness. The Unfair Contract Terms Act 1977 adopts both approaches and represents by far the biggest incursion by Parliament into controlling the use of exemption clauses.

The Unfair Contract Terms Act 1977

This Act is of the utmost importance in relation to the control of exemption and limitation clauses and the reader may therefore ask why it should be considered last in this section dealing with the contents of contracts. The reason for its somewhat ignominious position is that its provisions have to be read in conjunction with the existing law and thus the Act cannot be fully understood until this aspect has first been dealt with.

Clearly the Act cuts a deep furrow right across the doctrine of freedom of contract, but some degree of care is required here since the Act does not set up a general legal structure that deals with all exemption and limitation clauses in every context. The Act does not establish general regulatory measures based on a concept of fairness but declares certain types of clauses to be totally ineffective whilst others are to be subject to a requirement of reasonableness.

It also needs to be established from the very start that the title of the Act is most misleading. In the first place, the Act applies to liability arising both in contract and in tort and, secondly, it applies to exemption and limitation clauses contained in any contractual term or notice. The Act will thus apply equally to a situation where an exemption clause is contained in a contract or to one arising where no contract is entered into, such as an exemption clause displayed in a free car park. Certain types of contracts, contained in Schedule 1 of the Act, are specifically excluded from the operation of ss. 2, 3, 4 and 7; these are:

(i)   contracts of insurance (including contracts of annuity);
(ii)   contracts relating to the creation, transfer or termination of interests in land;
(iii)   contracts relating to the creation, transfer or termination of rights or interests in intellectual property such as patents, trade marks, copyrights, and the like;
(iv)   contracts relating to the formation or dissolution of a company or the constitution or rights or obligations of its members;
(v)   contracts relating to the creation or transfer of securities or of any right or interest therein;
(vi)   contracts of marine salvage or towage; or charterparties of ships or hovercraft or of carriage of goods by sea, by ship or hovercraft, with the exception of liability arising by virtue of s. 2(1) below, or in favour of a person acting as a consumer;
(vii)   international supply contracts, as defined in s. 26 of the Act;
(viii) sections 2–7 of the Act do not apply where, in an international contract, the parties agree to adopt English law as 'the proper law of the contract' (s. 27).

(The latter two provisions were brought in to preserve mercantile legal practice.)

(a) *'Business liability' and dealing as a consumer.* The Act only applies to actions in contract and tort arising in relation to 'business liability'. This is defined by s. 1(3) as: 'liability for breach of obligations or duties arising – (a) from things done or to be done by a person in the course of a business (whether his own business or another's); or (b) from the occupation of premises used for business purposes of the occupier'.

A 'business' is stated by s. 14 to include a profession and the activities of any government department or local or public authority.

The Act is principally aimed at protecting the person who 'deals as a consumer'. Section 12 provides:

1   A party to a contract 'deals as consumer' in relation to another party if –
     (a) he neither makes the contract in the course of a business nor holds himself out as doing so; and
     (b) the other party does make the contract in the course of a business; and
     (c) in the case of a contract governed by the law of sale of goods or hire purchase, or by section 7 of this Act, the goods passing under or in pursuance of the contract are of a type ordinarily supplied for private use or consumption.
2   But on a sale by auction or competitive tender the buyer is not in any circumstances to be regarded as dealing as a consumer.
3   Subject to this, it is for those claiming that a party does not deal as consumer to show that he does not.

Whilst the definition of 'deals as consumer' appears fairly conclusive this is not necessarily the case since items may be bought by means of a business account but they will have both a private and a business use, such as, for example, company cars or mobile telephones. In the past it was thought that the question of private or business use could be resolved by simply investigating the source from which the item was purchased. Thus if it was purchased via a business account then it was a purchase in the course of a business, but it was a consumer contract if paid for via a private account. In *Peter Symmons & Co* v *Cook* (1981) 131 NLJ 758 it was held that a purchaser acting on behalf of a business may still be regarded as dealing as a consumer if the subject of the purchase is neither integral nor necessarily incidental to the business.

In *R & B Customs Brokers Co Ltd* v *United Dominions Trust Ltd* (Saunders Abbott (1980) Ltd third party) [1988] 1 All ER 847 a rather different approach was adopted by the Court of Appeal. In the case the plaintiff company purchased a secondhand vehicle on a conditional sale agreement for the use of one of its directors. The car was to be used partly for business and partly for private use. Rather surprisingly the Court of Appeal decided that this was a consumer sale, basing its reasoning on the fact that the transaction was only incidental to the business activity of the company. The court stated that a degree of regularity was required before a transaction could be regarded as integral to the business activity so that it becomes exercised in the course of a business. The car in question was only the second or third vehicle obtained by the plaintiff company and therefore there was held to be an insufficient degree of regularity to establish that the contract was anything but a consumer contract. The decision has been heavily criticised, not surprisingly since on the above reasoning any unusual item bought irregularly by any business may now be regarded as a consumer contract. It appears that the court had been persuaded to use a definition of business contained in the Trade Descriptions Act 1968, though this Act is concerned with sellers, to whom a regularity test is rather more appropriate than it is to purchasers.

Two further points are worth examining in relation to the definition. The first is concerned with the proposition of a person holding himself out as acting in the course of business in s. 12(1)b. It would seem rather unusual for a consumer to jeopardise his protection under the Act by taking such an action. The type of scenario possibly envisaged here is where a consumer, having acquired access to a wholesaler, represents himself as acting in the course of a particular trade or business in order to acquire goods at a 'trade' price.

Secondly, it should be noted that the requirement contained in s. 12(1)c does not apply to contracts falling outside ss. 6 or 7, that is, to consumer services, as distinguished from contracts for consumer goods which are contained in those two sections.

(*b*) *Liability arising in negligence.* As has already been stated, the Act deals with liability arising under the tort of negligence by virtue of s. 2. 'Negligence' is, however, defined by s. 1(1) as a breach:

(a) of any obligation arising from the express or implied terms of a contract, to take reasonable care or exercise reasonable skill in the performance of the contract;
(b) of any common law duty to take care or exercise reasonable skill (but not any stricter duty);
(c) of the common duty of care imposed by the Occupiers' Liability Act 1957.

This provision clearly relates to negligence as it arises in tort but also to that arising in contractual relations.

(c) *Terms rendered totally ineffective.* The Unfair Contract Terms Act makes certain types of terms or notices totally ineffective. Terms affected in this way arise in relation to:

(i)   negligence;
(ii)   manufacturers' guarantees;
(iii) the sale of goods and hire purchase;
(iv)   contracts for the transfer of goods and contracts of hire;
(v)   terms governed by the Consumer Protection Act 1987.

(i) **Negligence** (s. 2(1)): a person cannot by virtue of a contractual term or notice exclude or limit his liability in negligence for death or personal injury caused to another.

(ii) **Manufacturers' guarantees** (s. 5(1)): where goods are 'of a type ordinarily supplied for private use or consumption, where loss or damage (a) arises from the goods proving defective while in consumer use; and (b) results from the negligence of the person concerned in the manufacture or distribution of the goods, liability for the loss or damage cannot be excluded or restricted by reference to any contract term or notice contained in or operating by reference to a guarantee of the goods'. This provision is aimed at preventing manufacturers of goods from excluding or restricting their liability by virtue of so-called guarantees supplied with their products. The provision is therefore aimed at regulating the relations between manufacturers and consumers. This is clearly apparent from s. 5(3) which states that s. 5(1) does not apply to contracts in which possession or ownership of goods passes, such contracts being regulated by ss. 6 and 7. It should be noted that by virtue of s. 5(2)b 'anything in writing is a guarantee if it contains or purports to contain some promise or assurance (however worded or presented) that defects will be made good by complete or partial replacement, or by repair, monetary compensation or otherwise'.

(iii) **Sale of goods and hire purchase** (s. 6(1)): the implied undertaking as to title contained in the Sale of Goods Act 1979, s. 12, and the Consumer Credit Act 1974, sch. 4, para. 35 cannot be excluded or restricted in any such contracts. Similarly the implied undertakings as to description, quality, fitness for purpose or sample contained in the Sale of Goods Act 1979, ss. 13–15 and the Consumer Credit Act 1974 sch. 4, para. 35 cannot be excluded against a person acting as a consumer.

(iv) **Contracts for the transfer of goods and contracts of hire** (s. 7(1)): this provision relates to contracts regulated by Part I of the Supply of Goods and Services Act 1982. The provision broadly reflects s. 6(1) as described above. Thus the implied term as to title cannot be excluded and the implied terms as to conformity of goods with description and sample, or as to the quality of the goods or their fitness for purpose, cannot be excluded against a person dealing as a consumer.

(v) **Terms governed by the Consumer Protection Act 1987**: by virtue of Part I of the above Act producers of goods and certain others engaged in the distribution of defective or unsafe goods are liable if the defect causes death or personal injury or certain types of damage to property. Section 7 of this Act provides that such product liability cannot be excluded or limited by any contractual term, notice or other provision. Such product liability may arise irrespective of the existence of any contractual relationship or proof of negligence.

By virtue of Part II of the above Act a criminal liability is imposed if any goods supplied fail to meet the general safety requirement laid down by the Act or any regulation made under its authority. Failure to comply with this requirement gives rise to civil liability enforceable by a person adversely affected by the breach, which cannot be excluded or limited by any contractual term, notice or other provision.

(d) *Terms subject to the requirement of reasonableness*. The Unfair Contract Terms Act also renders certain terms subject to a requirement of reasonableness. This arises in relation to:

(i)   negligence;
(ii)   liability arising in contract;
(iii)   unreasonable indemnity clauses;
(iv)   the sale of goods and hire-purchase;
(v)   contracts for the transfer of goods and contracts of hire;
(vi)   misrepresentation.

(i) **Negligence** (s. 2(2)): in respect of loss or damage caused by negligence other than that causing death or personal injury a person cannot exclude or restrict his liability except in so far as the term or notice satisfies the requirement of reasonableness.

(ii) **Liability arising in contract** (s. 3): s. 3 deals with the provisions relating to liability arising in contract and provides:

(1) This section applies as between contracting parties where one of them deals as a consumer or on the other's written standard terms of business.
(2) As against that party, the other cannot by reference to any contract term:
  (a) when himself in breach of contract, exclude or restrict any liability of his in respect of the breach; or
  (b) claim to be entitled –

    (i) to render a contractual performance substantially different from that which was reasonably expected of him, or
    (ii) in respect of the whole or any part of his contractual obligation, to render no performance at all,

  except insofar as (in any of the cases mentioned above in this subsection) the contract term satisfies the requirement of reasonableness.

We have already dealt with the definition of the expression 'deals as a consumer' but this section also talks in terms of another distinct contract made between two parties, one of whom deals on the 'other's written standard terms of business'. There is no definition of this expression within the Act, though there would clearly appear to be an overlap between the two contracts. The second contract goes further than consumer contracts and would seem to apply simply where two businessmen deal with each other on one or the other's standard terms. This begs the question as to what a standard-term contract is. At what point does a standard-term contract become an individual contract, for instance? The point is at present undecided.

Section 3(2)(b)(i) would seem most appropriate to holiday operators who often attempt to reserve the right to vary the date, destination or flight times of holidays booked with them. Such clauses are allowed under the Act though they are subject to the test of reasonableness.

A further aspect to s. 3 is that it will also apply to attempts to exclude liability under Part II of the Supply of Goods and Services Act 1982, which related to contracts for the supply of services. Part I exclusion of liability relating to contracts for the supply of goods is dealt with by s. 7(1) in the case of consumer contracts and s. 7(3) in the case of non-consumer contracts.

(iii) **Unreasonable indemnity clauses** (s. 4): a person dealing as a consumer cannot by reference to any contractual term be made to indemnify another person (whether a party to the contract or not) in respect of liability that may be incurred by the other for negligence or breach of contract, except insofar as the contract term satisfies the requirement of reasonableness.

(iv) **Sale of goods and hire-purchase** (s. 6(3)): as against a person dealing otherwise than as a consumer any contract term purporting to exclude or restrict liability in respect of the implied terms contained in the Sale of Goods Act 1979 ss. 13–15 and the Consumer Credit Act 1974, sch. 4, para. 35 is subject to the requirement of reasonableness. It should be noted that this provision is not confined to cases where the seller or hirer acts in the course of a business. Any term thus purporting to exclude or restrict liability in respect of the implied terms as to description and sample contained in ss. 13 and 15 by a private seller will also be subject to the requirement of reasonableness. The same is not true of the terms as to quality and fitness for purpose under s. 14(2) and (3), since these provisions only apply where the seller sells in the course of a business anyway.

(v) **Contracts for the transfer of goods and contracts of hire** (s. 7(3)): the above provision contained in s. 6(3) has a similar application in contracts for the supply or hire of goods, as contained in s. 7(3). It should be noted that s. 7(3) only operates where the supplier or hirer acts in the course of a business by virtue of s. 1(3) and thus, where such a private individual purports to exclude or restrict ss. 13–15, the term is not subject to the requirement of reasonableness.

(vi) **Misrepresentation** (s. 8): this provision amends the Misrepresentation Act 1967, s. 3, and thus any term which seeks to exclude or restrict liability for misrepresentation is now subject to the requirement of reasonableness.

(*e*) *The requirement of reasonableness.* It can be seen that the requirement of reasonableness stands at the core of the operation of the Act. One of the great problems with such a concept is that of actually defining what is reasonable. It is of course impractical simply to produce this requirement and leave it to the courts to formulate guidelines, and in any event the requirement could vary considerably from one case to another. The Act predicts such problems and not only attempts to explain what the requirement is but lays down guidelines for the application of the requirement. Section 11 provides what the requirement of reasonableness is in various situations. It provides:

(1) In relation to a contract term, the requirement of reasonableness for the purposes of this Part of this Act, section 3 of the Misrepresentation Act 1967 is that the term shall have been a fair and reasonable one to be included having regard to the circumstances which were, or ought reasonably to have been, known to or in the contemplation of the parties when the contract was made.

(2) In determining for the purposes of section 6 or 7 above whether a contract term satisfies the requirement of reasonableness, regard shall be had in particular to the matters specified in Schedule 2 to this Act; but this subsection does not prevent the court or arbitrator from holding, in accordance with any rule of law, that a term which purports to exclude or restrict any relevant liability is not a term of the contract.

(3) In relation to a notice (not being a notice having contractual effect), the requirement of reasonableness under this Act is that it should be fair and reasonable to allow reliance on it, having regard to all the circumstances obtaining when the liability arose or (but for the notice) would have arisen.

(4) Where by reference to a contract term or notice a person seeks to restrict liability to a specified sum of money, and the question arises (under this or any other Act) whether the term or notice satisfies the requirement of reasonableness, regard shall be had in particular (but without prejudice to subsection (2) above in the case of contract terms) to –

(a) the resources which he could expect to be available to him for the purpose of meeting the liability should it arise; and
(b) how far it was open to him to cover himself by insurance.

(5) It is for those claiming that a contract term or notice satisfies the requirement of reasonableness to show that it does.

Whilst it can be seen that s. 11 itself provides some guidelines as to the application of the requirement of reasonableness, particularly s. 11(4) (although this relates to limitation clauses only), these are only of a general nature.

In examining how the courts assess what is reasonable or not it should be first of all noticed that they may only take into account 'circumstances which were, or ought reasonably to have been, known to or in the contemplation of the parties **when the contract was made**. Secondly, the burden of proving that a clause is reasonable rests on the person seeking to rely on the clause.

Since reasonableness is not specifically defined in the Act, the courts have a wide discretion to determine this issue, taking into account the circumstances of a particular case, though not circumstances that arise after the contract, such as the seriousness of the breach. The result of this 'hands off' approach by the legislature is that the courts will have to refer to guidelines built up by way of judicial precedent.

Judicial guidelines are, of course, quite diverse and of necessity relate to the facts of particular cases; nevertheless they do provide broad points of reference which a judge may take into account. Thus, in the *Photo Productions* case the question as to who is in a better position to insure against a risk was held to be a relevant consideration in assessing whether or not an exemption clause was reasonable or not. It will be noticed that s. 11(4) could not be relied on for authority here since this only relates to limitation clauses not exemption clauses.

In *Levison* v *Patent Steam Carpet Cleaning Co Ltd* [1977] 3 WLR 90, the Court of Appeal considered that the clarity of a term was an important consideration, deciding that a clause stating: 'All merchandise is expressly accepted at the owner's risk' was 'in the context of [the] contract, insufficiently clear or strong' to exclude liability in respect of a fundamental breach of contract. Again, in *Stag Line Ltd* v *Tyne Ship Repair Group Ltd* [1984] 2 Lloyd's Rep 211, it was considered that terms expressed in small print or using complex terminology may be considered to be unreasonable. These considerations will be particularly relevant in consumer contracts, as in the *Levison* case itself. It should also be noted that in *Stag Line Ltd* v *Tyne Ship Repair Group Ltd* Orr LJ thought that it was easier to establish that a clause is reasonable when it merely attempted to limit liability rather than to exclude it altogether.

The only specific guidelines in the Act that relate to the requirement of reasonableness are to be found in Schedule 2. However, these guidelines are limited to the requirement of reasonableness as it applies to ss. 6(3), 7(3) and 7(4). Schedule 2 provides:

> The matters to which regard is to be had in particular for the purposes of sections 6(3), 7(3) and 7(4), 20 and 21 are any of the following which appear to be relevant –
>
> (a) the strength of the bargaining positions of the parties relative to each other, taking into account (among other things) alternative means by which the customer's requirements could have been met;
> (b) whether the customer received an inducement to agree to the term, or in accepting it had an opportunity of entering into a similar contract with other persons, but without having to accept a similar term;
> (c) whether the customer knew or ought reasonably to have known of the existence and extent of the term (having regard, among other things, to any custom of the trade and any previous course of dealing between the parties);
> (d) where the term excludes or restricts any relevant liability if some condition is not complied with, whether it was reasonable at the time of the contract to expect that compliance with that condition would be practicable;
> (e) whether the goods were manufactured, processed or adapted to the special order of the customer.

An early case in which the requirements of reasonableness and the guidelines were considered is that of *R. W. Green Ltd* v *Cade Bros Farm* [1978] 1 Lloyd's Rep 602. It should be noted that the case was based on the provisions of the Supply of Goods (Implied Terms) Act 1973, though these are not significantly different from the relevant provisions of the 1977 Act. The facts were that there was a contract on standard written terms for the sale of seed potatoes from the potato merchants to the farmers. A clause in the contract purported to exclude liability if the buyers failed to give notice of any defects within three days of the delivery of the potatoes. Yet another clause purported to restrict the liability of the merchants to that of the contract price in respect of consequential loss. The potatoes were planted and when they had come through were found to be infected with a virus.

It was held by Griffiths J that the limitation clause in respect of the consequential loss was found to be reasonable on the basis of grounds (a) and (c) quoted above. This term had been in operation for many years and had been discussed and approved between the National Association of Seed Potato Merchants and the National Farmers' Union. As regards the exemption clause the judge found this to be unreasonable. Whilst he agreed that the clause might be reasonable as regards apparent defects this was not the case in relation to a hidden defect such as a virus.

Whilst the guidelines in Schedule 2 are confined within the Act to ss. 6(3), 7(3) and 7(4), there is evidence that the courts are willing to use them in deciding whether a particular clause is reasonable or not, as indicated in the *Levison* case (where the relative strengths of the parties were considered, although this factor did not prove decisive in the decision); and in *Woodman* v *Photo Trade Processing Ltd* (1981) 131 NLJ 933 (where the alternative means by which a customer's needs could have been met were regarded as a relevant factor).

In *George Mitchell (Chesterhall) Ltd* v *Finney Lock Seeds Ltd* [1983] 2 AC 803, the plaintiff farmers ordered 30lb. of cabbage seed from the sellers. The seed arrived with invoices amounting to £201.60 containing a limitation clause restricting the liability of the sellers to either replacing the seed or repaying the contract price. The farmers planted the seed which produced a useless crop when it grew, thereby causing the farmer to suffer losses amounting to some £61,000. The sellers sought to rely on the limitation clause. The House of Lords found that the clause was unreasonable, relying substantially on the fact that the suppliers very often made '*ex gratia*' payments in cases they regarded as justified, rather than rely on the clause. This conduct was regarded as indicative of the fact that the suppliers themselves did not consider their own terms to be reasonable. Secondly, the House of Lords considered that it was unreasonable to allow the suppliers to rely on the clause when the breach was a result of their own negligence. Thirdly, their Lordships considered that the seller could have insured against claims resulting from the supply of defective seed and that this would not have significantly increased the contract price.

The *George Mitchell* case was not based on the provisions of the 1977 Act but on s. 55(3) Sale of Goods Act 1979 which contained a test of reasonableness similar to that contained in the Unfair Contract Terms Act (UCTA). The *George Mitchell* case is nevertheless of use in providing extra-statutory guidelines in assessing whether a clause is reasonable or not.

The House of Lords has also made an assessment of the requirement of reasonableness in relation to a clause purporting to exclude liability for negligence in two cases: *Smith* v *Eric S. Bush (A Firm)* and *Harris* v *Wyre Forest District Council* [1990] 1 AC 831 which were handled as joint appeals. The two cases are of particular interest since whilst the facts are not so dissimilar from each other, they were decided differently by the Court of Appeal.

In the *Smith* case the plaintiff had applied to a building society for a mortgage, signing the application form which required the plaintiff to pay a fee of £38.89 for a survey valuation report from the defendants, a firm of surveyors. The application form stated that the plaintiff would be given a copy of the survey report and the valuation contained in it. The form contained an exemption clause to the effect that neither the building society nor the surveyor warranted the accuracy of the report and that no responsibility would be accepted for any inaccuracy contained within it. Eventually the plaintiff was supplied with a copy of the report in which the terms of the exemption clause were also repeated. The report valued the property at £16,500 and stated that no essential repairs were required to be done. The plaintiff did not obtain an independent survey but chose to rely on the contents of the report supplied by the defendants, eventually purchasing the property for £18,000 after accepting an advance of £3,500 from the building society. The defendants, in producing the report, had noticed that a number of chimney breasts had been removed but had not inspected whether or not the chimneys above had been adequately supported. Some one and a half years later the chimneys collapsed causing considerable damage to the property. The plaintiff sued the defendants in negligence, who sought to rely on the exemption clause as a defence. At first instance it was held that the defendants were liable. They appealed to the Court of Appeal who affirmed the first instance decision and held that the exemption clause did not satisfy the requirement of reasonableness within the Unfair Contract Terms Act 1977. The defendants appealed to the House of Lords.

In the *Harris* case the facts were very similar except that the application form contained an exemption clause to the effect that the local authority would not accept any responsibility for the contents of the survey and valuation report and that the report produced by the surveyors engaged by the local authority was confidential and intended only to be for the benefit of the local authority. The plaintiff was warned to obtain his own independent survey, although he did not do so, preferring to rely on the report supplied to the local authority. Some three years later it transpired that the property was subject to subsidence and that repairs costing more than the purchase price were required. The plaintiff sued the local authority and the firm of surveyors in negligence, claiming that even if the exemption clause was sufficiently wide to cover such liability, it was nevertheless ineffective since it did not comply with the requirement of reasonableness under s. 2(2) of the Unfair Contract Terms Act 1977. At first instance the judge decided in favour of the plaintiff. The defendants appealed to the Court of Appeal which reversed the first instance decision. The Court decided that the right to claim under the principles contained in *Hedley Byrne & Co Ltd* v *Heller and Partners Ltd* [1964] AC 465 (see Chapter 9 below) whereby a person may be liable for a negligent misstatement, only applied where the person making the statement had assumed responsibility for that statement. The Court of Appeal considered the effect of the exemption clause in the present case was to prevent responsibility from arising in the first instance and that since s. 2(2) only applied where a duty of care already existed, the exemption clause was not subject to the requirement of reasonableness.

The decision of the Court of Appeal in the *Harris* case was clearly very alarming since it would enable a major provision of the Unfair Contract Terms Act 1977, namely s. 2(2) to be circumvented simply by constructing one's exemption clause in such a way as to prevent a duty of care from arising in the first place.

The House of Lords dismissed the appeal by the valuer in the *Smith* case and allowed the appeal by the plaintiff purchaser in the *Harris* case. Their Lordships found that the surveyors/valuers in each of the cases clearly did owe a duty to take care within the principles of the *Hedley Byrne* case, approving the case of *Yianni* v *Edwin Evans & Sons* [1982] QB 438, and that both the exemption clauses were subject to the requirement of reasonableness contained in s. 2(2). In considering the requirement of reasonableness Lord Griffiths drew attention to the four matters which should always be considered when determining the reasonableness of a clause. These were:

(a)   'Were the parties of equal bargaining power?'
(b)   'How far was it reasonably practicable for independent advice to be obtained taking into account the costs and time that may be taken up in obtaining such

advice?' His Lordship drew attention to the fact that such consideration could be of great importance to the first time buyer with limited resources, though this would diminish as the price of the house and the resources available to the purchaser increase proportionately.

(c)   'How difficult is the task being undertaken for which liability is being excluded?' In the two cases the surveyors were only required to exercise such reasonable degree of care and skill as is normally required of such professional men. The result might have been different if they had been subject to a burden in excess of that particular duty.

(d)   'What are the practical consequences of the decision on the question of reasonableness?' The purchasers in the two cases were exposed to potentially very substantial losses which they would be unlikely to insure against. The surveyors on the other hand could easily offset their potential losses if found liable by means of professional indemnity insurance. This was an important aspect of the case since it made the concept of insurance an important consideration in assessing the requirement of reasonableness in cases involving exemption clauses. Insurance as a guideline to reasonableness is not to be found in sch. 2 of the 1977 Act but is to be found in s. 11(4) which, as we have seen, relates only to limitation clauses.

A case that illustrates the approach of Lord Griffiths in his application of the requirement of reasonableness is that of *St Albans City and District Council* v *International Computers Ltd* (1994) *The Times*. The facts of the case were that a local authority suffered serious financial losses to the extent of £1,314,846 as a result of an error in a computer program purchased from the defendants. The company's standard terms and conditions in its contract contained a limitation clause that limited its liability to £100,000 unless the 1977 Act applied. The court found that, by the Unfair Contract Terms Act 1977, s. 3, a party who was in breach of contract could not rely on a term restricting liability in respect of that breach except where the term satisfied the requirement of reasonableness. In order to fall within s. 3 the plaintiffs had to show that they had contracted on the defendants' 'written standard terms of business', which on the facts they were able to do. The court also found that either s. 6 or s. 7 applied. The court did not think that it mattered which of these two sections applied, since it considered that the relevant provisions were identical for all practical purposes. In relation to these provisions the court stated that regard had to be paid to the five matters within Schedule 2 in deciding whether the requirement of reasonableness was fulfilled or not. Since the term in the defendants' contract was a limitation clause, s. 11(4) applied and in deciding the requirement here of reasonableness, regard had to be paid to the defendants' resources to meet potential liability and how far it was open to them to obtain insurance cover.

Taking all these factors into account, the court decided that the determining factors were: firstly, the parties were of unequal bargaining power; secondly, the defendants had not justified the figure of £100,000 in the limitation clause, which the court considered to be small in relation to the potential risk and the loss actually sustained; thirdly, the defendants were insured for an aggregate sum of £50 million worldwide; and, fourthly, the practical consequences. In relation to the last factor Scott Baker J thought that this followed on from the third and produced the question as to who was better able to bear the loss of the size in question, the local authority or the company? He thought that the company was well able to insure and pass the premium on to its customers. On the other hand, if the loss fell on the local authority, the losses would ultimately be borne by the local population either by way of reduced council services or by increased local taxation. He considered that it was not unreasonable that he who made the profit should carry the risk. He decided that the practical consequences favoured the local authority and that these factors outweighed the fact that local authorities, like businessmen, should be free to negotiate their own contracts with their eyes open. The defendants failed therefore to discharge the burden imposed on them by the Act of proving that the limitation clause was a reasonable one.

(f) *Anti-evasion provisions.* The Act has three anti-evasion provisions within it designed to prevent the Act from being circumvented. The first – unreasonable indemnity clauses falling under s. 4 – has already been considered above. The other two are secondary contracts and choice of law clauses.

With respect to **secondary contracts** (s.10): this provides:

> A person is not bound by any contract term prejudicing or taking away rights of his which arise under, or in connection with the performance of, another contract, so far as those rights extend to the enforcement of another's liability which this Part of this Act prevents that other from excluding or restricting.

Whilst the terminology seems somewhat obscure, the provision appears to apply where two related contracts are entered into, the second attempting indirectly to exclude liability in respect of rights which a person could have enforced directly in the first contract.

As regards **choice of law clauses** (s. 27 (2)): one method of evading the provisions of the Act could be to nominate the laws of a foreign country as being the proper law applying to the contract – where the laws of that country contain no rules governing the use of exemption clauses, or where that other country's rules are less strict. Section 27(2) provides:

> This Act has effect notwithstanding any contract term which applies or purports to apply the law of some country outside the United Kingdom, where (either or both) –
>
> (a) the terms appear to the court, or arbitrator or arbiter to have been imposed wholly or mainly for the purpose of enabling the party imposing it to evade the operation of this Act; or
> (b) in the making of the contract one of the parties dealt as consumer, and he was then habitually resident in the United Kingdom, and the essential steps necessary for the making of the contract were taken there, whether by him or by others on his behalf.

European limitations on unfair contract terms

In 1993 Directive 93/13 on unfair terms in consumer contracts was adopted by the Council of Ministers. The preamble indicates that the Directive has two aims: firstly, the Single European Act, in attempting to provide a Single European Market, will require the wide divergence in consumer protection in Member States to be approximated so that consumers are not deterred from entering into contracts within the Single European Market; secondly, the Directive is attempting to harmonise the rules relating to consumer protection on a Community-wide basis. It has, however, to be questioned whether the Directive will achieve these objectives since by virtue of Article 1(2) 'mandatory statutory or regulating provisions' are excluded from the Directive. The apparent reason for this is that if a Member State has provided that certain contract terms should be implied into particular types of contracts, then such terms should not be regarded as unfair. For example, the implied conditions under the Sale of Goods Act 1979 would not be subject to the Directive. There is thus plenty of scope for individual Member States to 'customise' their consumer protection legislation, such legislation being excluded from the operation of the Directive. The result of this is that the two main objectives of the Directive are immediately subverted.

The extent to which the Directive regulates unfair terms

It should be noted that the Directive is both narrower and wider than the Unfair Contract Terms Act 1977. Firstly, it is narrower in the sense the UCTA will already cover some aspects of the Directive and in respect of these provisions Parliament will not be required to take any action to adopt such provisions. Similarly, by Article 8 where English law imposes stricter duties than those set by the Directive these strict duties may be retained. Where, however, the Directive is wider in application or sets stricter duties than in the United Kingdom, legislation will have to be introduced to provide compliance with the Directive. Article 10 requires such compliance to be implemented by 31 December 1994. In fact, the regulations contained in the Directive will come into effect on 1 July 1995. The consequence of this six-month delay is unclear but it may be possible for a consumer to take direct action against the Government if he or she suffers loss as a result of the Directive not being implemented by the date stipulated in Article 10.

By Article 1 the Directive is aimed at harmonising consumer protection in relation to 'unfair terms in contracts concluded between a seller or supplier and a consumer'. A 'consumer' is defined in Article 2(b) as 'any natural person who, in contracts covered by this Directive, is acting for purposes which are outside his trade, business or profession'. This definition clearly eliminates sole traders, partnerships or companies from the scope of the protection of the Directive. Thus circumstances such as those seen in *Peter Symmons & Co v Cooke* and *R & B Customs Brokers Co Ltd v United Dominions Trust Ltd* above would be outside the scope of the Directive.

A 'seller or supplier' is defined in Article 2(c) as 'any natural or legal person who, in contracts covered by this Directive, is acting for purposes relating to his trade, business or profession, whether publicly owned or privately owned'. It will be seen immediately that this definition is wider than that adopted by UCTA in relation to 'business liability' as defined in s. 1(3) of that Act.

A term is regarded as being unfair if it falls within the definition set out in Article 3(1):

> A contractual term which has not been individually negotiated shall be regarded as unfair if, contrary to the requirements of good faith, it causes a significant imbalance in

the parties' rights and obligations arising under the contract, to the detriment of the consumer.

Further, Article 3(2) introduces a presumption that pre-printed terms are *prima facie* to be regarded as not being individually negotiated. Whilst a seller or supplier might attempt to rebut the presumption, it is clear that the burden of proof lies on them to prove that the contract was individually negotiated. It should be noted that the Directive is wider than s. 3 UCTA which applies 'between contracting parties where one of them deals as a consumer or on the other's written standard terms of business'. Under the terms of the Directive *both* these factors must exist before the provisions operate.

The Directive preserves the notion of freedom to contract. Firstly, if the contract is individually negotiated then, as seen previously, the contract will fall outside the Directive. Secondly, if a consumer has exerted any influence on a contract term within a standard form contract it will be assumed that the term will not be unfair, although the Directive will apply to the rest of the contract. Thirdly, the Directive, by Article 4(2), excludes terms that define the main subject matter of the contract and relate to the adequacy of the contract price, though such terms still have to comply with the general requirement in Article 5 that they are drafted in 'plain intelligible language'.

The general requirement of 'plain, intelligible language' is a peculiar one in that this expression is not defined within the Directive. No sanction is provided for non-compliance with this provision other than that where there is doubt an 'interpretation most favourable to the consumer shall prevail'. This provision is thus similar to the *contra proferentem* rule that applies in relation to exemption clauses in English law. The main difference with Article 5 is that it applies to all terms, whether or not they fall within the scope of the Directive, and whether or not they are exemption clauses.

Assessing whether a contract term is unfair

It can be seen from Article 3(1) above that a term is regarded as unfair if it causes a 'significant imbalance in the parties' rights and obligations . . . to the detriment of the consumer'. Further the term must be 'contrary to the requirement of good faith'. In assessing these requirements it it clear that the expression 'to the detriment of the consumer' has little substantive reference except to indicate the party to whom the unfairness has to be directed.

The Preamble states that 'good faith' is satisfied by dealing equitably and fairly with the consumer whose legitimate interests must be taken into account. The expression 'significant imbalance' is not defined within the Directive and the concept appears to have been left deliberately vague, as does its relationship with the requirement of good faith. It may be that a significant imbalance is merely evidence of bad faith. Alternatively, one might argue that for a term to be unfair there must not only be a significant imbalance between the parties but also a lack of good faith, i.e. if it can be shown that the parties enter into the contract in good faith, the fact that there is a significant imbalance will be inconsequential.

It may be that the vagueness of the relationship between these two expressions is deliberate in order to give a wide discretion to the courts to make an assessment of each case. Such an analysis would be consistent with Article 4(1) which provides that the unfairness of a term is to be assessed by:

> . . . taking into account the nature of the goods or services for which the contract was concluded and by referring, at the time of conclusion of the contract, to all the circumstances attending the conclusion of the contract and to all the other terms of the contract or of another contract on which it is dependent.

A further aid to deciding what terms may be regarded as unfair is that in the Annex to the Directive there is a list of 17 terms that may be regarded as being 'unfair'. Article 3(3) describes ths list as being 'indicative and non-exhaustive'. The terms contained in the Annex appear to break down into two broad areas: firstly, those that equate with such exempting or limiting terms as are already controlled by the Unfair Contract Terms Act 1977, e.g. terms that exempt or limit liability for death or bodily injury within s. 2 of UCTA; secondly, the Annex sets out terms that are outside the scope of UCTA, e.g. terms relating to penalty clauses, or those which allow a seller or supplier unilaterally to change the terms of a contract without a valid reason, though it may be argued that the latter example, contained in paragraph (j), could fall under s. 3 of UCTA (i.e. excluding or limiting liability for breach of contract).

The effect of a term being found to be 'unfair'

By Article 6(1) a term that is found to be unfair within Article 3 'shall . . . not be binding on the consumer'; however, the rest of the contract will continue in existence and bind the parties 'provided it is capable of continuing in existence without the unfair terms'.

It is possible that severance to this level may make the contract commercially unbalanced or uncertain. It is considered possible that only the unfair element of a term should be severed so that there is a greater possibility of the contract as a whole surviving the severance exercise.

State regulation of unfair terms

By Article 7(1) States have to ensure that 'adequate and effective means exist to prevent the continued use of unfair terms in contracts concluded with consumers'. It would seem, therefore, that Member States will have to provide some mechanism whereby alleged unfair contract terms can be challenged other than by the consumer in civil litigation. No guidance is given in the Directive as to the form that such mechanism should take, except insofar that Article 7(2) provides that there must be a means by which any person or body, that has a legitimate interest in protecting consumers, can challenge whether 'contractual terms drawn up for general use are unfair'. Thus the means will have to be provided for bodies such as the Consumers' Association to challenge the validity of standard form contracts, whether imposed by individual bodies or by groups of sellers or suppliers, such as trade associations. The Consumers' Association in past years has been very critical of British Rail's notorious Condition 25, whereby British Rail is almost totally excluded from liability in respect of losses caused to customers by British Rail's failure to transport them to their destinations on time, if at all. Presumably the Association would wish to challenge this condition if British Rail (or its successor) continued to make use of it. Package holiday firms and banks could also find their standard form contracts under siege by such a mechanism.

Further reading

Adams and Brownsword, 'The Unfair Contract Terms Act: A Decade of Discretion', 104 *Law Quarterly Review* 94, 1988

Beale, Bishop and Furmston, *Contract – Cases and Materials* 2nd ed. 1990, Butterworths

Brown and Chandler, 'Unreasonableness and the Unfair Contract Terms Act', 109 *Law Quarterly Review* 41, 1993

Cheshire, Fifoot and Furmston, *The Law of Contract* 12th ed. 1991, Butterworths

Guest, *Anson's Law of Contract* 26th ed. 1984, Oxford University Press

Macdonald, 'Incorporation of Contract Terms by a "Consistent Course of Dealing" ', 8 *Legal Studies* 48, 1988

Palmer, 'Limiting Liability for Negligence', 45 *Modern Law Review* 322, 1982

Palmer, 'Clarifying the Unfair Contract Terms Act 1977', 7 *Business Law Review* 57, 1986

Spencer, 'Signature, Consent, and the Rule in *L'Estrange* v *Graucob*', 32 *Cambridge Law Journal* 104, 1974

Treitel, *The Law of Contract* 8th ed. 1991, Sweet & Maxwell

Part III
FACTORS THAT VITIATE A CONTRACT

9 | Misrepresentation

INTRODUCTION

In Chapter 7 we saw that prior to the making of a contract the parties often make statements to each other with the intention of inducing the other party to make the contract. Some of these statements may well be translated into terms of the contract, breach of which will give the innocent party certain rights in an action for breach of contract, depending on either the relative importance or status of the term within the contract or the seriousness of the consequences of its breach. Some statements, however, will not themselves become terms of the contract but remain as 'mere representations', that is, statements of fact which are only intended to induce the other party to enter into the contract. The process of discerning between statements which are terms and those that are 'mere representations' may not be an easy one, as seen earlier in the *Oscar Chess* case.

Of itself a breach of a mere representation is not actionable and it may amount to nothing more than a trade 'puff'. Should the 'mere representation' turn out to be a false statement, however, calculated to induce a party to enter into a contract, then an action may lie in the law of tort for misrepresentation, the effect of which is to render the contract voidable, giving the injured party a possibility of either rescinding the contract or claiming damages, or both, though more will be said about remedies later.

A misrepresentation may be defined then as a false statement of fact made with the intention of inducing another to enter into a contract.

THE NATURE OF THE INDUCEMENT

As our definition indicates, the false statement must be a statement of fact. It is extremely important to distinguish between statements that are statements of fact and those which are merely statements of law, opinion or intention.

Statements of law

It is simple to state that a misrepresentation cannot be a statement of law, though it is substantially harder to distinguish between these and statements of fact in practice.

The rule is justifiable since the law is equally accessible to everyone and if one is not sure as to the state of the law he should seek the advice of his own legal adviser. Statements relating to the contents and meaning of an Act of Parliament or statutory instrument are clearly statements of law. The position is not so clear in relation to other documents since whilst the meaning of the nature of a particular document might be a statement of law, a statement as to its contents might be a statement of fact. For example, a statement that all contracts for the sale or other disposition of an interest in land must be in writing to be enforceable is a statement of law. A statement that the contract for the sale of land between A and B is in writing and is therefore enforceable is a statement of fact in that it is declaratory of the rights of the parties to the contract.

Some observers consider that this rule exists because statements of law must of necessity be mere statements of opinion as to the state of the law.

Statements of opinion

Cheshire, Fifoot and Furmston (1991) define a statement of opinion as a 'statement of a belief based on grounds incapable of actual proof'. The point is easily illustrated by the case of *Bisset* v *Wilkinson* [1927] AC 177 where the vendor of a farm in New Zealand, when asked about the number of sheep the farm could sustain, declared that in his judgment it would support 2,000 sheep. In fact the farm had never held sheep and thus it was held that the statement could amount to nothing more than an honest statement of opinion and not a statement of fact. The action for misrepresentation thus failed.

The rule that a statement of opinion cannot form the basis of an action in misrepresentation may nevertheless be overturned if it can be shown that a reasonable man in possession of the same knowledge as the representor could not have honestly held such an opinion. In such a circumstance the statement will be regarded as one of fact rather than one of opinion. In *Smith* v *Land and House Property Corporation* [1884] 28 Ch D 7 a vendor described his property as being 'let to Mr Frederick Fleck (a most desirable tenant) . . . thus offering a first class investment'. In fact the tenant was in arrears with his rent at the time of the sale and soon after it he declared his bankruptcy. The purchasers refused to complete the sale on finding out the truth and were sued for specific performance of the contract. The court held that since the vendor was in the position to know the true facts of the situation his statement could not be regarded as one of opinion but as one of fact.

The decision in the *Smith* case has more recently been affirmed in the case of *Esso Petroleum Ltd* v *Mardon* [1976] 2 All ER 5 which distinguished the *Bisset* case. In the case Esso represented to a prospective purchaser of a petrol station that was being built that it was likely that possible sales of petrol could reach 200,000 gallons a year. In fact the local authority refused planning permission for the proposed layout of the garage, so that the pumps had to be placed to the rear of the site with an entrance via a back street. Despite these changes the market researchers at Esso confirmed that the selling capability of the garage would not be affected and on this basis the defendant bought the petrol station with the help of a loan from Esso. The garage sold a maximum of only 78,000 gallons and as a result incurred such losses that the purchaser could not afford to repay Esso the instalments on the loan. Esso sued to repossess the petrol station and the defendant counter-claimed on the basis of negligent misrepresentation and breach of contract. Esso argued that their estimate as to the maximum sales was one of opinion, since, as in the *Bisset* case, there had never been a petrol station at this location before and therefore any statement as to the potential sales could only be an expression of opinion. The Court of Appeal rejected this contention and found the statement as to the maximum sales to be one of fact. In contrast to the *Bisset* case, Esso had substantial experience and skill in the form of their market research analysts as to the potential sales a petrol station in such a location could expect to achieve. In the circumstances they had failed to exercise reasonable care and skill in relation to the potential sales of the petrol station in question and were thus held to be liable to the defendants. In the *Bisset* case the parties were of equal bargaining strength and thus both were able to formulate their own opinions as to the maximum number of sheep the farm could support.

Statements of intention

Often a promise to do something in the future may not only amount to consideration in a contract but also comprise of a term of the contract. Failure to carry out the promise in such circumstances will amount to a breach of contract. A mere representation as to future conduct is not actionable either as a breach of contract or as a misrepresentation since such statements do not amount to statements of fact. A statement of intention that induces a person to enter into a contract is, however, actionable as a misrepresentation of fact where it can be shown that the maker knew that his promise would not be carried out.

In *Edgington* v *Fitzmaurice* (1885) 29 Ch D 459 the directors of a company issued a prospectus inviting subscriptions for debentures. The money raised from the loan capital arising from the sale of the debentures was, according to the prospectus, to be used to complete alterations to the company's premises, to purchase horses and vans and to develop the business. The plaintiff advanced money in the wrong belief that debenture holders would have a charge over the company's premises. The object of raising the loan capital was in fact to enable the company to pay off pressing debts. It was held that the plaintiff could rescind the contract because there was found to be a misrepresentation of fact. The company directors had not simply made a promise as to the future use of the money which they may or may not have fulfilled, but consciously told an untruth in order to induce members of the public to subscribe to the debentures. Bowen LJ justified the decision as follows:

> The state of a man's mind is as much a fact as the state of his digestion. It is true that it is very difficult to prove what the state of a man's mind at a particular time is, but if it can be ascertained it is as much a fact as anything else. A misrepresentation as to the state of a man's mind is, therefore, a mis-statement of fact.

Silence as a misrepresentation of fact

As a general rule silence cannot amount to a misrepresentation since there is no duty to disclose facts which may influence a person not to enter into a contract. This rule has its origins in the classical theory of contract where the notion of freedom to contract and equality of bargaining power reigned supreme.

There are, however, three exceptions to the above rule:

Change of circumstances

It may happen that later events cause a previously true representation to become untrue. Where a representor knows that the subsequent events or circumstances have this effect he is under a duty to disclose the change of circumstances. In *With* v *O'Flanagan* [1936] Ch 575, for example, a doctor was negotiating the sale of his practice and made certain representations regarding the income that could be earned from it. At the time the misrepresentation was made the figures were true. Subsequently the doctor fell ill so that the income earned from the practice decreased substantially. The reduction was not made known to the purchaser who purchased the practice on the basis of the original earnings. When the purchaser discovered the true state of affairs he sought to rescind the contract. It was held that the purchaser should succeed in his action for rescission on the grounds of misrepresentation, as the doctor should have declared the change of circumstances.

The statement made is only half the truth

A representor must take care not to mislead the representee by only revealing part of the circumstances prevailing. In other words, the representor must not suppress anything disadvantageous which may be considered relevant by the representee.

In *Dimmock* v *Hallett* (1866) LR 2 Ch App 21, a landlord selling property which he disclosed in the negotiation as fully let was under a duty to reveal that in fact the tenants had served notice to quit on the representor landlord.

Confidential/fiduciary relationships

A fiduciary relationship exists where a person has placed a confidence in another person, whereby that person, having been privy to such information, is under a duty not to disclose information gained from such a relationship. Such relationships exist between a trustee and a beneficiary, or a doctor and his patient or a solicitor and his client.

A fiduciary relationship also arises in certain types of contract irrespective of the nature of the relationship between the parties, where one party has the sole access to information forming the basis of the contract. Such contracts are known as contracts *'uberrimae fidei'* (utmost good faith). An example of a common contract *uberrimae fidei* is a contract of insurance. It is clear in such a contract that the decisions of an insurer to insure, or as to what premiums to charge a person seeking insurance, depend entirely on the nature of the information supplied by that individual. The law therefore requires persons applying for insurance to be placed under a duty of utmost good faith, so that anything likely to affect the decision of a prudent insurer as to whether to insure at all or, if he will insure, what premiums to charge, must be declared.

THE FACT OF THE INDUCEMENT

Our definition of a misrepresentation indicates that the statement of fact must have induced the innocent party to enter the contract. In order to prove the inducement we must take certain factors into consideration.

The misrepresentation must be material

The misrepresentation, to be actionable, must be important enough to influence a reasonable man in considering whether or not to enter into a contract or on what terms he is prepared to enter into the contract. It should be noted that an objective test is used here and thus, even if the representor does not consider the false statement to be material it may nevertheless be held to be so.

The objective approach to testing materiality is important because it is largely this factor which distinguishes this rule from the need for reliance on the misrepresentation, which is discussed below. In deciding whether a person has relied on a misrepresentation one examines the actual state of the representee's mind with regard to the false statement at the time he enters into the contract. Materiality, on the other hand, rests on the importance of an untrue statement to the reasonable man of business when he is deciding whether or not to enter into a contract.

In *J. E. B. Fasteners Ltd* v *Marks Bloom & Co* [1983] 1 All ER 583, the plaintiffs decided to launch a takeover of a company for the purpose of obtaining the services of two directors. The plaintiffs inspected the accounts of the company but these were inaccurate because of the negligence of the defendant firm of accountants. Whilst the accounts were regarded as a material misrepresentation the plaintiffs' action failed as they had not relied on the accounts. This conclusion was reached since the principal objective of the plaintiffs was not to acquire the company for commercial reasons but to secure the services of the two directors in question. The case therefore represents a good illustration of the distinction between reliance and materiality.

Nevertheless, the requirement of materiality has been recently called into question in the case of *Museprime Properties Ltd* v *Adhill Properties Ltd* [1990] 2 EGLR 196 where there was a sale by auction of three properties. During the auction certain representations were made to the effect that a rent review was outstanding and that it was still possible for the purchaser to negotiate higher rents. In fact, new rents had already been fixed for the next review period. The plaintiffs sued to have the contract rescinded on the grounds of misrepresentation. The defendants argued, *inter alia*, that they could not do so because the misrepresentation was not material since no reasonable bidder would have allowed such a misrepresentation to affect his bid. The Court held that the materiality was not determined objectively on the basis of whether a reasonable person would have been induced to enter into the contract. It was sufficient if the purchaser could show that he was actually affected by the representation.

It is considered that the test of reasonableness in relation to materiality was only important in relation to the representee proving to the court that he had in fact been induced by the misrepresentation. In other words, the more unreasonable the misrepresentation, the more difficult it will be for him to prove that he was actually induced by the statement. Thus, if the representor had made the statement in good faith and the representation would not have influenced a reasonable person, then the representee may find it exceedingly difficult to prove that the statement was in fact material to him. Even if the representee can show that he was actually influenced by the statement, it may be that a court would not award him rescission but only nominal damages in such a situation.

It should be noted that all statements are deemed material where a contract expressly provides for this. Contracts of insurance, for instance, commonly provide that statements made in proposal forms are deemed to be material, no matter how minor or trivial they may be.

Reliance

The misrepresentation must have been relied on

In other words, the person to whom the misrepresentation is made must have taken cognisance of the statement so that it influences him in the making of his decision to enter into the contract. An example might occur if X is offered a car for £2,500 and he is told by Y that the car had only done 20,000 miles but in fact it had done 40,000 miles. Here there is a clear misrepresentation, but one which is only actionable if X had been induced into the contract by the statement as to the mileage of the car. If X was not bothered about the mileage or in fact chose the car because of its colour, age or model then he will have no action for misrepresentation.

In *Attwood* v *Small* (1838) 6 Cl & Fin 232 the appellant negotiated the sale of certain mines and works to the respondents. The respondents asked questions regarding the capacity of the mine and subsequently had the appellant's answers confirmed by the reports of their own mining engineers. Some six months after the sale the respondents discovered that the answers supplied by the appellant were inaccurate and claimed to rescind the contract for misrepresentation. It was held that their action would fail since the respondents had not relied on the statements made by the appellant but on the reports of their own mining engineers.

A person is not precluded from claiming in misrepresentation merely because he relied on other factors as well as the false statement. As we have already seen in the case of *Edgington* v *Fitzmaurice*, above, the plaintiff there relied not only on the false statements made in the prospectus but also on his own wrong assumption that subscribing to the debenture would give him a charge over the company's property. He was nevertheless held to be entitled to rescind the contract for misrepresentation.

Truth known to the representee?

A person cannot claim in misrepresentation if, in fact, he was aware of the untruth of the statement of fact before or at the time of entering into the contract. It is clear that if one is aware of the untruth of the statement then one could not have relied on it. The burden of proof that the representee knew of the untruth of the statement lies with the representor, who cannot establish this merely by showing that the representee had the means of discovering the falsehood. Clearly it would be a nonsense to allow a person to make a false statement and then to escape liability by stating that the representee should have discovered the untruth because he had the means to do so.

The point can be seen in *Redgrave* v *Hurd* (1881) 20 Ch D 1 where a solicitor was induced to buy a practice on the basis of an innocent misrepresentation as to the value of the practice and the property attached to it. The solicitor had the accounts made available to him though he did not examine them. It was held that he was able to rescind the contract despite the fact that the accounts would have revealed the untruth of the statements made to him.

It would appear that in cases involving negligent misrepresentation it is possible that it may be reasonable for a representee to make use of an opportunity to discover the truth of a representation, with the effect that failure to do so will defeat the claim, or at least raise a spectre of contributory negligence. Such a possibility was indicated in the case of *Smith* v *Eric S Bush* [1990] 1 AC 831 where the plaintiffs, who were purchasing a house, relied on a negligently-prepared survey carried out by the surveyors engaged by their lender. They would have discovered the truth about the property if they had engaged their own surveyor. However, the House of Lords stated that where the value of a house was modest it was unlikely that such purchasers would engage their own surveyor and, indeed, it was not reasonable for them to do so. The case thus followed *Redgrave* v *Hurd* in that their failure to engage their own surveyor did not prevent them from taking action. However, if the house was of a substantial value or comprised of commercial property, the House of Lords indicated that the position would have been different and failure to take the opportunity to discover the truth of a state of affairs would have prevented them from taking action. It is, however, uncertain whether the same principles could be applied to cases of innocent misrepresentation. Presumably the decision in *Redgrave* v *Hurd* will still stand since, as Treitel points out, 'there is actual, and reasonable, reliance on the misrepresentation in such a case'.

Representee unaware of the misrepresentation?

As already indicated the misrepresentation, to be actionable, must have acted on the mind of the representee. It follows therefore that if the representee is unaware of the misrepresentation he cannot take action on the basis of it. Thus in *Ex Parte Briggs* (1859) 28 LJ Ch 50 a purchaser of shares in a company could not rescind the contract on the basis of false reports as to the state of the financial affairs of the company because he could not prove that he had actually read or been aware of the contents of the reports before or at the time he purchased the shares.

THE NATURE OF THE MISREPRESENTATION

The remedies available for misrepresentation vary according to the nature of the misrepresentation alleged. In this section therefore we will look at the nature of the various types of misrepresentations and the particular remedies available for each and in the next section we will look at the various factors which may affect the remedies themselves or their availability.

Originally at common law only two types of misrepresentation were recognised: fraudulent and innocent; however, in recent years we have seen the development of negligent misrepresentation at common law under *Hedley Byrne & Co Ltd* v *Heller & Partners Ltd* [1964] 8 AC 465 and in statute by virtue of the Misrepresentation Act 1967, s. 2(1).

Fraudulent misrepresentation

Fraudulent misrepresentation was stated by Lord Herschell in *Derry* v *Peek* (1889) 14 App Cas 337 to be a 'false statement made knowingly or without belief in its truth or recklessly careless whether it be true or false'. Carelessness of itself does not amount to dishonesty, but where a person acts recklessly it is open for the court to find dishonesty in that he could not reasonably have believed in the truth of his statement. Great care needs to be exercised here since the terms 'careless' and 'recklessly' are today very often regarded as synonymous with negligence, and negligence must never be confused with fraud. Fraudulent misrepresentation is a dishonest statement but it is not necessarily dishonest to state a belief that would not convince a reasonable man, though this may, of course, amount to a negligent mis-statement. Thus a statement made recklessly or carelessly may only amount to evidence of fraud, though if the maker of the statement believes it to be true then he cannot be liable for a fraudulent misrepresentation.

Proving that the representor has made a fraudulent misrepresentation by suing in the tort of deceit is not easy and is likely to be hotly disputed. Failure to prove it may result in an action in defamation so the decision to pursue such an action should never be taken lightly. These factors and the difficulty of proving one's case mean that an action under s. 2(1) of the Misrepresentation Act 1967 (below) is often more advisable.

Common law negligent misrepresentation

The case of *Hedley Byrne & Co Ltd* v *Heller and Partners Ltd* [1964] AC 465 fundamentally changed the nature of misrepresentation which until then was based on the principle that all misrepresentations that were not fraudulent were in fact innocent misrepresentations. The decision in *Hedley Byrne* extended the common law tort of negligence to cover negligent mis-statements that result in loss. The facts of the case were that the plaintiffs had been asked for credit by a particular company and decided to ask for advice as to the financial standing of the company from the company's own bankers, the defendants. The defendants, who were aware of the purpose behind the plaintiff's request, stated carelessly that the company was financially sound. The House of Lords decided that whilst the defendants owed the plaintiffs a duty to take care, they were not liable because of a disclaimer enclosed with the credit reference which stated that the advice was given 'without responsibility'.

The decision established that a representor had a duty of care to do all that is reasonable to make sure that his statement is accurate irrespective of the existence of a fiduciary or contractual relationship. The duty arose in any situation where there was a 'special relationship' between the parties. Unfortunately the House of Lords was not very specific as to what a 'special relationship' was. Certainly there was no need for a direct contractual link between the parties, though there had to be a sufficient degree of proximity between the parties for the action to be sustained, a principle recently reaffirmed in *Caparo Industries plc* v *Dickman and Others* [1990] 1 All ER 568.

At first it was thought that the degree of proximity between the parties only arose between professional men whose business involved the giving of advice to clients such as solicitors, accountants and surveyors (see *Yianni* v *Edwin Evans & Son* [1982] QB 438) and barristers (see *Rondel* v *Worsley* [1969] 1 AC 191). This approach was confirmed by the Privy Council in *Mutual Life and Citizens Insurance Co Ltd* v *Evatt* [1971] AC 793, though rejected in *Esso Petroleum Co Ltd* v *Mardon*, above. In the latter case it was held that a special relationship also exists in a purely commercial transaction where the representor has superior knowledge and experience to that of the representee and where it is reasonable for the representee to rely on the statements made to him by the representor. Ormrod LJ pointed out, however, that liability would not have arisen in a case where a representor could assume that the representee would seek the advice of his own professional advisers.

It is more difficult to bring a claim for negligent misrepresentation at common law than to bring an action under s. 2(1) of the Misrepresentation Act 1967 (see below). The burden of proof lies on the representee who must prove not only the existence of the so-called 'special relationship' but also the existence of a duty of care and its breach, coupled with resulting and foreseeable loss. Such an action does have one advantage, though, since it is not limited to actions in respect of mis-representations that induce a contract.

Misrepresentation Act 1967, section 2(1)

Section 2(1) provides:

> Where a person has entered into a contract after a misrepresentation has been made to him by another party thereto and as a result thereof he has suffered loss, then, if the person making the misrepresentation would be liable to damages in respect thereof had the misrepresentation been made fraudulently, that person shall be so liable notwithstanding that the misrepresentation was not made fraudulently unless he proves that he had reasonable grounds to believe and did believe up to the time the contract was made that the facts represented were true.

Immediately it will be seen that there are significant differences between this and negligent misrepresentation at common law. Firstly, there is no need to prove a 'special relationship'; secondly, the misrepresentation must result in a contract being entered into; thirdly, the burden of proof is reversed so that the representor is liable unless 'he had reasonable grounds to believe and did believe up to the time the contract was made that the facts represented were true'.

Clearly the provision imposes a form of liability for negligent misrepresentation; this is subject to the special conditions stated above which make actions under this provision far more desirable for the representee, in that he has a procedural advantage given the reversed burden of proof. It should be stressed that a contract must result between the representor and the representee. Provided a contract results, the vast majority of actions will be framed within this provision.

Innocent misrepresentation

Prior to *Hedley Byrne* v *Heller* this type of misrepresentation encompassed all misrepresentations that were not fraudulent. Given the developments since *Hedley Byrne*, this category of misrepresentation is confined to those that are wholly innocent.

THE REMEDIES AVAILABLE FOR MISREPRESENTATION

Rescission and indemnity

Rescission

The general rule is that the effect of misrepresentation is to render the contract voidable **not** void and thus the contract is still valid and subsisting until the representee decides to set it aside. Of course, the representee may decide to carry on with the contract, that is, to affirm it. A representee may affirm the contract either by expressing his intention to do so or by simply performing such an act as would indicate to a reasonable person that he intends to proceed with the contract.

A further remedy available to the representee is to cease his performance of the contract and allow himself to become liable for breach of contract, then raising the misrepresentation as a defence to the action for breach. This occurs commonly where a person fails to declare matters of importance when filling in a proposal form to an insurance company. As we have already seen (above) such contracts are contracts *uberrimae fidei* and therefore a person is bound to declare matters of interest to a prudent insurer. The insurer on finding out about the omission may rescind the contract. Very often insurers will refuse to return any premiums paid but if sued for their return may successfully raise the misrepresentation as a defence to the action. Misrepresentation thus acts as a bar to an order for a decree of specific performance of the contract.

As an alternative to the above approaches the representee may decide to rescind the contract which he may simply do by making clear to the other party that he no longer considers himself bound by the contract. Once the representee has elected either to treat the contract as rescinded or affirmed then he cannot retract from that election. If he delays in making the election he will be deemed to have affirmed since, as we shall see later, delay defeats equity and since rescission is an equitable remedy the representee will be precluded from claiming.

Whilst the communication to the representor of the representee's election to rescind the contract is crucial, this communication is relaxed in two instances.

Firstly, it may be that the representor cannot be contacted so that communication of the election is impossible, as where a person making a fraudulent misrepresentation to acquire goods makes off with them and disappears. In such circumstances all that the representee is required to do to effect rescission is to show by some overt act that he intends to rescind. In *Car and Universal Finance Co Ltd* v *Caldwell* [1964] 1 All ER 290, a car was sold and delivered to a rogue whose cheque was dishonoured the next day, by which time the rogue and the car had disappeared. In order to attempt to recover the car the owner informed the police and the Automobile Association. The rogue then sold the car to a garage which knew that the rogue had a defective title to the vehicle. The garage subsequently sold the car to a buyer who purchased the car in good faith. It was held that the owner, by informing the police and the Automobile Association, had made it clear that he sought to rescind the contract, with the result that the rogue no longer had title to the goods so that no title could pass to the garage or to the innocent buyer, and the latter had to return the car to the owner.

Secondly, if the representee seizes or otherwise retakes possession of the goods from the representor, this action of itself amounts to rescission and there is no requirement for the representee to communicate his election to rescind formally.

So far we have been considering the exercise of rescission out of court but it is possible and, indeed, desirable in some cases, to apply to the court for a formal order of rescission. Such a situation might arise where a representee has been induced to buy shares by way of a misrepresentation. Since the representee has paid money to the representor it is useless to think in terms of repossessing the monies paid and whilst it may be possible to declare one's intention to rescind to the other party this is unlikely to have any great effect. In the sale of goods, the reason for informing the rogue of one's election or informing the police, etc is often to prevent title being passed to some third party, but this is not the case with money. Whatever one's motives for applying for a formal order, it should be noted that even here rescission is regarded as an act of the representee, and the result is that the rescission takes effect from the date of the communication of the application of the order to the representor rather than from the award of the order by the court.

The effect of rescission for misrepresentation is to render the contract void *ab initio*, which requires that the parties should be restored to their original positions. It follows that if this so-called *restitutio in integrum* cannot be achieved then rescission is not possible. A problem, might arise, however, in that whilst the parties can be substantially returned to their status quo ante, the representee might have incurred other expenses which would not necessarily figure in the mutual handing back of what each party has received under the contract. In fraudulent misrepresentation this presented no problem since damages were available at common law for this type of misrepresentation and the expense element was often included within the damages element. In innocent misrepresentation, however, damages were not available at common law and thus the courts, to make an award for such expenses incurred, had to manipulate the rules so as to produce a substantial return of the parties to their status quo ante. The courts achieved this by making an award, not of damages, but of an indemnity, whereby the representee was awarded a sum that equated with expenses or obligations necessarily incurred as a result of the representation.

One final point that should be noted with regard to rescission is that it is available for **any** type of misrepresentation.

Indemnity

As already stated, an indemnity is a means whereby, as part of the process of *restitutio in integrum*, the representee can recover expenses necessarily incurred by the creation of the contract induced as a result of the misrepresentation. It is important that an indemnity is not confused with one's common law right to damages. The distinction may be seen in the case of *Whittington* v *Seale-Hayne* (1900) 82 LT 49.

In this case the plaintiffs were lessees of premises which they used for breeding poultry. They alleged that they were induced to take up the lease because of representations made by the defendant's agents that the premises were in a sanitary condition and in a good state of repair. They further alleged that as a consequence of the premises being in an insanitary condition their farm manager and his family became seriously ill and that much of the poultry either died or became valueless for breeding purposes. The local authority also condemned the premises as being unfit for human habitation because of defective draining. The plaintiffs claimed that they were entitled to an indemnity as regards the losses in respect of the stock and the medical expenses of the farm manager and his family since these were incurred as a consequence of entering into the contract. It was held that the claim would fail as it really amounted to a claim for damages, which could not be awarded for an innocent misrepresentation. The plaintiffs were, however, entitled to those expenses which were incurred as a requirement of entering into the lease, such as rent, rates and repairs. The contract did not require the plaintiffs to appoint a manager so the expenses claimed in respect of his medical condition were not an expense necessarily incurred by the contract. Similarly the contract did not require the farm to be used as a poultry farm and therefore these expenses also were not necessarily incurred by the contract.

Bars to the remedy of rescission

A person may be barred from exercising the remedy of rescission in four circumstances:

(a) Affirmation. We have already seen that when a person elects to affirm the contract that election cannot be retracted and rescission will cease to be available to the representee. It should, however, be remembered that the election may be made expressly or made impliedly by conduct and that, further, affirmation can only take place if the representee knows of the truth of the situation. As regards the latter mere rumours or vague hints as to the untruth of the representations made are not regarded as discovery of the truth.

An example of affirmation can be seen in the case of *Long* v *Lloyd* [1958] 1 WLR 753 where the vendor of a lorry falsely stated that it was in good condition and the vehicle was subsequently purchased by the plaintiff. After the first journey some defects were found, but, when they were pointed out to the defendant he offered to meet half the costs of the repairs and this offer was accepted by the plaintiff. The following day on the second journey the lorry broke down and serious defects were discovered to the extent that it was unroadworthy. The defendant's representations as regards the vehicle were clearly untrue, though honestly made and the plaintiff sought to rescind the contract for innocent misrepresentation. It was held that by accepting the offer of assistance with the repairs after the first journey the plaintiff had accepted the lorry and therefore lost any rights he may have had to rescind the contract.

(b) Lapse of time. Rescission is not barred by lapse where the misrepresentation is fraudulent; it simply provides evidence of affirmation of the contract. In this type of misrepresentation time only becomes relevant from the discovery of the truth of the misrepresentation. Similarly, once the misrepresentation has been discovered, any time spent negotiating a solution to the dispute does not count towards debarring a claim.

In misrepresentations other than fraudulent misrepresentations the rule is that rescission must take place within a reasonable time, even though there is no evidence of an intention to affirm the contract. Thus in *Leaf* v *International Galleries* [1950] 1 All ER 693, the plaintiff bought a painting after accepting it to be a genuine Constable on the basis of misrepresentation made by the defendants. Five years after the sale the plaintiff discovered that the painting was not by Constable and sought to rescind the contract on the grounds of innocent misrepresentation. It was held that his right to rescind was barred. Even though there was no evidence that the plaintiff had affirmed the contract the lapse of time nevertheless debarred him from his remedy.

(c) Where restitutio in integrum has become impossible.   The basis of the remedy of rescission is that of restitution, that is, a mutual handing back of what has been given and received under the contract. The principle then is that rescission cannot take place if the parties cannot be returned substantially to their original positions. Clearly there should be no problem if the representee merely has to hand back money received, but the position may be very different with other types of property or benefits received. One example could be if the representee has been induced to purchase a car by the misrepresentation but, prior to the exercise of rescission, he has had an accident and written it off. Similarly the benefit received might have deteriorated in value, as in a sale of shares induced by a misrepresentation where prior to the exercise of rescission the value of the shares had fallen substantially, as in *Armstrong* v *Jackson* [1917] 2 KB 822. Still further rescission would not be possible if the representee had consumed the goods misrepresented to him.

Of course there are various degrees by which the property or benefits might have changed. At common law the rule relating to rescission was strict in the sense that the restitution had to be precise. Equity was not so strict and it allowed rescission if the property or benefit returned was substantially the same as when it was received, minor charges being compensatible by damages in all but innocent misrepresentations. The same is also true where the representor has enhanced the value of the item received, since here he may be able to claim the cost of such enhancement as damages, though not (as stated earlier) for innocent misrepresentation.

(d) The intervention of third parties.   In a broad sense this bar to the right of rescission is really only an extension of the principles discussed in *(c)* above. Here the right to rescind will be lost if an innocent third party acquires the subject matter of the contract in good faith and for value. The situation commonly arises in a case of fraudulent misrepresentation where a person is induced to sell certain items to the representor by fraud. If the representor sells the items to an innocent third party then the remedy of rescission will be barred by the acquisition of title to the goods by the third party. It can be seen, as in *Car and Universal Finance Co Ltd* v *Caldwell*, for instance, that it is extremely important for the representee to exercise the right of rescission as soon as possible after discovering the fraud, since this will preclude a third party from acquiring the title to the subject matter of the contract and enable the representee to recover the goods from the third party by way of an action in the tort of conversion. This area is dealt with more fully in Chapter 10 under unilateral mistake as to identity.

Damages in lieu of rescission

Before we proceed to analyse the remedy of damages in relation to misrepresentation fully it needs to be pointed out that the right of rescission may be lost where the court decides to exercise its discretion under s. 2(2) of the

Misrepresentation Act 1967 and award damages in lieu of rescission. Section 2 (2) provides:

> Where a person has entered into a contract after a misrepresentation has been made to him otherwise than fraudulently, and he would be entitled by reason of the misrepresentation to rescind the contract, then, if it is claimed in any of the proceedings arising out of the contract, that the contract ought to be or has been rescinded, the court or arbitrator may declare the contract subsisting and award damages in lieu of rescission, if of the opinion that it would be equitable to do so, having regard to the nature of the misrepresentation and the loss that would be caused by it if the contract were upheld, as well as to the loss that rescission would cause the other party.

It is important to note that the discretion to award damages in lieu of rescission cannot be exercised in relation to fraudulent misrepresentation. The reason for this can be found in the general reasoning for the introduction of the discretion, which is to extinguish the use of rescission in cases where the consequences of the misrepresentation are trivial and where damages would provide an adequate remedy. This poses a particular problem in innocent misrepresentation where the only remedy available is rescission and therefore the Act permits the court to award damages in lieu of rescission in an appropriate case. Fraud, however, is never regarded as trivial and thus the discretion does not arise in that type of misrepresentation.

Another important aspect of s. 2(2) is that it only applies where a person 'would be entitled by reason of the misrepresentation to rescind the contract'. The effect of this is that if a person's entitlement to claim rescission is barred by one of the factors discussed above then the court cannot exercise its discretion in relation to an award of damages under s. 2(2). In the case of innocent misrepresentation this may of course result in the representee being without any remedy, with the exception of claiming indemnity.

In the case of *Thomas Witter Ltd* v *TBP Industries Ltd*, ChD (unreported 15 July 1994), it was suggested that the power to award damages under s. 2(2) does not depend on an existing right to rescission but only on the right having existed in the past. There may be some sympathy with such a view in that as a matter of policy there seems to be no reason why the operation of one of the bars to rescission should restrict the discretion to award damages. For instance, whilst it may be inappropriate to allow rescission where the contract has been affirmed or third party rights have intervened, there seems to be no reason why this should prevent a court from making an award of damages. A reading of s. 2(2), however, seems to indicate that the reasoning of the court is incorrect. Section 2(2) only operates where on the facts the representee '. . . would be entitled, by reason of the misrepresentation, to rescind the contract . . .'. On this wording it would appear that the representee must still be able to avail himself of rescission at the time he brings his action. This would clearly not be the case if one of the factors that bar one's right to rescission exists.

Further authority for this proposition may be found by analogy in *Law Debenture Trust Corporation plc* v *Ural Caspian Oil Corporation Ltd and Others* [1993] 2 All ER 355, where Hoffman J considered that damages could not be awarded in lieu of injunctive relief by virtue of the Supreme Court Act 1981, s. 50, if injunctive relief itself was unavailable.

In deciding whether or not to exercise its discretion the court has to take into account the degree of seriousness of the breach and the likely consequences of the exercise of the discretion on the representee and the representor, particularly in cases involving an innocent misrepresentation where the degree of loss is minimal.

Damages for misrepresentation

Fraudulent misrepresentation

Damages are available at common law for fraudulent misrepresentation, the measure being a tortious one since the claim is based on the tort of deceit. The difference between a tortious measure and a contractual one is that in the latter the principle behind the award is to place the injured party in the same position he would have been in had the contract been completed. A tortious measure is based on the principle of placing the injured party in the same position he would have been in had the wrongful act not been committed.

Whilst the measure of damages in tort is limited by the concept of remoteness of damages, that is, that one is only liable for damages that are reasonably foreseeable, this has no application in fraud where the damages are awarded on a causation basis. Lord Denning in *Doyle* v *Olby (Ironmongers) Ltd* [1969] 2 QB 158 stated the position to be as follows:

> The defendant is bound to make reparation for all the actual damage following from the fraudulent inducement. . . . It does not lie in the mouth of the fraudulent person to say that they could not have been reasonably foreseen.

The result is that the court will award damages for all losses including consequential losses. It is this factor, the lure of heavier damages, that may encourage representees to pursue a claim under fraudulent misrepresentation. This is not an inevitable result. In *East* v *Maurer* [1991] 2 All ER 733 the Court of Appeal stated that the 'reparation for all actual damage' as indicated by Lord Denning would include loss of profits. The assessment of loss of profits, however, was to be made on a tortious basis. The result is that the assessment of damages for loss of profits caused by a fraudulent misrepresentation must be based on the level of profits that might have been expected had the false representation not been made, rather than on the basis of a contractual warranty. The effect of such an approach may well result in the amount of damages to be awarded for loss of profits being reduced, as indeed they were in this case.

Negligent misrepresentation at common law

Clearly the measure of damages here is based on a tortious measure and is thus subject to the test of remoteness, that is, damages which are reasonably foreseeable.

Negligent misrepresentation under s. 2(1)

As with s. 2(2), there is no specific statement as to the measure of damages to be applied though the wording clearly suggests that a tortious measure is intended. In *Watts* v *Spence* [1976] Ch 165 a contractual measure was used, but it would seem settled that this is wrong since, in *Andre et Cie SA* v *Ets Michel Blanc et Fils* [1977] 2 Lloyd's Rep 166 and latterly in *Sharneyford Supplies Ltd* v *Edge* [1985] 1 All ER 976, it was decided that a correct measure was one based on tort.

Having decided that a tortious measure is appropriate, we must next ask whether the measure is based on negligence or on the tort of deceit. As we have already seen, damages under the tort of deceit are wider, being based on causation and not being limited to those which may be reasonably foreseen as in negligence. Whilst there has been considerable debate over this question in the past, recently the Court of Appeal in *Royscot Trust Ltd* v *Rogerson* [1991] 3 All ER 294 stated that s. 2(1) was clear in that the correct measure was that based on the tort of deceit. Lord Justice Balcombe stated that the plaintiff was entitled to recover all losses even if those losses were unforeseeable, provided they were not otherwise too remote.

The difference between the calculation of damages in tort and the calculation in contract can be seen in the case of *Naughton and Another* v *O'Callaghan* [1990] 3 All ER 191. The facts of the case were that in September 1981 the plaintiffs bought a thoroughbred yearling for 26,000 guineas from the Newmarket sales. The horse was trained in England and Ireland for two seasons but was unplaced in all the races it was entered for. The horse's lack of success meant that its value fell to £11,500. In June 1983 it was discovered that the horse's pedigree had been incorrectly described in the sales catalogue because of an error at the stud farm where the horse was foaled. Subsequent to this discovery further expenses were incurred and the following year the plaintiff purchasers purported to repudiate the contract, seeking the purchase price and training fees and expenses amounting to £14,734. Judgment was entered by default against the defendants and the stud farm. In assessing the damages, evidence was produced that if the yearling had been correctly described it would only have fetched approximately 23,000 guineas at the sale. The defendants and the stud farm contended that the plaintiffs had bought a horse of practically the same value as the one they had intended to buy and that therefore they were only entitled to the difference in value. Further they contended that they were not liable for the training fees and other expenses since such expenses would have been incurred whatever horse had been purchased.

It was held that the correct measure of damages was the difference between the purchase price and the value of the horse at the time of the discovery of the misrepresentation, *not* the difference between the purchase price and the horse's actual value at the time it was purchased. As regards the expenses, it was decided that the plaintiffs were entitled to these since the plaintiffs were entitled to say that this was not the horse they thought they had bought and, as such, was not a horse that they would have spent money on training or keeping. The expenses were monies spent in reliance on the misrepresentation. In other words, plaintiffs are entitled to be put into the same position they would have been in had they not entered into the transaction.

It should further be noted that in *Gran Gelato Ltd* v *Richcliff (Group) Ltd* [1992] 1 All

ER 865 it was held that damages awarded under s. 2(1) may be reduced by virtue of the contributory negligence of the plaintiff.

Innocent misrepresentation

Damages are not recoverable for innocent misrepresentation unless the court decides to exercise its discretion under s. 2(2) and award damages in lieu of rescission. The measure of damages for this is discussed below.

The measure of damages under s. 2(2)

As with s. 2(1) this provision gives no express indication as to the measure of damages though both Treitel (1991) (p. 326) and Cheshire, Fifoot and Furmston (1991) (p. 298) indicate that the measure should be somewhat lower than those that may be awarded under s. 2(1). There are two reasons for this proposition. Firstly, s. 2(3) tends to suggest that a lower measure be adopted. Section 2(3) provides:

> Damages may be awarded against a person under subsection (2) of this section whether or not he is liable to damages under subsection (1) therefore, but where he is so liable any award under the said subsection (2) shall be taken into account in assessing his liability under the said subsection (1).

Secondly, damages under s. 2(2) are to be awarded in lieu of rescission and since the purpose of this remedy is to effect a restitution between what the representee handed over and what he received then the damages awarded under s. 2(2) should reflect such a measure. Such a measure would therefore preclude sums representing consequential losses.

Surprisingly, there has been very little judicial consideration of the measure of damages under s. 2(2). The issue has, however, been discussed in *William Sindall plc v Cambridgeshire County Council* [1994] 1 WLR 1016 (CA), where both Hoffman LJ and Evans LJ concurred that the measure is different from that which arises under s. 2(1) since s. 2(3) indicates this. They considered that the measure should be an amount that compensates the plaintiff 'for the loss he has suffered on account of the property not having been what it was represented to be'. Evans LJ was a little more explicit and stated that the measure of damages should be based on 'the difference in value between what the plaintiff was misled into believing that he was acquiring, and the value of what in fact he received'. This measure was to be calculated at the time of the contract and consequential losses should not be taken into account.

EXCLUSION OF LIABILITY FOR MISREPRESENTATION

This area of exclusion is now covered by s. 8 of the Unfair Contract Terms Act 1977, which replaced and repealed s. 3 of the Misrepresentation Act 1967. This has already been discussed in Chapter 8 above.

Further reading

Beale, Bishop and Furmston, *Contract – Cases and Materials* 2nd ed. 1990, Butterworths
Brinkworth and Powell, 'Fraudulent Misrepresentation: Dead or Simply Resting?' 13 *Business Law Review* 3, 1992
Cheshire, Fifoot and Furmston, *The Law of Contract* 12th ed. 1991, Butterworths
Guest, *Anson's Law of Contract* 26th ed. 1984, Oxford University Press
Spencer, Bower and Turner, *The Law of Actionable Misrepresentation* 3rd ed. 1974
Treitel, *The Law of Contract* 8th ed. 1991, Sweet & Maxwell

10 | Mistake

INTRODUCTION

We saw in Chapter 1 that in the nineteenth century the theory of contractual obligation was based on that of *consensus ad idem*. The courts were willing to intervene if it could be shown that the contract lacked consensus, on the basis that genuine consent to the agreement was non-existent. This being the case the courts would find that there was no valid contract thereby relieving the parties of their rights and liabilities under the contract.

The twentieth century has seen a marked change in the willingness of the courts to allow a mistake of the parties to vitiate the existence of a contract. The courts began to realise that many contracts coming before them where mistake was alleged were for the most part commercial contracts entered into by businessmen at arm's length. The attitude of the judiciary was that such people ought to be held to the bargain they had freely entered into and that, initially, the power lay with these individuals to draft their contracts in such a way as to account for factors that might only come to light after the contract was entered into.

A further aspect that promoted the change of attitude was the effect of the finding of mistake at common law on third parties. At common law where a mistake was found to exist the finding would be that the contract was void *ab initio*, that is, the common law refused to recognise the existence of a contract at all. The effect of this was that if goods were sold to an individual under a contract which was void for mistake then no title to the goods would pass to the other party, and he would then have to return them to the seller.

Between the parties to the alleged contract this created no significant problem. However, if the party who had 'purchased' the goods had sold them to a third party then that third party could be compelled to return the goods to the seller. The reason for this was that if the purchaser did not acquire title to the goods then no title could be passed from him to the third party. The principle is summed up in the maxim *nemo dat quod non habet*, that is, no one has power to transfer the ownership of that which he does not own. The result was that a third party's rights to title could be prejudiced by a mistake in a prior contract, the existence of which he may not even be aware of. Thus a third party could be compelled to return goods to the original seller, whilst at the same time being left with no or very limited rights against the person who had sold him the goods.

The constraints that the courts placed on their finding for an operative mistake were clearly well justified in view of the above factors, yet, nevertheless, instances did arise where it was unjustifiable to hold the parties to their contracts. The courts thus evolved an equitable doctrine of mistake where the contract was held not to be void *ab initio* but voidable, thus preserving at least some of the rights of an innocent third party, though not always so.

It should be noted that for a mistake to be an operative one the mistake must be one relating to a fundamental, underlying fact that existed at the moment the contract was entered into.

This was so in *Amalgamated Investment and Property Co Ltd* v *John Walker and Sons Ltd* [1976] 3 All ER 509 where a contract was entered into for the purchase of a warehouse which the purchasers wished to redevelop and for which redevelopment both parties knew that planning consent would be required. In the pre-contract enquiries the purchasers asked the vendors whether the building was designated as a building of special architectural interest. This was important because it would render the obtaining of planning consent substantially more difficult. The vendors answered in the negative, a statement which was true on 14 August 1973. In fact later, unknown to both parties, the Department of Environment decided to give the building such a designation as from 25 September 1973. The parties actually signed their contracts on that date and the purchasers were informed by the Department of Environment of the change of designation on 26 September 1973. The purchasers claimed that the contract should be rescinded for mistake. The Court of Appeal refused the application on the basis that on the date of the contract both parties believed the property to have no such designation and that since that was in fact the case at that time, there had been no mistake.

The case also illustrates another important point in that there are often great similarities between mistake and misrepresentation. Whilst this latter concept was not pleaded in the case it is not too difficult to see why very often claims will arise mainly in relation to misrepresentation rather than to mistake.

Given the two divergent approaches of the common law and equity to mistake it is logical and convenient to divide our study of mistake into these two areas.

MISTAKE AT COMMON LAW

The courts at common law have become reluctant to grant relief for mistake for the reasons already indicated, but they could be persuaded to find the contract void *ab initio* if satisfied that the mistake was one which was fundamental to the contract. Such a fundamental mistake can occur in two broad ways.

Firstly, a mistake may arise where the parties have entered into a contract on an assumption that a certain state of affairs exists but which it is subsequently discovered does not exist. In this type of mistake there is an undoubted agreement between the parties, but they have both made the same or a common mistake as to a fundamental fact on which the agreement is based. This is referred to as **common initial mistake** in what follows.

Secondly, a mistake may arise in relation to the terms of the agreement and this may preclude the formation of an agreement. This is a mistake that precludes the *consensus ad idem* of the parties. Such a mistake might arise where the parties are at cross purposes with one another, as, for example, where A is offering one thing, whilst B is accepting something else. This type of mistake will be referred to as **mutual mistake**. This type of mistake may arise where only one party makes a fundamental mistake of fact as to a term of the agreement, the other party being aware, or being presumed to be aware, of the mistake being made by the first individual. This type of mistake will be referred to as **unilateral mistake**. Mutual and unilateral mistake will be grouped under the heading **consensus mistake**.

One word of warning needs to be made at this point in that the terms common, mutual and unilateral mistake are used interchangeably by different authors, particularly the first two terms. No confusion should arise, however, if one bears in mind the circumstances in which each arises rather than simply relying on the label given to each type by the different authors.

One last point that should be noted is that in all types of mistake, however labelled or described, the mistake must be a fundamental mistake of fact.

Common initial mistake

To reiterate, this type of mistake arises commonly where the parties make a mistake that a certain state of affairs – on which the agreement is based – exists, but which it is subsequently discovered does not exist. Clearly if, unknown to both parties, a fact which is fundamental to the agreement either never existed or ceased to exist prior to the entering into of the contract then no contract can arise and therefore any agreement entered into is void *ab initio*.

It is important to emphasise that the state of affairs must cease to exist prior to the entering into of the contract. Should the state of affairs actually exist at the time the contract is entered into, but then subsequently cease to exist, the contract will be binding, though it may be discharged for subsequent impossibility under the doctrine of frustration. The doctrine of frustration will be examined in Part IV of the book and it is well to bear in mind the difference between initial mistake and subsequent impossibility when reading Chapter 15 on frustration.

One should point out that initial mistake rarely causes a contract to fail at common law and it is generally left to equity to provide a remedy for this type of mistake. Nevertheless the common law has seen fit to attempt to intervene in two circumstances.

Mistake as to the existence of the subject matter

This type of mistake is often referred to as *res extincta* and it arises where, unknown to both the parties, the subject matter of the contract had ceased to exist at the time the contract was entered into. This principle also has support in the form of the Sale of Goods Act 1979, s. 6 which provides:

> Where there is a contract for the sale of specific goods, and the goods without the knowledge of the seller have perished at the time when the contract was made, the contract is void.

The application of the principle can be seen in *Couturier v Hastie* (1856) HL Cas 673 where the plaintiff merchants sold a cargo of Indian corn to the defendant. Unbeknown to either party, a few days before the contract was made, the cargo, which was on board a ship, had overheated and started to ferment, and as a result the captain had sold the cargo in order to prevent it from deteriorating further. The buyer contended that since the subject matter of the contract, the corn, had ceased to exist prior to the entering into of the contract, then the contract was void and he was not liable to pay the price. The vendor, however, argued that the contract was based on the handing over of the shipping documents and that the defendant had not simply bought a cargo of corn but a whole venture in which he took all the risks regarding the shipment of the cargo. It was held by the House of Lords that the purchaser was not bound to pay for the cargo. The contract contemplated that the goods sold actually existed, and since they did not, the seller could not be required to deliver the goods, nor the buyer to pay for them. Lord Cranworth stated:

> The whole question turns upon the construction of the contract . . . Looking to the contract itself alone, it appears to me clearly that what the parties contemplated, those who bought and those who sold, was that there was an existing something to be sold and bought . . . The contract plainly imparts that there was something which was to be sold at the time of the contract, and something to be purchased. No such thing existing . . . there must be judgment . . . for the defendants.

One of the problems with the use of this case to illustrate mistake as to the existence of the subject matter is that nowhere in the judgment is mistake mentioned, let alone discussed. Furthermore the contract was not held to be void at all, the judgment being based on the fact that since the seller was unable to produce the goods, he was unable to recover the price for them. The result of such a decision is that in reality this was not a case based on *res extincta* but one based on a total failure of consideration, where the question as to whether the contract is a nullity or valid would not arise. The reasoning is clear in that, if the cargo has ceased to exist then it cannot be delivered, in which case the seller can neither claim the contract price from the purchaser, nor, indeed, retain any monies paid. The position however becomes very different if the action becomes that of the purchaser who claims for non-delivery of the goods. This might easily have been the case in *Couturier v Hastie* if the case had been regarded as simply a case of a sale of specific goods from the outset, rather than an attempt by the seller to claim that it was a sale of a venture. Whether the purchaser can claim here depends largely on the terms of the contract.

The position of the purchaser can be seen in the Australian case of *McRae v Commonwealth Disposals Commission* [1951] 84 CLR 377 where the Commission, the defendants, invited tenders for the sale of a wreck of an oil tanker which was said to be lying on the Jourmand Reef. The plaintiff, the successful bidder, was unable to find the reef on the marine charts and therefore asked for the ship's position, and this he was duly given. The plaintiff then spent a considerable sum of money equipping a salvage operation but, on arriving at the position given, found there was no tanker nor had there ever been such a tanker. The plaintiff sued for breach of contract and this was resisted by the defendants who claimed the contract was void for *res extincta* on the basis of *Couturier* v *Hastie*.

The plea of the defendants was accepted by the court at first instance but rejected on appeal to the High Court in which Dixon and Fullagar JJ decided that *Couturier* provided authority for the existence of *res extincta*. They stated that the case did not concern itself with the validity of the contract, being based on the existence of a total failure of consideration, but the court did consider the situation where the validity of the contract could be called into question. It was stated that this might arise if the purchaser had brought the action for non-delivery in *Couturier*. In this context Dixon and Fullagar stated:

> If it had so arisen, we think that the real question would have been whether the contract was subject to an implied condition precedent that the goods were in existence. *Prima facie*, one would think, there would be no such implied condition precedent, the position being simply that the vendor promised that the goods were in existence . . .

In the *McRae* case no such implied condition precedent arose, nor was it required, since the buyers clearly relied on an assertion made by the defendants that the tanker existed. It was not a case, as would have arisen in *Couturier*, had the purchaser brought the action, of a contract being entered into on the basis of a common assumption of fact as to the existence of the subject matter being a condition precedent to the entering into of that contract. In *McRae* the defendants had contracted on the clear basis that the tanker existed and therefore were liable for breach of contract.

The actual basis of *Couturier* v *Hastie* remains open and several theories have been expounded by as many commentators as to what this basis is. As was shown above, the decision could amount to authority either as to the existence of a common mistake as to the existence of the subject matter; or a case providing an example of a total failure of consideration; or a case involving an implied condition precedent as to the existence of the subject matter. Whatever that basis is, it would seem extreme to suggest that the analysis of the decision in *McRae* results in the questioning of the existence of *res extincta* itself as a legal concept. Both Dixon and Fullagar acknowledge the fact that in *Couturier*, Coleridge J in the Court of Exchequer Chamber and Cranworth LJ in the House of Lords talk in terms of the judgment turning 'entirely on the reading of the contract'. The true position is probably as stated by Anson when he comments:

> When properly construed, the contract may indicate that the seller assumed responsibility for the non-existence of the subject matter. This was so in *McRae*'s case, where the seller was held to have guaranteed the existence of the tanker. Or it may indicate that the buyer took the risk that the subject matter might not exist and undertook to pay in any event. This was the point at issue in *Couturier* v *Hastie*, where the House of Lords was called upon to decide whether or not the buyer had purchased merely the expectation that the cargo would arrive . . .

As in many areas of the law of contract, the whole question is ultimately reduced to deciding who should bear the loss in a contract based on the assumption that certain facts exist when they do not. In deciding the issue one asks if either party had accepted responsibility for the existence of the assumed facts. If one party did so, then clearly that is the end of the matter and the action lies for breach of contract against that individual. If neither party has assumed responsibility under the contract then ultimately the court has to decide whether either party can be regarded as having taken the risk. The court may consider, and it is submitted that this is a rare occurrence, that neither party can be regarded as having assumed the risk. Should this be the case the contract will be void for common mistake. This process of questioning would seem to have the support of Steyn J in *Associated Japanese Bank (International) Ltd* v *Crédit du Nord SA* [1988] 3 All ER 902, which is discussed more fully below, where he states:

> Logically, before one can turn to the rules as to mistake . . . one must first determine whether the contract itself, by express or implied condition precedent or otherwise, provides who bears the risk of the relevant mistake. It is at this hurdle that many pleas of mistake will either fail or prove to have been unnecessary. Only if the contract is silent on the point is there scope for invoking mistake.

A factor that complicates the above summary is the existence of s. 6 of the Sale of Goods Act 1979. This provision gives statutory authority for what was commonly assumed to be the position in *Couturier* v *Hastie* regarding the common mistake as to the existence of the subject matter of the contract. In *McRae* the judges considered that the provision did not apply to that case since s. 6 talks in terms of goods having perished and since the tanker in *McRae* never existed in the first place the facts of the case fell outside the provision.

In relation to s. 6 Atiyah (1989) at p. 237 argues that the provision only amounts to a prima facie rule which may be overturned by the express agreement of the parties. There is no suggestion whatsoever that Parliament intended this within the Act and therefore the assertion by Atiyah must be considered guardedly, though he is undoubtedly correct in the light of the above that s. 6 is something of an anachronism today.

Mistake as to title

This type of mistake is sometimes referred to as *res sua*. It is described by Lord Atkin in *Bell* v *Lever Bros* [1932] AC 161 as follows:

> Corresponding to mistake as to the existence of the subject-matter is mistake as to title in cases where, unknown to the parties, the buyer is already the owner of that which the seller purports to sell to him. The parties intended to effectuate a transfer of ownership: such a transfer is impossible: the stipulation is *naturali ratione inutilis*.

An example of this type of mistake may be seen in *Cooper* v *Phibbs* (1867) LR 2 HL 149 where an individual agreed to lease a fishery from another. Unbeknown to either party the purchaser already owned the fishery. In fact the case was not decided on common law principles at all, the court granting rescission of the contract, though Lord Atkin considered the contract to be void for *res sua* when he discussed the case in *Bell* v *Lever Bros*.

The principle so far seems very straightforward, but one must be careful not to jump to conclusions and immediately think in terms of invoking the principle. In many contracts the seller often warrants that he does have title, in which case the proper action is to sue for breach of contract. In contracts for the sale of goods, in particular, s. 12(1) of the Sale of Goods Act 1979 implies a condition that in such contracts the seller has the right to sell or that in executory contracts he will have the right to sell at the time when the property is to pass.

Mistake as to quality only arises where there is neither an implied condition nor a warranty as to title. At the same time title must be regarded as an integral part of the contract to the extent that the contract becomes meaningless without it.

Mistake as to the quality of the subject matter of the contract

The question that arises here is whether it is possible for the contract to be void on the basis that the subject matter of the contract does not have the quality it is thought to have by the parties to the contract.

The leading case on this area is that of *Bell* v *Lever Bros* [1932] AC 161, where the appellant was employed on a fixed-term contract as chairman of a subsidiary company of the respondents. The respondents decided to amalgamate the subsidiary with another company so that the appellant's services were no longer required, despite the fact that there was a substantial period of time of his contract to run. The respondents paid the appellant compensation amounting to £50,000 for the early termination of his contract. It later transpired that the appellant had been involved in certain speculative deals which would have entitled the respondents to dismiss the appellant summarily without compensation. Neither party had considered this as a possibility when the contract terminating his employment was entered into. The respondents, on discovering the truth, sought to have the contract rescinded and the monies paid returned. At first instance it was acknowledged that the appellant did not fraudulently conceal his breach of duty and did not consider it as a relevant factor when the severance agreement was being entered into. It was found that there was a mistake as to a fundamental fact that would enable the respondents to avoid the contract and recover the compensation money. The fundamental fact in question was that both parties assumed that the contract was one that could be terminated with compensation, whereas it was capable of being terminated without such compensation being payable. This decision was affirmed by the Court of Appeal who found that Lever Bros had clearly contracted under a fundamental mistake.

In the House of Lords it was held, by a majority decision that the contract was valid and binding. Lord Atkin's judgment is generally regarded as being the principal one. He concluded that 'it would be wrong to decide that an agreement to terminate a definite specified contract is void if it turns out that the contract had already been broken and could have been terminated otherwise'. He stated that Lever Bros got what they bargained for, that is, early release from the contract (the similarity of reasoning in *Saunders* v *Anglia Building Society* under *non est factum* should be noted here). He thought it was irrelevant that they could have arrived at a similar conclusion by some other means or that if they had known the true facts they would not have entered into the contract at all.

Both Lord Atkin and Lord Thankerton, who also considered there to be no mistake, went further and discussed the circumstances in which common mistake might arise. They considered that for an operative mistake to arise there had to be a mistake as to a fundamental assumption on which the contract was based and which *both* parties considered to be the basis of the agreement. As Lord Thankerton stated, mistake as to the subject matter of the contract 'can only properly relate to something which both must have necessarily accepted in their minds as an essential and integral element of the subject matter'. He considered that this test was not satisfied in the case since there was nothing to indicate that Bell regarded the validity of the original contract as vital to that of the severance contract – only Lever Bros considered this to be 'essential and integral' and therefore there was no common mistake.

Lord Atkin expressed, at least initially, an equally wide test. He stated:

> Mistake as to quality of the thing contracted for raises more difficult questions. In such a case a mistake will not affect assent unless it is the mistake of both parties, and is as to the existence of some quality which makes the thing without the quality essentially different from the thing as it was believed to be.

In isolation the test is very clear, but the waters have become muddy by the fact that this test was discussed in the context of *res extincta* and *res sua*, not mistake as to quality. Further Lord Atkin later on in his judgment produces a more restrictive test whereby the question is posed: 'Does the state of the new facts destroy the identity of the subject-matter as it was in the original state of facts?'

The inconsistencies set out have produced much debate as to whether *Bell* is authority for a separate concept of mistake as to quality or not. The fact that there was no finding as to this type of mistake in the case has caused much debate as to when this type of mistake will arise since the facts of *Bell* seem to fall within the first broad test enunciated by Lord Atkin. One hypothesis put forward by Cheshire, Fifoot and Furmston (11th edition, 1986, pp. 225–6 and repeated in the 12th edition, 1991, pp. 237–8) is that since there was no finding as to mistake as to quality in *Bell* within the tests of Lord Atkin, it follows that it is difficult to come to such a finding in any case, and that therefore the test confines mistake to that of the subject matter of the contract only: 'the only false assumption sufficiently fundamental to rank as operative mistake is the assumption that the very subject matter of the contract is in existence.'

On this basis Cheshire, Fifoot and Furmston cast doubt on whether common mistake as to the quality of the thing contracted for exists at all in law, and if it does it must be a very rare bird indeed! Further, they point to later cases as supporting their proposition, notably that of *Solle v Butcher* [1950] 1 KB 671 where the parties negotiated for the lease of a flat. There was a mistaken belief that the rent was not subject to the control of the Rent Acts and it was agreed that the rent should be fixed at £250 per annum. Later it was discovered that the flat was subject to a controlled rent of £140 per annum and the plaintiff claimed to recover the overpayments made as a result of his living in the flat for two years after entering into the contract. The defendant counter-claimed that the contract was void for mistake. It was held that the contract was not void for mistake, though it could be agreed, and was in Cheshire, Fifoot and Furmston that this was a case clearly falling within Lord Thankerton's expression of mistake as being something 'which both must necessarily have accepted in their minds as an essential and integral element of the subject matter'.

Further evidence was also produced in the form of *Leaf* v *International Galleries* [1950] 1 All ER 693. It will be recalled that in this case the parties contracted for the sale and purchase of a picture which both mistakenly believed to be by Constable. At the end of the day the plaintiff based his claim in misrepresentation, but what would the result have been if the plaintiff had claimed as to common mistake as to the quality of the thing contracted for? This case would seem to fall squarely within Lord Atkin's test, that is, 'it is the mistake of both parties, and is as to the existence of some quality which makes the thing without the quality essentially different from the thing as it was believed to be'. The Court of Appeal did not consider the facts to amount to a mistake within the definition. Almost certainly Lord Atkin would have come to a similar conclusion since in *Bell* v *Lever Bros* he set out a series of examples where he thought there would be no operative mistake. One example bore remarkable similarity to the *Leaf* case:

> A buys a picture from B; both A and B believe it to be the work of an old master, and a high price is paid. It turns out to be a modern copy. A has no remedy in the absence of representation or warranty.

Lord Atkin's argument here no doubt is that A thinks that he is buying a painting from B and that was what he got, a painting, therefore there is no mistake. Treitel however considers this to be erroneous. He also quotes an example of where A purchases a painting from B for £5 million which both believe to be a Rembrandt. On the completion of the contract if one were to ask A what he has bought he will reply that he has bought 'a Rembrandt' not 'a painting'. If it transpires that the painting is not a Rembrandt then quite clearly there is fundamental common mistake as to the quality of the thing contracted for. Treitel considers that this contract is void despite Lord Atkin's comment and the *dicta* in *Leaf* v *International Galleries*.

The debate above has been the subject of much scrutiny by Steyn J in *Associated Japanese Bank (International) Ltd* v *Crédit du Nord SA* [1988] 3 All ER 902 in which the facts were that a fraudster, Jack Bennett, entered into a sale and lease-back transaction with the plaintiff bank. The bank agreed to buy four precision engineering machines for £1 million and then to lease them back to him, but before doing so required a guarantor, the defendant bank agreeing to this position. The whole arrangement was a fraud by Jack Bennett since the machines did not exist at all, and on receiving the £1 million he disappeared and made no attempt to keep up the repayments. The plaintiff bank then attempted to enforce the guarantee against the defendants. The defendants claimed that the transaction was void since it was based on four specific pieces of equipment which both believed to exist but which in reality did not.

On the face of things this appears to be a case based on *res extincta* and has all the hallmarks of the *McRae* case since Jack Bennett was actually guaranteeing that the machines existed, as did the Commission with regard to the tanker in *McRae*. In the *Associated Japanese Bank* case, however, the party alleging the mistake, the defendants, were not guaranteeing the existence of the machines. They had entered the guarantee contract on the basis that the machines did in fact exist, a conclusion which they had apparently reached from their discussions with Bennett. The subject matter of the contract was not therefore the machines themselves but the obligations undertaken by Bennett and in particular his representation that the machines actually existed. Steyn J concluded that the question to be asked was whether the subject matter of the guarantee was essentially different from what it was reasonably believed to be. He concluded that 'for both parties the guarantee of obligations under a lease with non-existent machines was essentially different from a guarantee of a lease with four machines which both parties at the time of the contract believed to exist' and dismissed the claim.

Steyn J in the course of his judgment made a close examination of *Bell* v *Lever Bros* and of the proposition set out in Cheshire, Fifoot and Furmston. He considered the analysis by the latter to be 'too simplistic' and that the actual decision in *Bell* was founded on the particular facts of the case. He considered that the courts should attempt to uphold rather than destroy apparent contracts although this did not preclude the possibility of mistake. With regard to a plea of mistake he stated that for it to be operative in this context it had to be a mistake of both the parties and given this the judgments of Atkin and Thankerton LJJ were to be regarded as the *ratio decidendi* of *Bell*. He considered that mistake as to quality could produce a nullity in a contract but confined it to the test enunciated by Lord Atkin, that is that a 'mistake will not affect assent unless it is . . . as to the existence of some quality essentially different from the thing as it was believed to be'. At the end of the day, however, Steyn J considered that the tests for common mistake as to the subject matter and that of common mistake as to quality could be reduced to one single principle: 'the mistake must render the subject matter of the contract essentially and radically different from the subject matter which the parties believed to exist.' The use of the term 'subject matter' here apparently encompassed both type of mistake.

Steyn J added a final qualification in that a party seeking to rely on the mistake had to show that he had reasonable grounds for his belief that gave rise to the mistake. This qualification is useful since it produces an approach that is consistent with that of equity, where the fault of either party precludes the quality of equitable relief.

Consensus mistake

It has already been stated that this type of mistake arises because there is a mistake as to the terms of the contract. The effect of this is to preclude an agreement from arising, that is, there is a lack of *consensus ad idem*. There are two basic categories, mutual mistakes and unilateral mistakes, though prima facie these types of mistake do not render the contract void unless the mistake induces the contract and constitutes a mistake of fact which is fundamental to the contract.

Mutual mistake

This type of mistake occurs where the parties are at cross purposes where, to use the example given above, A is offering one thing whilst B is accepting something else. It is clear in such a circumstance that the contract is void because the offer and acceptance of A and B respectively do not coincide.

An example of the above principles can be seen in the case of *Raffles* v *Wichelhaus* (1864) 2 H&C 906 where the defendants had agreed to purchase '125 bales of Surat cotton . . . to arrive ex *Peerless* from Bombay . . .'. From the agreement it appeared that the defendants thought they were purchasing a cargo of cotton from the SS *Peerless* which had set sail from Bombay in October. In fact the plaintiffs thought they had sold a cargo of cotton on another ship called the SS *Peerless* which had set sail from Bombay in December. It was held that the contract was void for a fundamental mistake of fact that had prevented the formation of agreement – the offer and acceptance of the parties had failed to coincide.

In order to establish a mutual mistake one has to show that there is such a degree of ambiguity that it is impossible, on applying the objective test of a reasonable man, that the parties intended to be bound by one set of terms or the other. If, on an objective view, the parties could only have come to a single, common understanding of the terms of the contract then they will be bound by the contract, despite the actual view of a party that he was mistaken as to the terms. The test was expressed by Blackburn J in *Smith* v *Hughes* (1871) LR 6 QB 597. He stated:

> If whatever a man's real intention may be, he so conducts himself that a reasonable man would believe that he was assenting to the terms proposed by the other party, and that other party upon that belief enters into a contract with him, the man thus conducting himself would be equally bound as if he intended to agree to the other party's terms.

The application of the objective test approach can be plainly seen when the case of *Scriven Bros & Co* v *Hindley & Co* [1913] 3 KB 564 is compared with that of *Smith* v *Hughes* (above). In the former case the defendants wanted to purchase a quantity of hemp being sold at auction by the plaintiffs. Two lots were put up for sale from the same ship, however, one lot consisted of hemp and one of tow, though the identification marks on the bales were precisely the same. Closer examination would have revealed the distinction, but the defendant, having inspected the first lot and found it to contain hemp, immediately mistakenly considered that the other lot also contained hemp. The auction catalogue itself did not reveal the distinction and as a result the defendant paid a high price for a lot thought to contain hemp but in fact containing tow, which would normally have attracted a far lower price. The auctioneer at the time of the sale realised that the defendants had made a mistake, but one which related to the market value of tow rather than as to the nature of the lot *per se*. The defendants refused to pay, alleging mutual mistake. On applying the objective test the court found that one could not state with any degree of certainty which commodity formed the basis of the contract since it was clear that a reasonable person would have been misled as to the nature of each lot. The contract was thus held to be void for mistake.

In *Smith* v *Hughes* the defendant, a racehorse owner, wished to purchase a quantity of oats. A sample of the oats was inspected and the defendant agreed to purchase the whole amount. When the oats were delivered it was discovered they were 'green', that is, that season's oats. The defendant refused to pay for them, saying he thought he was buying 'old', or the last season's oats. When sued for the price the defendant argued that the contract was void for mistake. The court held that on an objective test basis there was a valid contract. On a finding of fact the seller had not misrepresented the oats as being old nor was there any suggestion that there was a term of the contract to this effect. The purchaser could not establish mistake on the basis of the fact that he had been careless and as a result misled himself as to the nature of the oats.

A further matter that may be seen to operate in these two cases is that of negligence. It is possible to discern a line of authority that appears to present evidence of an underlying policy that the courts will find for mistake, or, as the case may be, because of the negligence of one of the protagonists to the contract. Thus in the *Scriven* case the contract was held to be void, not only on the basis of a lack of consensus, but also because the mistake was in effect promoted by the inaccurate or incomplete description attached to the two lots in the catalogue. In the *Smith* case, however, the purchaser, who was no doubt mistaken as to what he thought he was purchasing, was nevertheless held to his bargain, bad though it was, because his mistake was carelessly self-induced. Certainly in the latter case this line of reasoning conforms to the common law notion of *caveat emptor* and is seen in the judgment of Cockburn CJ when he states:

> I take the true rule to be, that where a specific article is offered for sale, without express warranty, or without circumstances from which the law will imply a warranty . . . and the buyer has full opportunity of inspecting and forming his own judgment, if he chooses to act on his own judgment, the rule *caveat emptor* applies . . . The buyer persuaded himself they were old oats, when they were not so . . . He was himself to blame.

In both cases, carelessness precludes the rights of a party from arising and must therefore be regarded as a relevant consideration in applying the objective test as to whether he has entered into a contract or not.

Unilateral mistake

In this type of mistake the objective test discussed above is replaced with a subjective one since we are concerned here with a situation in which one party is actually aware of the other party's mistake. This type of mistake arises directly out of the classical analysis of contract in that where one party contracts on the basis of a mistake as to the nature of a promise made by the other party and that other party is aware of the mistake of the first, the contract is void for there is no conjoining link between the offer and the acceptance of the parties concerned.

It should be noted carefully that for this type of mistake to operate there must be a fundamental mistake as to the nature of the promise made by the other party – a mistake as to quality will not suffice. The mistake must also be one which induces the other party to enter into the contract. It should also be borne in mind that, as with other types of mistake, the overwhelming presumption is to find for the existence of a valid and binding contract. It is for the person seeking to avoid the contract to rebut this presumption. This burden or proof is indeed an onerous one and the reported instances of this being done are few and far between.

The instances of unilateral mistake fall into two categories, mistake as to the terms of the contract and mistake as to the identity of the person contracted with.

(a) *Mistake as to the terms of the contract.* Such a mistake will arise where one party makes an offer to another and he is aware that that other person is fundamentally mistaken as to the nature of the promise contained in the offer. An example is the case of *Hartog* v *Colin and Shields* [1939] 3 All ER 566 where the defendant mistakenly offered to sell a number of hareskins, the price to be determined at a certain sum per pound, an offer which the plaintiffs accepted. In fact, preliminary negotiations had been concluded on the basis that the skins would be sold at a certain sum per piece, which accorded with normal trade usage. The plaintiffs attempted to enforce the contract on the basis of a price per pound since this was financially advantageous to them. It was held the plaintiffs could not do so since they must have known when they accepted the offer that the defendant had made a mistake.

It should be stated that this type of mistake is now very rare indeed. The common law rule of *caveat emptor* and the development of statutory provisions relating to consumer protection have substantially reduced the need to plead this type of mistake.

(b) *Mistake as to the identity of the person contracted with.* A contract may become a nullity where a party is mistaken as to the identity of the person contracted with and the other party is aware of that mistake. It should be stressed that the question of the other party's identity must be of fundamental importance to the innocent party for the type of mistake to operate. It is a question of fact as to whether the identity of the other party is fundamental or not. It is for the person seeking to have the contract set aside for mistake to rebut this presumption. As with other types of mistake the presumption is that there exists a valid contract between the parties to the contract.

The last point is particularly important in this type of mistake, which is perhaps the most common of all alleged mistakes. Related to this point is the fact that the courts have in mind the protection of third parties who may be adversely affected by the finding of a contract being void *ab initio* for mistake, as was indicated at the start of this chapter. The courts, however, are often faced with a conflict of interest since frequently the problem of identity arises because a rogue misrepresents his identity to obtain goods from the innocent party. The balance that the courts have to make between mistake as to identity, fraudulent misrepresentation and the rights of innocent third parties produces some interesting results.

The typical situation that arises occurs where A accepts an offer to buy goods from B, who pretends that he is X. B, having obtained the goods now sells them to an innocent third party, Z. At this point B usually disappears although, even if he can be traced, any rights that A has against him are very often worthless since such rogues are usually 'men of straw'. A's action will therefore be framed in terms of an action in the tort of conversion against Z, alleging that he, A, has a better title to the goods than Z. In order to prove his case A will attempt to prove that the contract with B is void *ab initio* for mistake as to identity. If A is able to do this then it follows that B never acquired good title to the goods, in which case he cannot convey good title to Z – *nemo dat quod non habet* – so Z will have to surrender the goods to A. Z's action here will lie against B for breach of the implied conditions to title under s. 12 of the Sale of Goods Act 1979.

If A is unable to prove that the contract is void for mistake as to identity he will generally be able to show that there is a fraudulent misrepresentation on the part of B. As we have already seen (in Chapter 9), this renders the contract voidable. In these circumstances timing becomes crucial, since here A must take steps to show that he intends to rescind the contract as soon as he has discovered the deception perpetrated upon him. Invariably he will be seeking to rescind out of court and, as already indicated in *Car and Universal Finance Co Ltd* v *Caldwell* [1964] 1 All ER 290 (also discussed in the last chapter), he may display such intention by informing the police, for instance. If A manages to avoid the contract *before* B sells the goods to Z then the same situation as for mistake exists, since ownership in the goods will revert to A and B will not have any title to convey to Z, who again will have to surrender the goods to A. If, however, A only rescinds the contract *after* B has sold the goods to Z, then up to this point B will have had good title to the goods which he will have transferred to Z. In such a case A will be unable to recover the goods from Z and would have to sue B for breach of contract for non-payment which, as has already been noted, is not usually worth while. In any event A should consider tracing the proceeds of the sale to the bank accounts or some other fund of B, assuming he has one! Tracing would give A a procedural advantage since if B has other creditors the effect of a tracing order will be to give A priority over other creditors. The right to trace will be lost if the fund has been dissipated, though here it may be possible to trace in equity. It should also be borne in mind that A may be able to trace against Z even in these circumstances if he can show that Z was not a *bona fide* purchaser in that he knew of the defective title of B.

In order to prove unilateral mistake as to identity, the person alleging mistake must prove *each* of the following:

(a) an intention to deal with some other person;
(b) that the other party knew of this intention;
(c) that the identity was of fundamental importance;
(d) that reasonable steps had been taken to verify the identity.

One has to show that there was **an intention to deal with some other person** than the one with whom he appears to have made the contract. In other words, it has to be shown that there is confusion between two identities.

The point is well illustrated by the case of *King's Norton Metal Co Ltd* v *Edridge, Merrett & Co Ltd* (1897) 14 TLR 98. In the case a rogue by the name of Wallis set up a business under the name of Hallam & Co with the sole purpose of defrauding the plaintiffs. He had letterheads drawn up and printed which depicted the firm as being one of some substance; he then obtained goods from the plaintiffs after sending an order on one of the letterheaded notepapers. Wallis then sold the goods to the defendants, who bought them in good faith. The plaintiffs now sued the defendants alleging that the contract with Hallam & Co was void for mistake and that no title could be conveyed to the defendants. It was held that their action should fail since there was no mistake as to identity – they had intended to contract with Hallam & Co and that was who they had in fact contracted with. The plaintiffs failed to show that there was some other person with whom they had intended to do business; the court therefore rejected their claim.

The mistaken party must prove that **the other party was aware of the above intention.** Usually there is little problem in proving this since, where mistake as to identity is pleaded it is usually the result of a fraud being perpetrated on the mistaken party. It is clear that one cannot present oneself as a party to a contract knowing that the other party had no intention of entering into a contract with that person. It follows from this that an offer can only be accepted by the party to whom it is addressed.

The case of *Boulton* v *Jones* (1957) 2 H & N 564 illustrates the point and provides a rare example of a case in which no fraudulent misrepresentation arose. The facts were that the plaintiff, Boulton, had bought the business belonging to Brocklehurst. The defendant, Jones, had formerly dealt with Brocklehurst with whom he had a running account. One feature of the business relationship between Jones and Brocklehurst was that Jones could set against the account monies owed to him by Brocklehurst. Jones sent an order for goods from Brocklehurst but on the day the order was received the business was sold to Boulton, who executed the order. When Jones was presented with the bill he refused to pay since he had intended the order to go to Brocklehurst so that he could set off against the value of the order, monies owed to him by Brocklehurst. It was held that Jones was not liable for the price.

The actual basis for the decision in *Boulton* v *Jones* is ambiguous in that it could be based on either unilateral or mutual mistake. If the decision is based on unilateral mistake then it is undoubtedly correct, but if based on mutual mistake then it is highly questionable. In mutual mistake the finding of mistake in the contract is assessed in objective terms rather than subjectively as in unilateral mistake. Translated into a test the question that has to be asked is whether the reasonable man in the position of the offeree would have considered the offer to be intended for him, *not* whether the offeror intended to deal with the person to whom the offer was made. On this basis a reasonable man would no doubt have concluded that the identity of the seller was a matter of indifference to the purchaser. Such a conclusion would result in there being no *operative* mistake, and thus Jones would have been bound by the contract despite the fact that he could prove that he had made a mistake. The point is affirmed in *Upton on Severn RDC* v *Powell* [1942] 1 All ER 220.

In order to prove mistake the party alleging it must show that at the time of contracting **the identity of the person he was dealing with was of fundamental and crucial importance to him**. This is not easy to prove since the mistaken party clearly has to produce evidence of the fact from his conduct before or at the time of contracting. In these circumstances such individuals are generally mistaken more as to the attributes of the person they are dealing with, such as his creditworthiness, rather than as to his identity. Further it should be noted that it is usually easier to prove this where the parties contract *inter absentes,* for example by post. Where the parties contract *inter praesentes*, for example in a shop, the presumption is that the mistaken party intends to deal with the person before him whoever he is and very strong evidence indeed is required to rebut the presumption.

If we look at cases involving alleged mistake, *inter absentes* first of all, in the case of *King's Norton Metal Co*, the facts of which have already been discussed, it is clear that the party alleging mistake was not mistaken as to the identity of the person they had contracted with. They were merely mistaken as to the creditworthiness of that party. They thought they were contracting with a solvent and substantial business as portrayed on the letterhead not some insolvent rogue. They were ready and willing to deal with anyone and were concerned not as to the identity *per se* but as to whether they would get paid on the contract.

The case can be contrasted with that of *Cundy v Lindsay* (1878) 3 App Cas 459 where a rogue set up a business by the name of Blenkarn at 37 Wood Street and sent an order for goods to the plaintiffs. The order was signed by the rogue in such a way that it looked like the name Blenkiron and Co which traded at 123 Wood Street, a firm which the plaintiffs knew to be highly respectable. The plaintiffs accepted the order and despatched them to 'Messrs Blenkiron and Co, 37 Wood Street'. The rogue, having received the goods, sold them to the defendants, who took the goods in good faith. The plaintiffs now attempted to recover the goods from the defendants in conversion. The House of Lords held that they would succeed in their action in that they had intended only to contract with Blenkiron and Co and nobody else and that the identity of the person they were to contract with was of fundamental and crucial importance at the time of entering into the contract. The position was summed up by Lord Cairns:

> I ask the question, how is it possible to imagine that in that state of things any contract could have arisen between the Respondents and Blenkarn the dishonest man? Of him they knew nothing, and of him they never thought. With him they never intended to deal. Their minds never even for an instant of time rested on him, and as between him and them there was no consensus of mind which could lead to any agreement or any contract whatsoever.

In *Cundy v Lindsay* there was clearly confusion as to which two distinct entities had been contracted with. In the *King's Norton* case this was not apparent since there existed only one entity, Hallam & Co. On this basis, then, to establish mistake it is not enough for the party alleging mistake merely to show that he did not intend to contract with a particular individual. He must show also that he intended instead to contract with some other person capable of being identified, though it may be questionable whether this person must actually exist or whether he may remain completely fictitious.

Turning our attention to cases where the parties are *inter praesentes* we find, as already indicated, that it is particularly difficult to refute the presumption that the party alleging mistake intended to deal with the person in front of him. As a result, successful actions are fairly rare.

One of the early cases exemplifying this problem is that of *Phillips v Brooks Ltd* [1919] 2 KB 243. The facts of the case were that a rogue named North entered the jewellery shop owned by the plaintiff and selected some pearls valued at £2,500 and a ring valued at £450. He then proceeded to write out a cheque and as he did so stated, 'You see who I am, I am Sir George Bullough', giving an address in St James' Square. The plaintiff had heard of Sir George Bullough and on checking the telephone directory confirmed the address given. The plaintiff then asked if he would like to take the articles with him, to which the rogue replied, 'You had better have the cheque cleared first, but I should like to take the ring, as it is my wife's birthday tomorrow'. The plaintiff let North take the ring, and North then pawned it to the defendant who took it in good faith. The plaintiff on discovering the fraud now sued the pawnbroker defendant in conversion alleging that the contract was void for mistake. It was of course imperative that he successfully establish mistake since otherwise the contract would only be voidable for fraudulent misrepresentation, in which case the contract would be valid until disaffirmed and rescinded by the jeweller. In such a case the plaintiff would not be able to recover the ring from the jeweller since the rescission would have come after the goods and the ownership to them were transferred to the pawnbroker, thereby leaving the plaintiff with a worthless claim against the rogue North.

It was held that whilst the jeweller believed he was dealing with Sir George Bullough he would in fact have contracted with anyone present in the shop. Evidence of this decision can be seen in the fact that the contract had already been completed when the question of identity arose. The rogue had selected the items and offered to buy them. The plaintiff had accepted the offer and the rogue was writing out the cheque in payment for the goods when the question of identity arose. The identity of the person in front of the jeweller was not of fundamental or of crucial importance before or at the time of contracting. The jeweller thus failed in his action in conversion against the defendant.

Two other cases also illustrate the problems that arise in this context. The first is that of *Ingram v Little* [1960] 3 All ER 332, where two sisters jointly owned a car which they advertised for sale. A rogue called and agreed with one of the sisters to purchase the car for £717. When he proffered a cheque for the amount the sister adamantly refused to accept it, whereupon the rogue stated that he was P. G. M. Hutchinson and that he had substantial business interests. Whilst the discussions were taking place the other sister checked the name and address of P. G. M. Hutchinson in the telephone directory which seemed to corroborate his story. The sisters then agreed to let him have the car and accept his cheque. The cheque was subsequently dishonoured and the rogue, who was of course not P. G. M. Hutchinson, sold the car to a third party who purchased the vehicle in good faith. The plaintiffs sued the defendant in conversion alleging that the contract was void for mistake as to the identity and succeeded. The case however is largely regarded as being at best decided on the facts of the particular case and at worst, wrongly decided. It is suggested that in fact the latter is the only appropriate description of the case. It has been clearly established that the mistake as to identity must be of fundamental or crucial importance before or at the time of contracting to be operative. In this case the contract was complete, the sale agreed, and it was only when the rogue proffered a cheque that the question of identity arose. There may have been a dispute as to the mode of payment but identity was not at issue until this point.

The second case is that of *Lewis v Averay* [1971] 3 All ER 907 where the facts were very similar to those of *Ingram v Little*. Here again the plaintiff was the owner of a car that he wished to sell, and to do so he advertised it in the local newspaper. A rogue arranged to see the car and on doing so offered to buy it at the stated price. The plaintiff accepted the offer and the rogue then wrote out a cheque signing it 'R. A. Green'. The rogue asked if he could take the car straightaway but at this the plaintiff became hesitant and did not want to part with the car until the cheque had cleared. The plaintiff asked the rogue whether he had some evidence as to his identity. The rogue produced a pass to Pinewood Studios as proof that he was Richard Greene the well-known actor. The plaintiff on examining the pass allowed the rogue to take the car. The rogue then sold the car to an innocent third party and the cheque was subsequently dishonoured. The plaintiff then claimed the goods from the third party in conversion on the basis that the contract between himself and the rogue was void for mistake as to identity.

The Court of Appeal held that his action must fail since the plaintiff intended to deal with the person in front of him irrespective of his identity and that the contract was subsequently only voidable for fraudulent misrepresentation. Since the plaintiff had only disaffirmed the contract after the third party had purchased the car, the third party acquired a good title in the vehicle. Megaw LJ based his decision on the traditional analysis that the identity of the rogue was not of fundamental and crucial importance before or at the time of contracting and only became relevant when the rogue paid by cheque and wanted the car immediately. Lord Denning MR arrived at the same decision though on a somewhat different basis. He considered that the fine distinction between identity and attributes, or creditworthiness, and the time when the identity became important was to miss the point of the principle of mistake, which was ultimately to protect innocent third party purchasers. He considered that the effect of mistake as to identity was not to render the contract void but merely voidable, 'that is, liable to be set aside at the instance of the mistaken person, so long as he does so before third parties have in good faith acquired rights under it'. There would appear to be considerable merit in such an approach since the cases clearly tend to reflect this situation in any event.

A rather more modern case that deals with the distinction between identity and attributes is that of *Citibank NA* v *Brown Shipley & Co Ltd*; Midland Bank v *Brown Shipley & Co Ltd* [1991] 2 All ER 690. Here a rogue claimed to be a signatory on a company account held with the plaintiff bank. The rogue telephoned the defendant bank and asked to purchase some foreign currency which he would pay for by a banker's draft drawn on the company account held by the plaintiff. The rogue then telephoned the plaintiff requesting the banker's draft, which it handed to a 'messenger' whom the plaintiff thought was from the company.

In exchange for the draft, a forged letter of authority was given. The draft was then paid to the defendant who, after confirming that the draft had in fact been issued by the plaintiff in the ordinary course of business, paid the cash to the rogue. In due course the defenant presented the draft to the plaintiff bank and was subsequently paid. When the fraud was eventually discovered, the plaintiff bank brought an action to recover the value of the draft from the defendant. The action was based on the allegation that title had never passed to the defendant bank as it could not derive a good title from the rogue and that there was no contract between the two banks. The court held that the fact that the plaintiff had mistakenly dealt with a rogue instead of the company which the plaintiff bank thought they were dealing with did not prevent the formation of a contract between the two banks. The court agreed that the rogue had no title because of mistaken identity but they found that he was a 'mere conduit'. Title did not pass from the rogue to the defendant. The important factor was the identity of the paying bank, the defendant, and that there was no mistake here.

The party alleging mistake must last of all show that he has taken **reasonable steps to attempt to verify the identity** of the person with whom he is about to contract. This requirement must be shown whether or not the contract is made *inter absentes* or *inter praesentes*.

MISTAKE IN EQUITY

It has been seen that the effect of mistake at common law is to render the contract void *ab initio*, whereas mistake in equity has the effect of merely rendering the contract voidable. Furthermore equity is generally prepared to come to such a conclusion despite the fact that the common law itself might refuse to intervene. The circumstances in which equity grants relief tend to be categorised, not on the nature of the mistake *per se*, but according to the manner of the relief that is within the discretion of the court.

Rescission

This remedy is available widely outside the sphere of mistake, as may be seen in relation to misrepresentation. As with all equitable remedies its award is discretionary and it thus follows that the courts can apply rescission subject to any terms they feel appropriate in order to fulfil the principle of *restitutio in integrum*. It may also be used where the contract has been held to be void and an order of the court is required to place the parties back in their original positions, as has already been seen in *Cooper v Phibbs*, the facts of which have already been discussed above. In that case the court in deciding to grant rescission considered that *restitutio in integrum* could only be achieved by making the order of rescission subject to the respondents having a lien over the fishery to the value they had spent improving it.

In the case of *Cooper v Phibbs*, Lord Westbury commented:

> If parties contract under a mutual mistake [sic] and misapprehension as to their respective rights, the result is that the agreement is liable to be set aside as having been proceeded upon a common mistake.

The effect of the case is thus often upheld as providing a general authority for the use of rescission in cases of a common and material mistake irrespective of the presence of *res extincta* or *res sua*.

The case of *Huddersfield Banking Co Ltd v Henry Lister & Son Ltd* [1895] 2 Ch 273 also provides authority for this proposition. In that case the defendant's company had mortgaged its mills and the fixtures contained in them to the bank. Eventually the company went into insolvent liquidation. The bank claimed that it was entitled to 35 looms in the mills on the basis that since these were bolted to the floor they represented fixtures and thus fell within their security for the loans. If this was the case they could not fall into the hands of the Official Receiver to be sold to pay off the general creditors. On touring the factory premises, the agent of the bank and of the liquidator found that the looms were not in fact bolted to the floor and thus fell outside the fixtures capable of being claimed by the bank. The bank therefore gave a consent order for the looms to be sold. It then became apparent that the looms had in fact been bolted to the floor but had been wrongfully disconnected by some unauthorised person. The bank immediately applied for the consent order to be rescinded. The court held that the order had been made on the basis of a common and mutual mistake and gave an order for rescission. Lord Kay stated:

> It seems to me that, both on principle and on authority, when once the Court finds that an agreement has been come to between parties who were under a common mistake of a material fact, the Court may set it aside, and the Court has ample jurisdiction to set aside the order founded upon that agreement.

A similar decision was arrived at in *Solle* v *Butcher* [1950] 1 KB 671 where, as we have already seen, the contract was not held to be void for common mistake at common law. In equity however it was decided that the lease should be set aside. If equity had allowed the contract to be void, as in common law, this would clearly have resulted in an inequitable solution as far as the tenant was concerned since he would be dispossessed of his lease. The court thus offered him a choice of either surrendering the lease or continuing it but on the basis of paying the full rent allowable, which would have been £250 once statutory notices allowing for the increase had been served. The decision was similar in *Grist* v *Bailey* [1966] All ER 875 where the mistake, whilst not being fundamental enough to render the contract void at common law, was sufficiently fundamental to render the contract voidable in equity.

The problem with the above cases is that they are difficult to reconcile with the case of *Bell* v *Lever Bros*, where the contract was held to be valid and binding rather than void at common law or voidable in equity. Following the case of *Associated Japanese Bank (International) Ltd* v *Crédit du Nord* it may be possible to find that in *Bell* the case should have been void at common law. Failing this, why should it not have been held to be voidable in equity?

The latter point was considered in the case of *Magee* v *Pennine Insurance Co Ltd* [1969] 2 All ER 891 in which the plaintiff bought a car on hire purchase terms for his son. At the time of purchase a proposal form for the insurance of the vehicle was filled out by the manager, who made several errors amounting to innocent misrepresentation. Some time later the car was written off in an accident and the plaintiff claimed £600, though he agreed to accept a lesser sum of £385 after negotiations with the defendant. The defendant then discovered the misrepresentations and claimed to repudiate the agreement. The majority of the Court of Appeal found that the agreement had been reached on the basis of a common mistake though not one that was so fundamental as to render the contract void at common law, as in *Bell* v *Lever Bros*. The court however considered that the mistake was sufficiently fundamental to render the contract voidable in equity, though no terms were imposed on the parties. Lord Winn dissented and considered the case no different from *Bell* v *Lever Bros* and as such it should be regarded as binding. Lord Denning MR reconciled the decision in *Magee* with *Bell* by stating that there was an underlying doctrine of equity, that was never expressly referred to in *Bell*, that allowed equity a discretion to set a contract aside on the basis of a common mistake as to quality. Such a proposition is somewhat radical given the stature of the judges sitting in the *Bell* case since, if such a doctrine existed, then surely such judges would have referred to it. The view put forward by many commentators is that such a doctrine is a figment of Denning's lively and radical legal imagination.

So far we have been considering the effect of rescission in the context of shared mistakes, that is, those arising in both mutual mistake and common mistake. In assessing the intervention of equity in unilateral mistake in relation to the exercise of rescission, we find that there also arises a level of doubt as to the circumstances in which equity will exercise its discretion. One view is that such discretion should only be exercised where there has been some misrepresentation or fraudulent conduct by the other party. Another view is that rescission is available in a unilateral mistake where the other party is guilty of conduct that would make any insistence on his part that the contract be performed inequitable.

The Court of Appeal decision in *Riverplate Properties Ltd* v *Paul* [1975] Ch 133 tended to suggest the first narrower approach and held that equitable relief was not available simply on the ground of unilateral mistake unless the party against whom relief was being sought knew that the other party had contracted under a mistake. The case tended to lean against the establishment of a general doctrine of equitable relief in mistake, whereby the court would exercise its discretionary jurisdiction where the circumstances of the case and justice demanded it. Such a proposition was suggested in *Solle* v *Butcher* by Lord Denning when he stated:

> It is now clear that a contract will be set aside if the mistake of one party has been induced by a material misrepresentation of the other, even though it was not fraudulent or fundamental; or if one party, knowing that the other is mistaken about the terms of the offer, or the identity of the person by whom it is made, lets him remain under his delusion and concludes a contract on the mistaken terms instead of pointing out the mistake . . . A contract is also liable in equity to be set aside if the parties were under a common misapprehension either as to facts or as to their relative and respective rights, provided that the misapprehension was fundamental, and that the party seeking to set it aside was not himself at fault.

Until the House of Lords has the opportunity of thoroughly reviewing the subject and Denning's proposals it is difficult to state precisely when the equitable discretion will be exercised. It is, however, fair to say that Denning's proposals provide a degree of flexibility that is highly desirable when balancing the interests of the contracting parties together with those of third parties. Indeed in the *Associated Japanese Bank* case, Steyn J stated that:

> a narrow doctrine of common law mistake (as enunciated in *Bell* v *Lever Bros Ltd*), supplemented by the more flexible doctrine of mistake in equity (as developed in *Solle* v *Butcher* and later cases), seems to me to be an entirely sensible and satisfactory state of the law . . .

It is suggested that this is the way forward and indeed in *William Sindall plc* v *Cambridgeshire County Council* [1994] 1 WLR 1016, Evans LJ considered that there must be: 'a category of mistake which is "fundamental", so as to permit the equitable remedy of rescission, which is wider than the kind of "serious and radical" mistake which means that the agreement is void and of no effect in law'. He suggested that the difference between these two types of mistake lies in the fact that mistake at common law is confined to those types of mistake that have regard to the subject matter of the contract. Mistake in equity, however, he considered to be a wider concept that arose where the mistake was sufficiently 'fundamental' as regards a material fact and that this category appeared to have unlimited application.

Before leaving rescission it needs to be stated that the remedy will be lost where a party fails to apply for it within a reasonable time, or where the granting of rescission would have the effect of depriving a third party of his rights in the subject matter; or where *restitutio in integrum* is impossible.

Rectification

The equitable remedy of rectification arises where a written document does not represent the agreement reached between the parties. As in all equitable remedies the exercise of it by the courts is discretionary. It should be noted that the remedy does not lie where there is a mistake as to the subject matter of the contract but where there is an error on the face of the record. It is thus erroneous to talk in terms of rectification of a contract since the remedy only allows alteration of the instrument reflecting the contract.

In order to obtain rectification, three conditions have to be satisfied:

(a) the instrument that the application is made to rectify must have failed to reflect the agreement of the parties. It follows that if one party considers that the instrument reflects his intentions but the other does not, then rectification is unavailable;

(b) the party seeking rectification has to provide evidence that the instrument does not reflect the common intention of the parties at the time of contracting;

(c) there must be a literal disparity between what was agreed and what was recorded. It follows from this that the terms of the agreement must have remained static to the time the instrument was executed. This does not mean that the prior agreement must have amounted to a binding contract. Thus in *Joscelyne* v *Nissen* [1970] 2 QB 86 the plaintiff sought to have the written contract, whereby he made over his car-hire business to his daughter, rectified. It had been expressly agreed that in return for the business she would pay certain coal, gas and electricity bills. This agreement was not contained in the written document and when the daughter failed to pay these bills the plaintiff sought a declaration that she should do so and that the written document should be rectified to this effect. It was held that the agreement should be rectified despite the fact that prior to the written contract being executed there had been no binding contract concluded. Further the father could show that up to the contract being executed both parties were agreed that the daughter would pay the bills.

Originally rectification could only apply to shared mistakes since the remedy depended on the fact that the written record failed to reflect the intentions of both parties. In *A. Roberts & Co Ltd* v *Leicestershire CC* [1961] 2 All ER 545 however, it was held that the remedy could be used where a plaintiff could show that a term, beneficial to himself, which both parties had intended to be included in the document, had been omitted and that the other party was aware of the omission at the time of the document being executed. This latter point has recently been reinforced in *Agip SpA* v *Navigazione Alta Italia SpA* [1984] 1 Lloyd's Rep 353.

Refusal of specific performance

If a person refuses to perform his side of the bargain it is open to the other party to apply to a court of equity for a decree of specific performance to compel that person to carry out his contractual obligations. Since this remedy, like the others, was discretionary, the court would refuse to grant such a decree where the common law remedy of damages was regarded as adequate redress, as it very often was, except where the goods could be regarded as unique goods. Specific performance could, however, also be refused where one of the parties has contracted under such a mistake that it would be regarded as inequitable to compel him to carry out his contractual obligations. The effect of this then is to prevent a contract being enforced in circumstances where a mistake is insufficient to render the contract void *ab initio* at common law.

In *Webster* v *Cecil* (1861) 30 Beav 62 the plaintiff was offered several plots of land by the defendant for £1,250. Soon after sending the offer the defendant realised that he should have stated the price as £2,250 and informed the plaintiff immediately. Unfortunately his revocation arrived too late as the plaintiff had already accepted the offer. The court refused to give the plaintiff a decree of specific performance since it decided that he must have been aware of the defendant's mistake as he (the defendant) had already refused an offer of £2,000 from the plaintiff.

MISTAKE AS TO THE NATURE OF THE DOCUMENT SIGNED

This category of mistake forms a separate and distinct category of mistake at common law. Cases arising in this type of mistake might occur where a person is induced by a false statement made by some other person to sign a written contract that is fundamentally different from the one he thought he was signing. Whilst the person inducing the signing may well be a party to the contract it might be the case that he is a third party to the contract, for instance, where X by some fundamental statement induces Y to sign a guarantee of Y's indebtedness to X's bank, Z. If Z attempts to enforce the guarantee against Y, Y may attempt to avoid liability on the basis of mistake as to the nature of the document signed. It is obvious here that X is not a party to the contract between Y and Z. It is this feature that separates this type of mistake from the others.

Traditionally this type of mistake was often referred to as *non est factum*, literally translated as 'it is not my deed'. The rule originated as a limited defence to the proposition that a person was bound by any document signed by that person, as we have seen in *L'Estrange* v *Graucob* in Chapter 7. In fact the rule developed in medieval times when few people could read or write and were thus dependent on others accurately to describe the contents and meaning of a deed. Thus if the terms of a deed were read or explained in such a way that the deed did not in fact represent the true intention of the signor, he could escape liability on the basis that he would not have signed had the true situation been revealed to him.

The growth of literacy as educational opportunities increased raised serious doubts as to whether the plea continued to exist. In the nineteenth century, however, the scope of the plea was widened to include persons who had been tricked into signing a document which they would not have signed had they understood its true nature. The scope of the plea thus widened to include persons who were of low intelligence or mentally infirm, as well as blind persons. Persons of full capacity and literacy cannot generally rely on *non est factum*.

The modern leading authority on *non est factum* is *Saunders* v *Anglia Building Society* [1970] 3 All ER 961 (formerly known as *Gallie* v *Lee*), where the plaintiff was an elderly widow who had decided to give the title deeds of her house to her nephew, so that he could use the property as security for a loan in order to go into business. The widow made one stipulation, which was that, whatever he did she would be allowed to live in the house for the rest of her life. A document was prepared by a friend of the nephew's, Lee, who was a dishonest managing clerk, whereby the property was to be assigned to the nephew. In fact the document prepared by Lee was a deed of conveyance giving effect to a sale of the property to Lee for £3,000, though this sum was never paid. At the time the deed was signed by Mrs Gallie. She had broken her glasses and thus relied on Lee's explanation of the nature of the document. Lee then mortgaged the property to the building society but never repaid any of the mortgage instalments.

On discovering the truth of the matter the plaintiff sought a declaration that the conveyance of the property was void on the ground of *non est factum*. She alleged that she had signed the document under a fundamental mistake as to its nature. She thought that she was signing a deed of gift to her nephew, whilst what she in fact signed was a deed of conveyance to Lee.

It was held by the House of Lords, affirming the earlier decision of the Court of Appeal, that her plea would fail. Whilst on the face of things the two documents appear to be very different, the court thought that in assessing whether the nature of the document was different, one had to have regard to the 'object of the exercise'. The object of the exercise in assigning the property to the nephew was to enable him to use it as security to raise money by way of a secured loan. Their Lordships considered that this object would also have been arrived at had Lee acted honestly. There was thus no difference in the nature of the document Mrs Gallie signed and what she thought she was signing.

The case of *Saunders* v *Anglia Building Society* however established that three principles had to be proven before the defence would apply. Firstly, the plea can only rarely be relied upon by a person of full age and capacity; such a person will generally be bound by the document. Generally in order to succeed one has to show that one is signing under some disability, such as illiteracy, blindness or senility. Secondly, the person relying on the defence has to show that the document signed was different in nature from the one he thought he was signing within the concept of *non est factum* as discussed above. Finally, the person attempting to rely on the defence has to show that he was not careless in signing and that he took all reasonable precautions to ascertain the contents and significance of the document to be signed.

It has to be stated that *non est factum* is rarely pleaded and even more rarely is it successful. A recent example can be seen in *Lloyds Bank PLC* v *Waterhouse* [1990] Fam Law 23.

Further reading

Atiyah, '*Couturier* v *Hastie* and the Sale of Non-Existent Goods', 78 *Law Quarterly Review* 340, 1957

Beale, Bishop and Furmston, *Contract – Cases and Materials* 2nd ed. 1990, Butterworths

Cartwright, '*Solle* v *Butcher* and the Doctrine of Mistake in Contract', 103 *Law Quarterly Review* 594, 1987

Cheshire, Fifoot and Furmston, *The Law of Contract* 12th ed. 1991, Butterworths

Guest, *Anson's Law of Contract* 26th ed. 1984, Oxford University Press

Phang, 'Common Mistake in English Law: The Proposed Merger of Common Law and Equity', 9 *Legal Studies* 291, 1990

Treitel, *The Law of Contract* 8th ed. 1991, Sweet & Maxwell

11 | Duress, undue influence and inequality of bargaining power

INTRODUCTION

The essence of an agreement and hence a legally binding contract is founded upon the parties giving their free consent to be bound by the terms of the agreement. It follows that where a party is coerced into a contract by threats or undue pressure that stifles the principle of free consent, that individual should not be bound by that contract. Both the common law and equity concurred in this fact, the common law through its strict doctrine of duress and equity through the doctrine of undue influence, which had a wider sphere of operation than duress. Mere inequality of bargaining power is, as a general rule, insufficient to vitiate a contract entered into, though in recent years Lord Denning has attempted to develop a general concept under this heading whereby relief would be given to an individual who had not entered into a contract as a free agent. Finally, in recent years, statute has intervened to protect individuals in certain types of contracts.

THE COMMON LAW CONCEPT OF DURESS

Duress at common law relates to contracts induced by violence or the threat of violence. The act or threatened act must be illegal in that it may amount to either a tort or a crime. It follows that if the threatened act amounts to one which would otherwise be lawful then this could not amount to duress as, for example, a threat of lawful imprisonment as in *Williams v Bayley* (1886) LR 1 HL 200. The effect of duress at common law is to render the contract voidable.

At common law it was always considered that duress had to be directed against the person and that a threat to goods could not amount to duress. It follows that in *Skeate* v *Beale* (1840) 11 A & E 983 a promise given in return for goods that had been unlawfully detained was held to be valid. This principle has been criticised, however, and in *Maskell* v *Horner* [1915] 3 KB 106 it was held that money that had been paid in order to recover goods unlawfully detained could itself be recovered on the basis of money had and received under the law of restitution.

The notion of duress not including duress to goods has also been the subject of a great deal of criticism in more recent years when there has arisen a wider concept of economic duress. An early example of this being recognised was the case of *D. & C. Builders* v *Rees* [1966] 2 QB 617 which has already been examined in the context of sufficiency of consideration. In that case Lord Denning considered that the actions of the wife had amounted to improper pressure in order to compel the building firm to accept a sum substantially less than the one they were truly owed. In such a situation Lord Denning refused to exercise estoppel because of the wife's inequitable actions since she knew the builders needed the money. The case thus amounted to a crude but crucial step towards the development of the wider doctrine.

A more formal doctrine began to emerge in the case of *Occidental Worldwide Investment Corporation* v *Skibs A/S Avanti, The Sibeon and The Sibotre*, [1976] 1 Lloyd's Rep 293, the facts of which were that there was a worldwide recession in the shipping industry with the result that the charter rates had fallen substantially. The charterers of two ships renegotiated the rates of the charters having warned the owners that they would become insolvent unless this was done, although it was shown that the existing rates would probably not have had this effect on the charterers. They also stated that should action be taken against them for breach of contract no benefit would accrue to the owners since they, the charterers, had insignificant assets against which a claim could be made. The charterers were also cognisant of the fact that, should the charterers break their contract, the owners would be highly unlikely to be able to re-charter the vessels given the depth of the recession. This would result in the ships being laid up and the owners themselves would probably be forced into liquidation. In the case Kerr J developed a test for economic duress by stating that the question to be asked was, 'Was there such a degree of coercion that the other party was deprived of his free consent and agreement?' He considered that two questions had to be asked before the test could be satisfied. Firstly, did the victim protest at the time of the demand and, secondly, did the victim regard the transaction as closed or did he intend to repudiate the new agreement?

The tests propounded by Kerr J were considered more fully in the case of the *North Ocean Shipping Co Ltd* v *Hyundai Construction Co Ltd, The Atlantic Baron* [1979] QB 705.

The facts of the case were that the defendants had agreed to build a tanker for the plaintiffs at a price to be payable in five instalments in dollars. The plaintiffs paid the first instalment but then the dollar suffered a 10 per cent drop in the international money market. The defendants demanded a 10 per cent increase in the contract price, stating that they would not complete the ship unless this was forthcoming. At the time the defendants were not aware that this threat was particularly damaging to the plaintiffs since they had an agreement to charter the ship when it was completed. The plaintiffs agreed to pay the extra money despite the fact that, as they pointed out to the defendants, they were not legally obliged to do so. Eventually all four of the further instalments were paid, increased by 10 per cent, and the plaintiffs took delivery of the ship. Eight months later the plaintiffs sought to recover the extra monies paid, but failed in their action. Whilst Mocatta J considered that this was a case of economic duress, he held that they would be unable to recover since their delay in seeking the recovery of the extra monies paid amounted to affirmation of the contract, even if they had no intention of affirming the contract as such.

Whilst the judgment of Mocatta J undoubtedly gave additional support to the test propounded by Kerr J, it also produced a serious deficiency in the concept of economic duress as stated by Kerr J. The problem was that the victim was placed on the horns of a dilemma. If he protests too vehemently the other party will walk away from the contract, leaving the victim economically disadvantaged, despite his right to sue for breach of contract. A mild protest, however, may be read by the courts as not being sufficient. On the other hand if he fails to refute the contract quickly he will be regarded as having affirmed the contract and will be bound by it.

To a large degree the decision of Kerr J was affirmed in the case of *Pao On* v *Lau Yiu Long* [1979] 3 All ER 65 where Scarman LJ stated:

> there is nothing contrary to principle in recognising economic duress as a factor which may render a contract voidable provided always that the basis of such recognition is that it must amount to a coercion of will, which vitiates consent. It must be shown that the payment made on the contract entered into was not a voluntary act.

Further, in assessing whether or not a coercion of will had taken place, he stated:

> it is material to inquire whether the person alleged to have been coerced did or did not protest; whether, at the time he was allegedly coerced into making a contract, he did or did not have an alternative course open to him such as an adequate legal remedy; whether he was independently advised; and whether, after entering the contract, he took steps to avoid it.

It can be seen that his Lordship's judgment did little to remove or reconcile the dilemma set out above; quite the contrary. The judgment presents a significant problem when it talks in terms of the payment made or the contract entered into 'not [being] a voluntary act . . .'. Quite clearly if one does agree to a situation like this then such an act must of necessity be a voluntary act since the party coerced must have formed an intention to enter the situation. Lord Scarman's statement is thus an over-simplification and fails to address this aspect of his judgment in enough detail. He would have done better to express it not merely as a voluntary act but as a voluntary submission compelled by the fact of no other available course of action.

The question arose again in the case of *Universe Tankships Inc of Monrovia* v *International Transport Workers' Federation, The Universe Sentinel* [1983] 1 AC 366 where both Lord Scarman and Lord Diplock concluded that economic duress may arise where there is an intentional submission to the inevitable and that the pressure used to secure such submission was illegitimate in that there was a suppression of the will of the victim. The problem with the case is that it really failed to address how one tested the differences between legitimate and illegitimate pressure, or how a court is supposed to deal with the dilemma of a victim in the face of such pressure.

Whilst difficulties arise in testing the differences between legitimate and illegitimate pressure, the case did establish that the pressure compelling submission can be legitimate pressure and Lord Scarman specifically stated that duress can exist even if the threat is one of lawful action. In *Alec Lobb (Garages) Ltd* v *Total Oil Great Britain Ltd* [1983] 1 WLR 87 the Court of Appeal stated that no duress could arise where legitimate rights were threatened. Presumably the views of the Court of Appeal will now give way to those of the House of Lords.

It is clear from the above that the law as regards economic duress is very uncertain and this probably arises because the boundaries of the doctrine are still being formed. That economic duress is here to stay cannot be doubted and in fact the doctrine has received further judicial recognition in *Atlas Express Ltd* v *Kafco (Importers and Distributors) Ltd* [1989] 1 All ER 641.

The facts of this case were that the plaintiffs, a firm of road hauliers, contracted with the defendants to deliver cartons of basketware to branches of Woolworths throughout the United Kingdom. Prior to entering into the contract a manager of the plaintiffs, having inspected the cartons, estimated that each load would comprise of between 400 and 600 cartons. On this basis he agreed a contract rate of £1.10 per carton. The first load fell well below his estimations, comprising of only 200 cartons. The manager then went back to the defendants and stated that his firm would be unable to transport any more loads unless the defendants agreed to a minimum price of £440 per load. The defendants were a small concern that was heavily dependent on their contract with Woolworths, who were unable to find another carrier willing to transport their goods, and so they reluctantly agreed to pay the minimum charge. The defendants later refused to pay the minimum charge and when sued claimed economic duress as a defence. It was held that where a defendant had no alternative but to accept revised terms that were detrimental to its interests, this amounted to economic duress that vitiated the apparent consent to the renegotiated terms.

A similar case to the Atlas case is that of *Vantage Navigation Corporation* v *Suhail and Sand Bahawn Building Materials LLC (The Alev)* [1989] 1 Lloyd's Rep 138.

The facts of the case were that a ship, *The Alev*, was chartered to carry a cargo of steel by the plaintiffs. The defendants had an interest in the cargo. The charterers of the ship in fact had substantial financial problems, with the result that they defaulted in paying instalments under the terms of the charterparty. This default rendered the plaintiffs, by virtue of the bill of lading, liable to carry the cargo to its destination at considerable loss to themselves, which compounded their losses sustained by the default of the charterers. In order to offset some of the losses, the plaintiffs entered into negotiation with the defendants, with the result that a contract was entered into whereby the defendants would bear the port costs (together with some other costs) and agreed not to detain or arrest the ship whilst it was in port. This agreement was reached in part by the plaintiffs threatening not to transport the cargo. In fact, when the ship entered port and began unloading its cargo, the defendants arrested the ship and in defence to a claim for breach of contract by the plaintiffs, pleaded economic duress. It was held that the contract could be avoided by the defendants on the basis of economic duress. The court held that the threat to refuse to transport the cargo was illegal, that the plaintiffs knew this and, as a result, the contract was voidable.

Both the above cases indicate that there has been a considerable relaxation in the criteria required to prove economic duress. Whilst it is only necessary to prove a suppression of will and voluntary consent to the transaction by the victim, the concept is now very vague and it is not an exaggeration to state that the law in this area is in an unsatisfactory state. The truth is that the concept of economic duress is still evolving and is some way off being formulated into a hard set of principles. It should, however, be noted that, following *The Universe Sentinel* case, the effect of economic duress is to render a contract voidable, the proper remedy therefore being rescission.

THE EQUITABLE CONCEPT OF UNDUE INFLUENCE

Equity was, and is, always more flexible in the way it grants or refuses relief. Whilst the common law required concepts to be strictly defined, this was never the case in equity which, partly because it was discretionary and partly because it acted according to the principles of good consciousness, developed concepts that fell short of the requirements of the common law. An instance of such a concept is undue influence, where equity would grant relief from a contract that had been entered into because improper pressure had been placed on one of the parties.

With regard to undue influence, the courts will intervene where a relationship between the two parties has been exploited by one party in order to gain an unfair advantage. It follows that the exploitation can arise where there is an abuse of a particular confidence placed in a party or where that party is in a position of dominance over the victim. It should be stressed, however, that with regard to the latter category, it was held in *Goldsworthy v Brickell* [1987] 1 All ER 853 that domination is not a prerequisite of undue influence and that this was merely an example of conduct that might amount to undue influence. In the case of *Bank of Credit and Commerce International SA v Aboody* [1990] 1 QB 923 it was held that whatever category of undue influence is alleged it is a requirement that the transaction entered into must have been for the manifest disadvantage of the victim though this must now be read in the light of the House of Lords' decision in *Barclays Bank plc v O'Brien and Another* [1993] 4 All ER 417 and *CIBC Mortgages plc v Pitt and Another* [1993] 4 All ER 433.

In classifying the different categories of undue influence, it should be noted that undue influence may be either actual or presumed. In *BCCI v Aboody* [1990] 1 QB 923 the Court of Appeal adopted the following classification:

Class 1: actual undue influence;
Class 2: presumed undue influence, which has two sub-classifications.

Since this classification was adopted in the leading cases of *O'Brien* and *Pitt*, it is useful if this topic is dealt with by reference to the *Aboody* classification.

Class 1: actual undue influence

In this classification it is necessary for the claimant to prove affirmatively that the wrongdoer exerted undue influence on the complainant to enter into a particular transaction which is thus impugned. This type of undue influence arises where there is no special relationship between the parties so that there is no abuse of a particular confidence.

It was originally defined in *Allcard* v *Skinner* (1887) 36 Ch D 145 as some unfair and improper conduct, some coercion from outside, some overreaching, some form of cheating and generally, though not always, some personal advantage obtained by the guilty party.

The leading case on this area is that of *Williams* v *Bayley* (1866) LR 1 HL 200 where a father, to save his son from being prosecuted and possibly transported for giving his bank promissory notes on which he had forged his father's signature, was forced to give security for the debts of the son. It was held that the father's agreement had been extracted by virtue of undue influence being exerted on the father. The agreements were held to be invalid.

Other examples of such undue influence include taking advantage of persons acting under religious delusions, as in *Norton* v *Reilly* (1764) 2 Eden 286; or a young man's mentor influencing him to incur liabilities, as in *Smith* v *Kay* (1859) 7 HLC 750.

In *National Westminster Bank plc* v *Morgan* [1985] 1 All ER 821 it was held that in presumed undue influence (i.e. Class 2 undue influence) a claim to set a transaction aside for undue influence could not succeed unless the claimant could prove that the transaction was manifestly disadvantageous. This requirement was taken up and applied to cases of actual undue influence (i.e. Class 1 undue influence) by the Court of Appeal in *BCCI* v *Aboody*. In *CIBC* v *Pitt*, Lord Browne-Wilkinson did not agree with *Aboody* and considered the requirement that the undue influence had to be manifestly disadvantageous as laid down in *Morgan* had no application to cases of actual undue influence. He stated:

> Actual undue influence is a species of fraud. Like any other victim of fraud, a person who has been induced by undue influence to carry out a transaction which he did not freely and knowingly enter into is entitled to have that transaction set aside as of right. . . . A man guilty of fraud is no more entitled to argue that the transaction was beneficial to the person defrauded than a man who has procured a transaction by misrepresentation. The effect of the wrongdoer's conduct is to prevent the wronged party from bringing a free will and properly informed mind to bear on the proposed transaction, which accordingly must be set aside in equity as a matter of justice.

Thus, where there is no special relationship and the claimant proves actual undue influence, he is not under a further burden of proving that the transaction induced by this undue influence was manifestly disadvantageous to him and he may have it set aside as of right. It should be noted that the onus of proof is on the claimant to prove the presence of undue influence.

This type of undue influence is becoming much more rare today since there is a continuing blurring of this area with duress. An example of this may be seen in *Flower* v *Sadler* (1882) 10 QBD 572 where a promise to pay a sum of money extracted by the threat of criminal prosecution was held to be invalid for undue influence. Today such conduct would no doubt fall within the ambit of duress.

Class 2: presumed undue influence

In this classification all the victim has to show is that there is a relationship of trust or confidence between himself and the wrongdoer. Once this is done, undue influence is presumed to have occurred. Not every type of fiduciary relationship gives rise to such a presumption since it has to be shown that the confidence placed in the wrongdoer gives that person some authority over the victim or that it creates an obligation on the wrongdoer to offer or recommend the victim to seek independent advice. The person in whom the confidence is reposed is in such a position that he has an obvious opportunity of enhancing that position, to the extent that he must prove that he has not exercised his position of influence in that manner.

There is thus no need for the victim to prove that actual undue influence has taken place, since all he has to do is to prove that a confidential relationship has arisen. Once the victim has done that the burden of proof shifts to the wrongdoer to prove that the victim entered into the transaction of his own volition, for instance by showing that the victim had received independent advice.

The Court of Appeal in *BCCI* v *Aboody* established that a confidential relationship could arise in two ways, thus creating two sub-classes:

Class 2A. Whilst the categories of special relationship are not closed certain types of relationship automatically presuppose the existence of undue influence, for instance, the relationship between trustee and beneficiary (*Benningfield* v *Baxter* (1886) 12 App Cas 167); solicitor and client (*Wright* v *Carter* [1903] 1 Ch 27); parent and child (*Powell* v *Powell* [1900] 1 Ch 243); religious leader or adviser and disciple or parishioner (*Allcard* v *Skinner* (1887) 36 Ch D 145).

Class 2B. Where there is no special relationship that falls within Class 2A it may be the case that the victim can prove the existence of a relationship in which he has placed a trust and confidence in the wrongdoer as a fact. The victim will therefore be able to have the transaction set aside merely by proving that he has placed a trust and confidence in the wrongdoer, without the need to prove that an actual undue influence arose.

The husband and wife relationship is a good example of a category of relationship within Class 2B that does not exist *per se* but which has to be proven as a fact. This was established in *Howes* v *Bishop* [1909] 2 KB 390 and *Bank of Montreal* v *Stuart* [1911] AC 120, and again confirmed in *Midland Bank plc* v *Shephard* [1988] 3 All ER 17. In *Kingsnorth Trust Ltd* v *Bell* [1986] 1 All ER 423 the wife was able to prove undue influence as a fact where the husband was regarded as an agent of the Bank in procuring the agreement of the wife to a particular transaction. Similarly, in *BCCI* v *Aboody* a wife was able to avoid liability to the bank in respect of a surety transaction, which she was induced to enter by her husband, on the basis that the bank had notice, actual or constructive, of the husband's actions in either exercising undue influence over his wife or misrepresenting the extent of his indebtedness to the bank.

Whilst the cases which cause most concern arise out of the husband and wife relationship, Class 2B undue influence may arise in any transaction where the victim can prove as a fact that he or she entered into a transaction that was manifestly disadvantageous at the instigation of the dominant wrongdoer. This being done, a court will presume that the victim has been subject to undue influence.

Thus in *Lloyds Bank Ltd* v *Bundy* [1975] QB 326 the defendant was an elderly farmer whose only asset comprised a farmhouse that was also his home. The defendant shared the same bank as his son and his son's company. The company ran into financial difficulties and so the defendant gave a guarantee in respect of the company to the bank, the guarantee being secured by a charge over the farmhouse. In fact the fortunes of the company failed to improve and the defendant was then approached by his son and the manager of the bank, who informed him that the bank was unwilling to continue to support the company without additional security. In response to this approach, and without seeking independent advice, the defendant extended the guarantee and with it the charge over his property. Eventually a receiver was appointed in respect to the company and as a result the bank sought to enforce its security against the farmhouse. The defendant pleaded undue influence based on the fact that there was a long-standing relationship between himself and the bank, and as such he had placed confidence in it in that he looked to the bank for financial advice. Clearly the bank in having a financial interest in the company could not present itself as being able to give independent financial advice. It was incumbent upon the bank to advise the defendant to seek such advice, which they failed to do, and as such could not rebut the presumption of undue influence.

It has to be stated that the *Bundy* case is a somewhat exceptional one and turns on its own facts, since the presumption of undue influence does not normally arise between banks and their customers.

Thus in the leading case *National Westminster Bank Ltd* v *Morgan* [1985] 1 All ER 821 a husband and wife were the joint owners of the family home which was mortgaged to a building society. The husband became unable to meet the mortgage repayments because his business began to fail. When the building society began to take proceedings for possession of the property in order to enforce the mortgage, the husband decided to seek new finance from the bank, which had agreed to help. The bank manager then called at the family home to have the relevant documents executed by the wife, who did not receive any independent legal advice before signing the new mortgage. Although the husband was initially present the wife insisted that she wished to discuss the mortgage with the bank manager privately. During her discussions with the manager she stated that she had little confidence in her husband's business ventures and that she did not want the legal charge to cover her husband's business liabilities. The manager assured her, incorrectly, that the legal charge would only cover the refinancing of the mortgage and that it did not extend to the business liabilities. The financial difficulties of the husband and wife continued and they again fell into arrears with the mortgage repayments, although the husband's business was not in debt to the bank. The bank sought to enforce their security on the charge by seeking possession of the property. Soon afterwards the husband died. The wife then appealed against the order for possession on the grounds that the mortgage had been obtained by virtue of undue influence and therefore the legal charge should be set aside. The Court of Appeal allowed her appeal but she failed in the House of Lords.

The House of Lords rejected the contention that undue influence arose simply out of the relationship of the parties and that the presence of such undue influence allowed the transaction to be set on one side. Lord Scarman (who delivered the only judgment) referred to the judgment of Sir Eric Sachs in *Lloyds Bank Ltd* v *Bundy* [1975] QB 326 where he considered that undue influence does not simply arise because of the relationship of banker and client, as in a simple case of the bank going about its normal duties where it is, for instance, obtaining a guarantee and in the course of that explains the legal effect of the guarantee and the sums involved. For the presumption of undue influence to arise the bank must normally 'cross the line' into the area of confidentiality. Lord Scarman did not approve of the latter expression, preferring to find whether or not a dominating influence was present by a 'meticulous examination of the facts', an expression used by Sir Eric Sachs in determining whether or not an area of confidentiality had been crossed into. He considered that on the facts the bank had not exercised a dominant influence over the wife.

Lord Scarman decided that on a 'meticulous examination of the facts' the bank in the *Morgan* case had not crossed the line to where a presumption of undue influence existed. In any event he considered that the presence of this presumption was not of itself sufficient in any event. He stated that one also had to show that the transaction was of itself wrongful in that it constituted a manifest disadvantage to the person influenced. He found that the transaction had not been unfair to the wife; indeed, quite the contrary, since it had allowed Mr & Mrs Morgan to stay in their house on terms that were not substantially different from those of the building society. The transaction, if anything, was to their advantage and thus the bank had no duty to ensure that Mrs Morgan received independent advice.

It can easily be seen that the need to prove a 'manifest disadvantage' is a substantial factor in limiting the application of undue influence since the courts will be prepared to enforce a transaction where the potential benefits of the transaction outweigh the disadvantages, as in the *Morgan* case.

It should be noted that even if undue influence is not found to be present it is always possible for an action to be taken against the bank in misrepresentation or negligence as regards the nature of the transaction being entered, as seen in *Cornish* v *Midland Bank Ltd* [1985] 3 All ER 513. Similarly, as in *Lloyds Bank plc* v *Waterhouse* [1991] Fam Law 23, a defence of misrepresentation may be combined with one of *non est factum* in appropriate circumstances.

Whilst it has been seen that the presumption of undue influence may be rebutted by the person having the dominating influence showing that the other party had had access to independent advice or at least been in a position to exercise his free judgment, such advice is not always successful in saving the situation. It must be competent advice and made in the knowledge of all the facts of the case: *Inche Noriah* v *Shaik Allie bin Omar* [1929] AC 127.

The effect of undue influence on third parties

So far the examination of undue influence has been looked at in the context of where the victim is attempting to avoid a transaction entered into with the wrongdoer. However, it sometimes arises, particularly in the context of a husband and wife relationship, that the victim is persuaded to enter into a guarantee or surety contract with a bank or some other creditor on the basis of some undue influence, misrepresentation or other legal wrong, not by the bank or creditor, but by some third party, for instance a husband. The question arises, therefore, to what extent that undue influence will affect the transaction between the victim and the bank/creditor? If one adopts the usual rule of privity of contract, the actions of the wrongdoer should have no effect on the transaction; however, in certain instances the courts have allowed the victim to have the transaction set aside.

Creditors have been affected by the actions of the wrongdoer and thus unable to enforce the surety contract/guarantee in the following three situations.

(a) Agency

The process used by the courts here is based on the reasoning that the wrongdoer (i.e. the principal debtor) was acting as the agent of the creditor in persuading the victim (i.e. the guarantor or surety) to enter into the guarantee or surety contract. Where the principal debtor obtains the compliance of the victim by undue influence, misrepresentation or other legal wrong, then the principal creditor is also faced with this wrongdoing and is therefore unable to enforce the guarantee or surety contract against the victim.

Such a situation arose in the case of *Kingsworth Trust Ltd* v *Bell* [1986] 1 All ER 423 where a husband wanted to borrow £18,000 against a second mortgage on the matrimonial home in order to expand a business that he operated in partnership with his son and daughter-in-law. The husband was aware that his wife, who was his second wife and not the mother of the son, would not be willing to mortgage the home for this purpose. The plaintiff finance company instructed their solicitors to prepare the necessary documents, which were then sent to the husband's solicitors, asking them to act as their agents in order to complete the transaction. The husband's solicitors then handed the documents to the husband himself who misrepresented their contents in order to persuade his wife to sign them. The Court of Appeal held that the transaction should be set aside on the basis that the husband had effectively acted as the plaintiff's agent and therefore his wrongdoing should also be attributed to the plaintiff.

A similar reasoning was also adopted, *inter alia*, in *Avon Finance Co Ltd* v *Bridges* [1985] 2 All ER 281, though not adopted in *Coldunell Ltd* v *Gallon* [1986] QB 1184.

The use of agency in the manner described now seems to have been firmly put to bed by the latest and now leading case on this area of undue influence: *Barlays Bank plc* v *O'Brien*. Here Lord Browne-Wilkinson stated that the agency device was highly artificial. He said, reiterating comments made in the Court of Appeal:

> . . . the reality of the relationship is that, the creditor having required of the principal debtor that there must be a surety, the principal debtor on his own account in order to raise the necessary finance seeks to procure the support of the surety. In doing so he is acting for himself not for the creditor.

(b) Special equity

In *O'Brien* in the Court of Appeal ([1992] 4 All ER 983) the leading judgment was given by Scott LJ who, as already stated, did not approve or adopt the agency theory discussed above. He preferred instead to apply a line of authority that provided that equity confers special protection to a protected class of surety. Such a protected class arises where the relationship between the debtor and surety is such that any influence exercised by the debtor over the surety and the fact of reliance on the debtor by the surety are natural features of the relationship. Scott LJ stated that as a matter of policy married women who gave security for their husband's debts fell within this special protected class of sureties. Given this relationship, any security provided by such a surety would, in certain circumstances, be unenforceable despite the fact that the creditor was not aware of or responsible for the vitiating conduct of this debtor.

The Court of Appeal held that security given by a surety in the protected class was unenforceable when: firstly, the relationship between the surety and the debtor, and thus the possibility of influence and reliance, was known to the creditor; secondly, the surety's consent to the transaction was procured by undue influence or a material misrepresentation by the debtor, or the surety lacked an 'adequate understanding of the nature and effect of the transaction'; and thirdly, the creditor, whether or not he had left matters to the debtor, had failed to take reasonable steps to ensure that the surety had an adequate understanding of the nature and effect of the transaction and ensured that the surety's consent to the transaction was a true and informed one. On the facts, which will be dealt with later, the Court of Appeal found that the bank had failed to take reasonable steps to ensure that the wife had an adequate understanding of the effect of the charge, which was therefore unenforceable against her, except to the amount that she had agreed to secure.

Lord Browne-Wilkinson in the House of Lords, whilst expressing some sympathy with the views expressed above, considered that although wives deserved the protection of the law, the reality being that in a substantial proportion of marriages the wife was still dependent on her husband's financial decisions and advice, there were wider policy considerations to take into account. He stated that, if wives were given special protection, this might have the effect of rendering vulnerable any loans granted on the security of matrimonial homes. This would result in financial institutions becoming unwilling to accept matrimonial homes as being an adequate security for a loan, thereby reducing the stock of venture loan capital to businesses. He thought it was essential that the matrimonial home remained acceptable to financial institutions as security for loans.

Lord Browne-Wilkinson rejected the special equity theory, giving four reasons. Firstly, he could find no basis for affording special protection to a narrow class of persons in relation to one type of transaction only. Secondly, he considered that a requirement that the creditor had to prove knowledge and understanding by the wife in all cases was a means of extending Class 2A presumptive undue influence to the husband and wife relationship. Thirdly, apart from the Court of Appeal decision, there was only one other case that supported the theory, *Yerkey v Jones*

(1939) 63 CLR 649. Finally, he considered that it was possible to protect the interests of wives by way of a more wide-ranging doctrine of notice.

(c) Notice

Lord Browne-Wilkinson considered that the key to whether a creditor is bound by the wrongdoings of the principal debtor, and thereby unable to enforce security as a guarantor or surety, lay in whether the creditor had actual or constructive notice of the equitable right of the surety to have the transaction set aside on the basis of the debtor's wrongdoings. He stated that 'the doctrine of notice lies at the heart of equity' and 'provides the key to finding a principled basis for the law'. He went on to state that where there are two innocent parties, both of whom enjoy rights, the earlier right prevails against the later one if the holder of that later right has actual notice of the earlier one or has constructive notice of it and he would have discovered it by making proper inquiries. Translating this to the husband and wife scenario, where the wife has agreed to stand as surety for the debts of her husband by virtue of some undue influence or misrepresentation, then the creditor will be deemed to have constructive notice of the equitable right of the wife to have the surety agreement set aside, provided the circumstances are such as to put the creditor on inquiry.

Lord Browne-Wilkinson considered that it was at this point that the special position of wives became important since, even today, many wives place a confidence and trust in their husbands in relation to their financial affairs. Thus the relationship between a husband and wife in these circumstances gave rise to an 'invalidating tendency' which meant that a wife was in a better position to be able to establish class 2B presumed undue influence by her husband. The informality of the dealings between a husband and his wife meant that there was a higher likelihood of the husband misrepresenting the liability of the undertaking to the wife in order to secure her assent to the surety contract. His Lordship considered that the informality of the business dealings between a husband and his wife would be sufficient to put a creditor on notice if two factors are satisfied:

> (a) the transaction is on its face not to the financial advantage of the wife; and (b) there is a substantial risk in transactions of that kind that, in procuring the wife to act as surety, the husband has committed a legal or equitable wrong that entitles the wife to set aside the transaction.

Thus where a creditor is put on inquiry it is incumbent on him to ensure that the wife's consent to act as surety has been properly obtained, since otherwise he will be deemed to have constructive notice of the wife's right to have the surety agreement set aside, either on the basis of undue influence or misrepresentation.

But what of the situation outside the husband and wife relationship? Lord Browne-Wilkinson stated that the special position of wives does not arise out of the status of the husband and wife relationship but out of the emotional ties that arise within that relationship. These emotional ties also arise in the case of cohabitees, whether of a heterosexual or homosexual nature. Where the creditor knows that a surety or guarantor is cohabiting with the principal debtor, the nature of the surety contract and the relationship of the parties means that the possibility of undue influence or misrepresentation can be inferred, with the consequence that the creditor will have constructive notice of the equitable right of the surety to have the transaction set aside, just as in the husband and wife situation.

Of course, these principles are not confined to cohabitees but will arise in any situation where a creditor is aware that the surety places a confidence and trust in the principal debtor.

Lord Browne-Wilkinson gave as an example of this type of relationship *Avon Finance Co Ltd* v *Bridges* [1985] 2 All ER 281. In this case a son persuaded his parents to act as surety for his debts by means of a misrepresentation. It was held that the surety contract was unenforceable by the finance company, *inter alia*, because the finance company had knowledge of the trust the parents reposed in their son with regard to their financial dealings. One may discern a difference of approach here since there would appear to be a requirement to prove actual knowledge by the creditor of the confidence and trust reposed in the debtor by the surety, whilst in the cohabitee scenario undue influence or misrepresentation may be inferred.

The problem now remains as to how creditors can avoid the consequences set out above. Lord Browne-Wilkinson considered that the answer to this question lies in good banking practice by the various financial institutions. He thought that such institutions can lend in confidence on the basis of a surety contract provided the surety is warned, independently of the principal debtor, of the extent of his or her liability and the risks involved. Furthermore, the surety should be advised to seek independent advice. His Lordship also considered that notices in the documentation did not provide an adequate warning, no matter what prominence such warnings are given, since very often such written warnings were not read by potential sureties or they were intercepted by the principal debtor. There is thus a legal requirement on financial institutions to explain the matters indicated above to the potential surety in a personal interview from which the principal debtor is excluded.

The application of the doctrine of notice in the *O'Brien* case

The facts of *Barclays Bank plc* v *O'Brien* were that Mr O'Brien wanted to increase the overdraft facility of a company in which he was a shareholder. The bank agreed a loan of £120,000 that was to be guaranteed by Mr O'Brien, his liability in turn being secured by a second charge over the matrimonial home, which was jointly owned by Mr O'Brien and his wife. The bank manager gave instructions for the relevant documents to be prepared, including a legal charge to be signed by both Mr O'Brien and his wife, together with a guarantee to be signed by the husband alone. Instructions were also given that both Mr O'Brien and his wife should be advised as to the nature of the transactions and that, if they had any doubts, they should obtain independent advice. These instructions were not complied with and subsequently both husband and wife signed the documents without reading them. The company's indebtedness then increased beyond the agreed limit and the bank took proceedings to enforce its security against the husband and wife. In her defence the wife contended that her husband had put undue pressure on her to sign the surety agreement and, secondly, that her husband had misrepresented the effect of the legal charge in that she believed it was limited to a sum of £60,000 over three weeks.

The judge at first instance, and the Court of Appeal and House of Lords dismissed the wife's contention that she had been subject to undue influence by her husband and therefore the case turned on the misrepresentation of the husband as to the extent and the duration of the liability and whether the bank's ability to enforce the surety contract against the wife was prejudiced by the actions of her husband.

In the House of Lords Lord Browne-Wilkinson gave the only substantive judgment, much of which has already been discussed. However, towards the end of his judgment he summarised his views as:

> Where one cohabitee has entered into an obligation to stand as surety for the debts of the other cohabitee and the creditor is aware that they are cohabitees: (1) the surety obligation will be valid and enforceable by the creditor unless the suretyship was procured by the undue influence, misrepresentation or other legal wrong of the principal debtor; (2) if there has been undue influence, misrepresentation or other legal wrong by the principal debtor, unless the creditor has taken reasonable steps to satisfy himself that the surety entered into the obligation freely and in knowledge of the true facts, the creditor will be unable to enforce the surety obligation because he will be fixed with constructive notice of the surety's right to set aside the transaction; (3) unless there are special exceptional circumstances, a creditor will have taken such reasonable steps to avoid being fixed with constructive notice if the creditor warns the surety (at a meeting not attended by the principal debtor) of the amount of her potential liability and of the risks involved and advises the surety to take independent legal advice.

On the facts, the bank was aware that the parties were husband and wife and as such were put on notice as to the circumstances in which the wife would have been asked to stand as surety. The bank failed to warn the wife of the risks she ran in entering into the surety contract or as to her potential liability in respect of her husband's debts. Furthermore, the bank had not advised her to seek independent legal advice. On this basis the bank was fixed with constructive notice of the misrepresentation made by the husband to induce his wife into the surety contract and therefore the wife was entitled to have the legal charge on the matrimonial home securing her husband's liability to the bank set aside.

In *Banco Exterior Internacional* v *Mann and Others* (1994) *The Times*, 19th December, the Court of Appeal (by a majority) held that there was no obligation on a creditor to ensure that the surety received entirely independent advice. This decision follows the cases of *Bank of Baroda* v *Shah* [1988] 3 All ER 24 and *Midland Bank* v *Massey* (1994) *The Times*, 23rd March, although it appears to considerably weaken the decision in *O'Brien*.

Class 1 actual undue influence and the doctrine of notice

The same day that the House of Lords gave its judgment in the *O'Brien* case, their Lordships also gave a ruling in the case of *CIBC Mortgages Ltd* v *Pitt* [1993] 4 All ER 433.

The facts of this case were that a husband and wife jointly owned the matrimonial home, which in 1986 was valued at £270,000. The only encumbrance on the property was a mortgage for £16,700. That year the husband told his wife that he wanted to borrow some money to buy some shares, using the house as security for the loan. The wife was not happy with this arrangement, though she eventually agreed after her husband had brought some pressure to bear on her. They both signed an application form for a loan of £150,000 from the plaintiff, who was told that the money was to be used to pay off the existing mortgage and purchase a holiday home. The wife did not read the documents and was not aware of the extent of the loan. She did receive independent advice on the matter. The husband invested the money in shares and was, for a time, very successful. However, after the Stock Exchange collapse of 1987 he was unable to meet the repayments on the loan. The plaintiff consequently sought possession of the matrimonial home. The wife contested the application on the ground that she had been induced to enter into the transaction by the undue influence and misrepresentation of her husband.

At first instance the judge found that there had been actual undue influence exercised by the husband over his wife to persuade her to enter into the transaction. The judge also found (following *National Westminster Bank plc v Morgan* and *BCCI v Aboody*) that the transaction was 'manifestly disadvantageous' to her. The judge found that the husband had not acted as agent for the plaintiff. However, he considered that the 'special equity' that applies to wives only arose in cases where a wife acted as surety for her husband and not in cases where there was a joint advance, as in this case. He decided, therefore, that the wife's claim should fail.

The wife appealed to the Court of Appeal, where her claim was dismissed on the basis that the transaction was not 'manifestly disadvantageous' to the wife. Further, the Court of Appeal found that the plaintiff had neither actual nor constructive notice of any irregularity by the husband and that as far as the plaintiff was aware the arrangement was a simple re-mortgaging transaction for the joint benefit of both the husband and the wife. The Court of Appeal on the question of notice was prepared to distinguish between joint loan transactions and surety transactions since, in the latter, the fact that the transaction favours the husband at the expense of the wife puts the creditor on notice of the possibility of undue influence by the husband. The wife then appealed to the House of Lords.

The House of Lords (Lord Browne-Wilkinson again gave the only substantive judgment), as indicated in the analysis of class 1 actual undue influence earlier, overruled *BCCI v Aboody* and decided that because actual influence was a species of fraud it was unnecessary to prove that the transaction was 'manifestly disadvantageous' to the wife.

The House agreed that Mrs Pitt had established actual influence by Mr Pitt and that Mr Pitt was not acting as agent to the plaintiff in procuring his wife's agreement, so that the plaintiff would not be affected by Mr Pitt's actions on this basis. The only other means by which Mrs Pitt could have the transaction set aside would be on an application of the doctrine of notice. As far as the plaintiff was concerned it had no direct actual knowledge of the undue influence Mr Pitt had exercised over his wife. Could it be said, however, that the plaintiff had sufficient knowledge of the relationship between the parties that the plaintiff should have been put on inquiry, and thereby fixed with constructive notice? The House of Lords thought not:

> So far as the plaintiff was aware, the transaction consisted of a joint loan to the husband and wife to finance the discharge of an existing mortgage on 26 Alexander Avenue and, as to the balance, to be applied in buying a holiday home. The loan was advanced to both husband and wife jointly. There was nothing to indicate to the plaintiff that this was anything other than a normal advance to a husband and wife for their joint benefit.

Lord Browne-Wilkinson distinguished between cases where there is joint advancement and those involving a surety transaction, as follows:

> What distinguishes the case of the joint advance from the surety case is that, in the latter, there is not only the possibility of undue influence having been exercised but also the increased risk of it having in fact been exercised because, at least on its face, the guarantee by a wife of her husband's debts is not for her financial benefit. It is the combination of these two factors that puts the creditor on inquiry.

The effects of undue influence

The effect of undue influence on a contract is to render it voidable rather than void. It follows that the victim must take steps to avoid the contract by rescinding it. As in other instances where rescission is the remedy it may be lost where *restitutio in integrum* is impossible or where the contract has been affirmed or where a bona fide third party has acquired the title to any property sold to him.

It should be noted that restitution does not have to be precise but merely substantial, as in *O'Sullivan* v *Management and Music Ltd* [1985] QB 428.

Problems can arise, however, where restitution is ordered but the value of the property in question has changed. Such a situation arose in the case of *Cheese* v *Thomas* (1993) *The Times*, 24 August.

In this case the plaintiff (Cheese) bought a house with his great-nephew (Thomas) for £83,000. The money for the purchase was raised by the plaintiff contributing £43,000 and the defendant £40,000 by way of a mortgage on the property for that amount. The house was purchased in the defendant's name, though it was agreed that the plaintiff would have sole use of the house for the rest of his life. It was further agreed that on the plaintiff's death the house would belong to the defendant exclusively. Eventually the plaintiff became worried that the defendant was not paying the mortgage repayments, conduct which inevitably would have placed his interest in the property at risk. The plaintiff thus sought to have the arrangement set aside on the basis of undue influence.

The judge at first instance ruled that the agreement could be set aside for undue influence. Normally, where restitution is ordered, the plaintiff should have been able to recover his full £43,000 contribution since the principle behind this remedy is that the parties should be restored to their original positions. In this case, however, the house was sold for £55,400, i.e. a £27,600 loss. Should the plaintiff receive his £43,000 in full or only a proportion of it to reflect the loss sustained on the sale of the property? The Court of Appeal held that it was appropriate that the loss should be shared since each party had contributed to the purchase of a house in which each would have an interest. Further, the defendant's personal conduct was not found to be open to criticism – he had acted as an 'innocent fiduciary' rather than in some unconscionable manner. Presumably the result of this decision is that if the parties can show that they have an interest in the property then, if the property has been sold at a profit, the parties would have likewise been entitled to a share of the profit.

INEQUALITY OF BARGAINING POWER

In *Lloyds Bank Ltd* v *Bundy* [1979] QB 326 Lord Denning propounded a wider doctrine of equitable intervention whereby relief would be given where some unfair advantage had been obtained of a party to a transaction because of a substantial difference in the bargaining powers between the parties.

The facts of the *Bundy* case were that the plaintiff was an elderly farmer who had guaranteed the liabilities of his son's business to the extent of a £7,500 guarantee charge against the plaintiff's farmhouse in favour of the defendant bank. He had been advised by his solicitor that he should not commit any more to the son's business. The business affairs of the son grew steadily worse and the son, together with the assistant bank manager, visited the plaintiff. The assistant manager stated that the bank could only continue to support the business if the guarantee and charge was increased to £11,000. The assistant manager knew that the plaintiff was relying on him for advice and that the farmhouse was the plaintiff's only asset, but he failed fully to explain the extent of the financial position of the business. The plaintiff signed the guarantee and the charge and later the bank brought an action for the possession of the house. It was held that there was a presumption of undue influence since, in the opinion of Sir Eric Sachs after a 'meticulous examination' of the particular facts of the case, a special relationship had resulted by the bank 'crossing the line into the area of confidentiality'.

Lord Denning MR rather than formulate a judgment in terms of undue influence decided, having examined various categories of unconscionable bargains, to base his decision on a general theory that the courts could, and should in this case, give relief where the parties were of substantially unequal bargaining strengths. He stated the theory in the following terms:

> Gathering all together, I would suggest that through all these instances there runs a single thread. They rest on 'inequality of bargaining power'. By virtue of it, the English law gives relief to one who, without independent advice, enters into a contract upon terms which are very unfair or transfers of property for a consideration which is grossly inadequate. When his bargaining power is grievously impaired by reason of his own needs or desires, or by his own ignorance or infirmity coupled with undue influences or pressures brought to bear on him by or for the benefit of the other.

The other members of the Court of Appeal, whilst expressing sympathy with the view of Lord Denning, did not see fit to follow it and based their decisions on an orthodox application of the principles to be found in the doctrine of undue influence. Further, Lord Denning's approach was not followed in *National Westminster Bank Ltd* v *Morgan* by Lord Scarman, who stated:

> The fact of an unequal bargain will, of course, be a relevant feature in some cases of undue influence. But it can never become an appropriate basis of principle of an equitable doctrine which is concerned with transactions 'not to be reasonably accounted for on the ground of friendship, relationship, charity or other ordinary motives on which ordinary men act' (Lindley LJ in *Allcard* v *Skinner*).

To set up a general doctrine of inequality of bargaining power, Lord Scarman further stated, would require a legislative enactment. Such a doctrine does exist within the United States Uniform Commercial Code, but the only indications of our Parliament moving in this direction has been in very specific instances of hire purchase and consumer protection legislation. For instance the Consumer Credit Act 1974, s. 137(1), gives a court wide powers to reopen 'extortionate credit bargains'. A bargain is regarded as being extortionate if it 'grossly contravenes the ordinary principles of fair dealing' or where the repayments are regarded as being 'grossly exorbitant' by virtue of s. 138(1). Other factors to be taken into account in coming to such a conclusion are the debtor's age, prevailing interest rates, the degree of risk incurred by the creditor, the business capacity of the debtor and the degree of financial pressure on the debtor at the time of entering into the transaction. Further there are criminal sanctions available under the Fair Trading Act 1973, s. 17, in situations where a business practice subjects consumers to undue pressure.

Whilst Denning's views have been virtually dismissed by the courts, some academics have expressed some sympathy with his exposition of a general doctrine. Nevertheless it seems highly unlikely such an approach will be adopted since it is all too easy to deal with cases on the traditional basis of duress (including economic duress) and undue influence. Further, Denning's general doctrine is far too wide and is marked by an absence of governing principles within it, since inequality of bargaining power can exist in a vast number of cases and it is inconceivable that each one of these could be avoided on this basis. There can be a world of difference between a case where a party exercises a superior bargaining position over another and a case where that person's bargaining power is impaired, thus putting the other party in a superior position. The superior or weaker position may also arise from the effects of a completely external commercial source. Finally, Denning failed to make clear that it is not the fact of inequality of bargaining power that will render a contract voidable, but a state of affairs whereby a party in a superior position has abused that position to the detriment of the weaker individual.

Further reading

Atiyah, 'Economic Duress and the Overborne Will', 98 *Law Quarterly Review* 197, 1982

Beale, Bishop and Furmston, *Contract – Cases and Materials* 2nd ed. 1990, Butterworths

Chen-Wishart, 'Loss Sharing, Undue Influence and Manifest Disadvantage', 110 *Law Quarterly Review* 173, 1993

Cheshire, Fifoot and Furmston, *The Law of Contract* 12th ed. 1991, Butterworths

Doyle, 'Borrowing Under the Influence', 15 *Business Law Review* 6, 1994

Guest, *Anson's Law of Contract* 26th ed. 1984, Oxford University Press

Thal, 'The Inequality of Bargaining Power Doctrine: The Problem of Defining Contractual Unfairness', 8 *Oxford Journal of Legal Studies* 17, 1988

Tiplady, 'The Judicial Control of Contractual Unfairness', 46 *Modern Law Review* 601, 1983

Treitel, *The Law of Contract* 8th ed. 1991, Sweet & Maxwell

12 | Illegality

THE CLASSIFICATION OF ILLEGALITY

Oliver Cromwell's assertion of the state of English land law in the seventeenth century that it was an 'ungodly jumble' would also be most apt when applied to this area of the law of contract today. The area is a minefield for the student of the subject since it has little in the way of uniform structure and what there is produces tremendous inconsistencies. Students may therefore be forewarned by the words of A.P. Herbert in 'Uncommon Law' who says of the effect of the law relating to lotteries and gaming, 'This department of the law is a labyrinth of which Parliament and the Courts may well be proud!'

This topic concerns the fundamental principle that the courts will not enforce contracts that are considered to be illegal. Although this principle seems simple enough, the problem is that illegality as a concept covers a multitude of sins. While it is clearly illegal to commission the murder of another, at the same time, at the other end of the spectrum, it is also illegal to commission the theft of a toy from a shop or commit some other minor transgression. Thus there is a wide disparity in the seriousness of illegal contracts, but the question arises as to whether the various illegal acts should all have the same degree of effect on the contract. In addition to the problems of reconciling the differences that arise in this broad spectrum there looms the spectre of decisions based on the notion of public policy. Thrown into this mêlée is the *coup de grâce* for many people studying this area in that the terms 'illegal', 'void' and 'unenforceable' are not used consistently by the judges and are often used interchangeably. Authors have attempted to classify the circumstances of illegality in many ways and rarely satisfactorily since it is a truism to state that the circumstances of illegality probably defy classification in terms of conceptual analysis.

In this work it has been decided to treat the subject matter under four broad categories: where the manner of the performance of the contract is unlawful, where an act is illegal by way of statutory intervention, where an act is illegal at common law and, finally, the effects of a finding of illegality on the contract. I must emphasise that these categories are to some degree arbitrary and must be seen merely as vehicles for providing a descriptive analysis of the law rather than as forming conceptual boundaries.

THE UNLAWFUL MANNER OF PERFORMANCE

Illegality may have two principal effects on a contract and the distinction between the two is of the utmost importance. Firstly, a contract may be regarded as illegal if the actual creation of the contract itself is prohibited. The position here is that the contract is void *ab initio*. Thus in *Cope* v *Rowlands* (1836) 2 M & W 149 it was provided by statute that anyone acting as a broker in the City of London had to have a licence or pay £25 to the City for any transaction conducted without such a licence. The plaintiff was an unlicensed broker, and when he sued the defendant for his commission in buying and selling the defendant's stock it was held that the action must fail. Parker B stated:

> The legislature had in view, as one object, the benefit and security of the public in those important transactions which are negotiated by brokers. The clause, therefore, which imposes a penalty, must be taken . . . to imply a prohibition of all unadmitted persons to act as brokers, and consequently to prohibit, by necessary inference, all contracts which such persons make for compensation to themselves for so acting.

Secondly, a contract may be created lawfully but nevertheless be illegal because of the way in which it is performed. In such a situation the validity or invalidity of the contract is not nearly so decisive. In *Anderson Ltd* v *Daniel* [1924] 1 KB 138 there was a statutory requirement that vendors of artificial fertilisers had to state on their invoice the chemical breakdown of the fertiliser. In the contract in question the vendors had sold 10 tons of fertiliser to the defendants but failed to comply with the statutory requirement. When the defendants failed to pay the plaintiffs sued for the price, but were met with the defence that the contract was unenforceable due to statutory invalidity. It was held that the plaintiffs would lose in their action since the court stated that where a contract is lawful in its inception but illegal in its execution, then the plaintiff vendors would be unable to rely on their contractual rights. In *Shaw* v *Groom* [1970] 2 QB 504, however, it was held that where a landlord had failed to give his tenant a rent book, thereby committing an offence, he could nevertheless claim the rent owed by the tenant. The aim of the legislation here was to punish the landlord rather than to render the lease invalid, which would clearly be detrimental to the tenant.

The test for deciding which approach to take was stated in *St John Shipping*

Corporation v *Joseph Rank Ltd* [1956] 3 All ER 683 where the defendants withheld part of the freight due to the plaintiffs on the basis that while carrying the cargo the master of the ship had overloaded the ship contrary to the Merchant Shipping Act 1932. The defendants contended that the plaintiffs in an action for the freight withheld could not enforce a contract that had been performed in an illegal manner. The court held that the plaintiffs could succeed, stating that the test in deciding the validity or invalidity was based on the question as to whether the statute intended to penalise the conduct of the offending party or to invalidate the contract itself.

It may also be seen that the courts often adopt a more relaxed attitude where the innocent party is attempting to enforce the contract, but is unaware of an illegal act perpetrated by the other party. This was so in *Archbold's (Freightage) Ltd* v *S. Spanglett Ltd* [1961] 1 All ER 417 where the defendants agreed to carry the goods of the plaintiff, who was unaware that the defendants did not have the requisite licence required by statute for such a transaction. The goods were stolen in transit and the plaintiff sued for compensation for the loss. It was held that he could succeed since the contract itself was not illegal in its inception and in any event the plaintiff was unaware of the illegal performance of the contract by the defendants.

A different attitude may, however, result where the innocent party condoned or otherwise participated in the illegal performance of the contract. This was so in *Ashmore, Benson, Pease & Co Ltd* v *A.V. Dawson Ltd* [1973] 1 WLR 828 where the plaintiffs engaged the defendant road hauliers to carry a 25-ton tube to a port. The transport manager of the plaintiffs helped to supervise the loading of the tube on to the lorry which had a maximum load weight of 20 tons. On the journey to the port the lorry overturned damaging the tube. The plaintiffs sued to recover the losses resulting from the damage to the tube. It was held that the plaintiffs' action must fail since the transport manager had participated in the illegal performance of the contract.

ACTS ILLEGAL BY STATUTE

Where a contract is expressly declared to be prohibited in a statute then there is little doubt that Parliament intended that the contract could not be enforced. In *Re Mahmoud and Isaphani* [1921] 2 KB 716, the Seeds, Oils and Fats Order 1919 prohibited the unlicensed dealing in linseed oil without a licence from the Food Controller. The plaintiff had a licence to deal in linseed oil with other such licensed dealers. He agreed to sell linseed oil to the defendant and asked him if he held a licence to deal in such oils. The defendant stated that he did but subsequently refused to accept the delivery of the linseed oil on the basis that he in fact did not have a licence. The plaintiff sued for damages for non-acceptance. Despite the fact that the plaintiff was unaware that the contract was illegal when the contract was made it was held that his action would fail. The Court of Appeal stated that the legislation was clear and unequivocal that such contracts could not be enforced. Frequently statutes expressly specify the effects that a breach of a particular Act of Parliament has on a contract today.

Where a statute only impliedly declares a contract to be prohibited then the court must examine the Act to find the intention of Parliament in respect of the effects of the prohibition on the contract.

ACTS ILLEGAL AT COMMON LAW

The concept of a contract being illegal at common law is extremely wide and has its origins in the idea that a contract would not be upheld if its effect was contrary to the common good or it was injurious to society generally. The presence of such a concept in the nineteenth century and the early part of the twentieth century is rather contradictory to the idea of freedom of contract. Whilst the courts supported this idea, they recognised the need to qualify it so that contracts that were regarded as abhorrent or prejudicial to the interests of the community would not be upheld. Very often the decisions in cases falling within this area of concern were declared invalid by the judges on the basis of a vague notion of public policy, a concept which, of course, may cover a multitude of sins.

One of the great problems with the concept of public policy is that it is vague and has extremely wide borders. Even in the nineteenth century it had its critics, thus Anson quotes Burrough J in *Richardson* v *Mellish* (1924) 2 Bing 229 as stating: 'I, for one, protest . . . against arguing too strongly upon public policy; – it is a very unruly horse, and when you get astride it you never know where it will carry you.' Further Jessel MR in *Printing and Numerical Registering Co* v *Sampson* (1875) LR 19 Eq 462 counselled caution with its use. Lord Denning MR in recent times has not been reticent in handling the thorny stem of public policy and presented a reply to Burrough J in *Enderby Town FC Ltd* v *The Football Association Ltd* [1971] Ch 591 when he stated: 'With a good man in the saddle, the unruly horse can be kept in control. It can jump over obstacles.' The result has been something of a renaissance of public policy in recent times, though this is not perhaps so unusual since the concept lacks continuity. What one generation considers necessary for the common good is not necessarily true of the next generation, so it is inevitable that every so often a brush will make a clean sweep of areas that have, in the past, been subject to public policy and no doubt will introduce the concept to new aspects of commercial and social life.

Before we proceed to analyse contracts contrary to public policy in depth, a word about the organisation of the topic within this text would seem necessary. Some authors, including Cheshire, Fifoot and Furmston, discuss this area in two parts, namely contracts illegal on grounds of public policy and contracts void on grounds of public policy. However there is some disagreement as to which types of contracts are considered illegal and which are considered void. In particular, as was indicated in the introduction to this chapter, authors cannot agree on the effects of contracts being illegal or void at common law. In any event such a classification, as Treitel indicates, is an over-simplification since the effects of such contracts vary so much that it is almost impossible to group them under these two headings. In this work the contracts will be divided into contracts for the commission of an act that is wrong at common law and contracts which are contrary to public policy. However it must be stated that such a classification has been adopted in order to aid understanding of the subject matter rather than to place the contracts discussed into watertight compartments. With respect to contracts contrary to public policy, contracts in restraint of trade will be treated separately since this area of public policy is not only particularly important, but also somewhat lengthy.

Contracts for the commission of an act that is wrong at common law

It is clear that a contract to commit a crime must itself be illegal and the courts will not enforce such a contract. In *Bigos* v *Bousted* [1951] 1 All ER 92 it was held that a contract that was contrary to exchange control regulations would be unenforceable. Similarly it is well established that a person cannot benefit from his own crime, thus in *Beresford* v *Royal Insurance Co Ltd* [1937] 2 KB 197 it was held that the relatives of a person who had committed suicide could not claim under a life insurance policy, even though the insurance allowed a claim in such circumstances, provided the suicide (which was a crime at this time) did not occur within two years of the making of the policy. The court considered that to allow a claim to succeed would be to allow the deceased to provide for his relatives via a criminal act. The principle, however, must be treated guardedly since there are a great many statutory offences today which often do not require a guilty intention to secure conviction. In such cases it would be harsh to apply a general rule that no one can benefit from his crime. It should be noted that in the field of motoring insurance it is still possible for an insured to claim against his policy despite the fact that his actions might amount to a crime or incur civil liability, or both. In order for such a claim to be upheld, however, the act of the driver must not be a deliberate act but a negligent or reckless one, as was held in *Tinline* v *White Cross Insurance Association Ltd* [1921] 3 KB 327.

A contract will also be illegal if it has as its object the deliberate commission of a civil wrong. Thus a contract to commit an assault was held to be void in *Allen* v *Rescous* (1677) 2 Lev 174. Where, however, there is an unintentional commission of a civil wrong it would seem that if both the parties are unaware of the illegality then the contract is enforceable by and against each other. If, however, one party knows the contract to be illegal then it would seem that only the innocent party can enforce the contract.

Not surprisingly a contract to defraud the Inland Revenue or a rating/polling authority whether national or local is clearly illegal. Thus in *Alexander* v *Rayson* [1936] 1 KB 169 there was a lease of a flat in Piccadilly. The rent was £450 per annum but the lease provided that certain other services were to be provided. The 'other services' were detailed in a second document and the defendant had to pay another

£750 per annum for these services. A dispute arose and the defendant refused to pay the monies due under the agreement. When sued the defendant stated that the object of having two documents was to deceive the local authority as to the rent payable since the calculation of the rateable value, and hence the rates, depended on the rent payable. The Court of Appeal held that the plaintiff would not be entitled to recover the monies owed if the purpose of the two documents was indeed to perpetrate such a fraud.

Contracts contrary to public policy

Contracts prejudicial to the administration of justice

Such contracts are nearly always void and illegal no matter how slight the transgression. There are many examples of the application of this rule, for instance, an agreement not to proceed with divorce proceedings as in *Cooper* v *Willis* (1906) 22 TLR 582, an agreement by a wife that she would not apply for maintenance in divorce proceedings as in *Hyman* v *Hyman* [1929] AC 601, or an agreement by a witness not to give evidence as in *Harmony Shipping Co SA* v *Davis* [1979] 3 All ER 177.

It is, of course, most important that the exercise of the criminal law should not be capable of being suppressed by virtue of some private agreement. The courts will not hesitate to declare such a contract illegal and void where the agreement results in the withdrawal of a prosecution of a crime. In some cases, however, the courts will allow the question of liability to be compromised by agreement provided the offence is not one which is contrary to public interest. Thus in cases of libel, which may be the subject of a private suit or a criminal prosecution, an agreement compromising a prosecution may well be upheld since the choice of civil or criminal proceedings lies in the hands of the injured party. A similar situation arises in cases involving assault as seen in *Keir* v *Leeman* (1846) 9 QB 371. Though in this case it was held that the compromise was void, nevertheless Lord Denman CJ stated that normally a compromise is lawful where the criminal offence is one which also gives rise to civil liability. He stated that compromise is not possible where the offence involves the public interest. The case was not simply a case of assault but involved the public offence of riot and an assault on a public officer (a sheriff's officer) carrying out his duties.

So far our examination of contracts that are prejudicial to the administration of justice has been concerned with the situation where a party attempts by means of a contract to prevent the force of the law being brought against himself. There are, however, two categories of contract which the law regards as unlawful since they tend to promote litigation with the result that the action is not brought in good faith and may be regarded as speculative. It is regarded as contrary to public policy to allow a person to sell his right of action to another or, in fact, to allow a person to incite the bringing of litigation.

The two categories of contracts falling within this area are known as maintenance and champerty. A contract of maintenance arises where a person encourages and supports a course of litigation in which he has no interest. Such contracts will, however, be valid if a person can show that he has just cause or excuse in promoting and supporting the litigation. Thus in *Martell* v *Consett Iron Co Ltd* [1955] Ch 363 the action of a fishing club in supporting a riparian owner against the pollution of a river was held not to be a contract of maintenance.

Champerty is a contract in which a person is given assistance in bringing an action, either financially or by the provision of evidence, in return for a share in the rewards arising from the action if successful. Originally both maintenance and champerty gave rise to both criminal and tortious liability but both have now been abolished by the Criminal Law Act 1967, ss. 13 and 14. In relation to whether such contracts are treated as contrary to public policy or otherwise illegal, s. 14(2) of this Act specifically preserves such contracts.

A modern attempt at establishing a contract of champerty can be seen in *Picton Jones & Co* v *Arcadia Developments* [1989] 3 Estates Gazette 85, where the plaintiffs, a firm of chartered surveyors, agreed to act for the defendants in their attempt to acquire some amusement arcades. The contract required the plaintiffs to make applications for gaming licences and planning permission, but their fees were only to be payable 'in the event of ultimate success'. The plaintiffs successfully carried out their part of the contract but when they pressed the defendants for their fee they were told that the contract was one of champerty and unenforceable. Further they maintained that such a method of dealing was contrary to the rules of the plaintiffs' professional body and as such contrary to public policy and void. With regard to the latter defence it was held that an action that is contrary to the rules of a professional association was not necessarily illegal at law. With regard to the allegation that the contract was one of champerty it was held that such contracts only applied to the outcome of litigation. The plaintiffs were thus successful.

Contracts calculated to oust the jurisdiction of the courts

Such contracts have for many years been regarded as contrary to public policy and void. There is, however, no objection to a contract that requires the parties to attempt to resolve their dispute by reference to arbitration, provided there is no attempt to deprive the parties of their right to have their case heard before the ordinary courts of law. It is, however, not unusual for a right to take such action to be the subject of a condition precedent in the contract, whereby an arbitration award must first be made before the course of action can be placed before the ordinary courts of law. Such a clause is known as a '*Scott* v *Avery*' clause and is not *per se* regarded as ousting the jurisdiction of the courts.

The Arbitration Act 1979, which governs the rules regarding this area, specifically allows for an appeal to the High Court from an arbitrator's award on a point of law. The Act, however, allows the parties to oust this right of appeal in certain circumstances with the effect that it is possible under the Act for a dispute to be resolved by reference to arbitration only.

Contracts tending to corrupt the public service

It is clear that the public has a substantial interest in the negation of activities which tend to corrupt the administration of the state, both at a central or a local level, or which fetter the performance of public officers in exercising their duties. The object of the law here is clear in that it seeks to prevent the sale of public offices or the diversion of the salaries accruing to such offices by way of either assignment or mortgage. The reason for this latter point is thought to arise from the notion that should public officers assign their salaries, they will be open to the possibility of poverty which may lead them to compromise their positions. One wonders how such a principle has escaped the attention of public service pay negotiators in recent years!

Contracts prejudicial to the status of marriage and the family

The action for breach of promise to marry was abolished by the Law Reform (Miscellaneous Provisions) Act 1970, s. 1, but even when such contracts existed it was void as contrary to public policy for an individual to enter into a contract to marry whilst being already married. This being the starting point it is fairly easy to arrive at the point whereby a separation agreement made between parties still living together or contemplating marriage is also void as being inconsistent with the status and sanctity of marriage. Where the parties to the marriage are already separated the sanctity of the matrimonial state is no longer in jeopardy and agreements providing for separation here are valid. It should be noted that where the parties have separated but have become reconciled, any agreement providing for the possibility of future separation will also be valid, as held in *Macmahon* v *Macmahon* [1913] 1 IR 428. The apparent logic in finding such agreements to be valid is that unless such an agreement is arrived at the possibility of a reconciliation may be prejudiced.

A further type of contract that may arise in this context is the contract in restraint of marriage. Marriage has a peculiar position in the law and can itself amount to consideration. Historically much of the sanctity afforded to it revolves around the transmission of estates and interests in land. Given this state of affairs it is not surprising that a contract that unjustifiably restricts a person's ability to marry is void as contrary to public policy. Where the restraint is only partial, in that it is for a limited duration or where it merely limits the class or type of person that may or may not marry, then it is possible for the contract to be valid. Under the latter limitation, however, the persons capable or not of being married must be so small or large, as the case may be, as to render the ability to marry or not illusory. Further, a contract is not invalid if it operates not to restrain but merely to deter marriage, as, for example, an allowance of £500 per month until X marries.

The rule whereby a contract is void on the grounds of public policy also extends to the relationship between parent and child. Today there are statutory restrictions on agreements made between parents who are not living together as to parental rights and duties, in that such agreements to be enforceable must be for the benefit of the child. One statute providing such restrictions is the Guardianship Act 1973.

Sexually immoral contracts

It should be noted that the law does not render any immoral contracts void as being contrary to public policy, except those promoting sexual immorality. Many of the rules found in the common law revolve around the promotion of cohabitation. Contracts in this area have been held to be illegal and void, a conclusion which is not surprising given the attitude of the common law to marriage above. It is, however, a somewhat dated attitude given the present morality of society with regard to such matters. It was held in *Benyon* v *Nettleford* (1850) 3 Mac & G 94 that a promise by a man for a woman to become his mistress was illegal. However, it is not uncommon today to find unmarried couples making agreements as regards the purchase of houses and the distribution of their income within the relationship. There would seem to be nothing wrong in principle in these agreements being binding.

Clearly contracts involving prostitutes are void and unenforceable. It is thus highly unlikely that a prostitute could sue for her fees, though prostitution *per se* is not illegal, unlike the act of soliciting for clients by a prostitute. As already seen in *Pearce* v *Brooks* (1866) LR 1 Ex 213 a prostitute was held not to be liable for the charges arising from the hire of carriage to be used for the purpose of soliciting. Presumably the same would also apply to the hire of a room or a flat for such purposes. However a contract to hire a room, flat or house to an unmarried couple would be enforceable. The undoubted change in moral principles may well present the courts faced with such situations with something of a dilemma.

Contracts in restraint of trade

General principles

Such contracts are prima facie void as being contrary to public policy, which intervenes on two grounds. Firstly, the common law seeks to protect an individual from negotiating away his livelihood to another, possibly contractually stronger, party, particularly where the restraint is a general one. Secondly, the law understood, even in the earliest days of the doctrine in the sixteenth century, that it was not in the public interest for the state to be deprived of a valuable benefit in allowing a person to be restricted in carrying out his lawful trade or business. It is possible that the degree of interference in such contracts may be closely associated with the prevailing economic theory of the day, as regards the encouragement or discouragement of competition, though as Anson points out, there are no judicial authorities pointing out such fluctuations of policy.

Contracts in restraint of trade are defined in Cheshire, Fifoot and Furmston (1991) at p. 397 as:

A contract in restraint of trade is one by which a party restricts his future liberty to carry on his trade, business or profession in such manner and with such persons as he chooses.

The modern doctrine of restraint of trade is to be found in the case of *Nordenfelt* v *Maxim Nordenfelt Guns and Ammunition Co* [1894] AC 535 where a machine gun manufacturer sold his business and agreed in the contract of sale to restrict his future activities in that business worldwide for 25 years. The covenant was held to be valid and binding, even though prior to this case the general principle was that general restraints of this nature were prima facie void, whilst partial restraints were prima facie valid. The leading judgment in the case comes from Lord MacNaghten who stated:

> The true view at the present time I think, is this: The public have an interest in every person's carrying on his trade freely: so has the individual. All interference with individual liberty of action in trading, and all restraints of trade of themselves, if there is nothing more, are contrary to public policy, and therefore void. That is the general rule. But there are exceptions: restraints of trade and interference with individual liberty of action may be justified by the special circumstances of a particular case. It is a sufficient justification, and indeed it is the only justification, if the restriction is reasonable – reasonable, that is, in reference to the interests of the parties concerned and reasonable in reference to the interests of the public, so framed and so guarded as to afford adequate protection to the party in whose favour it is imposed, while at the same time it is in no way injurious to the public.

The result of this decision, together with a number of other later ones, is that the doctrine of restraint of trade can be reduced to a number of principles. Firstly, all contracts in restraint of trade are prima facie void. Secondly, it is a matter of the law for the court to decide whether any special factors exist which may or may not justify the restraint. If the view is taken that such special factors do not justify the restraint then the contract will be void as being contrary to public policy. Thirdly, however, if the special circumstances do point to the restraint being valid, then it must be reasonable not only as regards the parties to the contracting, but also as regards the interests of the public. Finally the burden of proving that the restraint is reasonable lies on the party alleging it to be so. If that burden is satisfied then it is always open for the party attempting to avoid the restraint to prove that the restraint is, in any event, contrary to the public interest and therefore void on this basis.

The above principles are now well established where the contract is in restraint of trade, though the obvious qualification is that the contract must be regarded as being in restraint of trade in the first place. In *Esso Petroleum Co Ltd* v *Harper's Garage (Stourport) Ltd* [1968] AC 269 Lord Wilberforce stated:

> It is not to be supposed, or encouraged, that a bare allegation that a contract limits a trader's freedom of action exposes a party suing on it to the burden of justification. There will always be certain categories of contracts as to which it can be said, with some degree of certainty, that the 'doctrine' does or does not apply to them. Positively, there are likely to be certain sensitive areas as to which the law will require in every case the tests of reasonableness to be passed; such as . . . contracts between employer and employee as regards the period after the employment has ceased. Negatively . . .

there will be types of contracts as to which the law should be prepared to say with some confidence that they do not enter into the field of restraint of trade at all.

The court must therefore decide whether the contract is in restraint of trade before considering the reasonableness or not of the restraint.

Reasonableness of the restraint

(a) Reasonableness as regards the parties to the contract. A covenant found to be in restraint of trade can only be regarded as reasonable if it is designed only to protect the legitimate interests of the covenantee. Whilst the basis for such a finding will undoubtedly vary from case to case, in *Herbert Morris Ltd* v *Saxelby* [1916] AC 688 Lord Shaw identified two types of contracts which illustrate the types of interests capable of being protected by a covenant in restraint of trade. Firstly, in contracts for the sale of a business, together with its goodwill, it is clearly proper for the purchaser to restrain the vendor from acting in competition with the business he had just sold to the purchaser since the goodwill is a proprietary interest legitimately capable of protection. Secondly, in contracts of employment an employer, whilst not legitimately able to prevent a former employee from acting in competition with him, is able to prevent the former employee from making use of trade secrets acquired during his period of employment. Similarly, the employer can prevent a former employee from soliciting his former employer's customers. In these two examples one can clearly see that the law is attempting to balance the rights of the individual and the requirements of the state in respect of trade.

Once it has been established that there is a legitimate interest capable of being protected it has to be remembered that the courts will only allow the covenantee to impose such a restraint as will do no more than protect his interest. If the covenant is excessive then it will be void. In assessing the reasonableness of the restraint the court will have regard to its nature, area and duration (see below). Finally the covenantee has to show that the restraint must be reasonable as regards both parties at the time of contracting. The effect is that the question of reasonableness is one which is directed towards the contract as a whole, and a contract will not be held to be reasonable if it is found to be unreasonable as regards one of the parties.

(b) Reasonableness as regards the public interest. Contracts that are void as being unreasonable as regards the public interest are extremely uncommon. One such example is that of *Wyatt* v *Kreglinger and Fernau* [1933] 1 KB 793 where the defendants promised the plaintiff a pension provided that he would not compete against them in the wool trade. The plaintiff eventually agreed and the pension was paid for nearly nine years, when the defendants then refused to pay. The plaintiff sued for breach of contract. The defendants denied that there was any such contract and stated that anyway such a contract was void since it was an unreasonable restraint of trade. The Court of Appeal held for the defendants and agreed that the restraint was too wide and in any event it was contrary to the public interest. One must, however, wonder to what degree the public was affected by this restraint. The

decision would seem to stretch the notion of public interest beyond the realms of reality.

(c) Other factors influencing the degree of reasonableness. The courts will also consider the following factors in deciding whether or not the covenant is reasonable or not:

(a) the duration of the restraint;
(b) the area of the restraint.

The restraint of trade covenant will be struck down if it is found to be unreasonably extensive as to its **duration**. It is clear that an employee's connections with his former employer's customers must wane in time, and similarly, one cannot protect one's trade secrets indefinitely. The question of duration is largely one of fact, depending on the nature of the business. Thus in the *Nordenfelt* case 25 years was upheld as being reasonable. It is nevertheless possible for the restraint to last indefinitely as in *Fitch* v *Dewes* [1921] 2 AC 158, where a covenant by a solicitor's clerk agreed that he would not practise within seven miles of Tamworth town hall was held to be reasonable, even though it was for an unlimited duration. The court considered that this restraint did no more than protect the legitimate interests of the solicitor, given the knowledge acquired by the clerk in respect to the clients of his former employer. On the face of things, however, this period seems excessive and the decision should probably be considered to be exceptional.

The covenant must not be excessive in respect of the **area** to which the restraint applies. Again in the *Nordenfelt* case a worldwide ban was appropriate given the reputation of the covenantor in that business. In *Forster & Sons Ltd* v *Suggett* (1918) 35 TLR 87 a covenant by a works manager, who had acquired knowledge of a secret glass-making process, not to engage in glass-making anywhere within the United Kingdom was held to be reasonable. On the other hand in *Mason* v *Provident Clothing and Supply Co* [1913] AC 724 a covenant by a canvasser not to work in a similar trade or business within 25 miles of London was held to be unreasonable given the covenantor's limited sphere of influence in his employment.

The construction of covenants in restraint of trade

In the case of *J A Mont (UK) Ltd* v *Mills* (1993) *The Times*, 7 January, the defendant was a man aged 43 who had been employed for twenty years in the paper tissue industry. It was the only work he knew and he had risen to become marketing and managing director of the company. In 1991 that company amalgamated with the plaintiffs and he became redundant. In 1992 he entered into a severance agreement with the plaintiffs in which he was paid a year's salary and relased from working for them for twelve months. This agreement was subject to a restriction that he was not to join another company in the paper tissue industry within one year of leaving the plaintiff's employment.

The defendant contended that the restraint was unreasonable as being too wide in that it not only operated worldwide but also that it restrained him from being involved in the paper tissue industry in any capacity at all. It was held at first instance that an interlocutory injunction should be granted in that there was a possibility that the defendant could have used confidential information in his new position. The judge, however, stated that the parties should co-operate with each other in drafting the restraint of trade clause in more reasonable terms. The plaintiffs contended that the judge should have construed the clause as being reasonable.

The Court of Appeal (Simon Brown LJ giving the leading judgment) found that there was no attempt to draft the covenant in terms that restrained the defendant from using confidential information, which was the only legitimate way in which the defendant could be restrained should he obtain future employment in the paper tissue industry. The Court of Appeal decided that as a matter of policy it would not attempt to discover whether there was any implicit limitation in the clause that rendered the clause narrower and, therefore, reasonable such that it could be enforced by injunction.

The Court of Appeal by the above decision took a highly restrictive views of its ability to construe restraint of trade clauses. Recently, however, the Court of Appeal in *Hanover Insurance Brokers Ltd and Christchurch Insurance Brokers Ltd v Schapiro* [1994] IRLR 82 indicated that a rather more liberal approach should be taken in construing such clauses.

The facts of the case were that the business of Hanover Insurance Brokers Ltd (the first plaintiff) was sold to Christchurch Insurance Brokers Ltd (the second plaintiffs) in June 1993. The defendants were all employees of the first plaintiffs (HIB); indeed three of the defendants were also directors of HIB, who all resigned once the sale had been completed. It was alleged by the plaintiffs that the defendants were attempting to solicit clients and employees of HIB both prior to and after leaving the employment of HIB. These activities were explicitly forbidden by a restrictive covenant in their contracts of employment. Subsequently the plaintiffs obtained an *ex parte* injunction against the defendants, which they then attempted to get discharged.

There was a difference in the wording between the restrictive covenants in the contracts of the first and second defendants and those of the third and fourth. In the latter the covenants were expressed to protect not only HIB, but also Hanover Acceptances Ltd (which was the holding company of HIB) and any of its subsidiaries. In the former the operation of the covenants was expressed to protect only HIB itself. The third and fourth defendants argued that by further restricting the non-solicitation of clients to Hanover Acceptances Ltd and its subsidiaries, there was an attempt to impose far wider protection than was necessary and that the clause was thus void for being an unreasonable restraint of trade. Their reasoning was based on the argument that the restrictive covenant could also operate in fields of economic activity other than the insurance brokerage business. The plaintiffs argued that the court should adopt a purposive approach to its construction of the clause, so that a narrow interpretation could be given to the clause in order that it reflect the intention of the parties, thereby rendering the clause enforceable.

Both the judge at first instance and the Court of Appeal considered that the only true intention of the parties was to restrict the defendants in soliciting insurance broking clients. Since HIB was the only subsidiary involved in this activity the Court decided that the parties only intended to protect the clients of this company, and therefore by applying this purposive approach the clause was enforceable to this degree. In arriving at this decision the Court of Appeal referred to *Littlewoods Organisation Ltd v Harris* [1987] 1 WLR 1472 where the Court of Appeal decided that a clause stating 'Great Universal Stores Ltd or any company subsidiary thereto . . .' limited the protection of the clause to that part of the plaintiffs' business activities to which they were reasonably entitled.

It should be noted that the decision of the Court of Appeal in the *Schapiro* case took place in relation to interlocutory proceedings. The Court considered that the cases of *J A Mont Ltd* and *Littlewoods* needed to be reconciled in a full hearing.

The application of covenants in restraint of trade in various situations

The categories of contract discussed below are merely examples of the application of such covenants. The categories of restraint are never closed.

(a) Contracts of employment. Covenants restraining an employee whilst actually engaged by his employer cannot usually be called into question since the employer can require an employee to maintain confidentiality in the course of his employment. Similarly in contracts of employment an employer can demand that an employee does not act in competition to his, the employer's, business. In these circumstances the doctrine of restraint of trade has no bearing on the validity or otherwise of the restraint.

It is only after an employee has left the covenantee's employment that the doctrine comes to bear. It has already been stated that an employer has a legitimate interest in protecting confidential information or preventing a former employee from soliciting customers so as to protect the goodwill of the employer's business. It is not legitimate, however, to prevent the former employee from exercising a personal trade or skill, even though that may have been acquired during the period of employment, as in an apprenticeship, for instance.

An interesting variation on this theme arose in *Hanover Investment Brokers Ltd and Christchurch Insurance Brokers Ltd* v *Schapiro* [1994] IRLR 82 as already discussed. One of the arguments put forward by the first defendant, who was the former chairman of HIB, was that he should not be restricted from soliciting clients that he brought to HIB when he began working there.

In putting forward this argument he relied on the case of *M & S Drapers (A Firm)* v *Reynolds* [1957] 1 WLR 9 where a salesman, when taking up employment with the plaintiffs, brought with him customers from his previous employment. On joining the plaintiffs he entered into a contract that contained a restrictive covenant which stated that on terminating his employment with the firm he would not, for the period of five years, solicit former customers on whom he had called during his employment. It was held that the clause was unenforceable in that the duration of the restraint was unreasonable.

The Court of Appeal in *Hanover* distinguished that case from that of *M & S Drapers* on the basis that in the latter case it was considered that a salesman's customer connections amounted to the equivalent of his tools of the trade, so that he could not be unreasonably deprived of them. In *Hanover*, however, the Court of Appeal considered that one of the reasons for employing the first defendant was the fact that he would bring clients into the business of the company; indeed, his salary reflected this commitment. The Court of Appeal therefore dismissed the arguments put forward by the first defendant.

One other aspect of the *Hanover* case that is relevant in the context of restraints in contracts of employment arose in relation to the third and fourth defendants, who argued that the restraint was unreasonable since it prevented them from soliciting clients with whom they had had no contract whilst employed by HIB. In arriving at its decision the Court of Appeal considered two apparently conflicting Court of Appeal cases: *G W Plowman & Son Ltd* v *Ash* [1964] 1 WLR 568 and *Marley Tile Co* v *Johnson* [1982] IRLR 75.

In *G W Plowman* the defendant, a sales representative, was employed under a contract that contained a restrictive covenant that he would not, for two years after the termination of his contract, solicit any farmer or market gardener who had been a customer of his employers at any time during the course of the defendant's contract. The defendant argued that this clause was too wide in that it sought to restrain him from soliciting customers who were not known to him. The court rejected this argument since it considered that he could easily avoid innocently breaching the covenant by simply asking a potential customer whether or not he had been a customer of the plaintiffs. If the answer was in the affirmative he could then avoid attempting to solicit business from that customer.

In *Marley Tile* there was a similar covenant against soliciting or dealing with former customers, but on this occasion the Court of Appeal held that this clause was too wide and unenforceable. The court found that of the 2,500 customers of the plaintiffs, the defendant could only have known or come into contact with a small proportion of them. In considering this case, though, it has to be noted that the restraining clause was wider than that in the *G W Plowman* case in two respects: firstly, the restriction prevented the defendant not only from soliciting former customers, but also from dealing with them; secondly, the restriction attempted to restrain the defendant from engaging in activities other than those for which he had been employed by the plaintiffs.

In the *Hanover* case Lord Justice Dillon, in considering *G W Plowman* and *Marley Tile*, thought that the decisions in these cases clearly showed that every case has to be decided on its own facts. His Lordship therefore resiled from making a decision, since in dealing with interlocutory proceedings the full facts were not known to him, i.e. he was not aware of what proportion of HIB's clients the defendants had contact with. This was not the problem in another case on this issue, *Austin Knight (UK) Ltd* v *Hinds* [1994] FSR 52, where Vinelott J had detailed knowledge of the extent of the employee's knowledge about her employer's clients. This information showed that she only knew a third of the clients and therefore Vinelott J distinguished the case before him from *G W Plowman*. The basis of the decision was that it is an unreasonable restraint of trade to prevent a defendant from approaching or dealing with customers of a former employer whom the defendant had no knowledge of or contact with during his or her employment.

The distinction between a personal skill or knowledge and confidential information obtained during employment can be exceedingly difficult to make, especially since 'know-how' is not widely regarded as a commodity in its own right. In *Leng & Co Ltd* v *Andrews* [1909] 1 Ch 763 a journalist covenanted not to work for any other newspaper within 20 miles of Sheffield. The principle behind the covenant was to protect so-called 'sources of information'. It was held that such interests could not be protected.

(b) Contracts for the sale of a business. Covenants in restraint of trade are far more likely to be upheld where they are contained in a contract for the sale of a business. It should be borne in mind, however, that restraints attempting to prevent competition *per se* are not valid, since there must be shown to be a legitimate interest worthy of protection. It follows from this that the restraint can only protect the legitimate interests of the business actually sold. This being the case in *British Reinforced Concrete Engineering Co Ltd* v *Schelff* [1921] 2 Ch 563 a manufacturer of a specialised road improvement product could not be restrained from engaging in the manufacture or sale of road reinforcements generally when he sold the business to the plaintiffs. The sale of the business concerned the specialised product only and therefore the restraint could only curb his activities in relation to that product.

Very often the restraint is designed to protect the goodwill that may be purchased with the business and this does, of course, form a proprietary interest capable of protection, though again, regard must be had to the area and duration of the restraint in assessing its reasonableness.

(c) Exclusive trading. Such contracts commonly arise where a manufacturer, or sometimes wholesalers, attempt to restrict the retailer in his method of distribution or pricing policy or simply to tie the retailer so closely to the chain of supply that he is prevented from selling similar goods produced by competing manufacturers or distributed by competing wholesalers. Such agreements are traditionally termed 'solus agreements', or, more recently, 'vertical agreements'. Technically there is no difference between the two in that they generally take the form of a person entering into an agreement to purchase all his requirements as regards certain types of goods from a particular manufacturer. Alternatively, he may be required to sell all that he produces of a particular item to an individual buyer.

The leading case in this area is that of *Esso Petroleum Co Ltd* v *Harper's Garage (Stourport) Ltd* [1967] 1 All ER 699 where the respondent owners of two garages entered a solus agreement with the appellants whereby they contracted to purchase all their petrol from the appellants. The agreement was to last for four years and five months in respect of one garage, during which the owners would receive a discount in the price of petrol purchased from the appellants. In respect of the second garage the 'tie' was to last for 21 years in return for a mortgage of £7,000 but covenants in the second agreement stated that they had also to comply with covenants contained in the agreement made in respect of the first contract. Further the respondents were not entitled to redeem the 21-year mortgage before the end of the term of the mortgage. When the respondents started to sell another brand of petrol they were sued by the appellants. The respondents argued that they were not bound by the contracts since they were an unreasonable restraint of trade.

The House of Lords held that both transactions fell within the doctrine of restraint of trade and were thus prima facie void. Their Lordships decided that there was nothing unlawful *per se* in a solus agreement since very often both parties benefited from the transaction. One party benefited from acquiring a chain of distribution which made the supply of its products efficient and economical. On the other hand, the other party, the respondents in this case, gained by acquiring extra capital finance and a preferential wholesale price. On this basis there were clearly interests that merited protection. Nevertheless the restrictions could only be enforced if they could be reasonable, not only between the parties, but also as regards the public interest. With regard to the first agreement they found that it was reasonable since it protected a legitimate interest of the parties and at the same time it was not contrary to the public interest. The court, however, decided that such agreements would become unreasonable if they operated for an excessive period and in this regard considered the second agreement to be unreasonable and void.

The stance taken by the House of Lords with regard to the second agreement is also consistent with the general principle in relation to the law of mortgages. Here equity will not allow a 'clog or fetter' on the equity of redemption. Any attempt to postpone the right of redemption or to render it illusory is void here. The court, however, stated that the doctrine of restraint of trade still applied even though it crossed into the field of land law. Their Lordships then adopted an unusual stance and stated that the doctrine did not apply where the restriction was applied to covenants contained in leases or conveyances of land. Thus if one purchases a garage, for instance, or takes a lease of such a garage and the oil company imposes covenants akin to those found in the *Harper's Garage* case, then such restrictions will be prima facie valid. This presumption as to validity will only be rebutted if it can be shown that the restrictions are contrary to the public interest, as stated in *Cleveland Petroleum Co Ltd* v *Dartstone Ltd* [1969] 1 All ER 201, where the Court of Appeal considered that to find otherwise would be to allow the doctrine of restraint of trade to be side-stepped by the adoption of a conveyancing device.

An attempt to make use of the above distinction between a person who is already in possession of his business premises entering into a solus agreement, thereby surrendering rights, and a person who enters into restrictions as he acquires his business premises can be seen in the case of *Alec Lobb (Garages) Ltd* v *Total Oil Great Britain Ltd* [1983] 1 WLR 87 where the plaintiff company was a petrol filling station. In 1969 it found itself in financial difficulties and turned to the defendants for help. This help took the form of the defendants taking a 51-year lease of the garage forecourt for £35,000 plus a nominal rent. There was an immediate lease-back arrangement whereby the directors of the plaintiff company acquired a 21-year sublease at a rent of £2,500 per annum, together with a solus clause whereby the plaintiffs agreed to buy all their petrol from the defendants. The reason the sublease was granted to the two directors of the plaintiff company was to avoid the solus clause being challenged, since if the clause was contained in what might be considered a separate transaction, namely the sublease, it would not be subject to the doctrine of restraint of trade.

The plaintiff company relied on an earlier decision of the Privy Council in *Amoco Australia Pty Ltd* v *Rocca Bros Motor Engineering Co Pty Ltd* [1975] AC 561 that a lease and a lease-back were held to be a single transaction, and that since the result of the solus clause was to render the sublease unenforceable, the effect was to render both transactions, that is, the lease and the sublease, unenforceable. This decision was followed in the *Alec Lobb* case, although the effect of the solus clause was not quite so fundamental as to render both transactions unenforceable. The Court of Appeal decided that the solus clause was severable from the sublease, with the result that both the lease and the sublease were upheld as valid but without the benefit of the solus clause.

(d) Restrictive trading agreements and monopolies. Despite the fact that the public interest must be considered in assessing the validity of an agreement in restraint of trade, most cases decide the validity of the restraints in such agreements by reference to their reasonableness as regards the parties. The result is that it is possible for restraints to go unchecked despite the fact that the public may be adversely affected by such an agreement. Since the validity is decided as a matter of private law should the case come to court (which it may not do, of course), there is no possibility of such restraints being challenged by third parties. The result of this state of affairs has been to prompt the intervention of Parliament by the passing of, firstly, the Monopolies and Restrictive Practices (Inquiry and Control) Act 1948 and the Restrictive Practices Act 1976.

The 1948 Act created a Commission, now known as the Monopolies and Mergers Commission, which may investigate references made to it by either the Secretary of State for Trade and Industry or the Director-General of Fair Trading. Its remit is to investigate and report on potential monopoly situations or on the potential implications of large mergers, either of which may require political decisions or legislative action. Latterly, under the Competition Act 1980, it also has had the power to investigate anti-competitive practices. It should be noted that the Commission does not possess the power of independent action and can only act on receiving a reference for investigation.

By virtue of Part III of the Restrictive Practices Act 1976 certain types of trading agreements are required to be registered with the Director-General of Fair Trading. If an agreement is required to be registered, then the Director brings it before a Restrictive Trade Practices Court so that its validity can be determined. If the agreement is found to be 'contrary to the public interest', it is declared void. The agreements falling within the Act are presumed to be void. The parties to the agreement have to rebut the presumption by bringing the agreement within one or more of eight tests laid down in s. 10(1) of the Act. Even if the parties are able to do this the agreement may nevertheless still be held to be void if the agreement is unreasonable between the parties or causes detriment to the general public, third party purchasers, consumers or users of the goods.

(e) Commercial agency agreements. A more extensive description of such agreements may be found in Chapter 20. However, it is appropriate to state at this point that the Commercial Agents Regulations 1993 control the use of restraint of trade clauses in such agreements. Regulation 20(1) provides that restraint of trade clauses in this context will only be valid if they are expressed in writing and are limited to the geographical area and/or group of customers and to the kind of goods covered by the agency contract. Furthermore, Regulation 20(2) provides that the restraint of trade clause must not last for more than two years after the termination of the agency contract. It should be noted that Regulation 20(3) preserves other enactments and rules of law and thus it would seem that, as regards the application of the Regulations in English law, the requirement that restraint of trade clauses have to be reasonable as between the parties is still a necessity for such clauses to be valid.

THE EFFECTS OF ILLEGALITY

The general effect

As was indicated at the start of the chapter, the expression 'illegal' covers a multitude of sins, some serious, some minor. It was also stated that the effect of illegality is widely disparate and not always consistent.

The fundamental rule of the courts was stated as long ago as the eighteenth century when Lord Mansfield declared in *Holman* v *Johnson* (1775) 1 Cowp 341 that no person who is aware of an illegality within a contract can enforce it. Furthermore, any money or property transferred under that contract is irrecoverable. Since illegality is founded on public policy such a rule is apparently sound in this context, but with regard to the parties themselves it produces great difficulties, mainly because it provides a defence to a defendant who may not merit such protection. The result of the rule is that the defence of illegality is available to both parties, whatever the rights and wrongs of their respective situations. Thus a plaintiff cannot base his claim on an illegal contract, though he may be able to do so if he can find an additional ground not based on the illegality. Further, a plaintiff will not be able to succeed where he is seen to benefit from the illegality.

The blind approach of the courts, whereby the relative fault of the parties is not taken into account, clearly is very unfair to the innocent party. The courts are now beginning to deal with this problem. Public policy still, however, remains at the forefront of judicial reasoning and under such policy the courts will not grant relief in cases where to do so would amount to aiding and abetting a criminal act, an action amounting to an affront to public conscience. This was indicated in *Thackerell* v *Barclays Bank plc* [1986] 1 All ER 676 and affirmed by the Court of Appeal in *Saunders* v *Edwards* [1987] 2 All ER 651.

The effect of this 'affront to public conscience' approach can be seen in *Howard* v *Shirlstar Container Transport Ltd* [1990] 3 All ER 366 where the plaintiff, a pilot, made a contract to recover an aircraft that had been impounded in Nigeria. The contract was illegal in that it was not so much a 'rescue' mission as a mission to steal the aircraft from under the noses of the Nigerian authorities. When he had successfully completed the contract the defendants refused to pay; when sued they raised the question of illegality as a defence. Even though the effect of his claim succeeding would have been to allow the plaintiff to benefit from an illegal act, the court decided that his claim should succeed since the conscience of the court in the opinion of Slaughter LJ was not compromised. Whilst this decision has been described and praised as the adoption of a 'pragmatic approach' it does not seem calculated to produce certainty within the law.

In *Tinsley* v *Milligan* [1993] 3 WLR 126 the House of Lords rejected the 'affront to public conscience' approach. The facts of the case were that both parties had provided money to purchase a house. The house was only put into the name of the plaintiff since the defendant wanted to make false claims in respect of social security payments. The defendant later claimed a share of the house, basing her claim on a resulting trust. The plaintiff's defence was that the defendant's claim should fail since the arrangement had been entered into to further an illegal purpose.

The House of Lords, by a majority, considered that the proper test was whether the action to assert the interest in the property relied on the illegality to support the action. On the facts this was not the case, since the action was brought simply to establish and enforce a property right that arose in the form of a trust. Lord Goff, representing the minority, took the view that, because 'he who comes to equity must come with clean hands', one could not use an equitable property right to subvert the consequences of illegality.

It may also be possible for an innocent party to succeed in his claim, provided the basic notion of public conscience is not broken in other situations. It may be that the contract itself is lawful but there is an intention to use it to further some illegal purpose or where one of the parties intends to perform it in some illegal manner. Here the innocent party will be able to recover damages or what is due to him under the contract, provided he was unaware of the illegal intention of the other party as in *Bloxsome* v *Williams* (1824) 3 B & C 232, though here it was the subject matter of the contract that was illegal. In *Cowan* v *Milbourn* (1867) LR 2 Ex 230 it was also stated that if he should discover the illegality before the transaction is performed then the innocent party can withdraw from the contract. An innocent party who discovers the illegality part of the way through performing the contract may withdraw from the contract and sue on a *quantum meruit* basis.

It should be borne in mind that a party to a contract will not be regarded as innocent if, while being fully aware of the facts, he is not aware of the illegality within the contract because he is ignorant of the law. Ignorance of the law is no excuse (*ignorantia juris neminem excusat*), thus in *J.W. Allan (Merchandising) Ltd* v *Cloke* [1963] 2 All ER 258 it was held that the fees for the hiring of a roulette wheel for purposes of a game that was illegal under the Betting and Gaming Act 1960 were not recoverable, despite the fact that both parties were unaware of the illegal nature of the game.

It was seen in our earlier examination of acts declared illegal, that a contract either expressly or impliedly prohibited by statute was void and unenforceable. In such a situation the innocent party is not necessarily precluded from obtaining a remedy since it may be that he has been induced into the contract by some misrepresentation. Had such an action been adopted in *Re Mahmoud and Isaphani* [1921] 2 KB 716 the result might have been different. Further it may be possible to avoid the effects of the illegality by alleging the existence of a collateral contract. Thus in *Strongman (1945) Ltd* v *Sincock* [1955] 2 QB 525 the plaintiffs, who were builders, contracted to modernise some houses for the defendant architect. At that time, due to shortages of materials, it was illegal to do such work without a licence. The plaintiffs were told by the defendant that he would obtain the necessary licences, but in fact he failed to do so. The defendant failed to pay for the work and when sued pleaded that the contract was void and unenforceable on the grounds that it was illegal. The court nevertheless held that there existed a collateral contract based on the promise of the defendant to obtain the appropriate licences and since he had failed to do so he was liable in damages. There are limits to the use of this device since the finding and enforcing of a collateral contract must not equate with the enforcement of the illegal contract. It may be, however, that an action could be sustained in misrepresentation despite such a finding, though of course the measure of damages would be different. Presumably the use of the fiction of collateral contracts would be subject to the 'public conscience' criterion.

Recovery of money or property

It has been seen in *Holman* v *Johnson* above that one effect of illegality was to render any money or property irrecoverable, just as a person is not allowed to benefit from an illegal contract, as we saw in *Beresford* v *Royal Insurance Co Ltd* above. In such a case even claims in quasi-contract (see Chapter 18) cannot be maintained. There are however three situations in which the parties will be relieved of the illegal nature of the contract.

Where the parties are not in pari delicto

Where the parties are not equally in the wrong it may be possible for the less culpable party to recover any property transferred or monies paid under the contract. This result may arise where the statute rendering the contract illegal is designed to give protection to a particular class of individuals, of whom the less guilty party forms a part. Thus under the Rent Act 1977, s. 125 allows a premium to secure a lease to be recovered where such a premium could not be lawfully required. This position also applies even if the tenant was a knowing party to a contract to evade the Rent Acts. This was so in *Kiriri Cotton Co Ltd* v *Dewani* [1960] AC 192 where a landlord's acceptance of a premium from the plaintiff to secure a flat was illegal, though the relevant statute did not allow for the recovery of such premium. The court found that the plaintiff had little choice but to accept the terms of the landlord, who fully intended to exploit the deficiencies in the legislation. In these circumstances the plaintiff could recover the premium paid despite its illegality.

The same criteria also apply where the less culpable party has been induced to enter the contract by virtue of some fraud or undue pressure by the other party. In *Hughes* v *Liverpool Victoria Legal Friendly Society* [1916] 2 KB 482 the plaintiff was induced by the fraudulent misrepresentation of the defendant's agent to take out a number of insurance policies against the lives of persons in whom she had no insurable interest, on the basis that such policies were valid and legal. In fact such policies were illegal and void, but nevertheless she could recover the premiums paid in respect of the policies. There is also authority that monies or property may also be recovered in similar circumstances where the defendant stands in a fiduciary relationship to the plaintiff.

Where the illegal contract has been withdrawn from

Money paid or property transferred under an illegal contract may be recovered if the contract did not take effect because of the plaintiff's decision to withdraw from it. In *Kearley* v *Thomson* (1890) 24 QBD 742 it was stated that recovery ceases to be possible once the illegal purpose has commenced, whether or not it is completed. This decision refutes an earlier one where it was suggested that recovery will be allowed provided withdrawal occurs before the illegal purpose is carried out. It is suggested that *Kearley* v *Thomson* now represents the true position.

In order to claim recovery under this head it must also be shown that the withdrawal from the contract is voluntary. If the execution of the contract is frustrated by the other party failing to carry out his side of the bargain, or where there is some other reason whereby withdrawal occurs other than by a voluntary act, then recovery will not be allowed. This was the case in *Bigos* v *Bousted* [1951] 1 All ER 92 in which, as we have already seen, there was an illegal contract to avoid the provisions of the Exchange Control Act 1947. The plaintiffs claimed that they could recover a share certificate deposited with the defendants as security for Italian currency because the currency was never forthcoming. It was held that the certificate could not be recovered because there was no voluntary withdrawal but merely a frustration of the contract by the defendant.

Where the illegal contract is not relied on for recovery

Here the recovery of goods transferred is not based on the illegal nature of the contract but on the existence of a proprietary interest in the goods. In other words, the plaintiff is relying on the fact that he retains some title to the property transferred. This being the case it is clear that recovery will not be allowed in a contract for the sale of goods, since here the property in the good passes on sale, unless, of course, the seller has retained title by virtue of a Romalpa or reservation of title clause. For the most part, however, recovery is limited to circumstances whereby something less than full ownership is delivered up to the other party, such as that found under a hire purchase agreement or lease. Thus in *Bowmakers Ltd* v *Barnet Instruments Ltd* [1945] KB 65 the defendants came into the possession of certain machine tools under an illegal hire purchase agreement. They failed to pay the instalments and in fact, contrary to their rights under the agreement, sold some of the tools. The plaintiffs sued under the tort of conversion to recover the value of the tools on the basis of asserting the proprietary rights they retained in the tools. They based their claim purely on the rules of hire purchase and bailment, making no reference to the illegality of the transaction. On this basis the court upheld their claim. If, however, they had made reference to the illegality of the transaction then the claim would probably have been rejected since it would have indicated that they were not relying on their proprietary rights but on the illegality. The decision has been subject to criticism since it is apparent that in pursuing the claim in conversion they must have had to rely on the contract – which was of course void and unenforceable for illegality.

SEVERANCE

Generally

Severance amounts to the removal of the illegal elements of the contract, leaving behind a valid and enforceable agreement. The application of severance is particularly important in contracts in restraint of trade enabling an objectionable restraint to be removed. There are, of course, limitations on the principle since, as we have seen in relation to implied terms, it is not for the court to rewrite the contract for the parties in order to produce something entirely different from what they intended. Should it be impossible to sever the objectionable parts of the contract so as to leave a contract that is capable of being carried out, then the whole contract will be void and unenforceable.

Before we assess the specific rules relating to the application of severance it should be noted that severance can only be used where it is consistent with the rule of public policy that renders the contract illegal in the first place. In *Napier v National Business Agency Ltd* [1951] 2 All ER 264 there was a contract in which an employee's wages were supplemented with an inflated figure for expenses far beyond those which he would normally incur. This arrangement was arrived at with the sole aim of defrauding the Inland Revenue. It was held that the contract was so tainted with illegality that the court refused to apply severance, with the result that the whole contract was vitiated. The employee could not recover wages owed to him despite the fact that he withdrew his claims in respect of 'expenses' outstanding.

The requirements necessary for the exercise of severance

The 'blue pencil' rule

The effect of this rule is that an objectionable part of a contract can only be severed where it leaves the remaining part verbally and grammatically correct and capable of standing alone. A case commonly quoted as an example of this rule is that of *Goldsoll v Goldman* [1915] 1 Ch 292 where a defendant sold his imitation jewellery business to the plaintiff, at the same time agreeing that he would not, for a period of two years, deal in real or imitation jewellery in the United Kingdom, France, the USA, Russia or within 25 miles of Potsdammerstrasse, Berlin, or St Stefans Kirche, Vienna, either on his own account or jointly. It was held by the Court of Appeal that the restraint was valid notwithstanding that the area of the restraint was too extensive. They therefore removed the restriction as to real jewellery and confined the area of the restraint to the United Kingdom.

The illegality must not comprise the main part of the contract

The objectionable part of the contract must not form the main part of the contract since the effect of severance would be to remove a central aspect of the contract. This is expressed by Anson in terms of the severance effectively reducing the consideration within the contract. The effect would be to compel the other party to continue with a bargain that represents far less than he originally contracted for.

In *Bennett* v *Bennett* [1952] 1 KB 249 a wife petitioned for a divorce, claiming maintenance for herself and her son. Prior to the hearing for the decree *nisi* she entered a deed with her husband whereby she agreed to withdraw the application for maintenance in return for the husband paying an annuity to her and the son and, at the same time, conveying certain property to the wife. The husband did not keep to the arrangement and was sued by the wife. The court found that the covenant entered into by the wife not to apply for maintenance was contrary to public policy and void. Severance of the offending covenant was considered but it was found that this played a central part in the agreement – it effectively represented the consideration for the agreement – therefore severance was not feasible. The agreement was thus held to be unenforceable and void, so that the wife could not claim the annuity.

The agreement must not be altered by the act of severance

It was stated in *Attwood* v *Lamont* [1920] 3 KB 571 by Lord Sterndale MR that the operation of severance must not 'alter entirely the scope and intention of the agreement'. In the above case, the plaintiff operated a general outfitter's business in Kidderminster, which was divided into different departments. The defendant had been employed as a tailor and cutter in the tailoring department. His contract of service contained a restraint of trade clause whereby he agreed that he would not, at any time, be concerned in the trade or business of a 'tailor, dressmaker, general draper, milliner, hatter, haberdasher, gentlemen's, ladies' or children's outfitter' within 10 miles of the plaintiff's store. It was held by the divisional court that the clause was too wide but that it could become enforceable by the severing of all the trades except that of tailor. The Court of Appeal also found the clause to be too wide in that it sought to restrain the defendant from trades in which he had not been employed. The court however refused to apply severance, stating that this was not possible where the covenant formed a single covenant, which they found to be the situation here, rather than a 'combination of several distinct covenants'.

The basis of the Court of Appeal's decision seems to be that severance would have altered the entire nature of the covenant. The original covenant was intended to protect the entire business, whilst severance would have had the effect of only protecting that part of the business, namely tailoring, in which the defendant had been employed. In other words the Court of Appeal considered the covenant to be entire, standing or falling in that entirety.

The case is extremely difficult to reconcile with *Goldsoll* v *Goldman*, which in many respects is virtually identical. On the face of things it would appear that the idea of dividing covenants into those which are entire and those which are several is unsatisfactory. One should examine each case on its own facts and decide whether the effect of severance is to alter the scope and intention of the agreement.

Further reading

Beale, Bishop and Furmston, *Contract – Cases and Materials* 2nd ed. 1990, Butterworths
Cheshire, Fifoot and Furmston, *The Law of Contract* 12th ed. 1991, Butterworths
Guest, *Anson's Law of Contract* 26th ed. 1984, Oxford University Press
Jefferson, 'Evading the Doctrine of Restraint of Trade', 134 *Solicitors Journal* 532, 1990
Treitel, *The Law of Contract* 8th ed. 1991, Sweet & Maxwell

Part IV

DISCHARGE OF CONTRACTS

13 | Discharge by performance and breach

PERFORMANCE

Introduction

The basic rule in relation to performance of a contract is that it must be carried out strictly in accordance with the terms of the contract. Failure to do so will entitle the innocent party to allege that the contract has not been performed and will give him the right to claim damages or to repudiate the contract and treat himself as discharged from it, as well as entitling him to claim damages, as we saw in Chapter 7. In the case of *Re Moore & Co* v *Landauer & Co* [1921] 2 KB 519 there was a contract for the sale of tins of canned fruit which were to be packed in cases of 30 tins. On delivery it was found that a number of the cases contained only 24 tins. It was held that the defendants could reject the entire consignment even though the total number of tins delivered was correct.

A similar case is that of *Arcos Ltd* v *E.A. Ronaasen & Son* [1933] AC 470 where there was a contract for a consignment of wooden staves to be used in barrel making, described in the contract as being half an inch thick. At the time of delivery the price of timber had fallen, and this meant that it was in the interests of the purchaser to be able to reject the cargo, since he could then renegotiate the contract at a lower price or go elsewhere for the timber. When the timber was measured it was found that most of it was 9/16 of an inch thick, though this difference would not have had any effect on the usefulness of the timber. The purchaser nevertheless was held to be entitled to reject the cargo. Lord Atkin stated the position in the following terms:

> A ton does not mean about a ton, or a yard about a yard. Still less when you descend to minute measurements does half an inch mean about half an inch. If a seller wants a margin he must, and

in my experience does, stipulate for it. . . . No doubt there may be microscopic deviations which businessmen and therefore lawyers will ignore. . . . But apart from the consideration the right view is that the condition of the contract must be strictly performed . . .

The position maintained by Lord Atkin needs qualifying in two ways. Firstly, and Lord Atkin hints at this qualification in the above passage, the law will not take notice of 'microscopic' deviations. This practice is sometimes expressed in the maxim *'de minimis non curat lex'*, though even where the deviation is minimal the innocent party may still reject where the contract expressly provides for precise performance. Secondly, in *Reardon Smith Line Ltd* v *Hansen-Tangen* [1976] 1 WLR 939, there was a reaction against an over-excessive exercise of the right to rescind the contract. In a contract for the sale of goods by description, words which merely identify the goods may not be regarded as being part of the description, thus preventing a breach of condition from arising. In the case there was a charter of a tanker ship that was under construction. Since the ship had not been named it was described as 'Yard No 354 at Osaka'. In fact the ship was not built at this place, though it met the contractual specifications and was built under the control of Osaka. The tanker market collapsed and the charterers sought to repudiate the contract. It was held that they could not do so since the phrase 'Yard No 354 at Osaka' was only a means of identifying the ship and a substitute for a name, not a description of the ship. Lord Wilberforce commented on the *Landauer* and *Ronaasen* cases stating that their decisions were 'excessively technical and due for fresh examination in this House'.

Despite the above means of limiting the strict approach to performance it should be borne in mind that the approach does have some statutory authority in certain circumstances. In contracts for the sale of goods, the Sale of Goods Act 1979, s. 30(1), provides that 'where the seller delivers to the buyer a quantity of goods less than he contracted to sell, the buyer may reject them, but if the buyer accepts the goods so delivered he must pay for them at the contract rate'. Conversely, s. 30(2) states that: where the seller delivers to the buyer a quantity of goods larger than he contracted to sell, the buyer may accept the goods included in the contract and reject the rest, or he may reject the whole'. However, s. 4(2) of the Sale and Supply of Goods Act 1994 now provides for an additional provision to be inserted into s. 30 of the Sale of Goods Act 1979. The new provision states:

'(2A) A buyer who does not deal as a consumer may not –
   (a) where the seller delivers a quantity of goods less than he contracted to sell, reject the goods under subsection (1) above, or
   (b) where the seller delivers a quantity of goods larger than he contracted to sell, reject the whole under subsection (2) above,
if the shortfall or, as the case may be, excess is so slight that it would be unreasonable for him to do so. . . .'

By s. 2B it is for the seller to show that a shortfall or excess is so slight that it would be unreasonable for him to reject the goods. There is thus now a statutory basis for the *de minimis* rule in non-consumer contracts.

The right to reject will still exist where there is a breach of the implied conditions that arise under the 1979 Act. In the context described above, s. 13 (implied condition as to description) is particularly appropriate, especially in a contract for the sale of unascertained goods, since these are invariably sales by description. One should be aware, however, that in non-consumer sales, s. 15A of the Sale of Goods Act 1979 (as inserted by s. 4(1) of the Sale and Supply of Goods Act 1994) limits the right to reject for a breach of condition where the breach is so slight that it would be unreasonable for the buyer to reject the goods, subject to contrary intention either express or implied in the contract.

The strict rule relating to performance is also relevant in what may be described as 'entire' contracts. In such contracts a person's contractual obligations are conditional on the other party performing his side of the contract completely and entirely. In *Cutter v Powell* (1756) 6 Term R 320 there was a contract by a seaman to serve on a ship bound from Jamaica to Liverpool. He was to be paid 30 guineas 'provided he proceeds, continues and does his duty . . . from hence to the port of Liverpool'. Unfortunately he died at sea prior to reaching Liverpool. The defendants refused to pay for the work he had completed prior to his death and were sued by the administratrix. It was held that her action would fail since the terms of the contract meant that he would only be paid if he sailed the ship to Liverpool and since he did not do so no pay was owed.

Clearly the application of the rule requiring strict performance is particularly harsh when seen in the light of the above case and for this reason the courts have developed several rules which have mitigated the effects of the general rule.

Mitigating the strict performance rule

The doctrine of substantial performance

In many respects this doctrine is really an offshoot of the *'de minimis'* rule outlined above. It arises where a person in fully performing his side of the bargain hopes that he has done all that he is required to do under the contract, or supplied everything he is supposed to supply, but there are nevertheless minor defects in his performance of the contract. In such a case the court will find that he has substantially performed his side of the contract and it will allow him to claim the contract price, less an amount by which the value of the contract has been diminished by his breach. Clearly such a solution is more equitable since it protects the interests of the innocent party whilst allowing the individual concerned an amount for work actually completed. If such a position was not adopted by the courts it could well mean that many sound businesses could be drawn into insolvency by virtue of minor breaches of contract. In any event it is unfair to allow a party to take the substantial benefit of the contract whilst at the same time escaping liability to pay for that benefit by reason of minor, technical breaches of the contract.

Clearly this area of performance is closely linked to the remedy of damages for breach of warranty or breach of an innominate term under the *Hong Kong Fir* principle, since in both situations it might be considered that there is substantial performance.

An example of the application may be seen in the case of *Hoenig v Isaacs* [1952] 2 All ER 176, where there was a contract by the plaintiff to decorate and furnish the defendant's flat for £750. The defendant alleged that the workmanship was poor and defective but paid £400. The plaintiff sued for the balance. The court found that there were defects in the work but that these could be cured for some £55, and thus awarded the plaintiff the full amount of the contract less the cost of putting right the defects and, of course, the amount already paid.

Partial performance

It may happen that an individual only partially performs his side of the contract yet nevertheless the other party, rather than reject the work, decides to accept the work that has actually been done. In these circumstances the promisee will be obliged to pay for the work done on a *quantum meruit* basis. It should be borne in mind that the promisee has complete discretion as to whether to accept the partial performance or not. In *Sumpter v Hedges* [1898] 1 QB 673 the plaintiff, who had agreed to erect certain buildings for the defendant, could not claim on a *quantum meruit* basis for work completed before he abandoned the contract. The defendant had gone on to the premises and completed the work himself, making use of materials left on the site by the plaintiff. The defendant had no option but to complete the buildings, though the plaintiff could recover for the materials used by the defendant since the defendant had the option of using those materials or not. Since he had decided to use them the court held that he should pay a reasonable price for them.

Tender of performance

To offer a tender to perform is regarded as equivalent to actual performance. It is clearly wrong to allow the promisee to avoid a contract for non-performance where he himself has refused to accept the offer of performance. Where such a situation arises it is open to the promisor to treat the refusal as discharging him from any further obligations under the contract. The promisor is also entitled to raise the promisee's refusal to accept his offer of performance as a defence to an action by the promisee for breach of contract. Thus in *Startup v Macdonald* (1843) 6 Man & G 593 the parties had contracted for the sale of 10 tons of linseed oil, which was to be delivered 'within the last fourteen days of March'. The plaintiffs delivered the oil at 8.30 p.m. on 31 March, a Saturday. The defendant refused to accept delivery and it was held that the plaintiffs were able to recover damages for the non-acceptance of the delivery of the oil. This decision needs however to be qualified in the context of the modern law contained in the Sale of Goods Act, s. 29(5), whereby 'Demand or tender of delivery may be treated as ineffectual unless made at a reasonable hour; and what is a reasonable hour is a question of fact'.

So far tender of performance has been examined in the context of performance of a service or delivery of goods. Performance may also be tendered by the payment of money. Where money is proffered for tender of performance but refused by the promisee, it should be borne in mind that the promisor is not discharged from the debt and he must remain willing and ready to discharge the debt, and that any special terms regarding payment must be complied with. Should the promisor tender payment and this is refused he should wait until he is sued on the debt and then pay the monies owed into court, raising his offer of payment as a defence to the action brought by the promisee. This will result in the promisee recovering the debt and no more, whilst the promisor will be entitled to claim his legal costs.

It may also arise that the promisor commences performance of the contract but is subsequently prevented from completing it because of the fault or actions of the promisee. In such a situation the promisor will be able to sue for breach of contract and gain damages on a *quantum meruit* basis for work actually completed. In *Planché v Colburn* (1831) 8 Bing 14 where the defendants had embarked on the publication of a series of books entitled *The Juvenile Library* the plaintiff was engaged to write a volume on ancient armour and costume for £100, the sum being payable on completion of the manuscript. When he had researched and written part of the book, the defendants abandoned the project. It was held that the plaintiff had accepted the abandonment of the project as discharging the contract, and that therefore he was entitled to be paid for the work actually completed at the acceptance of the breach. The court therefore awarded him £50 for his work.

Divisible contracts

The means of mitigating the rule requiring strict performance of a contract, as discussed above, have also been augmented by the development by the courts of a distinction between entire and divisible contracts. A divisible contract may be defined as a contract in which partial performance attracts an obligation to provide payment of part of the consideration. Such a state of affairs may be expressly provided for in the contract, where, for instance, large quantities of a particular commodity may be required. Here it could be agreed that the promisor will be paid for each ton of the commodity delivered or that a proportion of the contract price is payable on the delivery of each instalment of the item in question. If the promisor fails to complete the whole contract he will nevertheless be entitled to a proportion of the monies owed under the contract.

A further example of such a contract arises in contracts of employment where the terms of the contract state that a particular worker is to be paid weekly. If this term had applied to a case such as *Cutter v Powell*, the administratrix would have been able to claim the seaman's wages for each week of work completed before his death. Whether a contract is entire or divisible depends on the intentions of the parties as discovered by the courts.

The time of performance

At common law time was regarded as being 'of the essence' in a contract, unless the parties had agreed otherwise. Equity did not, however, regard time as being of the essence and would apply equitable remedies to the contract even where there was a failure to comply with the time fixed for completion of the contract.

The position is now governed by the Law of Property Act 1925, s. 41, which provides:

> Stipulations in a contract, as to time or otherwise, which according to rules of equity are not deemed to be or to have become of the essence of the contract, are also construed and have effect at law in accordance with the same rules.

The result of this provision is to fuse the rules of equity and those of the common law, producing the effect that if time is not of the essence there arises only a right to damages rather than a right to terminate the contract, as was held in *Raineri v Miles* [1981] AC 1050.

Equity did, however, regard time as being of the essence in three situations, stated in Halsbury's *Laws of England* (4th edition, Vol. 9, para. 481) to be where:

> (1) the parties expressly stipulate that conditions as to time must be strictly complied with: or (2) the nature of the subject of the contract or the surrounding circumstances show that time should be considered to be of the essence: or (3) a party who has been subjected to unreasonable delay gives notice to the party in default making time of the essence.

This statement of law has been stated to be correct and confirmed by the House of Lords in *United Scientific Holdings Ltd* v *Burnley Borough Council* [1978] AC 904 and, a little more recently, in *Bunge Corporation* v *Tradax Export SA* [1981] 2 All ER 513.

BREACH

Where a person fails to perform his side of the contract then, subject to the mitigating factors, he will be in breach of contract. A breach of contract will always give rise to a claim for damages, no matter how minor or serious the nature of the breach. Whether an innocent party is also entitled to treat the contract as at an end, so that he can treat the contract as discharged, depends on whether the breach is so serious that it goes to the root of the contract, that is, there is a breach of a primary obligation, or whether the other party has repudiated the contract prior to the performance of the contract.

Breach of primary obligation

It has already been shown in Chapter 7 that the innocent party may treat the contract as discharged where there has been a breach of a primary obligation of the contract. A primary obligation is often expressed as a condition. Such an obligation will give the parties this right if they have expressly agreed that it will do so, or where this effect is implied by the parties simply expressing a term to be a 'condition'. Such an effect may also be implied by the courts as in *The Mihalis Angelos* [1970] 3 All ER 125 or by statute as in the condition implied by the Sale of Goods Act 1979. Furthermore a contract may be treated as discharged where a term is found to be an innominate term and its breach has had the effect of depriving the innocent party of substantially what it was intended he should obtain under the contract, as in the *Hong Kong Fir Shipping* case.

Repudiation prior to performance of the contract

The types of breaches that have been discussed so far are those that have arisen by virtue of the fact that a party has not performed the contract in compliance with the terms of the contract when the time for performance has arrived. It may, however, occur that a party may indicate, either expressly or impliedly, by words or conduct, that he does not intend to honour his obligations under the contract. Such a repudiation is known as an anticipatory breach.

An example of an explicit repudiation can be seen in *Hochester* v *De La Tour* (1853) 2 E & B 678 where the defendant entered into a contract in April to employ the plaintiff in June as a courier. In May he wrote stating that he no longer required the plaintiff's services. The plaintiff brought his action prior to the date on which he was supposed to start work and succeeded. He was entitled to elect to treat the contract as discharged immediately and to sue for damages although the date of performance had not arisen.

An example of an implied repudiation may be seen in *Frost* v *Knight* (1872) LR 7 Exch 111 where the defendant promised to marry the plaintiff as soon as his father died. When the defendant retracted his promise by breaking off the engagement prior to his father's death, it was held that the plaintiff could immediately sue for damages for breach of contract, although the father was still alive.

Some care needs to be taken in deciding whether or not the anticipatory breach amounts to repudiation since it needs to be established beyond reasonable doubt from the circumstances of the case that the other party does not intend to perform his side of the contract. Thus in *Freeth* v *Barr* (1874) LR 9 CP 208, Keating J stated:

> It is not a mere refusal or omission of one of the contracting parties to do something which he ought to do, that will justify the other in repudiating the contract; but there must be an absolute refusal to perform his part of the contract.

Similarly Lord Selbourne in *Mersey Steel and Iron Co* v *Naylor Benzon & Co* (1884) 9 App Cas 434, stated:

> You must look at the actual circumstances of the case in order to see whether one party to the contract is relieved from its future performance by the conduct of the other; you must examine what that conduct is so as to see whether it amounts to a renunciation to an absolute refusal to perform the contract . . . and whether the other party may accept it as a reason for not performing his part.

Whilst an express intention may well be taken as amounting to repudiation it is always possible, just as where the repudiation is implied, that a misinterpretation may arise. If the innocent party treats such an anticipatory breach as an actual breach and treats the contract as at an end he would render himself in anticipatory breach no matter that his motives in taking such action were in good faith, as is illustrated in the *Hong Kong Fir* case. In *Federal Commerce and Navigation Co Ltd v Molena Alpha Inc* [1979] 1 All ER 307, a charter authorised the charterer to sign bills of lading stating that cargo had been prepaid. During the dispute the shipowners withdrew the authority of the charterers to sign the bills of lading so that the charterers were unable to issue bills of lading. Without these bills they would be unable to operate the ship. The shipowners believed they were entitled to take such action, but the charterers claimed that the action by the shipowners amounted to a wrongful repudiation of the contract. The House of Lords agreed with the charterers since even though the owners believed that they could take such action, this belief could not be reconciled with the disastrous effects of such a course of action on the business of the charterer.

The decision in the *Molena Alpha* case was however thrown open to doubt a year later by the House of Lords' decision in *Woodar Investment Development Ltd v Wimpey Construction (UK) Ltd* [1980] 1 All ER 571.

In this case there was a contract for the sale of land which allowed Wimpey, the purchasers, to rescind the contract should proceedings to compulsorily purchase the property commence before the completion of the sale. On the date the contract was signed the local authority had already commenced compulsory purchase proceedings in respect of part of the land. In the meantime the state of the market had changed, with land prices becoming depressed, so Wimpey wanted to escape from the contract. Just as in the *Molena Alpha* case, Wimpey took legal advice and proposed to Woodar that they should renegotiate the contract, but that if these negotiations failed they would rescind the contract. Woodar alleged that Wimpey had no right to take such action, at which point Wimpey wrote back rescinding the contract because they alleged that the contract had become discharged by way of the local authority's action. Woodar then alleged that the action of Wimpey amounted to repudiation which they (Woodar) had accepted and were therefore entitled to claim damages. The House of Lords held that Wimpey had not repudiated the contract. Lord Wilberforce stated:

> So far from repudiating the contract, Wimpey were relying on it and invoking one of its provisions, to which both parties had given their consent. And unless the invocation of that provision were totally abusive or lacking in good faith (neither of which is contended for), the fact that it has proved wrong in law cannot turn it into a repudiation.

On the basis of this judgment it would seem that if a party is mistaken as to his rights then this, provided he has acted in good faith, cannot amount to a repudiation of the contract. Lord Wilberforce was thus effectively drawing a distinction between a threatened breach, which would result in serious consequences for the other party, as in the *Molena Alpha* case, and a situation where a party exercised what he erroneously, but in good faith, believed to be a right under the contract, as in the *Woodar* case.

The decision in the case is a majority one, with Lord Salmon and Lord Russell dissenting, alleging that the case was identical to that of *Molena Alpha*. They stated that in both the cases one party was determined to depart from the terms of the contract on the basis that the contract entitled them to do so, though this view of the contract was an erroneous one. Cheshire, Fifoot and Furmston (12th edition, p. 538) point to three distinguishing factors between the cases. Firstly, in *Woodar*, the sellers could have waited and tested the correctness of their view of the contract by legal process rather than take immediate action. Secondly, in *Woodar*, the time for completion was some way off and if Wimpey had refused to complete on this basis their conduct would have amounted to completion. Thirdly, in the *Molena Alpha* case, the breach was anticipatory but the gap between repudiation and performance was short and thus greater pressure was placed on the charterers. That these differences exist cannot be doubted but in practical terms it leaves the parties, such as the charterers and Woodar, in an impossible position of having to make a qualitative decision as to whether a repudiation is based on a bona fide mistake as to rights contained in the contract, as in *Woodar*, or whether it is based on a decision by the other party not to carry on with the performance of the contract. On such a view it might be better to confine the decision in *Woodar* to the circumstances of that particular case.

A further hazard in this context is that it was held in *Vitol SA* v *Norelf Ltd (The Santa Clara)* [1994] 4 A11 ER 109 that there was no reason why an acceptance of an anticipatory breach by one party could arise either by words or conduct, provided these made it clear that the innocent party was responding to the repudiation by treating the contract as at an end. The court considered that whilst it might be more difficult to indicate acceptance of the repudiation solely on the basis of conduct, it was possible for this to arise if an innocent party did something completely incompatible with his own performance, or by simply not performing his own contractual obligations. Phillips J considered that there was an analogy to be drawn here with offer and acceptance in the formation of a contract.

A difficult question regarding repudiation arises in relation to contracts for the sale of goods where delivery is made by instalments, each instalment being paid for separately. Whether a failure to make or pay for an instalment amounts to repudiation largely depends on the terms of the contract and the circumstances in which the failure arises. In *Maple Flock Co Ltd* v *Universal Furniture Producers (Wembley) Ltd* [1934] 1 KB 148 it was stated by Lord Hewart in the Court of Appeal that:

> the main tests to be considered . . . are, first, the ratio quantitatively which the breach bears to the contract as a whole, and secondly, the degree of probability or improbability that such a breach will be repeated.

The principle contained in *Maple Flock* seems also to have been adopted in *Decro-Wall International SA* v *Practitioners in Marketing Ltd* [1971] 2 All ER 216 in that not just any breach of contract can be regarded as repudiation, but only those which deprive the injured party of a substantial benefit of what it was intended that he should receive under the contract. In the case the defendants were sole dealers for the plaintiffs in the United Kingdom, but as they were short of working capital, they were often late in paying for goods received from the plaintiffs. This caused inconvenience to the plaintiffs in that they had to pay interest to the bank when payments were not made promptly, though there was never any question that they would ultimately not be paid. On the face of things the Court of Appeal found that such a situation would almost certainly continue but found that the delays in payment could not amount to repudiation since they were not sufficiently serious as to bring the whole contract to an end. Lord Buckley suggested that the test to be applied was whether

> the consequences of the breach be such that it would be unfair to the injured party to hold him to the contract and leave him to the remedy in damages as and when a breach or breaches may occur? If this would be so, then repudiation has taken place.

The process has been more lately affirmed in the House of Lords in *Afovos Shipping Co SA* v *Pagnan and Lli, The Afovos* [1983] 1 All ER 449 where it was stated that the treatment of an anticipatory breach as repudiation could only arise if the breach related to a primary obligation or a fundamental breach.

The effects of breach

The right to affirm the contract

Where a party to a contract is in breach of a primary obligation or where he is guilty of conduct that amounts to repudiation then this will not bring about the automatic termination of the contract, and the innocent party is free to treat the contract as still subsisting. Where such a situation applies in a contract for the sale of goods the seller remains liable to deliver the goods in accordance with the contract, whilst the buyer remains liable to accept delivery and pay for the goods. Both parties also retain their right to sue on the contract.

In a situation where there has been an anticipatory breach of contract and the innocent party elects to affirm the contract, he is still required to perform his own obligations under the contract, but faces the danger that, should he subsequently become guilty of a breach of contract the other party may escape liability.

This point was discussed in *Fercometal SARL* v *Mediterranean Shipping Co SA, The Simona* [1989] AC 788 where there was a charterparty entered into in June 1982 whereby the shipowner agreed to take a cargo of steel coils from Durban to Bilbao. The charterparty contained an 'expected readiness to load' clause which entitled the charterers to cancel the charterparty should the ship not be ready to load on or before 9 July. On 2 July the shipowners asked for an extension to the expected readiness to load date as they wanted to load another cargo first and this meant that the ship would not be ready until 13 July. On receiving this request the charterers immediately cancelled the charterparty and chartered another vessel. The shipowners did not accept the repudiation and on 5 July gave notice to the charterers that the ship would be ready to load on 8 July. When the vessel subsequently arrived in Durban on that date, the shipowners gave notice that the ship was now ready to load. In fact this was not the case so the charterers rejected the notice and proceeded to load the cargo on to the second vessel. The shipowners brought an action for deadfreight.

In the arbitration proceedings that followed, the arbitrator upheld the shipowners' claim on the basis that the wrongful repudiation of the charterers relieved the shipowners from complying with their own obligations. The effect was that the shipowners' failure to tender the ship ready to load on time did not prevent them from recovering damages for wrongful repudiation by the charterers. On appeal this decision was set aside, though on further appeal to the Court of Appeal it was held that the unaccepted wrongful repudiation of the charterers did not prevent them from cancelling the contract when the shipowners failed to tender the vessel ready to load on 9 July.

The shipowners subsequently appealed to the House of Lords. Their Lordships confirmed the position that where a party wrongfully repudiated a contract, the innocent party could elect to affirm or treat the contract as discharged, subject to the criteria already discussed. If he elected to affirm the contract he was obliged to comply with his own contractual obligations under the contract. If an innocent party subsequently failed to comply with those obligations then the repudiating party could escape from his own liability for wrongful repudiation. The shipowners in question having affirmed the contract were subsequently in breach of contract themselves by not tendering the vessel ready to load on 9 July and thus remained bound by the cancellation clause in the charterparty which was exercised by the charterers when the ship arrived late in Durban. The shipowners' appeal was consequently dismissed.

A further danger with affirmation lies in the possibility that a frustrating event may occur after the innocent party has affirmed the contract. Frustration will be dealt with more fully in Chapter 15 but basically it amounts to an external event that renders the contract impossible. The effect of frustration is automatic and radical in that it brings the contract to an end so that both parties are excused further performance of the contract. Where an innocent party has decided to affirm a contract and there is an anticipatory breach, frustration will destroy the rights of that party to sue for the breach when the date of performance on the contract arrives. The point is well illustrated by the case of *Avery* v *Bowden* (1855) 5 E & B 714 where a ship was chartered to sail to the Russian Baltic port of Odessa and to take a cargo from the charterer's agent within 45 days. On the ship's arrival the agent stated that he could not provide a cargo and told the plaintiff to take the ship away. The plaintiff kept the ship at the port and repeatedly over the period in question asked the agent for a cargo and was in turn advised to take the ship away from the port. Before the 45-day period expired the Crimean War broke out and this rendered Odessa an enemy port and as a result the contract became frustrated. The effect of this was that the plaintiff lost the rights to sue for breach of contract since the frustrating event had destroyed the contract he had affirmed, together with his rights under it.

Once the innocent party has elected to affirm, or for that matter to treat the contract as discharged, he cannot retract his election. In *Panchaud Frères SA* v *Établissements General Grain Co* [1970] 1 Lloyd's Rep 53 it was held that affirmation is really a species of waiver that results in an innocent party being estopped from altering his election.

The fact that an innocent party can treat the contract as still subsisting and affirm his obligations under it so that he can go on to complete his obligations cannot be denied. In some circumstances, however, such a proposition is very unfair to the other party despite the fact that he was originally the offending party. The unfairness results from the fact that, in affirming the contract, the innocent party is entitled to continue to perform his obligations under the contract, thereby increasing his losses. When the date of performance arrives he can, despite having been told by the other party that he does not intend to perform the contract, use these losses as the basis of a claim for damages against the offending party.

In *White and Carter (Councils) Ltd* v *McGregor* [1962] AC 413 the appellants were suppliers of litter bins to local authorities, although the bins were paid for not by the local authorities but by businesses who had advertisements displayed on the bins. The respondents, who were proprietors of a garage, agreed to pay for advertisements on the bins for three years but on the same day that they entered into agreement they decided not to proceed and informed the appellants to that effect. The appellants refused to accept the cancellation (repudiation) and affirmed the contract even though they had at that stage taken no steps towards carrying out the contract. For the three years they prepared advertising plates, attached them to bins and displayed them throughout the locality agreed, making no attempt to mitigate their losses. At the end of the three-year period they sued for the entire contract price. It was held by a majority for the House of Lords that they were entitled to the contract price.

The decision is clearly unsatisfactory and all the judges considered that the appellants should not be allowed to succeed in such a claim, though none could find or develop a test which allowed the general rule relating to affirmation whilst qualifying its application in such a context. Lord Reid suggested that a plaintiff should not be allowed to affirm the contract and continue with it unless he could show that he had a legitimate interest, financial or otherwise, in performing the contract rather than claiming damages. The decision in *White and Carter* has been heavily criticised but it would seem that Lord Reid's approach has now been expressed judicially in the case of *Clea Shipping Corporation* v *Bulk Oil International Ltd, The Alaskan Trader (No 2)* [1984] 1 All ER 129 and that this will be the stance taken in future cases. It does, however, create a dilemma for the innocent party in that if he affirms but can show no legitimate interest then he will not be able to claim the full damages available to him – and that position is clearly fair. On the other hand, if he wrongly considers that there is an absence of a legitimate interest and decides to treat the contract as discharged, so that he can sue for his losses immediately, he may well find himself in breach of contract should he be unable to justify that stance in accordance with the rules discussed on pp. 260–4 above. Clearly some refinement of the rules is required.

A further limit on affirmation is that in certain contracts confirmation of the contract is only possible with the co-operation of the other party. If such co-operation is not forthcoming then clearly affirmation will not be possible. Such a situation often arises in contracts of employment. If an employer wrongfully dismisses an employee, that employee cannot claim that he is ready and willing to work but is being prevented from doing so by the employer and that the employer is liable for all losses of wages from the date of the dismissal. The employee's only remedy is to sue immediately for damages.

The right to treat the contract as discharged

The innocent party has the right to elect to accept the repudiation as discharging the contract with the result that all his future obligations under the contract come to an end, as do the obligations of the guilty party, though here his obligation to pay damages arises by operation of law, as stated in *Moschi v Lep Air Services Ltd* [1973] AC 331. It should also be noted that, just as in affirmation above, once the election to accept the repudiation has been made, it is not possible to retract it.

The decision to accept the repudiation and treat the contract as discharged is not one to be taken lightly since, as we have seen in cases such as *Woodar, Molena Alpha*, and so on, if the repudiation does not amount to a breach of a primary obligation then there is no right to treat the contract as discharged, with the result that the innocent party himself may be held to be in breach of contract.

Further reading

Beale, Bishop and Furmston, *Contract – Cases and Materials* 2nd ed. 1990, Butterworths

Beatson, 'Discharge for Breach: The Position of Instalment, Deposits and Other Payments Due Before Completion', 97 *Law Quarterly Review* 389, 1981

Cheshire, Fifoot and Furmston, *The Law of Contract* 12th ed. 1991, Butterworths

Guest, *Anson's Law of Contract* 26th ed. 1984, Oxford University Press

Treitel, *The Law of Contract* 8th ed. 1991, Sweet & Maxwell

14 | Discharge by agreement

INTRODUCTION

The general rule here is that since contracts are created by agreement then they may be extinguished by agreement. The rule thus stated is simple, but whilst the parties may agree to extinguish the contract there is always the possibility of one of the parties reneging on the agreement and taking action against the other for breach of contract. It is therefore advisable for the parties to formulate their agreement in terms of a second contract supported by consideration. But if the agreement is contained in a deed then no consideration will be required, regardless of whether the discharge is bilateral (i.e. where the contract is wholly or partly executory) or unilateral (i.e. where the contract is wholly executed by one party, but not by the other). For the most part, however, it is rare for such an agreement to be encompassed within a deed. It is therefore necessary to examine the nature of the consideration needed in the formulation of an agreement which purports to discharge a legally enforceable contract.

Whilst until now discharge by agreement has been expressed in terms of bringing the contract to an end, the principles apply not only where the parties are terminating the contract, but also where they are replacing it with a new one or simply varying the terms of the agreement.

BILATERAL DISCHARGE

Accord and satisfaction

As has already been stated, where both parties have yet to carry out their obligations under the contract, either wholly or partially, then their respective promises must be supported by consideration. This situation is often described by lawyers as 'accord and satisfaction' – which is just mystical legal parlance for describing the need for new consideration to support the discharge agreement. It was explained in *British Russian Gazette Ltd* v *Associated Newspapers Ltd* [1933] 2 KB 616 by Scrutton LJ in the following terms:

> Accord and satisfaction is the purchase of a release from an obligation, whether arising under a contract or tort by means of any valuable consideration, not being the actual performance of the obligation itself. The accord is the agreement by which the obligation is discharged. The satisfaction is the consideration which makes the agreement operative.

The 'satisfaction' supplied by the parties must not be something less than what was required under the original contract, as indicated in *Pinnel's* case and must amount to sufficient consideration, which was examined in Chapter 3. In this context, however, special attention must be given to the case of *Williams* v *Roffey Bros & Nicholls (Contractors) Ltd* [1990] 1 All ER 512 since here a variation of the terms of the contract was enforceable despite the fact that the promise of the contractors was not supported by any consideration supplied by the plaintiffs, but by the contractors obviating a disbenefit that arose because of a further obligation to a third party. Since such consideration falls well short of what is normally regarded as consideration it may be that the law is moving away from such a doctrine, possibly towards a position whereby discharge by agreement will come to rely more on the use of promissory estoppel as a means of enforcing the agreement. The discussions that arise in and out of the case of *Re Selectmove Ltd* (1994) *The Times*, 13 January, should also be considered here.

The form of discharge

Rescission and variation

Very often the problems relating to discharge revolve around the problems that arise because of the formalities required by certain types of contract. Thus it has been seen that certain contracts are required to be under seal, others to be evidenced in writing and yet others to be in writing. The rule here is that where it is intended to bring about the discharge of the contract then there is no need to comply with the formalities required at law. The position is different, however, where it is not only intended to discharge the contract but to substitute a new one, since in this situation the formalities would have to be complied with, as indicated in *Morris* v *Baron & Co* [1918] AC 1.

Waivers

The situation above is the position where the parties are entering into an agreement for their mutual advantage, but different considerations apply where the advantage is only to benefit one of the parties. Such a situation is termed a waiver and it normally arises where one party requests an alteration of the terms of the contract and the other party agrees not to insist on strict compliance with the terms of the contract, so, for example, he may allow late delivery at the request of the other party. The difference between a waiver and a variation is that in the former no new contract is created, it is simply that one party is agreeing to forgo his strict legal rights. This fact points to the historical basis for the existence of waivers in that it was a method of evading the requirement of evidence in writing under the Statute of Frauds, since no new contract was being created. So desperate were the judges to avoid the effects of the Statute of Frauds that they made no attempt to justify how a purely gratuitous promise could be enforceable.

The enforcement of purely gratuitous promises in waivers still poses a conundrum for lawyers when they are attempting to justify their existence, and it is probably better simply to regard them as a form of promissory estoppel. In truth waivers are slightly wider in application than promissory estoppel, which normally requires the promisee to alter his position in reliance on the promise of the other party; such a requirement is not necessary in waivers.

The modern authority on waivers remains *Charles Rickards Ltd* v *Oppenheim* [1950] 1 All ER 420 where a chassis for a Rolls-Royce was ordered from the plaintiffs, who later also agreed to build a body for it in 'six to seven months'. At the end of seven months the body had not been completed and the defendant agreed to wait another three months. At the end of this period it was still not ready so the defendant gave notice that if it was not ready within four weeks he would cancel the order. At the end of this period the body was still not ready so the order was cancelled. The Court of Appeal held that he was entitled to do so since, even though he had waived the stipulation as to time of delivery, he had given reasonable notice of his intention to make time of the essence. Lord Denning commented:

> Whether it be called waiver or forbearance on his part, or an agreed variation or substituted performance, does not matter. It is a kind of estoppel. By his conduct he evinced an intention to affect their legal relations. He made, in effect, a promise not to insist on his strict legal rights. That promise was intended to be acted on, and was in fact acted on. He cannot afterwards go back on it.

In fact some authorities distinguish between waivers and promissory estoppel, considering that they are related but separate doctrines that produce the same effects. Such a difference of opinion can be seen in *Brikom Investments Ltd* v *Carr* [1979] 2 All ER 753.

Express provision for discharge

The parties may agree either expressly or impliedly in their contract that it will become discharged should certain circumstances arise. A common example would be where the parties have agreed that the operation of some condition subsequent will have the effect of discharging the contract.

UNILATERAL DISCHARGE

Unilateral discharge usually arises where one party has fully performed his obligations under the contract, the other party having yet to do so. The situation may arise therefore that the first party agrees to release the other from any obligations that he has yet to perform. The problem with this type of discharge is that it is purely gratuitous and unenforceable, unless it is made by deed.

Further reading

Beale, Bishop and Furmston, *Contract – Cases and Materials* 2nd ed. 1990, Butterworths

Cheshire, Fifoot and Furmston, *The Law of Contract* 12th ed. 1991, Butterworths

Dugdale and Yates, 'Variation, Waiver and Estoppel – A Reappraisal', 38 *Modern Law Review* 680, 1976

Guest, *Anson's Law of Contract* 26th ed. 1984, Oxford University Press

Treitel, *The Law of Contract* 8th ed. 1991, Sweet & Maxwell

15 | Discharge by frustration

INTRODUCTION

It has already been seen in relation to the discharge of contracts by performance that the overriding principle is that compliance with the terms of a contract is strict. This principle, however, would be grossly unfair if a promisor becomes liable for breach of contract because he is prevented from performing his side of a bargain by the occurrence of some unforeseeable event that is beyond his control. In such circumstances the law provides the promisor with the excuse that the contract has become frustrated.

Frustration is really an expression indicating that the contract, once entered into, has subsequently become impossible to perform, as opposed to the doctrine of initial impossibility in relation to mistake as discussed in Chapter 10. The effect of frustration being proved is dramatic and radical, in that it brings about the immediate and automatic end to the contract, releasing the parties from the need to perform their obligations under it.

Originally supervening events that were beyond the control of either party had no effect on the obligations of the parties to perform their side of the contract, as we see in the case of *Paradine* v *Jane* (1647) Aleyn 26. Once the doctrine began to emerge, however, such was its radical impact on the contract that the courts strove to confine it within narrow limits. This confinement of the doctrine operated at two levels. Firstly, the courts would only allow frustration to be used as a defence to an action for breach of contract where the supervening event destroyed a fundamental assumption on which the contract was based. Secondly, the courts recognised that contracts themselves could provide for the consequences of the occurrence of such an event. The second point gave rise to so-called *force majeure* clauses that businessmen commonly began to draft into their contracts in order to restrict the effects of a frustrating event.

THE DEVELOPMENT OF THE MODERN DOCTRINE

Just as businessmen could insert in their contracts express provisions dealing with frustrating events, the courts were empowered to imply terms into contracts, as we have already seen in Chapter 7. In the nineteenth century the principles of freedom of contract and equality of bargaining power were very much in vogue, with the result that the courts were most reluctant to imply terms into contracts, though they could be persuaded to do so where the gravity of their failure to intervene would produce serious consequences. It should be recalled, however, that this intervention was not made on the basis of judicial intervention but on the fiction that they were giving effect to the unexpressed wishes or intentions of the parties.

The ability of the courts to imply terms into contracts produced the breakthrough that was needed in order to develop the modern doctrine of frustration. The case which produced this result was *Taylor* v *Caldwell* (1863) 3 B & S 826.

In this case the defendant agreed to hire a music hall to the plaintiff. After the contract was made, but prior to the day of the first concert, a fire broke out, completely destroying the music hall. By this time the plaintiffs had made extensive arrangements with regard to the productions they intended to perform. The loss of the music hall meant that their concerts had to be cancelled, resulting in substantial financial loss to the plaintiffs. The contract contained no express provisions dealing with this eventuality so the plaintiffs sued for non-performance of the contract in order to recover their losses. The defendants pleaded the destruction of the music hall through no fault of their own as a defence.

The court upheld the defence of the defendants, deciding that the principle contained in *Paradine* v *Jane* was confined to positive contracts. The contract in *Taylor* v *Caldwell* was found not to be a positive contract, where performance was guaranteed, but one that was subject to an implied condition that the hall would continue to exist until performance was due. Thus Blackburn J stated the position to be:

> that, in contracts in which performance depends on the continued existence of a given person or thing, a condition is implied that the impossibility of performance arising from the perishing of the person or thing shall excuse the performance. In one of these cases is the promise in words other than positive, nor is there any express stipulation that the destruction of the person or thing shall excuse the performance; but that excuse is by law implied, because from the nature of the contract it is apparent that the parties contracted on the basis of the continued existence of the particular person or chattel.

From this basis the doctrine of frustration began to expand, though it always relied on the basis of an implied term because of the continued fiction of equality of bargaining power. Eventually the implied term became almost as fictitious as the principle it sought to avoid, so wide was its area of application.

The fictitious nature of the implied term was discussed in *Davis Contractors Ltd* v *Fareham UDC* [1956] 2 All ER 145, in which both Lord Reid and Lord Radcliffe expressed dissatisfaction with the concept. Lord Radcliffe in particular thought that it was clearly illogical to imply a term into a contract. He stated:

> there is something of a logical difficulty in seeing how the parties could even impliedly have provided for something which, *ex hypothesi*, they neither expected nor foresaw.

The falsehood of the implied term concept is clearly exposed here, since in such circumstances it would be impossible to apply that other peculiar fiction in this area – the officious bystander test – since this relies, as expressed in *Shirlaw* v *Southern Foundries Ltd* [1939] 2 KB 206, on the parties reacting with an 'Oh, of course' to the suggestion that a particular term be contained in the contract. If the parties could not possibly have expected or foreseen the implied term expressed in *Taylor* v *Caldwell*, then it stands to reason they cannot fall within the officious bystander test.

The obvious inconsistency led both Lord Reid and Lord Radcliffe to find for some other basis for a doctrine of frustration. Lord Reid expressed this basis in the following terms:

> It appears to me that frustration depends, at least in most cases, not on adding any implied term but on the true construction of the terms which are, in the contract, read in the light of the nature of the contract and of the relevant surrounding circumstances when the contract was made . . .

Lord Radcliffe stated this position more fully:

> So, perhaps it would be simpler to say at the outset that frustration occurs whenever the law recognises that, without default of either party, a contractual obligation has become incapable of being performed because the circumstances in which performance is called for would render it a thing radically different from that which was undertaken by the contract . . .

Thus both Lord Reid and Lord Radcliffe stepped outside the concept of the implied term perpetuated by *Taylor* v *Caldwell* and found that the modern doctrine of frustration should be based on an objective rule within the law of contract that arose independently of the intentions of the parties, as formulated in cases such as *Shirlaw* v *Southern Foundries Ltd*. It may, of course, still be possible to base the application of frustration on an implied term today, but here it will arise as a term implied by law, an application of which was seen in *Liverpool City Council* v *Irwin* in Chapter 7, where the intentions of the parties also have no relevance. Lord Wilberforce in *National Carriers Ltd* v *Panalpina (Northern) Ltd* [1981] AC 675 was most reluctant to repudiate the continued existence of the implied term basis, preferring to think of it as having merged into the modern test and remaining almost dormant until the circumstances require its use.

The modern test is often expressed as a 'radical change in obligations' or a 'construction' test. The court is required to construe the contract in the light of its nature and surrounding circumstances so that the obligations of the parties can be determined. Once this has been done the court is then able to assess whether the obligations of the parties have changed because of the subsequent supervening events.

It should be noted carefully that it is not a radical change in circumstances that triggers the operation of the doctrine of frustration but a radical change in the obligations of the parties under the terms of the contract as construed by the court. As Lord Radcliffe pointed out in the *Davis Contractors* case:

> it is not hardship or inconvenience or material loss itself which calls the principle of frustration into play. There must be as well such a change in the significance of the obligation that the thing undertaken would, if performed, be a different thing from that contracted for.

Similarly, more recently, Lord Simon, in the *National Carriers Ltd* case, stated the test to be:

> Frustration of a contract takes place when there supervenes an event (without default of either party and for which the contract makes no sufficient provision) which so significantly changes the nature (not merely the expense or onerousness) of the outstanding contractual rights and/or obligations from what the parties could reasonably have contemplated at the time of its execution that it would be unjust to hold them to the literal sense of its stipulations in the new circumstances; in such a case the law declares both parties to be discharged from further performance.

Before we see how the doctrine of frustration has been applied in various types of situations, it should be noted that the test amounts to a question of law not fact, even though the issue of facts heavily overlays the considerations of the court.

APPLICATIONS OF THE DOCTRINE OF FRUSTRATION

It is not possible to discuss all the circumstances in which the doctrine of frustration applies since these are obviously innumerable, but it is possible to identify certain typical situations which cover most of the situations in which the doctrine has arisen.

Destruction and unavailability of the subject matter of the contract

Clearly this is the most obvious situation, an example of which has already been seen in *Taylor* v *Caldwell* above. The death of an individual on whom the execution of the contract depends would present another example.

A similar situation also arises where the subject, though not destroyed, ceases to be available for the purposes of the contract. To a large degree the finding of frustration here revolves around the period of unavailability. If this is only a short time then the courts might well determine that the contract still subsists, such a finding becoming less predictable the longer the period of unavailability. So for instance the absence of an artiste from a show for one night because of illness would almost certainly not frustrate the contract, whilst an absence of several weeks would. It is easy to see here how it is important for the courts to construe the contract in the light of its nature and circumstances before deciding the issue of frustration. In situations like that in the example above, the length of the overall contract balanced against the period of illness is of major consideration by the court.

A case displaying a particular problem in this respect is that of *Condor* v *The Barron Knights Ltd* [1966] 1 WLR 87 where a contract relating to a member of a pop group contemplated that he would be able to work seven evenings a week, should this work be available. The member fell ill and was advised to work only a limited number of nights a week. In fact he ignored this advice since he considered himself sufficiently well to work to the contract, and he did so. The court nevertheless held the contract to be frustrated because it was possible that the member's health could have broken down at any time, and therefore it was necessary to employ another musician to be available to take the regular member's place should this event occur. This was, however, impracticable since it meant that the group had to rehearse twice, in order to prepare the reserve member of the group should he be needed.

Non-occurrence of an event central to the contract

It may happen that whilst it may be physically possible to carry out the contract, the non-occurrence of an event specified in the contract, on which the contract is based, renders the contract pointless. The question that arises here is whether the non-occurrence renders the object of the contract defeated and thereby frustrated. One has to distinguish here between the situation where the specified event amounts to the object of the contract and that where it merely amounts to the motive for entering into the contract in the first place.

The distinction between object and motive is clearly seen in the so-called 'Coronation cases' of *Krell* v *Henry* [1903] 2 KB 740 and *Herne Bay Steamboat Co* v *Hutton* [1903] 2 KB 683. In the former, the plaintiff hired a flat to the defendant for 26 and 27 June 1902. The defendant intended to use the flat in order to watch and celebrate the coronation procession of Edward VII which would pass by the flat. No mention of this purpose was made in the contract. A prepayment of one-third of the rent was made. Due to the sudden illness of the King the coronation procession was cancelled and the defendant refused to pay the balance of the rent owing. It was held that the plaintiff could not recover these monies since the contract had been frustrated by the cancellation of the procession. The court found that the procession and the position of the flat formed the objective of the contract which was thus frustrated and discharged as a result.

In the *Herne Bay Steamboat* case the defendant hired a motor launch for 28 and 29 June 1902 for the purpose of seeing the coronation naval review of the fleet at Spithead and allowing the passengers themselves the opportunity of touring the fleet. Again the review was cancelled because of the King's illness, though the fleet remained at Spithead. It was held that the defendant was bound by the contract which had not been frustrated by the cancellation of the review. The coronation review was held not to be the object of the contract but merely the motive for the hiring of the motor launch on these dates. The court based its decision on two grounds. Firstly, it was still possible for the tour of the fleet to take place and, secondly, since the defendant intended to charge the passengers for the trip it was his venture and therefore he should bear the risks inherent in the venture.

Inability to comply with specified manner of performance

In commercial contracts it is common for the contract to require a party to carry out the terms of the contract in a particular manner, and if it should become impossible for him to comply with that specified manner then the contract will be frustrated. A distinction is made between mandatory stipulations and those which merely express an expected manner of performance. In the latter any supervening events that occur and prevent such an expected manner of performance rarely have the effect of rendering the contract frustrated.

Thus in 1956 and 1967 the closing of the Suez Canal meant that ships had to be diverted around the Cape of Good Hope in order to reach India and the Far East. This diversion obviously meant that extra costs were incurred by the shipping companies, which therefore sought to have their contracts set aside for frustration in order that they could renegotiate their freight contracts. In a number of cases, like that of *Tsakiroglou & Co Ltd* v *Noblee Thorl GmbH* [1962] AC 93 and *The Eugenia* [1964] 1 All ER 161, the courts held that the contracts were not frustrated since, while the shipowners had contemplated moving their ships through the Suez Canal when pricing their freight rates, such a manner of performance of the contract was not stipulated within the contract. The fact that their costs had increased substantially over what had been contemplated did not help the shipowners since, if we recollect the words of Lord Radcliffe in the *Davis* case, 'it is not hardship or inconvenience or material loss which calls the principle of frustration into play'.

Unavailability

It is clear that a delay in performing the contract caused by some supervening event may also frustrate the contract. The Gulf War cases produce an example here, where ships became trapped in the Gulf by virtue of hostilities there. Of course the degree of delay is important but in cases like that of *The Evia* [1983] 1 AC 736, *The Agathon* [1982] 2 Lloyd's Rep 211, *The Wenjiang (No 2)* [1983] 1 Lloyd's Rep 400 and *Finelvet AG* v *Vinava Shipping Co Ltd* [1983] 2 All ER 658, the ships were confined for such long periods that the contracts were found to be frustrated.

In the latter case the ship was a time chartered ship which became trapped on 22 September 1980. However the court upheld the decision of the arbitrator to find that the contract was frustrated, not on this date, but on 24 November 1980. The reasoning was that at the earlier date expert opinion considered that the war would be quickly won by Iraq, thereby reducing the period of confinement. At the time of the later date the expert opinion had changed to that of anticipating a protracted war, which clearly resulted in the contract being frustrated. The courts thus have to balance the length of time of the charter with the temporary unavailability of the vessel caused by the frustrating event. In the case of *Pioneer Shipping Ltd* v *BTP Tioxide Ltd, The Nema* [1981] 2 All ER 1030, a time charter envisaged that during a nine-month period the vessel would be able to make six or seven voyages. In fact a strike at the port where the ship was being loaded meant that the number of voyages within the contract period was reduced to two. It was held that the contract was frustrated since the degree to which the contract was capable of performance was inordinately small compared to that contracted for. Lord Wright stated the position:

> If there is a reasonable probability from the nature of the interruption that it will be of an indefinite duration, they ought to be free to turn their assets, their plant and equipment and their business operations into activities which are open to them, and to be free from commitments which are struck with sterility for an uncertain future period.

One difficulty with frustration in such instances is when one can treat the contract as discharged. The delay or unavailability of the subject matter might be for a short period or a long period, but of course one does not know which. In such a situation it is possible for the courts to wait and see in order to determine the possible length of unavailability, either as a matter of fact or as a matter of inference by reference to all the circumstances surrounding the contract and the frustrating event, as we saw in the *Finelvet* case above.

Supervening illegality

It occasionally happens that once a contract has been entered into the law, quite independently, may move to the position that the performance of contracts of the type entered into is illegal. The position here was simply and cogently put by Lord Macmillan in *Denny, Mott and Dickson Ltd* v *James B. Fraser & Co Ltd* [1944] 1 All ER 678. He stated: 'It is plain that a contract to do what it has become illegal to do cannot be legally enforceable.' Thus if a contract is made to ship goods to a country and it subsequently becomes illegal to import such goods then the contract becomes frustrated.

The problem of frustration in leases

The particular problem that arises with frustration in leases is that when a tenant takes a lease over property he is acquiring an estate in land that persists even if the building rented is completely destroyed by, for instance, fire or bomb damage or is completely demolished by a heavy goods vehicle. The logic is correct since, whilst the layman may think in terms of renting a house, flat, warehouse or factory, the lawyer knows that one is actually leasing the land, the rent that is paid reflecting the length of the lease, the type of property and its position and location. The result is that even if the building is completely destroyed, one still has to pay the rent *on the land* leased, regardless of the fact that it merely comprises a burnt-out shell or a hole in the ground. Evidence of this state of affairs lies in the fact that when one purchases a house, for instance, it is well established that the purchaser should take out building insurance from the time the contracts are signed and exchanged, since the risk in the property passes to him at that point. Is it possible, however, to claim that the lease has been frustrated by the occurrence of such an event?

In *Cricklewood Property & Investment Trust Ltd* v *Leighton's Investment Trust Ltd* [1945] AC 221 a plot of land was let in 1936 to the lessees for 99 years in order that they could build shops on the property. Before the lessees could begin construction the war broke out and the government subsequently passed regulations restricting such development. The effect was that the lessees could not build the shops they had covenanted to do and they thus claimed that the lease was frustrated. The House of Lords held that the doctrine of frustration did not apply, basing their decision in terms more appropriate to unavailability, as outlined above, in that the restrictions would only delay building for a comparatively short period when balanced against the full extent of the 99-year lease. Their Lordships were of divided opinions as to whether frustration could ever apply to leases. Lord Simon and Lord Wright considered it could, but only in the rather extreme circumstances of where the land is engulfed by the sea. Lord Russell and Lord Goddard considered that frustration could never apply, whilst Lord Porter declined to express an opinion.

The position not to allow frustration in leases is, however, more than just a little illogical since if one rents a property for a particular purpose then surely if that purpose becomes impossible the doctrine should apply? Certainly frustration does exist in the case of a contractual licence to hold land since it was fully accepted in the case of *Krell* v *Henry*, where the contract to rent a room for the coronation procession was held to be frustrated when the procession was cancelled. From here the argument can be taken to the point that the law would have to make a distinction between a legal lease and an equitable lease. The latter takes effect as a contract to grant a lease under the doctrine of *Walsh* v *Lonsdale* (1882) 21 Ch D 9, and it could therefore be discharged by frustration, whilst a legal lease could not be.

The issue relating to frustration and leases would seem to be now decided by the case of *National Carriers Ltd* v *Panalpina (Northern) Ltd* [1981] AC 675 where the House of Lords decided that frustration could apply to leases. They expressed the view, however, that its occurrence would be rare and probably confined to the situation where there was a joint intention that the property was to be released for a particular purpose, and that the purpose had become impossible because of events beyond the control of the parties. Lord Wilberforce stated:

> if the argument is to have reality, it must be possible to say that frustration of leases cannot occur because in any event the tenant will have that which he bargained for, namely, the leasehold estate. Certainly this may be so in many cases . . . But there may also be cases where this is not so. A man may desire possession and use of land or buildings for, and only for, some purpose in view and mutually contemplated. Why is it an answer, when he claims that this purpose is 'frustrated' to say that he has an estate if that estate is unusable and unsaleable? In such a case the lease, or the conferring of an estate, is a subsidiary means to an end, not an aim or end of itself.

The result in the case, however, was therefore that a lease for a warehouse which had four and a half years to run was not frustrated by a street closure order that prevented the warehouse from being used for 18 months.

FACTORS AFFECTING THE OPERATION OF THE DOCTRINE

Self-induced frustration

It has been seen that the basis of frustration lies in the fact that it amounts to a supervening event that is beyond the control of the parties to the contract. It follows therefore that if the event arises out of the actions of a party to the contract then the doctrine cannot be relied on.

In the leading case of *Maritime National Fish Ltd* v *Ocean Trawlers Ltd* [1935] AC 524 the appellants chartered a trawler from the respondents. The trawler was fitted with a type of net called an 'otter trawl', the use of which was illegal without a licence from the Canadian government, both the parties being aware of this fact. The appellants had four other trawlers all fitted with the same type of net. They applied for five licences but in fact were only awarded three. They had to stipulate to which trawlers the licences applied. The appellants nominated three of their own trawlers and then claimed that their charter of the trawler belonging to the respondents was discharged for frustration on the basis that no licence was forthcoming for that vessel. It was held, by the Privy Council, that their claim would fail since they could have nominated the vessel in question to have one of the licences but had declined to do so. The result was that the appellants had control of the supervening event and therefore frustration could not be relied upon as discharging the contract. Their claim was thus rejected.

The question of choice that arose in the case above with regard to the supervening event was again considered by the Court of Appeal in *J. Lauritzen AS* v *Wijsmuller BV* [1990] 1 Lloyd's Rep 1.

In this case the plaintiffs needed to transport a drilling rig from Japan to Rotterdam. The defendant possessed two specialist transportation systems capable of performing this task, *Super Servant One* and *Super Servant Two*. The contract was open as regards which vessel could be used, though the choice of vessel rested with the defendants. In fact, although they did not mention this to the plaintiffs at the time, the defendants intended to use *Super Servant Two* for the task and allocated other tasks to the sister ship. *Super Servant Two* sank some six months before the contract was to be performed. The defendants claimed that the contract was frustrated. The plaintiffs contested this application, stating that the contract would still have been capable of being carried out but for the decision of the defendants to allocate *Super Servant One* to other tasks. The supervening event thus lay in the hands of the defendants. The Court of Appeal held that the contract was not frustrated since the loss of a vessel to the contract was due to the actions of the defendants, even if they were neither negligent nor in breach of contract.

Where the supervening event arises because of the negligent actions of one of the parties then again frustration will not be deemed to have arisen. To take an example, if the music hall fire in *Taylor v Caldwell* had arisen because of a negligent act by the owners, then they could not have pleaded frustration and would have been liable for breach of contract. Negligent actions *per se* will not prevent frustration from arising since the onus of proving the existence of frustration lies on the party seeking to rely on the doctrine as a means of discharging his contractual obligations.

Frustration expressly provided for in the contract

The parties may make provision for what is to happen should a particular supervening contingency occur. These clauses are the so-called *force majeure* clauses mentioned earlier. If the clause, as a matter of construction, deals with the event that has occurred, then the courts will not deem that the contract has been frustrated. The clause must be capable of dealing with any form that the contingency may take, no matter how serious, otherwise it will not prevent the operation of the doctrine of frustration. In *Jackson* v *Union Marine Insurance Co Ltd* (1874) LR 10 CP 125, a ship was chartered to sail 'with all possible despatch' from Liverpool to Newport to pick up a cargo and then to proceed to San Francisco 'dangers and accidents of navigation excepted'. The ship ran aground one day out from Liverpool. The repairs took eight months to complete, during which time the charterers repudiated the contract. It was held that despite the *force majeure* clause the contract was still frustrated. Undoubtedly the clause took account of the contingency that had occurred but it was not designed to cover damages and delay of such an extensive nature. It was considered that if the contract had been upheld and a voyage to San Francisco had taken place the venture would have been entirely different commercially.

THE LEGAL EFFECTS OF THE DOCTRINE OF FRUSTRATION

The general rule

In Chapter 13 it was seen that where there is a breach of contract the injured party has to elect whether to treat the contract as discharged by the breach or not. Such discretion does not arise in the case of discharge by frustration since, as was pointed out by the House of Lords in *Hirji Mulji* v *Cheong Yue Steamship Co* [1926] AC 497, the effect of frustration is to bring about the automatic termination of all obligations incurred under the contract. In turn the effect of automatic dissolution of the contract at common law is to produce fundamental and often harsh repercussions on the parties to the contract.

The effect of frustration at common law

The effect of frustration at common law was that from the date of the supervening event the parties were released from all future contractual obligations. Any obligations that had already arisen under the contract had to be performed. This position is well illustrated by the case of *Chandler* v *Webster* [1904] 1 KB 493.

In this case the defendant agreed to let a room to the plaintiff for £141 for the purpose of viewing the coronation procession. The cost of the hire was payable immediately but in fact the plaintiff only paid £100 in advance. Before he paid the balance the procession was cancelled and the contract frustrated as a result. It was held that the plaintiff could not recover the £100 but additionally he was also liable to pay the balance since the obligation to pay this had already accrued prior to the supervening event. Counsel argued that he could recover the £100 in quasi-contract (see Chapter 18 below) in that there had been a total failure of consideration. The Court of Appeal, however, held that this line of argument could not be sustained since the effect of frustration was not to discharge the contract *ab initio* but only from the time of the supervening event, and there was no **total** failure of consideration.

It is useful to compare the effects of frustration in the *Chandler* case with the case of *Krell* v *Henry* since in the latter case the obligation to pay had not accrued at the time of the supervening event. The result here was that the defendant hirer of the room was not obliged to pay anything – all his future obligations ceased to exist at the time of cancellation.

The decision in the *Chandler* case that the 'loss lies where it falls' clearly could produce extremely harsh consequences for the parties. The position was no less satisfactory for the reason that the effects on the parties were completely unpredictable and it was largely a matter of luck as to whether one walked away from the situation unscathed or not. The decision was, however, overruled by the House of Lords in *Fibrosa Spolka Akcyjna* v *Fairbairn Lawson Combe Barbour Ltd* [1943] AC 32.

In this case the appellants ordered some machinery from the respondents for delivery to their factory in Poland, paying £1,000 in advance by virtue of the terms of the contract. In 1939 Germany invaded Poland and the contract became frustrated. The London agent for the appellants asked for the return of their £1,000 but the respondent refused on the basis that a substantial amount of time and money had already been expended on the order.

Clearly on the basis of the *Chandler* case the £1,000 would have been irrecoverable, but the House of Lords allowed the claim, which of necessity was based in quasi-contract since the contract had ceased to exist by virtue of the supervening event. The House of Lords decided that there had been a total failure of consideration, overruling the *Chandler* decision. The appellants had not received anything under the contract they had bargained for and could thus recover the monies they had paid.

In fact the decision is really no less unsatisfactory than that of the *Chandler* case, perhaps even more so in some circumstances. Parties in the position of the respondents could, just as in the case itself, have incurred considerable expenditure in preparing the subject matter of the contract only to find that they would receive no recompense for the time and money put into fulfilling the order. To add insult to injury they might also be left with a product that was so specialised as to be unsaleable to anyone else. Such a sale would have provided them with some degree of return on the energy expended on the contract. Indeed it is very likely because of these last two points that the deposit was charged in the first place so as to underwrite the expenses to be incurred in preparing the subject matter of the contract. In truth the House of Lords had merely shipped the burden of the effects of frustration from one party to the other. The continued unsatisfactory nature of the law led to the passing of the Law Reform (Frustrated Contracts) Act 1943.

The Law Reform (Frustrated Contracts) Act 1943

The operation of this Act is confined to circumstances where a contract is frustrated, although it has no effect on the decision as to whether the contract has been frustrated or not but merely deals with the consequences of frustration. The Act seeks to regulate firstly, the recovery of monies paid or payable under the contract; secondly, compensation payable for expenses incurred in the performance of the contract; thirdly, the financial readjustment of the parties where one has received a valuable benefit under the contract in the absence of any prepayment.

Recovery of money paid

The position here is enacted by s. 1(2) as follows:

> All sums paid or payable to any party in pursuance of the contract before the time when the parties were so discharged (in this Act referred to as 'the time of discharge') shall, in the case of sums so paid, be recoverable from him as money received by him for the use of the party by whom the sums were paid, and, in the case of sums payable, cease to be so payable.
>
> Provided that, if the party to whom the sums were so paid or so payable incurred expenses before the time of discharge in, or for the purpose of, the performance of the contract, the court may, if it considers it just to do so having regard to all the circumstances of the case, allow him to retain or, as the case may be, recover the whole or any part of the sums so paid or payable, not being an amount in excess of the expenses so incurred.

Two effects are immediately discernible from the provision. Firstly, the decision in *Fibrosa* is confirmed in that monies paid are recoverable despite the absence of a total failure of consideration; at the same time any monies that are owed cease to be payable. Secondly, the provision regulates the position of the payee, that is, the respondents in the *Fibrosa* case, since the court now has a discretionary power to award him a sum in respect of any expenses incurred by the payee in the performance of the contract prior to the discharge of the contract. It should be noted that the payee will not get his expenses but only what the court considers to be a just sum having regard to the circumstances of the case and, in any event, this will be no more than his actual expenses.

Financial re-adjustment where a valuable benefit is conferred

The position here is governed by s. 1(3) as follows:

> Where any party to the contract has, by reason of anything done by any other party thereto in, or for the purpose of, the performance of the contract, obtained a valuable benefit (other than a payment of money to which the last foregoing subsection applies) before the time of discharge, there shall be recoverable from him by the said other party such (if any), not exceeding the value of the said benefit to the party obtaining it, as the court considers just, having regard to all the circumstances of the case and, in particular –

(a) The amount of any expenses incurred before the time of discharge by the benefited party in, or for the purpose of the performance of the contract, including any sums paid or payable by him to any other party in pursuance of the contract and retained or recoverable by that party under the last foregoing subsection, and

(b) the effect, in relation to the said benefit, of the circumstances giving rise to frustration of the contract.

The leading case on the operation of s. 1(3) is that of *BP Exploration Co (Libya) Ltd v Hunt (No 2)* [1979] 1 WLR 783 (decision affirmed by the House of Lords [1983] 2 AC 352). The facts of the case were that there was a contract between BP and Hunt for the exploration and, ultimately, the exploitation of an oil concession in Libya that was held by Hunt. BP's part of the contract was that they were to get a half share in the concession, but that they were to provide the finance and conduct the exploration work, though their expenses would be recoverable at a rate of three-eighths of Hunt's share should oil be found until 125 per cent of their initial expenses had been recouped. In fact a large oil field was discovered and in 1967 it came on stream. In 1971 Libya expropriated Hunt's concession with the result that the contract between BP and Hunt became frustrated. At this point BP had recovered only a proportion of their expenses and thus brought an action based on s. 1(3) of the 1943 Act.

Robert Goff J decided that in the method of assessing the claim under s. 1(3) regard had to be paid, firstly, to identifying and valuing any benefit obtained and, secondly, to assessing what would be a just sum. In accordance with s. 1(3) this sum could not exceed the valuation placed on the valuable benefit. Goff J stated that the valuable benefit should not be assessed on what had been paid out by BP in the exploration work but on the benefit received by Hunt. Hunt's benefit amounted to the value by which his concession had been enhanced but this had to be reduced, because of the effect of s. 1(3)b, by the diminution to the value of the concession caused by the expropriation. On this basis the valuable benefit obtained by Hunt amounted to the value of the oil he had received plus the amount of compensation awarded to him by the Libyan government for the expropriation. The court, however, took into account that half of this benefit was attributable to BP's efforts, and thus the valuable benefit obtained by Hunt amounted to $85m.

Turning to the question of assessing what would be a just sum Goff J decided that this should be calculated on the basis of what BP had actually spent on developing the concession, namely, $87m, plus any monies paid to Hunt, that is, $10m, less expenses actually recovered, that is, $62m. On this basis the just sum was $35m and it was this figure that was recoverable by BP in full, since it did not exceed the figure for the assessment of the valuable benefit, which by s. 1(3) would otherwise have restricted the amount recoverable for the just sum.

That the provision goes some way towards correcting the inequities that existed prior to the Act cannot be doubted, but the Act itself contains defects. The subsection only allows recovery where a party has received a valuable benefit which has been obtained 'before the time of discharge'. Thus, if the expropriation had taken place prior to any financial reward arising from the concession, for instance in the form of profits from oil, BP could not have recovered anything under s. 1(3) since there would have been no valuable benefit. That this is the effect of s. 1(3) is not open to doubt, but very serious flaws appear in Goff J's reasoning where a party receives a valuable benefit but this is destroyed by the frustrating event. Such a situation did not arise in the *BP v Hunt* case since the valuable benefit had already accrued to Hunt at the time of the expropriation. If, however, one takes a case such as *Appleby* v *Myers* (1867) LR 2 CP 651 the defect becomes quickly apparent. In this case the plaintiffs had contracted to install machinery in the defendant's factory, and the defendant was to pay when the installation was complete. When some of the machinery had been installed a fire broke out, completely destroying the factory and the machinery. It was held that the contract had been frustrated. If the plaintiffs attempted to sue under s. 1(2) they would receive nothing since no money was payable at the time of the frustrating event and all that they could hope to recover would be an amount for expenses.

If the plaintiff had attempted to claim under s. 1(3) in respect of a valuable benefit being obtained by the defendant, he would be met by the argument that the frustrating event had destroyed this and therefore no valuable benefit accrued to the defendant in respect of which a just sum may have been recoverable in the discretion of the court. This is the position adopted by Goff J in his interpretation of s. 1(3)b. His view was that if 'the effect . . . of the circumstances giving rise to frustration of the contract' (s. 1(3)b) was to destroy the valuable benefit then nothing could be recovered for this. This interpretation has been widely criticised both by academic lawyers in the UK and judicially in a number of Commonwealth decisions and it is certainly wrong. A cursory glance at s. 1(3) indicates that the court has to assess the level of the valuable benefit before the frustrating event, that is, 'where any party . . . obtained a valuable benefit . . . before the time of the discharge'. Furthermore s. 1(3)b itself clearly indicates that the valuable benefit must first be assessed and then the court must consider the effect of the frustrating event, that is, 'the effect, in relation to the said benefit, of the circumstances giving rise to frustration'. The interpretation given by Goff J here is unnecessarily restrictive and it may be that his approach has been to regard the Act not as an attempt to apportion losses but as an attempt to prevent undue enrichment – and this was certainly not the original aim of the Act. Unfortunately the decision has been affirmed by the House of Lords, subject to one or two minor adjustments, and thus one will have to wait until their Lordships have the opportunity of reviewing the position in which *BP* v *Hunt* has placed the law.

Contracts falling outside the Act

Certain contracts fall outside the ambit of the Act. Thus s. 2(3) allows the parties to contract out of its provisions where they have made express provisions regarding the effect of a frustrating event on the contract.

By virtue of s. 2(4) the Act does not apply to those parts of a severable contract that have been wholly performed prior to the frustrating event. For example, if there is a contract for the installation of two machines, payment being effected when each machine is installed, and a fire breaks out that completely destroys the factory, the Act will not apply in respect of the machine that is installed and paid for. In respect of the second, partially installed machine the Act will apply and the plaintiff may succeed if the other party receives a valuable benefit, if any, in recovering a just sum for that benefit in the discretion of the court.

By s. 2(5)a and s. 2(5)b the provisions of the Act do not apply to any charterparty (except a time charterparty), carriage of goods by sea or any contract of insurance. The apparent reason for these exceptions is that they are largely concerned with the apportionment of risk themselves and should therefore lie outside the Act.

By s. 2(5)c, contracts falling within s. 7 of the Sale of Goods Act 1893 (now s. 7 of the Sale of Goods Act 1979), which renders void any agreement to sell specific goods whereby, without any fault on the part of the seller or buyer, the goods perish before the risks pass to the buyer, are excluded from the provisions of the 1943 Act. This exclusion is more general and does not relate only to s. 7 since s. 2(5)c also states that 'any other contract for the sale, or for the sale and delivery, of specific goods, whereby the contract is frustrated by reason of the fact that the goods have perished', are also excluded.

Further reading

Battersby, 'Frustration: A Limited Future', 134 *Solicitors Journal* 354, 1990

Beale, Bishop and Furmston, *Contract – Cases and Materials* 2nd ed. 1990, Butterworths

Cheshire, Fifoot and Furmston, *The Law of Contract* 12th ed. 1991, Butterworths

Guest, *Anson's Law of Contract* 26th ed. 1984, Oxford University Press

Hall, 'Frustration and the Question of Foresight', 4 *Legal Studies* 300, 1984

Haycroft and Waksman, 'Frustration and Restitution', *Journal of Business Law* 207, 1984

McKendrick, 'Self-Induced Frustration and *Force Majeure* Clauses', *Lloyd's Maritime and Commercial Law Quarterly* 3, 1989

Treitel, *The Law of Contract* 8th ed. 1991, Sweet & Maxwell

Part V
REMEDIES FOR BREACH OF CONTRACT

16 | The common law remedy of damages

INTRODUCTION

So far in our analysis of the doctrines, principles and rules that bind the law of contract we have talked in terms of enforcing contracts. In fact the notion of enforcement is somewhat erroneous since at common law the only remedy is damages or compensation for the breach of contract. Of course the result may be the same in monetary terms but this can be far removed from the notion of forcing compliance with the terms of the contract. It is true that a party to a contract can enforce compliance via decrees of specific performance and injunctions, but these are equitable remedies available only at the discretion of the court, whilst damages at common law are available as of right. Nor are damages limited to circumstances where a party to the contract suffers loss because of the breach. As we have already seen, liability in breach of contract is strict and a party may claim damages, albeit only nominal damages, despite the fact that he has suffered no loss.

Whilst a person may recover damages even where he has suffered no loss it has to be said that the majority of claims will be in circumstances where substantial loss has been suffered. The injured party cannot recover for all loss since a causal link must be shown to exist between the loss suffered and the breach of contract. Even where this causal link exists an individual will not in any event be compelled to pay for all loss, since the losses must not be 'too remote' from the consequences of the breach. The limitations on the availability of damages for breach of contract, together with causation and remoteness, will form the second part of the analysis of the common law remedy of damages. The third part of this analysis will be concerned with how the damages are measured in terms of quantum (amount). Initially, however, we need to make an assessment of the basis on which the courts award damages for breach.

ASSESSMENT OF THE BASIS ON WHICH DAMAGES ARE AWARDED

General principles

As has been indicated already, the basis of an award of damages is to compensate the injured party for the breach of contract. The underlying and fundamental principle here is to place the injured party in the same position he would have been in had the contract been carried out, insofar as money is able to do this. The injured party is thus claiming damages for the gains he could have reasonably expected from the execution of the contract. He is thus claiming for his loss of bargain or loss of profits. Such damages are often referred to as an 'expectation loss'.

Alternatively the injured party may decide not to claim for his loss of bargain/loss of profits but for the expenses he has incurred because of his reliance on the contract being performed. The circumstances in which a party claims what is euphemistically referred to as 'reliance loss' may arise where the profits that he hopes will materialise from the contract are too speculative or uncertain. In such circumstances the injured party may find it simpler and safer to claim any expenses that he has incurred in his performance of the contract.

An example of such an instance can be seen in *Anglia Television Ltd* v *Reed* [1972] 1 QB 60 where the defendant, an actor, had entered into a contract with the plaintiffs to produce a film. At the last moment the defendant withdrew from the contract with the result that the plaintiffs had to abandon the whole project. They decided not to sue for expectation losses since these would be clearly purely speculative, but for loss of expenses, or reliance losses, in respect of monies expended hiring other actors, finding locations and engaging script writers. The court allowed the claim for these items of expenditure.

The *Anglia Television* case is also authority for the fact that the courts will not allow the injured party to claim for both expectation and reliance loss. Thus Lord Denning MR stated:

> It seems to me that a plaintiff in such a case as this has an election: he can either claim for his loss of profits; or for wasted expenditure. But he must elect between them. He cannot claim both. If he has not suffered any loss of profits – or if he cannot prove what his profits would have been – he can claim in the alternative the expenditure which has been thrown away, that is, wasted, by reason of the breach. That is shown by *Cullinane* v *British 'Rema' Manufacturing Co Ltd*.

The *'Rema'* case [1954] 1 QB 292 indicates that to claim both reliance loss and expectation would in effect be to compensate the plaintiff twice for the same loss. However, this requires qualification since such a state of affairs only exists if the expectation loss consists of gross profits which will include expenditure on the contract. There would seem to be no objection to a plaintiff claiming reliance loss and expectation loss where the latter consists of a claim for net profits. Unfortunately Lord Denning does not clarify this situation.

Whilst the plaintiff generally can choose whether to claim expectation loss or reliance loss, this choice may nevertheless be imposed on him by the court in certain situations. For instance the courts look very warily on claims for reliance loss where the plaintiff has made a 'bad bargain', in that there would normally have been no profits made from the contract – because the return on the contract might not even have covered the expenses incurred, either wholly or partly.

Thus in *C & P Haulage* v *Middleton* [1983] 3 All ER 94 the court held that in the circumstances of this case there would be no recovery for reliance losses. It would clearly be wrong though to prevent a person from recovering for reliance loss simply on the basis that no profits were made on the contract. The court stated that reliance loss could be recovered provided that the losses claimed arose from the breach of contract and that it was anticipated that the return on the contract would have meant, under normal circumstances, that the expenditure on the contract would have been recovered. On the other hand, if it is shown that the wasted expenditure would have arisen whether or not the contract had been broken then the courts will disallow the claim for those losses.

The burden of proof in relation to the last matter is important since it was stated in *CCC Films (London) Ltd* v *Impact Quadrant Films Ltd* [1984] 3 All ER 298 that the onus of proof is not on the plaintiff to show that his reliance losses would be at least as much as his expected profits. Such a burden of proof would be almost impossible to sustain. The onus is on the defendant to show that the plaintiff would not have recovered his wasted expenditure even if the terms of the contract had been fully complied with.

A second situation where a plaintiff will be prevented from exercising his choice of expectation or reliance loss arises where the court itself considers that the claim for expectation loss is too speculative. An example of such a move by the courts occurred in *McRae* v *Commonwealth Disposals Commission*, where the court considered that the claim for loss of profits was incapable of calculation since there was nothing in the contract to indicate the size of the tanker in question nor the approximate quantity of oil on board. The court decided that only a claim for reliance loss would be entertained.

It is worth noting at this point that so far we have been concerned with compensation for loss of bargain or expenses incurred. However it is also possible to claim for the recovery of a benefit received by the defendant from the unperformed contract. Such claims are based in restitution and will be discussed more fully in Chapter 18 under quasi-contracts. Claims in restitution are conceptually different from those for damages for breach of contract since the aim is to place both the parties in the same position that they were in **before** the contract had been entered into, that is, as if the contract had not been made. It should be noted that restitution is not the same as claims for reliance loss either since, whilst the intention in the latter is to compensate for losses sustained before the contract was entered into, it is only intended to return the plaintiff to the precontract position and not the defendant, and the latter may be left in a significantly worse position than before. Restitution therefore does not amount to compensation at all but a method of returning both parties to the precontract status quo.

Before we embark on an analysis of the specific issues that may arise in assessing the basis on which damages are awarded, a distinction has to be drawn between actions for damages and actions for an agreed sum. The latter commonly arise where the contract provides that an agreed sum is payable in return for some performance under the contract by the other party, such as the sale of goods for a fixed price. Actions to recover the agreed price or sum are very different from actions for damages in two respects. First, such actions take the form of specific relief, though without the restrictions normally found in actions for decrees of specific performance. Secondly, not only does the remedy differ in nature from damages, but it also differs in respect of the limitations imposed upon its award. Such actions are truly speaking actions in debt, since a precise known sum is being claimed. The result is that claims for such sums are not subject to the limitations of remoteness, mitigation of loss, and so on, that are frequently imposed on awards of damages.

The assessment of damages by reference to the market

An area where expectation losses are commonly claimed arises out of contracts for the sale of goods. The assessment of damages here depends on whether the seller is in breach of contract for non-delivery or whether it is the buyer who is in breach for non-acceptance of the goods delivered. In either case the measure of damages is dependent on the difference between the contract price and the price of the goods in the market at the time of the breach of contract.

Breach caused by non-delivery

Such a breach will occur where the seller refuses or neglects to deliver the goods to the buyer. In such a case the buyer is expected to mitigate this loss by going into the market-place and buying goods of a similar nature, his damages being the difference between the contract price and market price, assuming that he has had to pay more for the goods, otherwise he is only entitled to nominal damages. Thus the Sale of Goods Act 1979, s. 51(3) states:

> Where there is an available market for the goods in question the measure of damages is *prima facie* to be ascertained by the difference between the contract price and the market or current price of the goods at the time or times when they ought to have been delivered or (if no time was fixed) at the time of refusal to deliver.

This measure, however, will change somewhat where the seller has contracted to resell the goods and this resale is within the contemplation of the seller (see the rule in *Hadley* v *Baxendale* below). If there is no available market-place then the resale price is taken as the market price and the measure of damages will thus be the difference between the contract price and the resale price, as was held in *Patrick* v *Russo-British Grain Export Co* [1927] 2 KB 535. If there is an available market-place then the damages remain the same as stated in s. 51(3), that is, the difference between the contract price and the market price, whether or not the resale was within the contemplation of the seller, as was held in *Williams* v *Reynolds* (1865) 6 B & S 495.

Where the delivery is late but is nevertheless accepted by the buyer the damages have to be assessed on a different basis entirely since here the buyer's complaint is that he will only be able to resell them at a lower price than that prevailing at the time the goods should have been delivered. In such an instance the measure of damages is the difference between the market value of the goods when they ought to have been delivered and the market value when they were actually delivered. Nevertheless it was held in *Wertheim* v *Chicoutimi Pulp Co Ltd* [1911] AC 301 that this rule will be displaced if the goods were resold at more than their market value at the time of delivery. Here the measure of damage will be the difference between the market price at the time fixed for delivery and the price for which the goods are resold. By way of illustration, if the market price of the goods was £20 per ton at the time fixed for delivery and £9 per ton at the time of actual delivery, then prima facie the loss is £11 per ton. If, however, the buyer was able to resell the goods for £15 per ton, then according to the *Wertheim* case the measure of damages should be £5 per ton, since otherwise, according to the court, the buyers would make a profit out of the breach. The decision has been heavily criticised (see, for instance, Treitel, 8th edition, pp. 839–40).

Breach caused by non-acceptance

Such a breach occurs where the buyer refuses or neglects to accept delivery of the goods. In a private sale the seller can recover from the buyer the difference between the value of the goods still in his possession and the agreed sale price, subject of course to his duty to take reasonable steps to mitigate his loss by attempting to sell them elsewhere. This position can been seen in the Sale of Goods Act 1979, s. 50(3) which states:

> Where there is an available market for the goods in question the measure of damages is *prima facie* to be ascertained by the difference between the contract price and the market or current price at the time or times when the goods ought to have been accepted or (if no time was fixed for acceptance) at the time of refusal to accept.

The situation is not quite so simple where the seller is a dealer. It is true that the dealer has to take reasonable steps to mitigate his loss, just as in a private sale, so that where there is an available market his loss is the difference between the contract price and the market price. The problem, however, may be that there is no difference between the contract price and the market price so that his claim will be for his loss of profits from the sale. The ability of the seller to recover such loss of profit depends, however, on the supply and demand for the goods in question.

In *Thompson Ltd* v *Robinson (Gunmakers) Ltd* [1955] Ch 177 there was a contract for the sale of a new Vanguard car but the defendants refused to accept delivery. The defendants contested that the plaintiff dealers were only entitled to nominal damages given that there was no difference between the contract price and the market price. The plaintiffs, however, claimed their loss of profits since they maintained that given that the supply of such vehicles exceeded demand, they had sold one car less than they would normally have been able to do. It was held that the plaintiffs were entitled to their loss of profits, the judge finding that since s. 50(3) was only a prima facie rule it could be displaced in such circumstances. On the other hand in *Charter* v *Sullivan* [1957] 2 QB 117 it was held that only nominal damages could be claimed where demand exceeds supply since there the dealer, being able to sell all that he could get his hands on, had suffered no loss.

The situations described above tend to arise where there is a fixed retail price for the goods, and it may be that in the competitive market that exists today the rule in s. 50(3) may be a more appropriate means of measuring the loss. Certainly the above rules do not apply to secondhand goods which do not have a fixed retail price. Such goods are unique and a failure to accept does not give rise to a claim for loss of profits here. The seller must again take reasonable steps to mitigate his loss by going into the market-place, should a market be available, and if he sells the goods at the same or a higher price he can recover no damages from his first buyer, as held in *Lazenby Garages Ltd* v *Wright* [1976] 1 WLR 459. If he can only sell at a diminished price then his damages are the difference between the contract price and the market price as provided in s. 50(3).

It should be noted that if the buyer delays in accepting the goods then by the Sale of Goods Act 1979, s. 38, the seller can recover any losses resulting from that delay, together with a reasonable charge for the care and custody of the goods.

'Available market'

The expression 'available market' in s. 50(3) and s. 51(3) appears to have no precise definition. Various rather unconvincing attempts have been made over the years to define the expression. In *Shearson Lehman Hutton Inc* v *Maclaine Watson & Co Ltd (No 2)* [1990] 3 All ER 723 it was suggested that (in the case of a breach by the buyer) a market arises where the seller actually offers the goods for sale and there is a buyer who offers a fair price on the day. Alternatively there will be a market where the seller does not actually offer the goods for sale but where, nevertheless, it can be shown that there are sufficient dealers potentially in touch with one another to evince the existence of a market. Presumably a market arises on a similar basis where it is the seller who is in breach.

The question of time in assessing an award of damages

Damages are usually assessed as at the time the contract has been broken and this principle is evidenced by both s. 50(3) and s. 51(3) of the Sale of Goods Act 1979, above. This principle is only a presumption and is largely based on the fact that a plaintiff's obligation to take reasonable steps to mitigate his loss assumes that he will act immediately. In *Johnson* v *Agnew* [1980] AC 367, however, it was stated that the plaintiff does not have to take such immediate action where it is reasonable for him to take some other course of action, such as attempting to persuade the defendant to carry out his side of the bargain or to seek confirmation from the defendant that he does intend to perform. Thus Lord Wilberforce stated:

The general principle for the assessment of damages is compensatory, ie that the innocent party is to be placed, so far as money can do so, in the same position as if the contract had been performed. Where the contract is one of sale, this principle normally leads to assessment of damages as at the date of the breach, a principle recognised and embodied in s. 51 of the Sale of Goods Act 1893. But this is not an absolute rule; if to follow it would give rise to injustice, the court has power to fix such other date as may be appropriate in the circumstances.

In cases where a breach of a contract for sale has occurred, and the innocent party reasonably continues to try to have the contract completed, it would appear to me more logical and just rather than to tie him to the date of the original breach, to assess damages as at the date when (otherwise than by his default) the contract is lost.

On this basis it would seem that the courts fully intend to give themselves substantial discretion as to the time when the assessment of damages should be made. It should, however, be noted that when a party is claiming damages in lieu of a decree of specific performance under the Chancery Amendment Act 1858 (otherwise known as the Lord Cairns Act) damages are assessed as at the date of the judgment, though it should be noted here that the damages claimed are not damages at common law.

The effect of tax on the assessment of damages

The principle that damages are merely designed to compensate the plaintiff for his actual losses means that his liability in respect of tax has to be taken into account.

In the case of the *British Transport Commission* v *Gourley* [1956] AC 185 there was a claim for loss of earnings that arose from personal injuries caused by negligence. He was awarded a sum of £37,720 which represented the claim relating to loss of gross earnings. It was held by the House of Lords that the damages had to be reduced by the amount the plaintiff would have had to pay in tax in respect of that sum. Consequently the plaintiff was awarded a sum of £6,695 representing net income.

The rule in *Gourley*'s case establishes that damages will be reduced to take into account taxation only if two criteria are met:

(a) the damages must represent taxable income or gains, **and**
(b) the damages themselves are not taxable by the Inland Revenue.

As a general guide the following are not taxable by the Inland Revenue:

(a) Compensation for personal injuries. Clearly these will not generally attract the application of the rule as they do not represent taxable income or gains. Thus if the hirer of a taxi successfully claims in contract for personal injuries sustained by the taxi owner's failure to take reasonable care and is awarded £100,000, then these damages would be payable in full. Similarly, if a person suffers emotional distress from a ruined holiday or wrongful demotion then the awards here will both be payable in full since neither of these awards represent income.

(b) In respect of compensation for loss of office or wrongful dismissal in employment the rule in *Gourley* has been modified by the Income and Corporation Taxes Act 1988, s. 148. Here damages for £30,000 or less do not attract taxation in the hands of the recipient and therefore must be reduced to take into account tax in accordance with the rule in *Gourley*. Damages above £30,000 are taxable in the hands of the recipient are therefore payable free of reduction for tax. Thus if A has a fixed-term contract of employment for one year for which he is to be paid £70,000 per annum and he is subsequently, in breach of contract, dismissed after six months, he may well successfully claim £35,000 compensation for the breach. In such a case the court will reduce the first £30,000 to take into account taxation, whilst the remaining £5,000 will be paid in full and left to be taxed by the Inland Revenue itself.

Income and capital receipts of a trade, profession, office or employment (subject to the above) are taxed by the Inland Revenue and therefore fall outside the *Gourley* rule. Thus if X, a motor dealer, successfully sues a customer for his loss of profit on the sale caused by the customer acting in breach of contract, X will receive the damages in full since they effectively represent a receipt of the trade. The damages will then be added to X's gross income and duly taxed by the Inland Revenue. Similarly if R contracts to buy certain goods from S for £1,000 and subsequently S fails to deliver in breach of contract so that R has to buy similar goods which cost him £1,500, then he may claim the £500 extra expense as damages. It is suggested that he will be awarded this amount in full since here the amount does not represent income but increased expenditure for an asset from which he might have made a profit eventually.

Whilst the logic of *Gourley* may be correct it has been criticised in its operation since it treats damages awarded for loss of earnings arising out of personal injuries as taxable income.

Thus in *Beach* v *Reed Corrugated Cases Ltd* [1956] 2 All ER 652 it was estimated that an employee who had been wrongfully dismissed would have received £58,000 by way of salary over the next 10 years. In fact the plaintiff had a large personal fortune and therefore his damages were reduced by reference to his tax liability in respect of both earnings and the personal fortune, despite the fact that the fortune might of course vary over that period. The plaintiff was eventually awarded £18,000, though Pilcher J admitted that this was no more than a rough estimation.

It would seem much more sensible for the courts to award the gross sum to the plaintiff and then allow him to make the necessary arrangements with regard to tax with the Inland Revenue. Whilst the principle in *Gourley* was considered in 1958 by the Law Reform Committee no recommendations arose out of the discussions. In the mean time it might be more convenient for the courts to follow the decision in *Shove* v *Downs Surgical Plc* [1984] 1 All ER 7 where Sheen J estimated the plaintiff's net loss of income after deduction of tax and to this he added an amount equivalent to income tax. A further way round the rule is to treat awards of damages for loss of earnings as loss of earning capacity since such damages are treated for tax purposes as representing losses to a capital asset and they do not attract income tax. As the law stands at the moment, however, it is possible for a defendant to rely on totally extraneous matters, such as private income, as in the *Beach* case, to reduce the damages payable by himself, a result that is hardly just.

LIMITATIONS ON THE AVAILABILITY OF DAMAGES

Causation

In order to claim damages the plaintiff must show that there is a causal link between the losses sustained and the breach of contract. The problem here is that circumstances might arise whereby a breach of contract occurs but the defendant argues that the level of loss sustained by the plaintiff has resulted, not from the breach of contract, but from some other intervening state of affairs.

It was stated in *Galoo Ltd and Others* v *Bright Grahame Murray* (1994) *The Times*, 14 January, that the nature of the causation necessary to establish liability for breach of contract (or in tort) was one of the most difficult areas of law. The Court of Appeal said that it was clear that if a breach of contract by a defendant was to entitle a plaintiff to claim damages, it must first be found to be the dominant cause of his loss. In considering whether a breach of contract was the cause of the loss or merely the occasion for the loss, a court had to arrive at that decision on the basis of common sense.

It may be the case that the loss is caused by the very nature of the contract itself so that it is this factor that results in the loss rather than the breach of contract itself.

In *C & P Haulage* v *Middleton* [1983] 3 All ER 94 the plaintiff hired a garage on a six-monthly-contract basis for use in his business. During the operation of one such contract he decided to equip the garage to meet his own particular needs. The garage owner then, in breach of contract, terminated the contract 10 weeks early and the plaintiff sued to recover his expenses in equipping the garage. It was held that his action would fail since the garage could legitimately have terminated the contract 10 weeks later whereupon the plaintiff would have sustained his losses in any event. Clearly it was not the breach that had caused the loss but the nature of the contract he had entered into, although the breach meant that he suffered his losses somewhat earlier than was intended.

A further situation which may break the causal link between the breach of contract and the losses suffered occurs where the loss results partly from a breach of contract and also from the intervening acts of a third party. In such circumstances the party who is in breach of contract will continue to be liable provided the actions of the third party are, on the balance of probabilities, foreseeable. Thus in *Stansbie* v *Troman* [1948] 2 KB 48 a painter was engaged to decorate some premises. On completion he left the house unlocked so that thieves were able to enter and burgle the premises. He was held to be liable for the value of the goods stolen since it was reasonably foreseeable that such an event might occur and that he should have guarded against the possibility by securing the premises. A case that contrasts with this position and is referred to extensively by Treitel (8th edition, pp. 865–6) is *Weld-Blundell* v *Stephens* [1920] AC 956.

In this case an accountant was employed to conduct an investigation into the affairs of a company. The plaintiff wrote a letter to the accountant in which he libelled a number of directors of the company in question. The letter was then negligently left in one of the company's offices by the accountant's partner and when found by a manager it was handed to the directors concerned. The directors subsequently brought an action in defamation and secured damages from the plaintiff who, in turn, brought an action against the accountant for breach of contract. The claim was dismissed by the House of Lords on the basis that the action in libel did not result from the breach of contract but from the unforeseeable actions of the manager.

Whilst this case illustrates the point in question the basis for the decision has to be questionable since it is clear that the accountant owed the plaintiff a duty of confidentiality. Similarly the actions of the manager are reasonably foreseeable since any employee is bound to disclose information that may be damaging to his employer's interests. Even though this reasoning would appear wrong the case is probably correctly decided on the basis that the action in defamation was in any event independent of the contract, although it resulted from the accountant's breach of contract in the first place.

Remoteness of damages

Having established that there is a causal link between the breach and the losses sustained by the plaintiff it must not nevertheless be assumed that the defendant will be liable for all losses arising out of the breach. The defendant will only be liable for losses that arise from the consequences of the breach and which can be said to be within the contemplation of the parties at the time of contracting, other losses being regarded as 'too remote'.

The case that forms the basis of the modern law as regards remoteness is that of *Hadley* v *Baxendale* (1854) 9 Exch 341, the facts of which were that the plaintiff's mill had ceased working because of a broken crankshaft. As there was no spare shaft the broken one had to be sent to the manufacturer for use as a pattern for a new one. To this end the plaintiffs engaged the defendant carriers to transport the shaft to the manufacturers. The defendants were told what the item was, a broken shaft from a particular mill, and that the plaintiffs were the proprietors of the mill. The defendants were negligent in their delivery of the shaft and their negligence resulted in the operation of the mill being shut down for longer than would have been ordinarily necessary had there been no delay in the transit of the shaft. The plaintiffs sued for their increased loss of profits caused by the delay. In his judgment Alderson B produced what has since become known as the rule in *Hadley* v *Baxendale*:

> Where two parties have made a contract which one of them has broken, the damages which the other party ought to receive in respect of such a breach of contract should be such as may fairly and reasonably be considered either arising naturally, ie according to the usual course of things, from such breach of contract itself, or such as may reasonably be supposed to have been in the

contemplation of both parties, at the time they made the contract, as the probable result of the breach of it.

It can be seen that the rule in fact has two limbs to it. Some authorities consider that there are two rules but this interpretation has largely been discounted today in favour of the notion of one rule with two limbs. The result is that there is a single test as regards the liability for damages for breach of contract based on a reasonable foresight test, and that the level of liability varies depending on the degree of knowledge that the party in breach has or is assumed to have. The effect is that the more remote the damage becomes the greater the degree of knowledge required of the guilty party. It can be seen that the two limbs represent two extremes, one dealing with normal (natural) loss, the other with abnormal (exceptional) losses. The two limbs thus comprise of damage:

(a) 'arising naturally, ie according to the usual course of things, from such breach of contract itself . . .'. This limb covers damage that is an inevitable consequence of the breach and which the defendant should have contemplated as arising from his breach, that is, he is deemed to have imputed notice of this type of damage since it is a normal consequence of the breach.
(b) 'such as may reasonably be supposed to have been in the contemplation of both the parties, at the time they made the contract, as the probable result of the breach of it'. This limb covers losses which would not normally be in the contemplation of the defendant as likely to result from his breach, but which he may nevertheless be liable for if he had actual knowledge of those consequences when he entered into the contract. The type of loss dealt with by this limb is special or abnormal loss.

Translating the rule into the facts of *Hadley* v *Baxendale* the court decided that the loss of profits could not be regarded as a normal loss since such loss was not an inevitable consequence of the delay, as the mill owners could well have had a spare shaft which would have prevented any loss from occurring. If the loss of profits was not a normal loss in the contemplation of the parties as being an inevitable consequence of the breach, then it must have amounted to a 'special loss'. Could the plaintiffs succeed here? The court again decided that they could not since this type of loss required actual knowledge on the part of the carriers that their delay would result in such losses being incurred. Since the carriers were not given actual knowledge of this potential consequence by the plaintiffs they could not be held liable for that consequence.

The rule in *Hadley* v *Baxendale* was given substantial airing by Asquith LJ in *Victoria Laundry (Windsor) Ltd* v *Newman Industries Ltd* [1949] 2 KB 528.

The facts of the case were that the plaintiffs, hoping to expand their business, bought a secondhand boiler from the defendants. At the time of contracting the boiler had yet to be dismantled but in carrying out that operation the defendants damaged it. The result of this was that it arrived at the plaintiffs 22 weeks late. The delay meant that the plaintiffs failed to reap the extra profits the new boiler would have produced. These were assessed at £16 per week.

The plaintiffs also lost a lucrative dyeing contract with the Ministry of Supply, the damages for the loss of profits here being assessed at £262 per week. The plaintiffs sued for breach of contract. It was held that the plaintiffs could recover the £16 per week. The loss of profits here clearly fell within the first limb, being normal losses which the defendants must have known, at the time of entering into the contract, that the plaintiffs would sustain by their failure to deliver the boiler on time. The claim in respect of the £262 per week failed. This item was a special or abnormal loss for which the defendants would only be liable if they had actual knowledge of the possibility that such loss might occur at the time of entering into the contract. Since the plaintiffs had not told or otherwise informed the defendants of the lucrative dyeing contract, the defendants had no actual knowledge of such potential loss and were not therefore liable for this item.

It was stated earlier that the two limbs of the rule represent two extremes and it thus remains to be decided how one determines liability for loss which is something more than a natural loss and yet falls short of a special loss, actual knowledge of which has been given to the defendant. Asquith LJ considered that the liability for loss here depended on a reasonable foreseeability test. Thus he stated:

> In cases of breach of contract the aggrieved party is only entitled to recover such part of the loss actually resulting as was at the time of the contract reasonably foreseeable as likely to result from the breach . . . In order to make the contract-breaker liable under either rule it is not necessary that he should actually have asked himself what loss is liable to result from a breach. . . . It suffices that, if he had considered the question, he would as a reasonable man have concluded that the loss in question was liable to result . . . Nor, finally, to make the particular loss recoverable, need it be proved that on a given state of knowledge, the defendant could, as a reasonable man, foresee that a breach must necessarily result in that loss. It is enough if he could foresee it was likely so to result. It is enough, . . . if the loss (or some factor without which it would not have occurred) is a 'serious possibility' or a 'real danger'. For short, we have used the word 'liable' to result. Possibly the colloquialism 'on the cards' indicates the shade of meaning with some approach to accuracy.

The result of the above was that Lord Asquith seemed to suggest that the test of remoteness in contract was the same as the test applied in tort. This approach was subject to sharp rebuke from their Lordships in *Koufos* v *Czarnikow Ltd (The Heron II)* [1969] 1 AC 350. They considered that it was insufficient merely to show reasonable foreseeability of the loss. Lord Reid, in particular, considered that the question of liability turned on whether:

> on the information available to the defendant when the contract was made, he should, or the reasonable man in his position would, have realised that such loss was sufficiently likely to result from the breach of contract to make it proper to hold that the loss flowed naturally from the breach of contract or that loss of that kind should have been within his contemplation.

Lord Reid thus for the most part confined liability to that of loss arising naturally from the breach or loss that should have been within contemplation, that is, special loss. He considered that loss that fell within these two extremes would only occur 'in a minority of cases' and that such loss was not recoverable.

Lord Reid went on to distinguish between foreseeability in tort and foreseeability in contract. He considered that reasonable foreseeability in tort imposed a wider liability and allowed for recovery of the most unusual losses – provided that they were reasonably foreseeable. In contract, however, he considered the situation was different since the parties were free to protect themselves in respect of unusual or special losses by specifically drawing the attention of the other party to that particular risk, thereby placing it within the contemplation of that individual.

The other judges within the House of Lords produced various ways of explaining the difference in the foreseeability test in contract and in tort, though these attempts were largely spurious exercises in semantics which failed to explain the difference adequately, although four of the five members of the House considered the 'on the cards' expression of Lord Asquith to be inappropriate.

The decisions in the *Victoria Laundry* and *Heron II* cases were extensively considered in the Court of Appeal in *H. Parsons (Livestock) Ltd* v *Uttley Ingham* [1978] 1 All ER 525, where there was a contract for the sale and installation of an animal feed hopper which was to have a ventilated top. During transit to the site the ventilation hatch had been sealed and when installation was completed the defendants forgot to open the hatch. The result was that some of the feed went mouldy and caused a rare intestinal disease to break out amongst the plaintiff's pigs, killing 254 of them. At first instance the plaintiff lost his claim for the loss of the pigs since the judge considered that such loss was not within the contemplation of the parties. The Court of Appeal reversed this decision.

Lord Scarman took a diametrically opposing view to that of the House of Lords in the *Heron II* case and was supported by Orr LJ. He stated that there was no difference between the test of remoteness in contract and that in tort. He stated that, in any event, whether it be in contract or in tort, the test of remoteness depended, not on the contemplation of the degree of injury, but that simply on proof that the loss could reasonably have been anticipated. He stated that if the defendants had merely manufactured the defective hopper which had then been sold to a retailer, who, in turn had resold it to the plaintiffs, then the action of the plaintiffs would have been in tort against the manufacturer. The test of remoteness here would have been based on a reasonable foreseeability test based in tort and clearly there was no reason why this should be any different from the test that should exist in contract. The arguments of Lord Scarman make a great deal of sense and certainly make for a simpler application of the law.

Lord Denning adopted a different solution to the problem, differentiating between economic loss, such as loss of profits, as occurred in *Victoria Laundry* and *Heron II*, and physical loss, which occurred in the *H. Parsons* case. He considered that the stricter test proposed by Lord Reid was appropriate where the loss amounted to economic loss, and to some degree this view has some credence since, as pointed out by Lord Reid himself, the parties can provide for such occurrence specifically within the contract itself. In respect of physical loss, that is, personal injury or damage to property, Lord Denning considered that the test of remoteness in contract should be the same as that found in tort. In such an instance the defendant is liable for any loss which he ought reasonably to be able to foresee at the time of the breach as being a possible consequence of the breach, no matter how slight that possibility. The views of Lord Denning undoubtedly reconcile the particular problems of cases like *H. Parsons* with those encountered in *Victoria Laundry* and *Heron II* but it is unattractively unwieldy and has no authoritative support.

The discussions that took place in the Court of Appeal in *H. Parsons* clearly stand in the shadow of the decision in *Heron II*. For the moment at least the reasoning of Lord Reid that liability for special loss only arises where that loss is contemplated must persist. It has one advantage in that the strictness of the rule should encourage parties to a contract to provide information as regards the possible extent of their losses, though it is clearly inappropriate in cases such as *H. Parsons*. Until the House of Lords has the opportunity and, given the opportunity, deigns to adopt a different approach, the rule as expressed by Lord Reid must be regarded as the authoritative one.

A recent application of the rule in *Hadley* v *Baxendale* can be seen in the Scottish case of *Balfour Beatty Construction (Scotland) Ltd* v *Scottish Power plc* (1994) *The Times*, 23 March, where Balfour Beatty were the main contractors for the construction of a section of the Edinburgh by-pass and its associated structures. In order to carry out the project it was necessary to build a concrete production plant to provide for a continuous pour of concrete. The defendants contracted to provide a temporary supply of electricity to the plant. During construction the electricity supply was interrupted which caused a break in the continuous pour process. As a result of this an aqueduct could not be constructed according to the civil engineering specifications and therefore had to be demolished and rebuilt. The plaintiffs sought to recover the costs of the demoliton and reconstruction from the defendants.

The House of Lords held that the loss was too remote. It applied the principles in *Hadley* v *Baxendale* (the rule also operates in Scottish law), i.e. was the loss of the type that might reasonably have been contemplated by the defendants at the time of the contract as a consequence of the breach. Their Lordships found there was no evidence that the defendants were aware of the need for a continuous pour process. They considered that it had always to be a question of fact what one contracting party was presumed to know about the business activities of the other. Jauncey LJ considered that there was no general rule to the effect that in all the circumstances contracting parties were presumed to have reasonable knowledge of the course of business conducted by each other, finding support for this view in the *Heron II* case. However, the simpler the activity, the more likely could it be inferred that the parties had a reasonable knowledge of each other's business activities. On the other hand, if one party was involved in complex manufacturing or construction processes, there was no reason why a supplier of a product to be used in those processes should be aware of the details of all the techniques to be used in the process and thus be aware of the effect of a failure or deficiency in the product supplied.

Mitigation of loss

It has been seen how the basic concept of damages in contract, that is, to place the plaintiff in the same position he would have been in had the contract been carried out, is subject to the test of remoteness. However the basic concept is also limited by the notion of mitigation of loss. Mitigation essentially means that a plaintiff will not be able to claim for losses which he could have avoided by the taking of reasonable steps to reduce those losses once he has elected to treat the contract as at an end.

The principle may be seen in the context of a fixed-term contract of employment, say, for two years. If the employee is wrongfully dismissed four months into the contract, he cannot sit back and do nothing for the balance of the two years and then claim his full salary for the period of the contract. He must attempt to reduce his loss as far as can be expected of a reasonable man. He should, as held in *Brace v Calder* [1895] 2 QB 253, attempt to take up other employment, thereby reducing his losses. As stated in Haldane LC in *British Westinghouse Electric and Manufacturing Co Ltd v Underground Electric Railways Co of London Ltd* [1912] AC 673:

> I think that there are certain broad principles, which are quite well settled. The first is that, as far as possible, he who has proved a breach of a bargain to supply what he contracted to get is to be placed as far as money can do it, in as good a situation as if the contract had been performed. The fundamental basis is thus compensation for pecuniary loss naturally flowing from the breach; but this first principle is qualified by a second, which imposes on a plaintiff the duty of taking all reasonable steps to mitigate the loss consequent on the breach, and debars him from claiming in respect of any part of the damage which is due to his neglect to take such steps.

The facts of the *British Westinghouse* case were that the appellants, Westinghouse, had contracted to supply turbines to the respondents. The respondents laid down that the turbines had to meet certain specifications. Whilst the appellants built and delivered the turbines they never met the specifications required by the contract. In due course the respondents had to replace the turbines with those produced by a different manufacturer. The new turbines were highly efficient, so much so that they quickly paid for themselves. Nevertheless the respondents sued for the cost of purchasing and installing the new turbines. It was held that they could not do so. The respondents were required to mitigate their losses and this they had done, but so efficiently as to eliminate the costs of replacing the original turbines, and therefore nothing could be recovered as regards these losses. They were entitled, however, for compensation for the losses sustained whilst the inefficient turbines were being used.

Whether a plaintiff has taken reasonable steps to reduce his losses is a question of fact, the question revolving around whether the plaintiff has done everything a reasonable man might be expected to do in the ordinary course of business. From this it can be seen that the plaintiff is not obliged to embark upon a difficult course of action in order to mitigate any losses. Thus it was held in *Pilkington v Wood* [1953] 2 Ch 770 that the plaintiff was not obliged to embark upon difficult and complicated litigation. Similarly, in *Selvanayagam v University of the West Indies* [1983] 1 WLR 585 it was held that the plaintiff was not required to undergo an operation which carried a risk of post-operative complications in order to mitigate the loss. According to *Payzu Ltd v Saunders* [1919] 2 KB 581 the burden rests on the defendant to prove that the plaintiff has not taken reasonable steps to mitigate his losses. In this context it should be noted that provided the plaintiff's attempts to mitigate are reasonable at the time, it is irrelevant if they are subsequently found to be inefficient, as stated in *Gebruder Metel Mann GmbH & Co KG v NBR (London) Ltd* [1984] 1 Lloyd's Rep 614.

The rules on mitigation present particular problems in relation to anticipatory breach since there is no duty to mitigate whilst the plaintiff treats the contract as still subsisting, as may be seen in the case of *White and Carter (Councils) Ltd* v *McGregor* [1962] AC 413. In this context, however, the attempts to restrict this rule as stated in *The Alaskan Trader (No 2)* [1984] 1 All ER 129 should also be noted carefully (both cases being discussed fully in Chapter 13). Thus the duty to mitigate in anticipatory breach only arises where the plaintiff elects to treat the contract as at an end.

One final point on mitigation is that there is no duty on the plaintiff to mitigate. A plaintiff is only under a duty to take reasonable steps to mitigate his loss, and if the plaintiff chooses to take no steps it simply means that he will fail to be compensated for those losses which he could have avoided by the taking of reasonable steps.

Contributory negligence

The apparent overlap between contract and tort in relation to the test of remoteness also arises in this fourth limitation on the availability of damages, contributory negligence. The limitation of contributory negligence on an award of damages in tort has been recognised for some time, initially as a complete defence to an action and latterly, since the Law Reform (Contributory Negligence) Act 1945, as a means of reducing the amount of damages that might be recovered. The question arises as to whether such a doctrine will apply equally to contract as to tort, given the different criteria by which damages are assessed in the two areas and the fact that the law of contract imposes strict liability.

The answer to the question appears to lie within ss. 1(1) and 4 of the 1945 Act. Section 1(1) states:

> (1) Where any person suffers damage as the result partly of his own fault and partly of the fault of any other person or persons, a claim in respect of that damage shall not be defeated by reason of the fault of the person suffering the damage, but the damages recoverable in respect thereof shall be reduced to such extent as the court thinks just and equitable having regard to the claimant's share in the responsibility for the damage . . .

For liability in contract to fall within this provision it would be necessary to show that it falls within the concept of 'fault' as expressed in s. 1. 'Fault' is defined in s. 4, which is the interpretation section of the Act. It states:

> 'Fault' means negligence, breach of statutory duty or other act or omission which gives rise to a liability in tort or would, apart from this Act, give rise to the defence of a contributory negligence.

In deciding whether liability in contract falls within the latter part of this provision Hobhouse J in *Forsikringsaktieselskapet Vesta* v *Butcher* [1986] 2 All ER 488 (affirmed by the Court of Appeal [1989] 1 All ER 404) identified three possibilities; firstly, the defendant is in breach of his strict obligations under the contract; secondly, the defendant is in breach of a duty to take reasonable care which is laid down in a contract, though there is no corresponding duty in tort; for example, such a duty may arise in a contract for services; thirdly, the defendant is in breach of a duty of care arising out of liability both in contract and in tort.

It was held in the *Butcher* case that the 1945 Act would only apply in regard to the third classification, thus allowing contributory negligence to have a bearing on the overall assessment of damages. Apparently the reason is that the defendant's liability in contract could also arise separately and independently within an action in negligence, in which, of course, the 1945 Act would apply. This position was also affirmed in *Barclays Bank plc v Fairclough Building Ltd* (1994) *The Times*, 11 May.

In *AB Marintrans v Comet Shipping Co Ltd* [1985] 3 All ER 442 and *Basildon District Council v J. E. Lesser (Properties) Ltd* [1985] 1 All ER 20, it was stated that the 1945 Act did not apply to the first possibility since s. 4 clearly placed 'fault' in the context of a claim in tort, thereby specifically excluding liability arising in contract solely from the provisions of s. 1. With regard to the second possibility, Neil LJ in the *Comet Shipping* case considered that the 1945 Act only applies where the breach complained of involves a breach of a duty in tort. This view thus also excludes this category from the provisions of the 1945 Act. This reasoning is also propounded by O'Connor LJ in the *Butcher* case.

Recently the case of *Gran Gelato Ltd v Richcliff (Group) Ltd* [1992] 1 All ER 865 considered whether contributory negligence should operate to reduce an award of damages made under an action for breach of the Misrepresentation Act 1967, s. 2(1). The facts of the case were that the defendant had given the plaintiff an underlease for 10 years in 1984. The head lease contained a break clause which was exercisable on the giving of 12 months' notice, expiring on or after June 1989. Neither Gran Gelato nor its solicitors was aware of this restriction. In reply to an inquiry, the defendant's solicitors had stated that there were no such rights in the head lease that would affect the tenant's enjoyment of the property 'to the lessor's knowledge'. In 1988 the lessor of the head lease exercised the break clause in order to redevelop the property. The plaintiff brought an action for misrepresentation and for negligent misstatement. The defendant claimed that the plaintiff was contributorily negligent in not asking for and examining the head lease. The plaintiff argued that the Law Reform (Contributory Negligence) Act 1948, s. 1, did not apply to a claim for damages under s. 2(1) of the 1967 Act. It was held that the 1945 Act applied to both the claim under s. 2(1) and that for negligent misstatement at common law. It was also stated that this would be the case if a claim was framed under s. 2(1) alone, otherwise plaintiffs could avoid apportionment by bringing a claim under the Misrepresentation Act 1967. Nicholls VC considered that 'fault' within the 1945 Act was wide enough to encompass the 1967 Act. On the facts, however, it was decided that it was not just and equitable to make a reduction in damages.

The Law Commission has proposed in Law Commission Working Paper No 114 that the 1945 Act should apply to a breach of the strict contractual duty, although this proposal has not found favour, probably because of the need to balance the interests of the parties within the contract, particularly with regard to the equality of their bargaining power.

In 1993 the Law Commission published its report 'Contributory Negligence as a Defence in Contract' (Law Com No 219). The Commission recommended that the possibility of apportionment should be rejected where there was liability for breach of a strict contractual obligation. It was stated that the reason for this conclusion related to a consideration of the position before a plaintiff is aware, or must be taken to be aware, of the defendant's breach of contract. If the defendant commits himself to a strict obligation regardless of fault (as arises in contract), then a plaintiff should be able to rely on the defendant fulfilling his obligations and should not have to take precautions against the possibility that a breach might occur. The Commission thus affirmed the present law and, whilst it considered that the rules on mitigation of loss were not a substitute for apportionment for contributory negligence, they nevertheless prevented the plaintiff from acting unreasonably once he became aware of his loss or the defendant's breach.

The Commission considered, however, that where a plaintiff suffered damage partly as a result of his own failure to take reasonable care for the protection of himself or his interests and partly as a result of the defendant's breach of a contractual duty to take reasonable care or exercise reasonable skill, apportionment should be allowed in respect of the plaintiff's damages. It was stated that whether a duty of reasonable care is classified as contractual or tortious does not affect the content of the duty and the Commission considered that the availability for apportionment should not depend on how the duty to take reasonable care is classified.

The report (which also contains a draft Bill) defines contributory negligence as a 'plaintiff's failure to take reasonable care for the protection of himself or his interests' (clause 1(1)b of the draft Bill). The criteria for apportionment would be the same as in the 1945 Act, i.e. the plaintiff's damages would be reduced by the amount the court thinks 'just and equitable having regard to the plaintiff's share in the responsibility for the damage' (clause 1(1) of the draft Bill). Whilst the Commission allowed for the parties to contract out of contributory negligence as a defence (clause 1(2)), it also stated that, if a contract made provision for liquidated damages in the event of a breach, this amount would not be subject to a reduction on the grounds of the plaintiff's contributory negligence (clause 1(2)). The Commission also made it clear that anything done or omitted to be done by the plaintiff prior to entering into the contract would be disregarded for the purposes of assessing whether his damages should be reduced for contributory negligence (clause 1(3)).

As the law stands, it may nevertheless still be possible, by the use of the common law rule to raise contributory negligence as a means of defeating a plaintiff's claim altogether. The effect of contributory negligence here, however, is to break the chain of causation and it is rather different conceptually since the basis here is that the plaintiff was solely responsible for his injury or loss, as was held in *Quinn v Burch Bros (Builders) Ltd* [1966] 2 QB 370.

Contractual provisions relating to the limitation of damages

It has been clearly demonstrated in this work that it was in the nineteenth century first and foremost that a philosophy of freedom of contract was established. Embedded in this philosophy was not only the freedom to enter into and negotiate the terms of contract, but also the right of the parties to determine the levels of compensation payable in the event of a breach. The courts therefore readily surrendered their right to make awards to the will of the parties themselves as expressed within the terms of the contract. There were substantial advantages to the judicial process by the adoption of this approach, such as savings in time and expense. Despite the adoption of this position by the courts there was no question of their completely abrogating their jurisdiction as regards awards of damages. The courts were not so naive as to think that freedom of contract and equality of bargaining power represented the same thing and would step in to regulate awards of damages despite the terms of the agreement. The regulatory nature of the courts may be encountered in two broad areas; firstly, in the areas of penalties and, secondly, in the regulation of deposits and forfeiture clauses.

Liquidated damages and penalties

The parties may decide to make a genuine pre-estimate of the losses they may encounter should the other party be in breach of contract and then agree that certain sums will be payable if such an event occurs. Where the sums payable are a genuine pre-estimate of loss then the courts will support claims for such sums, despite the fact that the actual losses may be more or less than the actual loss sustained by the breach. The sums agreed to be payable by the parties in these circumstances are termed 'liquidated damages'.

In some contracts, however, the sums agreed by the parties to be payable are not based on a genuine pre-estimate of the losses the parties may encounter should a breach occur. These sums are usually excessive in relation to the maximum possible losses the parties may sustain in such circumstances. Such sums, rather than being 'liquidated damages' and amounting to compensation, are termed 'penalties' and are placed in the contract as a punitive measure to hold a party *in terrorem* of (as a warning against) breaking the terms of the contract. The courts will not award sums which are considered to be penalties and will substitute a sum representing the actual losses sustained to a party by reason of the breach.

The basis on which the courts decide whether a pre-estimated sum is a penalty or not was laid down by Lord Dunedin in *Dunlop Pneumatic Tyre Co Ltd* v *New Garage and Motor Co Ltd* [1915] AC 79 as follows:

(a)   A sum will be a penalty if it is extravagant having regard to the maximum possible loss that may be sustained by the breach.

(b)   If the contract imposes a liability on a party to pay a sum of money and failure to do so results in that party incurring liability to pay a larger sum, then the latter will be regarded as a penalty. In such cases it is possible to measure fairly precisely what the loss will be, and thus the liability to pay the larger sum must of necessity clearly be a penalty.

(c)   If a single sum is payable upon the occurrence of one or several breaches of the contract, some being serious, some being minor, then that sum will raise the presumption of its being a penalty.

This presumption is weakened if it is almost impossible to prove the actual losses that may result from the various breaches, although the fact that an accurate pre-estimation of loss is not possible will not prevent a sum from being a penalty.

Thus in the *Dunlop* case itself there was a contract entered into for the supply and purchase of tyres. The agreement was said to be a 'Price Maintenance Agreement' under which the defendants were not to sell the tyres below certain prices, nor to sell to persons on a 'black' list, not to exhibit or export the tyres without consent and, finally, not to tamper with certain marks on the tyres. The defendants had to pay £5 by way of liquidated damages for every tyre cover or tube sold or offered in breach of the agreement. The defendants sold a tyre below the plaintiff's current list price, and he claimed the £5 damages. The court held that the sum amounted to liquidated damages, the reason being that, whilst the sum involved was disproportionate to the loss sustained, the motive behind the agreement was to prevent a price war, as this would have damaged Dunlop's selling organisation. The motive behind this clause therefore was not to hold the defendants *in terrorem* of breaking the agreement, but to maintain balance within the industry. From Dunlop's point of view this would amount to a genuine pre-estimate of their possible indirect losses.

It was held in *Robophone Facilities Ltd* v *Blank* [1966] 1 WLR 1428 that the burden of proving whether a sum is a penalty lies on the party from whom the sum is being recovered. The mere fact that a clause is described in the contract as being either a 'liquidated damages' clause or a 'penalty' clause is not conclusive. Thus in *Cellulose Acetate Silk Co Ltd* v *Widnes Foundry (1925) Ltd* [1933] AC 20 a pre-estimated sum of £20 per week which was payable on late performance was described in the contract as a penalty. In fact the amount was not excessive with regard to the actual losses that would be sustained by late performance and was thus awarded, despite the designation given to the term.

The case of *Phillips Hong Kong Ltd* v *Attorney-General of Hong Kong* (1993) *The Times*, 15 February, appears to advocate a rather more flexible approach than that laid down in *Dunlop Pneumatic Tyre Co Ltd* v *New Garage & Motor Co.* In that case Lord Dunedin stated:

> The question whether a sum stipulated is penalty or liquidated damages is a question of construction to be decided upon the terms and inherent circumstances of each particular contract, judged of as at the time of the contract not at the time of the breach . . .

Whilst on this basis the clause has to be viewed objectively, the *Phillips* case suggests that a court can examine what actually happened in the case to decide whether or not the clause represents a penalty or liquidated damages, since it allows an assessment to be made of what the parties expected the losses to be when the contract was made. This would allow a court to disregard a liquidated damages clause which in the particular circumstances of the case provides for a disproportionate sum in relation to the actual losses suffered, if the facts showed that the parties did not intend the clause to apply in those circumstances. This would therefore allow such clauses to stand, whereas previously, following the *Dunlop* case, they would have been entirely severed from the contract. It may be that this flexible approach is confined to commercial contracts, as in the *Phillips* case, since the court considered that such contracts (and clauses) are entered into by businessmen at arm's length who should normally be bound by what they have agreed. Such an approach would accord with the comments of Lord Roskill in *Export Credits Guarantee Department* v *Universal Oil Products Co* [1983] 2 All ER 205.

It should be noted that the rules regarding penalties and liquidated damages are only applicable where there has been a breach of contract. Where a sum becomes payable because of the occurrence of some other event the above rules have no application, leaving the stronger of the two parties in a position to apply and enforce what would otherwise amount to a penalty. In *Export Credits Guarantee Department* v *Universal Oil Products Co* [1983] 2 All ER 205 Lord Roskill explained the reasoning for the principle in the following way:

> My Lords, one purpose, perhaps the main purpose, of the law relating to penalty clauses is to prevent a plaintiff recovering a sum of money in respect of a breach committed by a defendant which bears little or no relationship to the loss actually suffered by the plaintiffs as a result of the breach by the defendants. But it is not and never has been for the courts to relieve a party from the consequences of what may, in the event, prove to be an onerous or possibly even imprudent commercial bargain.

Whilst the rule is easy to understand when placed in such a context, nevertheless in practical terms it is perverse and illogical since it is likely that the defendant will find it cheaper to breach the contract than to labour on under harsh and onerous conditions.

In *Jobson* v *Johnson* [1989] 1 All ER 621 this rule does not seem to have been followed. The facts of the case are fairly complex but basically there was a contract for the purchase of shares, the purchase monies to be paid in seven instalments, including the initial payment. One clause in the contract stated that should the defendant default on any instalment then he would be required to re-transfer the shares back to the vendor, or his assignee, at a price substantially lower than the value of the shares or the amounts he might have paid in instalments. It was held that the reduced price payable, whilst clearly within the contract, was nevertheless a penalty. The court therefore refused specific performance of the re-transfer clause unless measures were taken to make adjustment for the amounts already paid in previous instalments. Patently, the court seems to have ignored the rule contained in the *Universal Oil Products* case and its predecessors.

Deposits and forfeiture clauses

Deposits are essentially the converse of penalties in that they are payable before a breach occurs, rather than after as in the case of a penalty. Deposits are normally regarded as a part satisfaction of the contract price which may be retained should the purchaser fail to perform his side of the bargain.

Forfeiture clauses normally arise where there is a purchase of goods by instalments and the contract provides that should the purchaser default on any instalment then he must surrender the goods, at the same time forfeiting any instalments already paid. Both deposits and forfeiture clauses are regarded as guarantees that the contract will be performed.

The normal rule in relation to deposits is that if the money has been paid and the party to whom it is paid breaks the contract, then the payer may recover the deposit either for breach of contract or in quasi-contract (see Chapter 18 below). Deposit monies payable in the future usually cease to be payable.

Where the person who has paid the deposit is in breach of contract then one must distinguish between sums paid as a deposit and those which amount merely to prepayments made on account. As regards the latter, it has been held in *Dies v British and International Mining and Finance Corporation* [1939] 1 KB 724 that in a contract of sale the advance payments on account can be recovered, subject to any rights of set-off possessed by the seller in respect of actual losses. In *Hyundai Heavy Industries Co Ltd* v *Papadopoulos* [1980] 2 All ER 29, the House of Lords held that such advance payments could not be recovered. The apparent reason for the distinction is that in the latter case the prepayment on the shipbuilding contract was regarded as an unconditional payment for the work that had already been completed, whilst generally in contracts of sale prepayments are conditional on performance taking place subsequent to the prepayment. The position was stated by Kerr LJ in *Rover International Ltd* v *Cannon Film Sales Ltd (No 3)* [1989] 3 All ER 423 as:

> The question is whether there was any consideration in the nature of part performance for which the instalment was payable, as in the *Hyundai Heavy Industries* case, or whether the instalment was payable in advance of any performance which was required from the party in default.

There does not appear to be any reason why a shipbuilding contract (as in the *Hyundai* case) should be different from any other type of contract of sale. Cheshire, Fifoot and Furmston (1991), p. 626 suggest that the distinction can be justified in three ways: firstly, the *Dies* case is wrong; secondly, shipbuilding contracts should be viewed differently from other contracts of sale; and, thirdly, more convincingly, it is suggested that distinction lies in the fact that in *Dies* there was a total failure of consideration but that this was not the case in *Hyundai*.

Where a person who has paid money is in breach of contract, the deposit, or prepayment may be made subject to a right of forfeiture. In such circumstances the payee is entitled to keep all of the deposit despite the fact that his losses may be less than the amount of deposit paid, as stated in *Howe v Smith* (1884) 27 Ch D 89. It should also be noted that if the deposit is payable but so far unforthcoming, the innocent party can (it has been held in *Damon Cia Naviera SA* v *Hapag-Lloyd International SA, The Blankenstein* [1985] 1 All ER 475) take action to recover the deposit. The same principles have also been held to apply to money paid as a prepayment.

It may be noticed that the effect of a payee being able to keep a deposit which in fact exceeds his losses is not very different from the effect of a penalty. Despite the similarity there is no, or little, relief available in cases of forfeiture which corresponds to that already seen in relation to penalties. Such relief as does exist tends to arise in specialist contracts, as in the termination of hire purchase and conditional sale agreements under the Consumer Credit Act 1974, s. 100, or in contracts for the sale of land under the Law of Property Act 1925, s. 49(2). The latter provides:

Where the court refuses to grant specific performance of the contract, or any action for the return of a deposit, the court may, if it thinks fit, order the repayment of the deposit.

The question arises, however, as to whether relief against forfeiture can be given outside these rather specialist areas. In equity the court will normally grant relief where the payer is overdue in the payment of instalments. Relief here normally takes the form of extending the time for payment, though occasionally the court may order the repayment of monies paid. Relief here is dependent on the buyer being ready and willing to pay an instalment or the balance of monies owed within a period fixed by the court, as stated in *Starside Properties Ltd* v *Mustapha* [1974] 2 All ER 567.

In *Stockloser* v *Johnson* [1954] 1 All ER 630 Lord Denning and Lord Somervell considered that there existed a more general equitable principle that gave relief against forfeiture. This principle, they thought, arose where the sum to be forfeited by reason of the forfeiture was out of all proportion to the losses sustained by the innocent party, in other words that the clause was penal in character and that it was unconscionable for that party to retain the monies paid. Lord Romer, however, took a far more restrictive view and considered that equity could only intervene in this way if the seller had acted in a fraudulent or unconscionable manner.

The view of Lord Romer is the one that seems to have gained prevalence in recent cases. In *Scandinavian Trading Tanker Co* v *Flota Petrolera Ecuatoriana, The Scaptrade* [1983] 2 AC 694, the House of Lords held that relief against forfeiture could not be invoked by a time charterer of a ship where he had failed to pay the hire instalments on time in order to prevent the shipowner withdrawing the ship from the charterparty. The reason given was that such relief would not be granted where specific performance would not be granted and it would not normally be given in the case of a time charter, since damages are an adequate remedy where there has been a breach of such a contract. The effect of relief against forfeiture here would be tantamount to a decree of specific performance. From this it follows from the decision of the House of Lords that relief against forfeiture is only available where proprietary or possessory rights are being forfeited. In *The Scaptrade* they clearly were not, since a time charter was regarded as merely a contract for the use of a ship, that is, a contract for services. This position has recently been affirmed in *Sport International Bussum BS* v *Inter-Footwear Ltd* [1984] 2 All ER 321, though in *BICC plc* v *Bundy Corporation* [1985] 1 All ER 417 the Court of Appeal considered that such relief could extend to proprietary and possessory rights in goods, rather than being confined to contracts for the sale of land as envisaged by Lord Diplock in *The Scaptrade*.

One further point in relation to relief from forfeiture needs to be made in that it is only available in respect of prepayments subject to a forfeiture clause **not** deposits, despite the fact that the distinction between the two, as already seen, is non-existent.

Speculative damages and damages for non-pecuniary losses

The fact that damages cannot be accurately assessed is in no way a bar to the recovery of compensation, provided that they do not fall foul of the rules regarding remoteness. A clear example of this can be seen in *Chaplin v Hicks* [1911] 2 KB 786 where the plaintiff who had entered a beauty contest and won the earlier stages was prevented from competing in the final stages of the contest contrary to the terms of the contract. It was held that she could claim damages for the loss of opportunity caused by the defendant's breach of contract.

Whilst damages are available for losses which are clearly speculative it is equally clear that damages are not available as a punitive measure, being purely compensatory. Nevertheless damages are not confined to financial loss, though it is true that in most of the cases discussed so far the actions revolve around commercial contracts in which such losses provide the main cause of the actions. Despite the fact that damages are not confined to financial loss the law is not as flexible as might first be supposed, since for many years the principle was that physical inconvenience had to arise from the breach and not simply mental distress, as affirmed in the case of *Addis v Gramophone Co Ltd* [1909] AC 488, where loss of reputation caused by the abrupt dismissal of the plaintiff was held to be irrecoverable.

In recent years a number of cases have arisen that have undermined the principle and allowed damages for mental distress and anxiety to be claimed. This position developed out of the case of *Jarvis v Swans Tours Ltd* [1973] 1 QB 233 and was affirmed in *Jackson v Horizon Holidays Ltd* [1975] 1 WLR 1468.

In both cases the plaintiffs suffered considerable disappointment as to the quality of the holidays they had bought, which did not live up to their expectations based on the holiday brochures of the respective tour companies. In both cases the courts decided that damages for disappointment, mental anxiety and distress could be compensated. In the *Jarvis* case Lord Denning stated:

> What is the right way of assessing damages? It has often been said that on a breach of contract damages cannot be given for mental distress . . . I think those limitations are out of date. In a proper case damages for mental distress can be recovered in contract, just as damages for shock can be recovered in tort. One such case is a contract for a holiday, or any other contract to provide entertainment and enjoyment. If the contracting party breaks his contract, damages can be given for the disappointment, the distress, the upset and frustration caused by the breach. I know it is difficult to assess in terms of money, but it is no more difficult than the assessment which the courts have to make every day in personal injury cases for loss of amenities.

The *Jarvis* and *Jackson* cases produced a considerable widening of the scope for awarding damages for mental distress caused by the breach of contract. Thus in *Cox v Phillips Industries Ltd* [1976] 3 All ER 161 an employee was able to recover damages for distress and anxiety caused by his wrongful demotion, the judge distinguishing it from the *Addis* case on the basis that the decision there arose out of a dismissal, though why this is any the less distressing remains something of a mystery. Clearly, where the contract is of a personal nature it can be expected that there will be some degree of anxiety and distress if a breach of contract occurs. However the principle soon expanded to cover other areas. In *Perry v Sidney Phillips & Son (a firm)* [1982] 3 All ER 705, for example, damages were awarded for the mental distress caused by the failure of a negligent surveyor to discover major structural defects in a dwelling house.

In recent years there has been a movement in the courts towards a considerable tightening up of awards of damages for such types of losses. Thus in *Shove* v *Downs Surgical plc* [1984] 1 All ER 7, the decision in *Addis* was reaffirmed and Sheen J found that damages for mental distress caused by wrongful dismissal were irrecoverable. More importantly in *Bliss* v *South East Thames Regional Health Authority* [1985] IRLR 308, the Court of Appeal reversed the decision at first instance that the mental distress and anxiety caused by the suspension of an orthopaedic surgeon for refusing to submit to an examination by a psychiatrist was recoverable. The decision substantially overruled the *Cox* case and also reaffirmed *Addis*. In the course of their judgments, the members of the Court of Appeal confined liability for damages for mental distress to facts such as those seen in the *Jarvis* and *Jackson* cases, where the provision of comfort, pleasure or 'peace of mind' was a central feature of the contract, or, indeed, where the relief of discomfort played such a prominent role in the contract. This decision has now received affirmation in *Hayes* v *James and Charles Dodd (a firm)* [1990] 2 All ER 815 where Staughton LJ stated that damages could not be recovered for the distress that might result from a breach of a commercial contract. In relation to the 'peace of mind' criterion discussed in *Bliss*, Lord Staughton stated:

> it might be that the class was wider than that. But it should not include any case where the object of the contract was not comfort or pleasure or the relief of discomfort, but not simply carrying on a commercial contract with a view to profit.

Further reading

Beale, Bishop and Furmston, *Contract – Cases and Materials* 2nd ed. 1990, Butterworths
Bishop, 'The Choice of Remedy for Breach of Contract', 14 *Journal of Legal Studies* 299, 1985
Burrows, *Remedies for Torts and Breach of Contract*, 1987, Butterworths
Cheshire, Fifoot and Furmston, *The Law of Contract* 12th ed. 1991, Butterworths
Guest, *Anson's Law of Contract* 26th ed. 1984, Oxford University Press
Hudson, 'Penalties Limiting Damages', 90 *Law Quarterly Review* 31, 1974
Hudson, 'Penalties Limiting Damages', 91 *Law Quarterly Review* 25, 1975
Taylor, 'Expectation, Reliance and Misrepresentation', 45 *Modern Law Review* 139, 1982
Treitel, *The Law of Contract* 8th ed. 1991, Sweet & Maxwell

17 | Equitable remedies and limitation of actions

EQUITABLE REMEDIES

Specific performance

The nature of the remedy

Specific performance is an order of the court which compels a defendant to carry out his obligations under a contract in accordance with the terms and conditions set out in the contract. Failure to comply with the order will render the defendant liable to criminal proceedings for contempt of court. The remedy is normally used to enforce positive obligations, negative ones being restrained with the use of a prohibitory injunction.

Specific performance is a remedy *in personam* and can be ordered even where the subject matter of the contract is outside the jurisdiction, provided the party subject to the order is within the jurisdiction. The remedy is awarded at the discretion of the court and it should be noted that it is only sparingly awarded, where the court considers it just and equitable to do so. The award will not be given, for instance, where its effect would be to cause hardship amounting to injustice to either party or an interested third party, as was held in *Patel v Ali* [1984] Ch 283.

In this case the vendor and her husband were the co-owners of a house which they had entered into a contract to sell in 1979. Completion was delayed by reason of the husband's bankruptcy. In addition the vendor contracted bone cancer which resulted in her having to have a leg amputated. These events also corresponded with the birth of their second and third children. The purchaser applied for, and was awarded, an order of specific performance, but the vendor appealed on the grounds of hardship. The vendor spoke little English and had to rely on friends and relatives for help. The effect of the decree would thus be to expose her to undue hardship. The court held that in an appropriate case relief could be given against specific performance where hardship arose once the contract had been entered into, even if the hardship itself was not related specifically to the subject matter and not caused by the plaintiff. The court decided that damages should be awarded instead of specific performance as the latter would amount to injustice, given the level of hardship that would be inflicted on the vendor.

Whilst an application for an award of specific performance will usually be made where a breach of contract has occurred, a breach is not an essential requirement for the application of an award. The award of the order is based on the existence of a contract, together with circumstances rendering it just and equitable to make an award, as stated in *Hasham v Zenab* [1960] AC 316, where an order of specific performance was given before the contractual date for completion since the defendant was in anticipatory breach of contract.

The award of an order of specific performance is not an arbitrary one and various factors might influence a court in the granting of the order.

Factors to be considered in making an order for specific performance

(a) Damages must not be an adequate remedy. If damages are an adequate remedy then an order of specific performance will not be awarded (the same principle also applying to the award of injunctions). The reason for this is that the remedies of the courts of chancery arose out of the inadequacy of the award of damages at common law. In the vast majority of contracts damages provide an adequate remedy as, for example, in contracts for the sale of goods, since here compensation will generally allow a purchaser to buy the goods elsewhere. In contracts for the sale of land, however, an order of specific performance will normally be awarded since, on just and equitable grounds, a simple award of damages would defeat the reasonable aspirations and expectations of the vendor.

Specific performance will be awarded for contracts for the sale of goods, however, where the goods in question are unique. A contract for the purchase of a valuable antique or painting clearly would not be compensated by damages since there is no or little prospect of a buyer being able to go into the market-place and purchase a similar item. This factor is another reason why contracts for the sale of land lend themselves readily to the award of such a remedy. Even in these circumstances the court will not make an order where the award would produce an injustice to the defendant.

The principle is illustrated by the case of *Wroth v Tyler* [1974] Ch 30 where a husband, who was the owner of a matrimonial home, entered into a contract to sell the property with vacant possession. Before completion could take place his wife, who did not want to move, registered her right of occupation under the Matrimonial Homes Act 1967 (now 1983) as a class F landcharge against the property, and this action had the effect of placing an encumbrance on the ability of the husband to give vacant possession. The husband withdrew from the contract and the purchaser sued for an order of specific performance.

It was held by Megarry J that the purchaser should fail in his action since to compel the husband to carry out his obligation he would have had to apply to the court to terminate the wife's right of occupation. In order to do this the husband would have had to embark on difficult and uncertain litigation against his own wife, which was clearly undesirable given the fact that they were still living together. Even if he was successful in such an action the court's decision to remove the right of occupation was in any event discretionary. Further, if the court awarded specific performance subject to the wife's right of occupation this would have entailed the purchaser in obtaining an order of eviction against the husband and his daughter, thereby resulting in the break-up of the family.

Contracts to pay money do not usually attract an order for specific performance since damages are normally an adequate remedy here. In certain circumstances the use of such an order can be justified where there is a contract under which money has to be paid to a third party. The case of *Beswick* v *Beswick* [1968] AC 58 (the facts of which are given in Chapter 19) is an obvious and extremely good illustration of the use of specific performance in such circumstances. An award of damages to Peter Beswick's estate would have been nominal since the contract to pay the annuity in question to his widow resulted in no loss to his estate, whilst the annuity payable to himself ceased on his death. The most appropriate remedy, therefore, was a decree of specific performance in order to compel the defendant to comply with his obligations under the contract to the third party.

(b) The requirement of mutuality. The general principle is that specific performance will not be awarded unless the order is available to both parties, that is, availability of the award is mutual. Thus in *Flight* v *Bolland* (1828) 4 Russ 298 an application for specific performance by a minor failed since the award would not have been available against the minor by the other party because of the incapacity of the applicant. The Landlord and Tenant Act 1985, s. 17, provides an exception to the rule requiring mutuality. It states that the court can make an order of specific performance in respect of a landlord's covenant to keep the premises in a good state of repair despite rules of equity restricting the award of the order 'whether based on mutuality or otherwise'.

One problem that has arisen in the past with respect to mutuality is the time at which mutuality should be present between the parties. It was suggested by Fry (1921) in *Specific Performance* that there had to be mutuality between the parties at the time an enforcement contract had been entered into. Ames (1913), however, in *Lectures on Legal History* pointed to several exceptions to this rule, stating that the rule should be expressed as:

> Equity will not compel specific performance by a defendant if, after performance, the common law remedy of damages would be his sole security for the performance of the plaintiff's side of the contract.

The rule, however, has recently been subject to extensive review in the case of *Price* v *Strange* [1978] Ch 337.

The facts of the case were that the defendant had contracted to grant a sublease to the plaintiff, provided the plaintiff did some external and internal repairs to the premises. The plaintiff did the internal repairs but, though he was ready and willing to do the external repairs, he was unable to do so because the defendant had then done them herself at her own expense. The defendant repudiated the contract and the plaintiff claimed for an order of specific performance. At first instance the application failed since the availability of the remedy was not mutual at the date of the contract because the defendant could not have compelled the plaintiff to carry out the repairs. The decision was reversed on appeal to the Court of Appeal. Goff LJ stated that the principle of mutuality is,

> that one judges the defence of mutuality on the facts and circumstances as they exist at the hearing, albeit in the light of the whole contract of the parties in relation to the subject-matter, and in the absence of any other disqualifying circumstances, the court will grant specific performance if it can be done without injustice or unfairness to the defendant.

It should be noted that the rule regarding the need for mutuality is one which affects the discretion of the court to award specific performance. The rule does not affect the jurisdiction of the court to award damages in lieu of specific performance under the Chancery Amendment Act 1858, which will be dealt with later.

(c) The exercise of discretion. As already stated the exercise of discretion is not an arbitrary one but is exercised within certain broad parameters in order to promote justice between the parties. Should the exercise of the discretion result in injustice being wrought upon an individual then the order of specific performance will not be given. The notion that governs this aspect of the exercise of discretion is sometimes expressed in the equitable maxim, 'he who seeks equity must do equity' or rather more graphically, 'he who comes to equity must come with clean hands'.

It has been seen how hardship can prevent the exercise of equitable discretion to give an order for specific performance, and the same is also true of mistake and misrepresentation. It should be noted, however, that a defendant cannot resist the granting of an order simply because he made a mistake. As a general rule the defendant will be held to his bargain, unless he can prove that this would lead to injustice. In *Webster* v *Cecil* (1861) 30 Beav 62 the vendor offered to sell some property to the purchaser for £2,250 but mistakenly wrote £1,250. The purchaser, who was aware of the mistake, immediately accepted the offer. The vendor on realising his mistake gave notice of it to the purchaser. It was held that in the circumstances he could not be compelled to carry on with the sale.

The rules relating to time (the doctrine of laches) in relation to performance of a contract have been fully discussed in Chapter 13. There it was seen that the rule in equity is that time is not of the essence in a contract and that therefore a plaintiff can obtain specific performance, despite the fact that he has not carried out his obligations under the contract at the time specified in the contract. Where, however, the parties have agreed that time will be of the essence then specific performance will not be awarded if the elements relating to time have not been met by the plaintiff. This principle applies even if time was only made of the essence by the service of notice during the ambit of the contract. Even where time is not of the essence specific performance may still be lost since the rule that 'delay defeats equity' may apply. Unreasonable delay then may defeat an application for equitable relief, including specific performance, but what is unreasonable depends substantially on the subject matter of the contract. At one time it was considered that specific performance had to be applied for within 12 months. However, in *Lazard Bros & Co Ltd* v *Fairfield Properties (Mayfair) Ltd* (1977) 121 Sol Jo 793 Megarry VC stated that specific performance should not be regarded as a prize to be awarded to the zealous and denied to the indolent. In that case a delay of over two years was held not to be a bar to the award of an order.

The exercise of the discretion to award specific performance is not given where the contract demands a personal service or work, for instance, in contracts of employment. The reason is that the order would require the constant supervision of the court, as was held in *Ryan* v *Mutual Tontine Westminster Chambers Association* [1893] 1 Ch 116 where the landlord of a flat agreed that he would appoint a porter who would be in constant attendance to maintain the common areas of the building, collect mail, and so on. The porter appointed also worked as a chef at a nearby club and was thus constantly absent. The plaintiff's action for specific performance failed since the exercise of the order would require the constant supervision of the court. It should also be noted that the courts are reluctant to order specific performance in personal contracts since as a matter of public policy it is considered undesirable to force a person to carry out obligations with another against his will.

(d) *'Equity will not assist a volunteer.'* In *Penn* v *Lord Baltimore* (1750) 1 Ves Sen 444, Lord Hardwicke declared that 'the court never decrees specifically without a consideration'. The requirement of consideration is a fundamental requirement for the granting of an order for specific performance, whether or not the contract is a simple one or one that is made under seal by deed.

Injunctions

The nature of the remedy

A further way in which a contract may be enforced is by the use of an injunction, which can be either prohibitory or mandatory in its application. A prohibitory injunction in the law of contract is only used to restrain a breach of a negative undertaking, for instance, where the defendant had broken an agreement not to carry on a particular trade, as in *Nordenfelt* v *Maxim Nordenfelt Guns and Ammunition Co Ltd* [1894] AC 535.

A mandatory injunction is an order to the defendant to do some positive act, such as demolishing a building, and is thus restorative in its nature. As a general rule such injunctions arise out of tortious acts rather than contractual ones, where specific performance is used. This type of injunction is quite uncommon and is not usually issued where damages are an adequate remedy or where the injunction would require the constant supervision of the court. Generally speaking, if a mandatory injunction should be claimed in a contractual situation, it will be subject to very similar limitations to those imposed on applications for specific performance.

Limitations on the use of prohibitory injunctions

The rule that damages must be shown to be inadequate before equitable relief will be granted does not apply to prohibitory (sometimes called 'ordinary') injunctions. That is not to suppose that the courts will allow this difference to be used in order to allow a plaintiff to gain a benefit that he would not ordinarily be entitled to claim in an application for specific performance. The courts will thus only grant the injunction where there is an express stipulation in the contract that the defendant should not do a particular act. Thus in *Lumley* v *Wagner* (1852) 1 De GM & G 604 the defendant agreed to sing at the plaintiff's theatre over a particular period. She eventually abandoned the contract and took engagements to sing elsewhere. It was held that the plaintiff could have an injunction restraining the defendant from singing anywhere else. The negative nature of the injunction should be noted in the case, since the court could not compel the defendant to work solely for the plaintiff, though it could prevent her from working for anyone else.

The decision in *Lumley* v *Wagner* was followed in the case of *Warner Bros Inc* v *Nelson* [1937] 1 KB 209 where the actress Bette Davis was restrained from working for anyone but the plaintiffs. Both cases have been criticised as being tantamount to forcing the defendants to work for the respective plaintiffs, an effect which in personal contracts has always been ruled against in the granting of equitable relief. Indeed, in the case of *Page One Records Ltd* v *Britton* [1968] 1 WLR 157 the courts refused to grant an injunction which would have had the effect of compelling the defendant, representing The Troggs pop group, to engage the plaintiffs as their agents and managers or to wind up the group. This approach was also followed in *Nichols Advanced Vehicle Systems Inc* v *De Angelis* (unreported, 21 December 1979) where Oliver J considered the proper approach was that taken in the *Page One Records* case, unless the period of the contract was very short, as in *Lumley* v *Wagner*.

Finally it should be stated that there are no restrictions on a court granting a prohibitory injunction to prevent an employee from breaking particular terms in his contract of employment. Recent examples of the use of an injunction in these circumstances are *Lansing Linde Ltd* v *Kerr* [1991] 1 All ER 418 and *Lawrence David Ltd* v *Ashton* [1991] 1 All ER 385 where prohibitory injunctions were used to prevent employees from disclosing the confidential information of their employers to a business rival.

Damages in lieu of specific performance and injunction

The Chancery Amendment 1858 gave the court of chancery the opportunity to grant damages in lieu of specific performance or injunction. It is possible for the court to grant damages in addition to these orders, provided the plaintiff can show that he has suffered some special loss or damage.

The position with respect to these types of damages is now governed by the Supreme Court Act 1981, s. 50. It should be noted that the damages that arise here are discretionary and that the discretion only arises where the contract is of a type for which an injunction or an order for specific performance is not available. Where the contract is of such a type then the court may exercise its discretion to award damages despite the fact that an injunction or an order for specific performance would not be given because of some discretionary reason, for example, the lack of mutuality. In order for the court to exercise its discretion, however, the plaintiff must have applied for either an injunction or an order for specific performance.

The measure of damages under the Act is calculated on the same basis as those at common law, as held by Lord Wilberforce in *Johnson* v *Agnew* [1980] AC 367.

LIMITATIONS OF ACTIONS

Limitation Act 1980

Whilst equity could exercise its discretion not to grant relief under the doctrine of laches, where a plaintiff unreasonably delayed in applying to the court, the common law developed no such rule, although stale actions were discouraged as a matter of policy.

The Limitation Act 1980 has laid down a framework of periods within which actions must be brought or be debarred. In actions for breach of contract the following periods are laid down by the Act.

Actions founded on a simple contract

Here the action must be commenced within six years from the date on which the cause of the action accrued, by virtue of s. 5. In contract the cause of action accrues from the time of the breach, rather than from the time any damage occurs, as in actions for negligence. Where the action can be framed in either contract or tort, or both, there may thus be a procedural advantage in framing the action in terms of a tortious claim.

Where the breach gives rise to personal injuries then s. 11 of the Act provides that the limitation period is reduced to three years from the date on which the cause of action accrued.

Actions founded on a speciality contract

By s. 8(1) an action upon a speciality shall not be brought after the expiration of 12 years from the date on which the cause of action accrued.

Action for an account

By s. 23 an action for an account shall not be brought after the expiration of any time limit which is applicable to the claim which is the basis of the duty to account, that is, six years in relation to breach of contract.

The suspension of the Act by virtue of disabilities

If the plaintiff is under a disability, for example, is a minor or of unsound mind, when the cause of action accrued then the limitation period does not begin to run until the disability has ceased to operate, by virtue of s. 28(1). It should be noted that by s. 28(2), if time under the limitation period had already started to run, then any subsequent disability has no effect on the running of time for the purposes of calculating the limitation period.

Postponement of the limitation period in cases of fraud or mistake

The position here is governed by s. 32(1) of the Act which provides:

> where in the case of any action for which a period of limitation is prescribed by this Act, either –
>
> (a) the action is based upon the fraud of the defendant; or
> (b) any fact relevant to the plaintiff's right of action has been deliberately concealed from him by the defendant; or
> (c) the action is for relief from the consequences of a mistake;
>
> the period of limitation shall not begin to run until the plaintiff has discovered the fraud, concealment or mistake (as the case may be) or could with reasonable diligence have discovered it.

Extension of the limitation period by acknowledgement or part-payment

It is provided by s. 29(5) that:

> Where any right of action has accrued to recover –
>
> (a) any debt or other liquidated pecuniary claim . . . and the person liable or accountable for the claim or makes any payment in respect of it the right shall be treated as having accrued on and not before the date of the acknowledgement or payment.

The result of the above provision is that if a person owes a debt to another then, every time the debtor makes a part-payment of the debt or acknowledges the debt, the limitation period begins to run afresh from the date of each part-payment or acknowledgement of the debt. By s. 29(7) however, once the debt is statute barred then the right of action cannot be revived by any acknowledgement or part-payment. An effective acknowledgement must be made in writing signed by the debtor, or his agent, and made to the other party or his agent by virtue of s. 30.

Further reading

Ames, *Lectures on Legal History*, 1913, Harvard University Press
Beale, Bishop and Furmston, *Contract – Cases and Materials* 2nd ed. 1990, Butterworths
Burrows, 'Specific Performance at the Crossroads', 4 *Legal Studies* 102, 1984
Cheshire, Fifoot and Furmston, *The Law of Contract* 12th ed. 1991, Butterworths
Fry, *Specific Performance*, 6th ed. 1921
Guest, *Anson's Law of Contract* 26th ed. 1984, Oxford University Press
Kronman, 'Specific Performance', 45 *University of Chicago Law Review* 351, 1978
Spry, *The Principles of Equitable Remedies: Injunctions, Specific Performance and Equitable Remedies*, 3rd ed. 1984, Sweet & Maxwell
Treitel, *The Law of Contract* 8th ed. 1991, Sweet & Maxwell

18 | Quasi-contract

INTRODUCTION

The doctrine of quasi-contract lies within a broader area of law known as the law of restitution. Historically actions based in quasi-contract arose individually, though they possessed a common procedure within the now defunct forms of action. Nevertheless it was always considered that there was some linking element between the cases which broadly fell into the category now known as quasi-contract. Eventually Lord Mansfield in *Moses* v *Macferlan* (1760) 2 Burr 1005 expressed the common link as being one of unjust advantage. In explaining the basis for an action for money had and received he stated that:

> This kind of equitable action, to recover back money, which ought not in justice to be kept, is very beneficial, and therefore much encouraged. It lies only for money which, *ex aeqo et bono*, the defendant ought to refund: It does not lie for money paid by the plaintiff, which is claimed by him as payable in point of honour and honesty, although it could not have been recovered from him by any course of law; as in payment of a debt barred by the Statute of Limitations, or contracted during his infancy or to the extent of principal and legal interest upon a usurious contract, or for money fairly lost at play: because in all these cases, the defendant may retain it with safe conscience, though by positive law he was debarred from recovering. But it lies for money paid by mistake; or upon a consideration which happens to fail; or for money got through imposition, (express or implied); or extortion; or oppression; or an undue advantage taken of the plaintiff's situation, contrary to laws made for the protection of persons under those circumstances. *In one word, the gist of this kind of action is, that the defendant, upon the circumstances of the case, is obliged by the ties of natural justice and equity to refund the money.* (emphasis added)

Lord Mansfield saw this action as one which arose independently of an action in either contract or tort, arising as an obligation imposed by the law on the basis of natural justice. This approach did not find favour after the abolition of the forms of action, with the passing of the Common Law Procedure Act 1852, for two reasons. Firstly, there developed a hardening of the categories into which legal obligations fell, those not being tortious of necessity being contractual, and vice versa. The result was that quasi-contractual obligations, being clearly not tortious, had to come within the law of contract. Secondly, since such obligations fell within the law of contract their existence within this category had to be justified in legal terms, especially as the tendency of nineteenth-century judges was to reject such nebulous concepts of natural justice. The result was that the existence of quasi-contractual obligations were justified in terms of contracts implied by law.

The implied contract approach has been subject to fierce criticism and largely rejected today in favour of a doctrine based on unjust enrichment which does not depend on the existence of a contract. In truth quasi-contract and the wider concept of restitution now exists as a subject in its own right, forming the middle ground between the narrow concept of the law of contract and the wide concept of the law of obligations. Thus Lord Wright in the *Fibrosa* case stated:

> It is clear that any civilised system of law is bound to provide remedies for cases of what has been called unjust enrichment or unjust benefit, that is to prevent a man from retaining the money of or some benefit derived from, another which is against conscience that he should keep. Such remedies in English law are generically different from remedies in contract and tort, and are now recognised to fall within the third category of the common law which has been called quasi-contract or restitution.

The broad parameters in which the courts will grant relief for unjust enrichment have been set out by Goff and Jones (1988) in *The Law of Restitution*. They state that the principle requires three factors to be present. Firstly, that the defendant has been enriched by some benefit given to him; secondly, that the enrichment has been acquired at the expense of the plaintiff; and thirdly, that the retention of the benefit by the defendant would be unfair or unjust.

Whilst claims in quasi-contract cover a myriad of situations, making it difficult to classify the instances in which the remedy arises, we will conduct our study of the subject by analysing claims to recover money paid and claims in *quantum meruit*. Such an analysis will not cover all the situations in which restitution arises, but it will cover the use of the remedy as it arises within the law of contract.

ACTIONS TO RECOVER MONIES PAID

An action will lie in quasi-contract to recover monies paid either under a contract or purported contract where there has either been a total failure of consideration or where the monies have been paid under a void contract.

Total failure of consideration

Generally

A party may recover monies paid in anticipation that the other will perform his contractual obligations in circumstances where there has been a total failure of consideration, that is, where he has received nothing that he bargained for, even where the other party is not in breach of contract. Thus any monies paid in advance in a contract that is subsequently frustrated, for instance, may be recovered in circumstances where there has been a total failure of consideration. The *Fibrosa* case (as discussed in Chapter 16) is a typical example of the operation of quasi-contract in such a situation, where a buyer was able to recover monies paid in advance for a contract that subsequently became impossible for the seller to carry out due to the outbreak of war. Since the buyer received no benefit from the contract there was deemed to be a total failure of consideration and it was clearly a case of the seller being unjustly enriched should he have retained those monies.

Consideration in this context refers, usually, to the performance of a promise, rather than the promise itself. This distinction is important since whilst (as already seen in Chapter 3 in our analysis of consideration) it is possible for an exchange of promises to amount to consideration, this definition is not appropriate in this context. Clearly if a promise could amount to a consideration then there will rarely, if ever, be a total failure of consideration. The position was explained by Lord Simon in the *Fibrosa* case as:

> In the law relating to the formation of contract, the promise to do a thing may often be the consideration, but when one is considering the law of failure of consideration and of the quasi-contractual right to recover money on that ground, it is, generally speaking, not the promise which is referred to as consideration, but the performance of the promise. The money was paid to secure performance and, if performance fails, the inducement which brought about payment is not fulfilled. If this were not so, there could never be any recovery of money, for failure of consideration, by the payer of the money in return for a promise of future performance.

As Lord Simon indicates, it is not always the case that quasi-contract requires an absence of performance of a promise, since it may be that the promise itself may form the basis of the consideration. Treitel (8th edition, p. 927) gives the example of a contract of insurance where the insured bargains for the promise of the insurer with the result that if his property is destroyed by some hazard other than that insured against, he cannot recover his premiums on the basis of a total failure of consideration since he has already enjoyed the benefit of the insurer's promise. Treitel points out that such premiums could only be recovered should the property insured against be destroyed before the insurance adopts the risk via the contract.

Partial failure of consideration

The rule here is that if a promisee has received part of the consideration due to him under the contract then he is unable to recover monies paid in advance, as held in

Whincup v *Hughes* (1871) LR 6 CP 78 where the plaintiff paid a watchmaker a premium of £24 to apprentice his son to him for six years. After one year the watchmaker died, though it was held that the plaintiff could not recover his money since the failure of the consideration was only partial. It should be noted, however, that the circumstances in this case would now be covered by the Law Reform (Frustrated Contracts) Act 1943 s. 1(2) as a sum 'paid . . . in pursuance of the contract before the time when the parties were so discharged . . .'.

Where there is a partial failure of consideration caused by a party failing to wholly perform his side of the bargain then the usual remedy is to sue for damages for breach of contract. The reason for the rule apparently is that the courts baulk at attempts to apportion the amounts due in relation to the partial performance of the contract. This rule, however, is not an absolute one and where apportionment is easy, as in the case of a divisible contract, or where the monies paid can be divided up on a pro rata basis in relation to the performance of the contract, then partial restitution may be allowed.

Converting a partial failure into a total failure of consideration

In certain circumstances it may be possible to convert a partial failure into a total failure of consideration by the promisee returning such benefits as he has already acquired under the partial performance of the contract. Such a situation may occur where the promisee has a right to rescind the contract because the performance itself is either partial or defective. The result of the act of rescission is to produce a total failure of consideration. Such a situation arises where there has been a breach of condition which is only discovered when the goods are delivered. The breach of condition may arise either through a term of the contract or by virtue of a condition implied by statute. Thus if a purchaser pays in advance for an item in a catalogue which, when delivered, does not correspond with the description in the catalogue, then he can quite clearly rescind the contract under s. 13 of the Sale of Goods Act 1979 and claim back his purchase monies on the basis of a total failure of consideration.

Rescission depends, however, on *restitutio in integrum* and where this is not possible then clearly there can be no total failure of consideration. Thus, for example, where there is a contract to rebuild a dilapidated vintage car that has been partially completed, it would probably not be possible for rescission to take place and the failure of performance could only remain as a partial one. The only alternative for the promisee here would be to sue for damages. One should, however, note that the principle of *restitutio in integrum* will not apply where the reason for the impossibility of rescission arises because of the very defect for which the right to rescind emanates in the first place.

In *Rowland* v *Divall* [1923] 2 KB 500, the plaintiff bought a car from the defendant and used it for some four months. The plaintiff then discovered that the defendant was not the owner of the car and had no right or authority to sell it. The plaintiff sued to recover the price and succeeded. He was entitled to treat the contract as discharged as there had been a total failure of consideration. Lord Atkin stated:

> There has been a total failure of consideration, that is to say, the buyer has not got any part of that for which he paid the purchase money. He paid the money in order that he might get the property and he has not got it.

It was clear from the case that the defendant could not claim that the plaintiff had derived some consideration from the contract in that the plaintiff had used the car or that the car was not worth as much at the time of rescission because of depreciation. The plaintiff had paid the price to acquire ownership, which he had not got and it was from this defect that his right to rescind arose. The use of the car in this context was totally irrelevant to the contract for the sale of the vehicle.

In certain circumstances the use of the benefit under the contract by the promisee may, despite the above decision in *Rowland* v *Divall*, prevent the failure of consideration from being total.

In *Hunt* v *Silk* (1804) 5 East 449 a contract for a lease provided that the landlord should carry out certain repairs, that immediate possession was to be given, that the lease be executed within 10 days of the agreement and that on execution the tenant would pay the landlord £10. The tenant duly went into possession and paid the £10 in advance and prior to the lease being executed. In fact the landlord failed to carry out the repairs or execute the lease within the 10-day stipulation, and as a result the tenant vacated the premises and claimed his £10 on the basis of a total failure of consideration. The court applied the strict rule that a person receiving part of the benefit he contracted for under the contract cannot recover his monies in quasi-contract. The tenant had occupied the premises albeit for a short period of time and thus he could not recover his £10, though, of course, he might have been able to claim damages for breach of contract and thus the decision is probably correct and proper in such circumstances.

In truth the *Rowland* v *Divall* case is a means of mitigating the rule as applied in *Hunt* v *Silk*. Its application in this way can result in great harshness simply because a party has received a benefit, no matter how slight. Nevertheless the principle in *Rowland* v *Divall* can itself produce great unfairness.

Thus in *Butterworth* v *Kingsway Motors Ltd* [1954] 1 WLR 1286 a person who was buying a car on hire purchase, and thus had no title to the car, sold it before all the instalments had been paid. The car was then bought and sold by several persons until it was eventually sold by the defendant to the plaintiff for £1,275. The plaintiff used the car for 12 months before being told by the finance company that the car belonged to them but that he could acquire the title by paying off the final amount owing on the hire purchase agreement, a sum of £175, otherwise they would want the car returned to them. The plaintiff claimed the return of his £1,275 even though the car was now worth only £800 due to a slump in the secondhand car market. Further, eight days after the plaintiff heard from the finance company and after he had claimed the return of the £1,275 the original hirer paid off the final instalment so that the title to the vehicle should have 'fed' to the plaintiff. The court nevertheless allowed the plaintiff the full £1,275 despite the fact that the court considered his claim had little merit.

The case represents an unfair and illegitimate extension of the *Rowland* v *Divall* case, and has led to substantial criticism of the *Divall* case itself. Nevertheless, there is nothing wrong with the principle within it if it were to be confined to dealers who are making the purchase in order to resell the item in question and who therefore require good title. In the case of the consumer, however, it would seem that the better principle is to be found in *Hunt v Silk*, since the consumer will generally be able to maintain an action for damages for breach of contract.

Recovering monies paid in a void contract

The basic rule here is that money paid under a void contract is recoverable, though this rule is not an absolute one and depends largely on the reason for the contract being held to be void. Thus it has been seen in our discussions on illegal contracts that the effects can vary considerably. Suffice it to say that in cases where the contract is void for mistake then it is possible to recover monies paid under such a contract.

Quantum meruit

A *quantum meruit* claim is defined by Anson (1984) at p. 596 as a claim arising 'where goods are supplied or services rendered by one person to another in circumstances which entitle him to be recompensed by that other by receiving a reasonable price or remuneration'.

Quantum meruit claims arise in two situations:

Restitutionary quantum meruit *actions*

Very often the contract will contain express terms setting out what remuneration is payable on the occurrence of certain events. In such circumstances the court has no option but to award such sums. However, it may occur that the remuneration expressly provided for does not become payable because the contract has ceased to exist.

Lord Greer in *Craven-Ellis v Cannons Ltd* [1936] KB 403 explained the nature of restitutionary *quantum meruit* as:

> an interference which a rule of law imposes on the parties where work has been done or goods have been delivered under what purports to be a binding contract but is not so in fact.

In such circumstances restitutionary *quantum meruit* actions will arise independently of the existence of any promise or agreement. The circumstances in which such *quantum meruit* awards are made may be as follows:

(a) *Void contracts.* An example of such a case can be seen in the case of *Craven-Ellis v Cannons Ltd* [1936] 2 KB 403 itself.

Here the plaintiff was employed as the managing director of the defendant company. By virtue of the articles of association of the company the plaintiff was required to take qualification shares within two months of taking office, failure to do so rendering him unable to act. The plaintiff failed to take up the shares but nevertheless the company executed an agreement under seal in which it agreed to pay the plaintiff. In fact, the resolution of the directors to affix the company's seal to the agreement was invalid, which rendered the agreement void. The plaintiff's action to recover the promised remuneration in contract must, of course, have failed since the contract was void. He could, however, succeed in *quantum meruit* for services already rendered.

(b) Frustrated contracts. Where a contract becomes frustrated then by virtue of s. 1(3) of the Law Reform (Frustrated Contracts) Act 1943 a party is able to recover such sum as the court considers just where the other party has a valuable benefit conferred on him. Clearly this would appear to be a statutory based type of *quantum meruit*. The rule would also apply outside the 1943 Act where work is done after the frustrating event and still carries on, with the result that it may be said that the plaintiff's actions are voluntary. The effect of this will be to deny him a claim in *quantum meruit*, though it is, of course, possible that a new contract will be implied, giving him a right to damages for breach of contract.

(c) Contracts discharged by breach. Where a contract has been broken so that the innocent party can elect to treat the contract and his obligations under it as discharged, the innocent party can elect to claim in *quantum meruit* for work done rather than to sue in damages for breach of contract. It should be noted that it is only the innocent party who may claim in *quantum meruit*. The remedy is not available to those in default. Secondly, the breach must entitle the innocent party to treat the contract as discharged.

The use of *quantum meruit* is particularly useful in such circumstances where the actions of the party in default allow the other party to treat the contract as discharged half-way through his performing the obligations under the contract. It is clear that the innocent party could not claim the sum fixed for completing the work since it has not been completed, but *quantum meruit* allows him to claim for the reasonable value of the work actually completed. An example of *quantum meruit* in such circumstances can be seen in *Planché* v *Colburn* (1831) 8 Bing 14, where the defendants were in the process of compiling a series of books to be entitled *The Juvenile Library*. They engaged the plaintiff to write a book on medieval costume and armour. When the plaintiff had written several chapters the series was cancelled. It was held that he was entitled to refuse the publisher's offer to publish the book separately and claim in *quantum meruit* for work completed on the book.

(d) Services rendered in contemplation of a contract. It sometimes occurs that a party undertakes work on the basis that a formal contract will be entered into at some future time. If the contemplated contract fails to materialise then the party who has undertaken the work may claim in *quantum meruit* for the work done, as seen in the case of the *British Steel Corporation* v *Cleveland Bridge and Engineering Co Ltd* [1984] 1 All ER 504 where construction work had begun in contemplation of a contract that never materialised. Here the plaintiffs on ceasing further performance could claim on a *quantum meruit* basis for work carried out. However, it should be noted that the effect of the decision in *G Percy Trentham Ltd* v *Archital Luxfer* [1993] 1 Lloyd's Rep 25 suggests a broader approach to the finding for a contract, particularly where the

whole or part of it is executed, and may mean that there will be less need to rely on quasi-contract in these circumstances. The decision in this case was fully discussed in Chapter 2.

The use of quantum meruit *within a contract*

Quantum meruit may arise within a contract in two situations.

(a) In circumstances where part-performance has been accepted. Where a party in breach of contract has only partly performed the contract and the other party elects to accept that performance, then he will be required to pay for that part-performance on a *quantum meruit* basis. By accepting the partial performance the innocent party implies that he will pay a reasonable sum for such performance. The same rules also apply where the party in default completes the contract in a manner different from that contemplated by the parties originally and where the innocent party accepts such performance. It should be noted that *quantum meruit* will **not** apply where the innocent party has no option either to accept partial performance or performance in a manner different from the original contract.

(b) In circumstances where there is an implied agreement to pay. It may be that the parties have entered into a contract but have failed to include provision for payment within the contract. In such a situation the law implies on a *quantum meruit* basis that a reasonable sum will be payable. In contracts for the sale of goods the Sale of Goods Act 1979, s. 8(2) provides that when goods are bought and sold without an express agreement as to price, then the buyer must pay a reasonable price, thus giving statutory authority to the rule in such contracts. A similar provision is also contained in the Supply of Goods and Services Act 1982, s. 15.

Further reading

Beale, Bishop and Furmston, *Contract – Cases and Materials* 2nd ed. 1990, Butterworths

Burrow, 'Contract, Tort and Restitution – A Satisfactory Division or Not?', 99 *Law Quarterly Review* 217, 1983

Burrows, 'Law Commission Report on Pecuniary Restitution on Breach of Contract', 47 *Modern Law Review* 76, 1984

Cheshire, Fifoot and Furmston, *The Law of Contract* 12th ed. 1991, Butterworths

Goff and Jones, *The Law of Restitution*, 3rd ed. 1988, Sweet & Maxwell

Guest, *Anson's Law of Contract* 26th ed. 1984, Oxford University Press

Law Commission, 'Law of Contract: Pecuniary Restitution on Breach of Contract', Law Commission Report No. 121

Treitel, *The Law of Contract* 8th ed. 1991, Sweet & Maxwell

Part VI

THE RIGHTS AND LIABILITIES OF THIRD PARTIES TO THE CONTRACT

19 | Privity of contract

THE GENERAL RULE

The rule in English law is that only the parties to the contract may enforce the contract against each other, even if the contract was entered into with the sole intention of benefiting or imposing liabilities on a third party. The rule was confirmed as being part of English law in the nineteenth century. However the modern authority for the rule is said to be the decision of the House of Lords in *Dunlop Pneumatic Tyre Co Ltd* v *Selfridge & Co Ltd* [1915] AC 847 where Viscount Haldane LC stated:

> My Lords, in the law of England certain principles are fundamental. One is that only a person who is a party to a contract can sue on it. Our law knows nothing of a *jus quaesitum tertio* arising by way of contract. Such a right may be conferred by way of property, as, for example, under a trust, but it cannot be conferred on a stranger to a contract as a right to enforce the contract *in personam*. A second principle is that if a person with whom a contract not under a seal has been made is to be able to enforce it consideration must have been given by him to the promisor or to some other person at the promisor's request.

It can be seen that the rule relating to privity is closely interlinked with the rule that consideration must move from the promisee. It is sometimes stated that the rule that only a party to a contract can sue on it is a different way of stating the above rule relating to consideration, and vice versa. This is not the case and both aspects are required to be shown in order to allow a person to sue on the contract. Very often when the rule relating to consideration arises it is assumed that there was an intention to include a person as party to the contract. If one translates this into the case of *Tweddle* v *Atkinson*, the facts of which were discussed in Chapter 3, it can be seen that even if the husband had furnished consideration for the promises of his father and father-in-law he would still not have been able to enforce the contract since the terms of the contract were not addressed to him; there was no intention to make the husband a party to the contract.

The precise reasons for the presence of the rule are somewhat unclear and over the years several different theories have emerged that have attempted to explain its existence. For instance, it is considered that to impose contractual liability on a person without his consent and in an arbitrary manner strikes at the liberty of the individual. Similarly it is considered unjust to allow a person to sue on a contract which cannot be enforced against himself. Finally, it is considered that gratuitous beneficiaries of a simple contract should not be entitled to enforce the contact. It may be that there is a vestige of an equitable principle in the latter point in that it is inequitable for a person who had nothing to be able to gain a benefit that is only accruing to him by way of the goodwill of the parties to the contract.

Whatever the reasons for the existence of the rule, it is now confirmed as part of the law though, as we shall see later, not without substantial criticism. The application of the rule can be seen in the following cases.

In *Dunlop Pneumatic Tyre Co Ltd* v *Selfridge & Co Ltd* [1915] AC 847, the appellants sold tyres to a distributor on the basis that he would not resell them below the appellants' list price and that if the distributor sold the tyres to a trade buyer, the distributor would ensure that the trade buyer would also have the price restriction clause imposed on him. The distributor sold the tyres to Selfridge & Co and imposed the price restriction clause in the contract and provided that Selfridge would pay £5 to Dunlop in respect of each tyre sold in breach of the price restriction clause. Selfridge sold the tyres to customers below Dunlop's list price and were sued by them in respect of each transgression and an injunction was issued restraining Selfridge from further sales of tyres below the list price. It was held that their action would fail since Dunlop had provided no consideration for Selfridge's promise. Privity of contract did not arise between Selfridge and Dunlop.

In *Beswick* v *Beswick* [1968] AC 58, Peter Beswick sold his coal business to his nephew who agreed to pay £6 10s. a week to Peter for the rest of his life. He further agreed that in the event of Peter predeceasing his wife, the nephew would pay the widow £5 per week for the rest of her life. On Peter's death the nephew made only one payment to the widow and refused to make any further payments. The widow sued but did so in two capacities; firstly, in her personal capacity as widow and beneficiary of the contract; and, secondly, as administratrix of her husband's estate. It was held that in respect of her personal capacity her action would fail as she was not a party to the contract and had not supplied any consideration under it. In her capacity as personal representative of Peter's estate she was successful since here she represented Peter's personal capacity rather than her own, such as it was.

THE EFFECT OF THE DOCTRINE OF PRIVITY OF CONTRACT

The basic effect

Where A and B contract with the intention that C will be the object benefiting from the contract then C will be unable to sue on the contract despite the intentions of the parties, as seen in *Tweddle* v *Atkinson*. The only way in which C can have the contract enforced is by seeking the assistance of a promisee. Lord Denning considered in *Beswick* v *Beswick* that the third party could compel a promisee to bring the action by starting the action himself and then conjoining the promisee as co-defendant. This process was rejected by the Court of Appeal who took a traditional stance in relation to the doctrine.

The basic position as regards third parties has a particular effect in relation to consumer protection. It was seen in Chapter 7 that in contracts for the sale of goods, for instance, the parties enjoy the benefit of certain implied conditions, such as the implied condition as to merchantable quality. If the third party receives the goods other than by way of entering into a consumer contract then he will be unable to benefit from the implied conditions and warranties imposed by the Sale of Goods Act 1979. Thus if C above receives the goods by way of a birthday present and they prove not to be of merchantable quality then he has no right of action against the seller since C is not a party to the contract. Again, C's only hope is to enlist the help of the purchaser of the gift. Contracts for the benefit of third parties do not affect the validity of the contract as regards the parties to the contract, who may take action to enforce it in the usual way. Such action may, however, affect the position of the third party.

Actions against the promisor for damages

It is clear that a third party cannot enforce the contract against the parties to the contract. Whilst it may be possible for the third party to persuade a party to the contract to enforce the contract, that party can only recover damages in respect of his own loss, unless he, or the third party, can bring the claim within one of the exceptions to the rule. Further the losses recoverable by the promisee are likely to be nothing more than nominal damages. This problem can be seen in the case of *Beswick* v *Beswick* since if the widow as administratrix had sued for damages in respect of the breach of contract as it affected Peter Beswick's estate, the amount of the damages would have been purely nominal given that the payments to Peter ceased on his death.

Even if the party to the contract can recover damages for losses incurred by the third party, there is always the problem of the third party recovering those damages from the promisee. Unless there is a contract between them, there would appear to be no legal basis for such a claim.

In the case of *Jackson* v *Horizon Holidays Ltd* [1975] 3 All ER 92, a husband booked a holiday for himself, his wife and his two children. His original booking proved to be unavailable and a substitute was found. The holiday proved to be a disaster and fell far short of what had been promised. The company admitted liability for breach of contract but appealed on the basis of the £1,100 damages awarded by the judge at first instance, since this figure was only just short of the full cost of the holiday. Lord Denning agreed that as regards the husband's losses alone the award was excessive, but that the assessment was correct as regards the loss sustained by the family as a whole. He considered that a promisee, as a matter of general principle, was entitled to recover damages on behalf of third parties who were beneficiaries of the contract entered into by the promisee and that the third parties could, in turn, compel the promisee to hand over to them such proportion of the damages as represented their losses. The other members of the court upheld the award but did not openly support Lord Denning's proposition.

Undoubtedly the decision of Lord Denning represented a substantial inroad into the doctrine of the privity of contract, but was one that was comparatively short-lived.

In *Woodar Investment Ltd v Wimpey Construction (UK) Ltd* [1980] 1 All ER 571, the vendors had contracted to sell land to the purchasers for £850,000 for themselves and £150,000 in respect of a third party. A dispute arose between the purchasers and the vendors who brought an action for breach of contract, claiming not only the £850,000 owed to themselves but also the £150,000 owed to the third party. The House of Lords decided that the purchasers were not liable for breach of contract. Their Lordships agreed that even if the purchasers had been liable then the vendors would not have succeeded in their claim in respect of the £150,000 since this was due, not to themselves, but to a third party. The vendors had not, in other words, suffered any loss in relation to the £150,000. The House of Lords stated that the principle stated by Lord Denning was not of general application but confined to a situation where a trust arose. Nevertheless, their Lordships considered that the decision in *Jackson v Horizon Holidays Ltd* was a correct one, albeit based on erroneous reasoning. Unfortunately whilst a number of their Lordships were highly critical of the doctrine of privity of contract they were not prepared to present a legal rule that would allow parties to a contract to sue on behalf of a third party. Lord Wilberforce considered that the *Jackson* case was a special one that called for 'special treatment'. He stated:

> I am not prepared to dissent from the actual decision in Jackson. It may be supported either as a broad decision on the measure of damages or possibly an example of a type of contract, examples of which are persons contracting for family holidays, ordering meals in restaurants for a party, hiring a taxi for a group, calling for special treatments. As I suggested in *New Zealand Shipping Co Ltd v A.M. Satterthwaite & Co Ltd*, there are many situations of daily life which do not fit neatly into conceptual analysis, but which require some flexibility in the law of contract. Jackson's case may well be one.

The decision in *Woodar* is not entirely satisfactory since rather than provide an answer to the problem of whether a party can sue on behalf of a third party and whether the third party can subsequently recover his share of the losses from the promisee, it tends to pose a problem as to when such a claim is sustainable. At the moment it can only be said that such a principle exists where a promisee, for instance, stands in a fiduciary relationship to the third party.

The promisee and specific performance

It was seen in *Beswick v Beswick* earlier that an action for damages by the widow as administratrix would only result in nominal damages being awarded. The claim here would be a representative action on behalf of the estate to recover any sums owed to Peter Beswick by the nephew under the contract. Since none were owed and the weekly payments to Peter were to cease on his death, the damages would only reflect a technical breach of contract. The real loss arising from the breach would be to the widow herself but, as we have already noted, as third party she could not claim in respect of this loss. The court, however, found that the widow in her capacity of administratrix could enforce the contract between the nephew and Peter Beswick by way of a decree of specific performance. The effect of the decree was to ensure that the widow in her personal capacity received the payments due to her under the contract.

The use of specific performance to enforce an undertaking in respect of a third party is not, however, without difficulties. The facts of the case were particularly beneficial to the widow in *Beswick* v *Beswick* because she had dual roles. Ordinarily the position of personal representative might reside in completely different hands from that of the third party, the result of which would be to leave the third party with the problem of persuading the personal representative to adopt the action. Further, it should be borne in mind that specific performance as an equitable remedy is a discretionary remedy.

Undertakings where the promisor promises not to sue the third party

There may arise a term in the contract between the promisee and the promisor, whereby the promisor undertakes either expressly or impliedly not to sue a third party. If the promisor reneges on the undertaking there is nothing the third party can do to restrain the action brought by the promisor since he was not a party to the contract. In such a case the promisee can obtain a stay of proceedings on the basis of the breach of the contractual undertaking by the promisor.

The obtaining of the stay of proceedings is not always a straightforward exercise. In *Gore* v *Van Der Lann* [1967] 2 QB 31 it was held that the grant of a stay of proceedings was dependent on the promisee being able to show that he had an interest to protect by enforcing the undertaking against the promisor.

In *Snelling* v *John Snelling Ltd* [1973] QB 87 the need to prove an interest worthy of protection by the promisee was ignored by the court. In the case the plaintiff, together with his two brothers, were directors and creditors of the family company. Arguments arose between the brothers who therefore agreed that should any one of them resign then that individual would forfeit all monies owed to him by the company. Despite the agreement, which was meant to put an end to the arguments, the plaintiff resigned. The plaintiff then brought an action for the debt owed to him by the company. The plaintiff's brothers were cited as co-defendants in the action against the company. The brothers counter-claimed on the basis that the brother by resigning had forfeited his rights in respect of the debts owed to him by the company. As a third party the company could not rely on the agreement in order to avoid the debt so the brothers sought a declaration that the agreement bound the plaintiff and that his action ought to be stayed. It was held by Ormrod J that the brothers should be entitled to have the action stayed as between themselves and the plaintiff. He further held that the brothers could have the action stayed against the plaintiff as regards the company also. The judge considered that the most convenient way of dealing with this situation was to dismiss the action against the company.

Clearly the *Snelling* case runs contrary to the principles contained in the *Van Der Lann* case. Treitel considers that the decision is consistent with the *Beswick* case and submits that in such a situation the most appropriate remedy is either a decree of specific performance or an injunction.

Total failure of consideration

Where the parties have entered into a contract for the benefit of a third party under which the promisee has paid money to the promisor, then, if the promisor has completely and totally failed to carry out his part of the contract, for example by delivering goods to the third party, the promisee can recover the monies paid on the basis of a total failure of consideration under quasi-contract (see Chapter 18).

AVOIDING THE DOCTRINE OF PRIVITY OF CONTRACT

Actions in tort

The law of torts, in particular the law of negligence, has developed to give relief to third parties in certain circumstances. Thus if X had been given a present that had been manufactured or produced in a negligent manner so that C is injured or otherwise suffers loss, then he will have a right of action against the negligent person, as seen in *Donoghue* v *Stevenson* [1932] AC 562. Very often the action for negligence will lie against the manufacturer and thus avoids the contracting parties altogether. This is not necessarily the case, however, since if, for instance, the defect in the goods arises because the seller has stored the goods in a negligent manner then the action will lie against him rather than against the manufacturer or the wholesaler. Thus in *Donoghue* v *Stevenson* the consumer of the adulterated ginger beer did not have to rely on the support of the purchaser in an action against the seller but could take direct action against the manufacturer.

The principle in *Donoghue* v *Stevenson* can also be seen in the case of *Junior Books Ltd* v *Veitchi Co Ltd* [1983] 1 AC 520 where the plaintiffs entered into a contract with X to build a warehouse. X employed the defendants as subcontractors for the flooring work. The defendants allegedly did this work in a negligent manner. Normally the plaintiffs would have sued X who, in turn, would have sued the defendants. The House of Lords held, however, that on the facts there was no reason why the plaintiffs, despite the fact that they would not suffer injury or damage as a result of the actions of the defendants, could maintain the action against them. It is unclear why the plaintiffs took such a course of action but the case created some disquiet and the decision has been subsequently confined to the facts of the particular case. In the case of *D & F Estates Ltd* v *Church Commissioners for England* [1989] AC 177 the court made it clear that it would be unlikely that a plaintiff could maintain an action against a subcontractor in the future. The change of attitude probably also reflects a feeling that to allow such actions as a matter of general policy would be likely to result in a formulation of a principle that every breach of contract could arise as an action in tort where the breach had arisen as a result of the negligence of the defendant.

The use of negligence by third parties has also been curtailed to some degree by the ruling that pure economic loss cannot be claimed in an action. Since physical injury or damage is less likely to occur in contract the ruling places some limitations on the use of tort as a means of securing a remedy and avoiding the doctrine.

Collateral contracts

The rule of privity of contract can be avoided by the finding of a collateral contract between the third party and the promisor, who may enforce the contract for and against each other. Such contracts must comply with the normal rule of contract and each party must, as a result, provide consideration.

The principle of collateral contract can be seen in the case of *Shanklin Pier Ltd* v *Detel Products Ltd* [1951] 2 KB 854 where the plaintiffs employed contractors to repair and repaint their pier. The plaintiffs specified in the contract with the contractors that they had to use the paint manufactured by the defendants, since they had been persuaded by the defendants that the paint would last seven years despite the harsh conditions to which it would be exposed. The contractors purchased the paint from the defendants but it soon became apparent that it did not match the specification represented by the defendants to the plaintiffs. In fact the paint only lasted three months and £4,000 approximately had to be spent remedying the defects. The problem for the plaintiffs was that, since the contract for the purchase of the paint was between the contractors and the defendants, they were third parties and clearly could not recover on the basis of that contract. The court, however, found that there was a collateral contract between the plaintiffs and the defendants and that the defendants were liable to pay damages for breach of the collateral contract. One problem faced by the court was that of finding consideration for the contract. The court held that the plaintiffs had provided consideration for the defendants' undertaking as to the longevity of the paint by entering into a contract with the contractors, in which they had stipulated that the defendants' paint had to be used.

EXCEPTIONS TO THE DOCTRINE OF PRIVITY OF CONTRACT

The doctrine of privity of contract has often been subject to sharp criticism, in particular by Lord Denning who considered it to be an outmoded nineteenth-century concept. The doctrine nevertheless continues to form part of the modern law, though it exists as a doctrine that is by no means absolute since the courts and Parliament have seen fit from time to time to create exceptions to the rule. One of the great problems of completely abolishing the rule is that whilst there is general agreement that third parties should be allowed to take action to enforce benefits due to them under a contract, the same is not true when the converse arises – where the parties to a contract wish to impose liabilities on a third party.

Exceptions allowing a third party to claim under a contract

Statutory exceptions

(a) Road Traffic Act 1988. The driver of a motor vehicle is obliged to take out a policy of insurance to cover possible claims by persons suffering injury by virtue of the actions of the driver of the vehicle. The Act permits an injured third party to make a direct claim against the insurance company despite the fact that he is not a party to the contract by virtue of s. 148(7).

(b) The Married Women's Property Act 1882. By virtue of s. 11 of this Act a husband can take out a policy of insurance on his own life for the benefit of his wife and children (and vice versa). The effect of this provision is that when the husband dies the proceeds of the policy are held on trust for the wife and the children. The result of this is that the proceeds do not fall into the estate of the husband and are thus outside the application of inheritance tax. If the insurance company does not pay out on the policy the wife and/or the children may take direct action against the company.

(c) The Companies Act 1985. By virtue of s. 14 the memorandum of association and articles of association form a contract between the company and its share-holders and between the shareholders *inter se*. The result is that an individual shareholder can sue another shareholder on the basis of the contract contained in the memorandum and articles of association.

(d) The Bills of Exchange Act 1882. Negotiable instruments provide an important exception to the privity of contract rule since the debt on the face of the instrument is enforceable not only by the original party to the transaction but by anyone to whom the debt is negotiated and who is deemed to be a 'holder in due course'. By virtue of s. 38(2) the holder in due course may take action not only against the original debtor on the instrument if he fails to pay, but also against any other previous signatories of the instrument who have had the debt negotiated to them. In order for the holder in due course to be able to enforce the instrument in this way, the instrument must be in a deliverable state which means that, if the instrument is made out to a named individual X, or 'to X or order', the instrument must be endorsed on to the third party by X. Where the instrument is not made out to a named individual but to the 'bearer' then the instrument is said to be a 'bearer bill' which is in a deliverable state and may be negotiated on without the need for endorsement.

Agency

The principle in agency is that 'he who does an act through another does it himself'. Thus if A contracts with B on behalf of C then the contract that results is between B and C. The law of agency will be dealt with extensively in the next chapter.

Assignment

This will be dealt with in greater detail in Chapter 21.

Trusts

If property is given to a person (the trustee) on trust for another (the beneficiary), then the former is the legal owner of the property, whilst the latter is said to be the equitable owner of the property. A trustee is in a fiduciary relationship to the beneficiary and this results in his being under a duty to protect the property appertaining to the trust. Such a duty extends to the trustee taking action against a third party to the trust who is in breach of obligation to the trust. Where the trustee fails to take action the beneficiary can require him to do so or alternatively have an action against the third party himself, at the same time joining the trustee into the action as co-defendant or, if he consents, as co-plaintiff.

The property that may be the subject of the trust can include intangible property, known generically as a chose in action, which includes a right to enforce a contractual obligation. Immediately one can see that this allows the possibility of a third party enforcing a contract, if the promisor simply declares that he holds the benefit of the contract on trust for the third party.

The principle set out above can be seen in the case of *Les Affréteurs Réunis SA* v *Leopold Walford (London) Ltd* [1919] AC 801, where Walford, acting as a broker, arranged a charterparty between the owners of a ship and a charterer. The charterparty provided that the shipowners would pay commission owed to Walford by the charterers. The shipowner subsequently refused to pay Walford's commission and so he brought an action for breach of contract as beneficiary under a trust. In such circumstances it was a normal practice of the shipping industry for the charterers to sue as trustees on behalf of brokers and this practice was acknowledged by the shipowners. It was thus possible for a broker to sue in the name of a trustee promisor, namely, the charterers. From that proposition the House of Lords found that the promisor could waive that requirement thus allowing the broker beneficiary to sue in his own name.

Clearly the trust idea could have been used to drive a large hole in the doctrine of privity of contract but this was not to be. The courts limited the application of the principle by imposing the requirement that to create a trust certainty of intention must be shown clearly from the circumstances of the case. Such certainty of intention to create a trust will not be regarded as arising simply where the parties enter into a contract for the benefit of a third party. Thus Lord Greene MR stated in *Re Schebsman, Official Receiver* v *Cargo Superintendents (London) Ltd and Schebsman* [1944] Ch 83:

> It is not legitimate to input into the contract the idea of a trust when the parties have given no indication that such was their intention.

Similarly, in the same case, Du Parcq LJ stated:

> It is true by the use possibly of unguarded language, a person may create a trust . . . but unless an intention to create a trust is clearly to be collected from the language used and the circumstances of the case, I think that the court ought not to be astute to discover indications of such an intention.

The above comments do not destroy the possibility of the occurrence of a constructive trust at all, but the burden of proving the certainty of intention has the effect of severely curtailing the use of this device.

The rule in Dunlop v Lambert

The rule in *Dunlop v Lambert* [1839] 6 Cl & F 600 was upheld by the House of Lords in *St Martin's Property Corporation Ltd v Sir Robert McAlpine Ltd* [1994] AC 85. The rule provides 'a remedy where no other would be available to a person sustaining loss which under a rational legal system ought to be compensated by the person who caused it'.

The application of this rule as an exception to the doctrine of privity of contract can be seen in *Darlington Borough Council* v *Wiltshier Northern Ltd* (1994) *The Times*, 29 June. The Council wished to build a new recreational centre but, to avoid some of the financial constraints, employed Morgan Grenfell (Local Authority Services) Ltd ('MG'). MG entered into contracts for the construction work with the defendants, Wiltshier Northern Ltd ('W'), for the benefit of the Council. A collateral agreement provided for MG to pay W and then the Council would reimburse MG, who would assign to the Council all rights which MG had against W.

On completion, serious defects were found to exist which would cost £2 million to remedy. At first instance it was stated that MG had no proprietary interest in the Centre and had suffered no loss or damage caused by the defects. The result of this was that MG could only assign rights to nominal damages for breach of contract, rather than a claim for substantial compensation for the defects. The Council was precluded by the rule of privity of contract from claiming the damages it suffered; indeed, it was agreed between the parties that the Council, as assignees of MG, could not recover any damages from W beyond those which MG could have recovered if there had been no assignment.

In the Court of Appeal Dillon LJ stated that damages for breach of contract were merely compensatory and that it remained the law that a third party could not sue for damages on a contract to which he was not a party. He affirmed the decision in *Woodar Investment Development Ltd* v *Wimpey Construction UK Ltd* [1980] 1 WLR 277 that a plaintiff could only recover for his own loss and that if a plaintiff entered into a contract with a defendant for the benefit of a third party, who was not a party to the contract, the plaintiff could not recover substantial damages from the defendant for breach of that obligation by the defendant. Dillon LJ, however, stated that it was obvious to W that the Centre was being constructed for the Council and that the rule in *Dunlop* v *Lambert* would apply as an exception to the rule that a plaintiff could only recover damages for his own loss. The Council, as assignee, had a valid claim against W for breach of contract and the damages would be assessed on the normal basis as if the Council had employed W. Further, the Court of Appeal held that in any event MG could have recovered from W the losses of the Council, to whom it stood in a fiduciary relationship.

The Law of Property Act 1925, s. 56(1)

This provides:

A person may take an immediate or other interest in land or other property, or the benefit of any condition, right of entry, covenant or agreement over or respecting land or other property, although he may not be named as a party to the conveyance or other instrument.

In *Beswick* v *Beswick* Lords Denning, Salmon and Danckwerts applied the literal rule to this provision and found that Mrs Beswick was entitled to enforce the contract in her personal capacity. They considered that s. 56 formed a general exception to the doctrine of privity of contract. Their arguments revolved around the interpretation of the words 'other property' since s. 205(1) of the Law of Property Act 1925 stated:

(xx) Property includes anything in action and any interest in real or personal property.

Since 'anything in action' or a chose in action, as we have already seen, can amount to a contractual obligation, the Court of Appeal proposed that s. 56(1) had abolished the doctrine of privity of contract. The House of Lords rejected this proposition and unanimously held that s. 56(1) did not have this effect. They added that s. 205(1)(xx) was to be construed in a restrictive way so that it had no application in the law of contract.

Exceptions imposing obligations on a third party

Obligations imposed by way of interests arising in land

(a) Obligations arising in leasehold land. Very often in leases the original parties, the landlord and the tenant, undertake to abide by certain conditions or covenants within the lease. These covenants are enforceable between the original parties to the lease since there exists privity of contract. Where the tenant assigns his lease to an assignee, X, then the landlord can continue to enforce covenants that are said to 'touch and concern' the land against X, as stated in *Spencer's* case [1583] 5 Co Rep 16a. For his part X can also enforce such covenants against the landlord. There is said to be privity of estate between X and the landlord.

The rules that render X liable for breaches of covenant above are also of application where the landlord assigns his reversion to a third party, Y, since the original tenant can enforce covenants that have 'reference to the subject matter of the lease' against Y, by virtue of s. 142 of the Law of Property Act 1925. For his part Y can also enforce covenants against the original tenant on the same basis by virtue of s. 141. Again between Y and the original tenant there is said to exist privity of estate. The same position also applies with respect to X and Y themselves, both being able to enforce the covenants against each other even though they were not parties to the original lease, again, by virtue of s. 141 and s. 142.

The above rules do not apply where the original tenant grants a sublease to a subtenant, Z. Although the original tenant can enforce the contracts against Z on the basis of privity of contract, neither this nor privity of estate exists between the original landlord or his assignee and Z, none of whom can enforce the covenants against each other, unless the covenant is a restrictive covenant. The rules regarding restrictive covenants are contained in the decision in *Tulk* v *Moxhay* [1848] 2 Ph 774 which will be discussed in relation to freehold land below.

(b) Obligations arising in freehold land.   The position in relation to the enforcement of restrictive covenants in both freehold and, in certain circumstances, leasehold land is to be found in the rules that arose out of the decision in *Tulk v Moxhay* [1848] 2 PL 774.

The facts of the case were that the plaintiff was the owner of a number of plots of land in Leicester Square. The plaintiff sold the gardens to a purchaser who entered a covenant to the effect that he would maintain the status of the gardens and that he would not build on the site. After the land in question had passed through the hands of several purchasers it came into the hands of Moxhay, the defendant. Despite the fact that Moxhay knew of the restrictive nature of the covenant in relation to the land, he nevertheless proposed to build on it. The original party could not, of course, obtain damages against Moxhay at common law for being in breach of the covenant since he was not a party to the contract with Moxhay. Instead the plaintiff sought the equitable remedy of an injunction to restrain Moxhay from building. The court issued the injunction on the basis that to allow the defendant to ignore an obligation of which he had knowledge at the time he purchased the property was contrary to the principles of equity and good consciousness.

The case thus established the notion of the restrictive covenant which will be binding, not only on the original parties, but also on the third parties who later acquire the land with knowledge of the restrictive covenant. It should be noted that it is not merely because there is knowledge of a covenant that is of a restrictive nature will the doctrine apply. In addition the person seeking the injunction (the covenantee) must show that he retained an interest in land adjoining the land being sold which was intended to benefit from the restrictive covenants.

Obligations imposed by way of interests in personal property

The problem that arises here is whether the principle as expressed in relation to covenants in land be extended to personal property. Thus where the owner of a car agrees to hire it to an individual and then sells the car to a third party, to what extent is the third party bound by the contract of hire, assuming he has knowledge of it when he purchases the car? Is it possible for the hirer to restrain the new owner from using the car in a manner which is inconsistent with the terms of the contract of hire by way of an injunction? The answer seems to be that equity will not assist the hirer in such circumstances. Equity will normally only grant an injunction where, firstly, damages are inadequate and, secondly, where the property in question is unique. In the example above it is clear that the hirer could be adequately compensated by an award of damages, unless the vehicle was unique in some way, such as a Rolls-Royce Silver Ghost which was to be used for a wedding. It is thus somewhat unlikely in the normal course of things that the courts will grant an injunction in such circumstances.

Despite the above it would appear that the courts have attempted to extend the principles seen in *Tulk v Moxhay* to charterparties, that is, personal property. This development was first seen in the case of *Lord Strathcona Steamship Co v Dominion Coal Co Ltd* [1926] AC 108.

In this case the Dominion Coal Co Ltd had a long-term charterparty of a ship, the *Lord Strathcona*. The owners of the ship sold it and after a series of transactions it came into the hands of the Lord Strathcona Steamship Co, the respondents, who were fully aware of the charterparty at the time of the purchase and in fact specifically agreed with the sellers to abide by it. The respondents later broke the charterparty when they refused to yield up the ship at the start of the charter period. The respondents were sued by the appellants but claimed as a defence that since they were not parties to the original charterparty they were not bound by it. The Privy Council rejected the contentions of the respondents and awarded an injunction restraining them from using the ship in a manner that was inconsistent with the charterparty.

The Privy Council applied the rules as expressed in *Tulk* v *Moxhay*, finding that the respondents were bound by the charterparty because they had notice of it at the time of purchase. This reasoning, however, has been heavily criticised since the rules in *Tulk* v *Moxhay* revolve not only around notice but also around the fact that the person attempting to enforce the restrictive covenant owns adjoining land which it was intended that the restrictive covenant should benefit. No such proprietary interest arose in the *Lord Strathcona* case since the charterer merely had a personal right to the use of the ship. This right rather than simply an action for damages, might be enforced by an injunction where the property in question is unique. There was no indication that the *Lord Strathcona* could be regarded as unique and damages would therefore have amounted to an adequate remedy. There thus appears to be no justification for the decision, especially when a ship only amounts to personal property and is no different from the car in the above example.

In *Port Line Ltd* v *Ben Line Steamers Ltd* [1958] 2 QB 146 Lord Diplock considered the *Lord Strathcona* case to be wrongly decided and stated that a proprietary interest was an essential element in *Tulk* v *Moxhay*, an interest that was noticeably absent in the *Strathcona* case.

Some judges have supported the decision in the *Lord Strathcona* case, notably Brown-Wilkinson J in *Swiss Bank Corporation* v *Lloyds Bank Ltd* [1979] Ch 548 who considered that the appellants were bound by the charterparty on the basis that they were constructive trustees of the ship and therefore obliged by equity to comply with their fiduciary obligations to the respondents.

Further consideration of this aspect of privity of contract arose in the case of *Law Debenture Trust Corporation plc* v *Ural Caspian Corporation Ltd and Others* [1993] 2 All ER 355. The facts of the case were that the minority shareholders in the first four defendants ('the Russian companies') agreed to sell their shareholdings to Leisure Investments (Overseas) Ltd (LIO Ltd). The Russian companies were in fact English registered companies which had traded in Russia prior to the 1917 revolution and whose assets had been confiscated by the Soviet authorities without compensation. The majority shareholding was held by Shell Petroleum Co Ltd who also agreed to accept the offer by LIO Ltd on condition that, should the Soviet authorities ever decide to pay compensation, that compensation would be applied for the benefit of the existing shareholders. In 1986 each of the Russian companies and LIO Ltd entered into covenants with the plaintiff, Law Debenture Trust Corporation plc, as trustee for the shareholders. The covenants also required the Russian companies to take whatever action was necessary to pursue the compensation claims. Further, the covenants required that, should LIO Ltd decide to dispose of its control of the companies, it would ensure that the transferee also entered into similar covenants. On this basis Shell and the minority shareholders relinquished control of the companies to LIO Ltd.

Later LIO Ltd sold the shares in the Russian companies to Hilldon Ltd but imposed no requirements in the contract that Hilldon should enter into covenants with the plaintiff. Hilldon subsequently sold its shareholdings to Caspian Resources Ltd, again without imposing the requirement that Caspian enter into the covenants with the plaintiff. In the meantime compensation amounting to some £13.2 million was paid to the Russian companies by the Soviet authorities by way of the Foreign Compensation Commission. The Russian companies then refused to pay any of the monies received to the plaintiff.

The plaintiff subsequently sought damages from the six defendants, alleging that Hilldon (the fifth defendant) had, with knowledge of the agreements between the Russian companies and LIO Ltd, caused LIO Ltd to breach the covenants and that therefore Hilldon was, by virtue of an implied collateral contractual agreement, bound to comply with the covenants. It was also argued that the sixth defendant, Caspian, by purchasing the shares from Hilldon, with the knowledge of the previous agreements, had also caused Hilldon to breach its implied collateral obligation and was, as a result, under an implied collateral obligation itself.

Hilldon and Caspian applied for the plaintiff's statement of claim to be struck out on the basis that it disclosed no reasonable cause of action. The plaintiff then applied to have its original statement of claim amended in order to include an allegation that, since both Hilldon and Caspian took the shares with knowledge of the covenants and LIO Ltd's breach of them, they also took the burden of the covenants and were therefore under either a legal or equitable obligation to perform the covenants and could be compelled to do so by way of a mandatory (positive) injunction. Alternatively, the plaintiff argued that it should receive damages in lieu of the award of an injunction or the shares should be re-transferred to the plaintiff so that the covenants could then be enforced against LIO Ltd.

It was held that the claim against Caspian depended on whether Hilldon was under a contractual duty to the plaintiff which Caspian had caused it to break. The court, however, considered that neither Hilldon nor Caspian were party to a contract with the plaintiff, nor were there any grounds for implying a collateral contract. There was thus no arguable claim against Caspian.

The court also considered the principles set out in *De Mattos* v *Gibson* [1843–60] All ER 803, as now set out in the *Lord Strathcona* case, as affirmed in the *Swiss Bank* case, namely, that where a person acquires property from another, who has entered into a legally binding contract with a third party to use the property for a particular purpose, the person acquiring the property is bound not to use the property in a manner inconsistent with the contract, provided he had full knowledge of the contract when he acquired the property. The Court admitted that neither *Lord Strathcona* nor *Swiss Bank* made it entirely clear when the above principle applied; however, the court decided to apply the principle nevertheless. It considered that the difficulty did not lie with the principle itself but with the remedy to be applied. In his judgment Hoffman J considered that the principle in *De Mattos* v *Gibson* only gave rise to a possibility of an award of a prohibitory (negative) injunction, that is to restrain an acquirer of this property from doing acts which are inconsistent with the performance of the contract by the original contracting party. He stated that the principle has never allowed the imposition of a mandatory injunction to compel the acquirer of the property to carry out an obligation to perform covenants imposed on his predecessor. To support his position Hoffman J referred to Lord Shaw in the *Lord Strathcona* case when he stated:

> It has sometimes been considered that *Tulk* v *Moxhay* . . . and *De Mattos* v *Gibson* . . .
> carried forward to and laid upon the shoulders of an alienee with notice, the obligations of the

alienor, and, therefore, that the former is liable to the covenantee in specific performance as by the law of contract, and under a species of implied privity. This is not so; the remedy is a remedy in equity by way of injunction against acts inconsistent with the covenant, with notice of which the land was acquired.

He pointed out that there was not one case in which the *De Mattos* v *Gibson* principle was applied that allowed an award of a mandatory (positive) injunction, a position that was confirmed by Browne-Wilkinson J in the *Swiss Bank* case. He also stated that it was this point that prevented the principle in *De Mattos*, as applied in *Lord Strathcona*, from being applied in *Port Line Ltd* v *Ben Line Steamers Ltd* since there the owner was under a positive obligation to provide the vessel. Injunctive relief, therefore, was only available to prevent the purchaser from doing an inconsistent act, that is chartering the vessel to someone else; it could not be used to compel a purchaser of the vessel to deliver it up to the charterer. Hoffman J considered that Diplock J in *Port Line Ltd* was wrong in concluding that just because positive injunctive relief was not available, the principle in *De Mattos*, as applied in *Lord Strathcona*, was entirely wrong.

As regards the claim that damages could be awarded in lieu of injunctive relief by reason of the Supreme Court Act 1981, s. 50, Hoffman J decided that this claim could not be sustained. He reasoned that damages in these circumstances were a substitution for injunctive relief and that, since this was not available for the reasons already given, so an award of damages under s. 50 could not be sustained.

Protecting third parties in exemption clauses

The question that arises here is to what extent third parties can rely on the protection of an exemption clause in a contract made between the promisor and the promisee. The principle can be seen in the case of *Scruttons Ltd* v *Midland Silicones Ltd* [1962] 1 All ER 1. In this case a shipping company had agreed to carry a drum of chemicals for the plaintiffs. The bill of lading limited the shipping company's liability to $500. The shipping company had contracted with the defendant stevedores for the latter to unload the drum, specifically stating that the defendants were to have the benefit of the limitation clause. The plaintiffs were unaware of the contract between the shipping company and the defendants. The drum was damaged to the extent of $1,800 by the negligent acts of the defendants, who were sued for this amount by the plaintiffs. The defendants claimed the protection of the limitation clause contained in the bill of lading.

It was held by the Court of Appeal and the House of Lords that the defendants should be liable for the full extent of the loss suffered. The courts held that since the defendants were not parties to the bill of lading, they could not rely on its protection. The fact that such clauses were commonplace in the commercial field did not exclude the operation of the privity rules, even in the case of an alleged implied contract between the plaintiffs and the defendants.

Whilst the privity rule was fatal to the claim Lord Reid stated that a third party could have the benefit of an exemption clause in agency. Whilst this exception to the doctrine of privity will be dealt with in the next chapter, the comments of Lord Reid are worth noting. He stated:

I can see a possibility of success of the agency argument if (first) the bill of lading makes it clear that the stevedore is intended to be protected by the provisions in it which limit liability, (secondly) the bill of lading makes it clear that the carrier, in addition to contracting for these provisions on his own behalf, is also contracting as agent for the stevedores that these provisions should apply to the stevedore, (thirdly) the carrier has authority from the stevedore to do that, or perhaps later ratification by the stevedore would suffice, and (fourthly) that any difficulties about consideration moving from the stevedore were overcome.

The arguments of the defendant pointing to the existence of an agency thus failed since Lord Reid found that there was nothing in the bill of lading that stated or implied that the parties to it intended the limitation of liability to extend to the defendant stevedores.

The remarks of Lord Reid were taken into account in the case of *New Zealand Shipping Co Ltd* v *A. M. Satterthwaite & Co Ltd (The Eurymedon)* [1975] AC 154 where there was a contract between a consignor and a carrier to ship drilling equipment to New Zealand. The contract contained an exemption clause exempting the carrier and his servants and agents, including any independent contractors that might be employed by the carrier from time to time, from liability in respect of damage to cargo. In respect of this exclusion it was stated that the 'carrier is acting as agent and all such persons shall to the extent be parties to the contract'. The defendants were employed as stevedores to unload the cargo and they negligently damaged the machinery. They attempted to rely on the exclusion clause in the contract between the consignor and the carrier.

It was held by the Privy Council that the stevedores could rely on the exemption clause. The first three factors set out by Lord Reid were found to be present. The case largely revolved around whether any consideration had been provided by the stevedores since, as we saw in Chapter 3 on consideration, the performance of unloading the ship was an existing contractual duty owed to the carrier. It was held that sufficient consideration had been provided by the stevedores since the court found that a promise to perform a duty to the carrier could also amount to consideration for the promise of the consignor.

The decision in *The Eurymedon* has since been affirmed in the case of *Port Jackson Stevedoring Pty Ltd* v *Salmond and Spraggon Pty (Australia) Ltd, The New York Star* [1980] 3 All ER 257 where Lord Wilberforce stated that the principle contained in Lord Reid's statement was now of general application. The principle is, however, always subject to the general principles contained in the law of agency. Thus, in *Southern Water Authority* v *Carey* [1985] 2 All ER 1077 the attempt to bring third parties within the scope of the exemption via agency failed on the basis that the third parties (who are the principals in the matter) did not exist when the agent entered into the main contract. The principle in agency by ratification is that this type of agency cannot arise without there being an ascertainable principal at the time of the contract. Since the third parties, who were subcontractors, could not possibly have been ascertained at the time the main contract was entered into, they could not ratify the acts of the agent and thereby gain the benefit of the exemption clause. The problem of agency arising in such circumstances must clearly point to a major weakness in the use of agency to bring third parties within the ambit of an exemption clause.

The effect of third party actions on contracts

It will have been noticed in Chapter 11 that it is possible for the actions of third parties to affect the validity of a contract between two persons. This very often occurs in the context of a husband and wife relationship where a wife is induced to enter into a contract of guarantee with a bank or some other creditor with respect to her husband's debts. If the wife is induced into the contract by the undue influence, misrepresentation or some other legal wrong of her husband, she will be entitled to rescind the contract. This therefore provides an exception to the rule of privity of contract in that a third party is, by his or her actions, able to affect the legal relationship between two parties to a contract. Previously this exception might have fallen into the category of agency, as already discussed above; however, since *Barclays Bank plc* v *O'Brien*, this is no longer possible as the effects of the third party's actions are now based on the doctrine of notice rather than an agency relationship.

PROPOSALS FOR THE REFORM OF THE DOCTRINE OF PRIVITY OF CONTRACT

The doctrine of privity of contract has been criticised, not so much with regard to the rule that no one can be made liable on a contract to which he is not a party, which is clearly correct, but for the fact that the rule prevents a third party who has an interest in a contract from enforcing it. Of course, the exceptions to the rule offset some of its major vagaries; nevertheless, it has been agreed that the doctrine ought to be abolished, or at least modified. In 1937 the Law Revision Committee (6th Interim Report, Cmnd 5449) recommended that:

> Where a contract by its express terms purports to confer a benefit directly on a third party it shall be enforceable by the third party in his own name subject to any defence that would have been valid between the contracting parties.

No action was taken in response to the call for the abolition of the rule and in the intervening fifty or so years the courts continued to exercise their imagination in finding means to avoid the rule. Recently, however, the Law Commission in its Consultation Paper No 121, 'Privity of Contract – Contracts for the Benefit of Third Parties' has again considered the need for the rule, which it referred to as 'the third party rule'.

The Paper took on board several pronouncements in decisions in the House of Lords; for instance the case of *Murphy* v *Brentwood District Council* [1991] 1 AC 398 that called for the rule to be reconsidered. The Law Commission agreed with the comments of Viscount Simonds in *Midland Silicones Ltd* v *Scruttons Ltd* [1962] AC 446 that reform of the rule should come by legislative enactment, given that the rule is an established principle of law involving complex issues and is already circumscribed by numerous exceptions. Further, the Law Commission considered that simply widening the scope of damages available to a promisee so as to encompass loss suffered by a third party, as in *Jackson* v *Horizon Holidays*, was an inadequate reform of the law. They took the view that the third party here was in the hands of the promisee, who might refuse to act, thereby depriving the third party of compensation. Thus in *Beswick* v *Beswick*, if the executor has been someone other than Mrs Beswick herself, she might have been without a remedy had the executor declined to act.

In deciding that the third party rule should be the subject of legislative reform, the Law Commission then went on to consider what form this should take. Firstly, they considered whether the contents of any enactment could simply be restricted to extending the exceptions to the third party rule in certain specific instances. This approach was rejected on the basis that the number and variety of exceptions had already produced a complex body of law and that the creation of further exceptions would simply further complicate the position. Secondly, the Law Commission considered simply abolishing the rule preventing the promisee from recovering the third party's loss in damages. This approach was rejected on the grounds already discussed above. Thirdly, it was considered whether any enactment could provide that no third party be denied enforcement of a contract made for his benefit on the grounds of lack of privity. The Law Commission considered that such a general approach could not address in a satisfactory manner all the situations in which third party rights arise. For instance, the Commission considered that the problem of defining the class of third party beneficiaries would not be solved by such a piece of legislation and that it was incorrect to leave this and other complex matters to the judiciary to solve without more complete legislative guidance.

Finally, the Law Commission considered that reform could take place by means of a full legislative scheme that defined matters such as the rights of contracting parties to modify or terminate the contract, promisor's defences and the types of remedy available to third parties. It considered that this approach had the advantages of clarity and certainty. The Commission considered, however, that simply giving third parties the right to enforce contracts made for their benefit would be unacceptably wide in that it would open the floodgates to litigation and leave promisors open to a potentially indeterminate class of third party plaintiffs. In attempting to limit the position of third parties, the Commission considered that only allowing them to sue where it was expressly intended they should be able to do so within the contract was not sufficiently wide since it excluded the enforcement of contracts by third parties who, whilst it was intended that they should benefit, could not do so because there was no express term to this effect. Similarly the Commission found themselves faced with the floodgates argument if third parties could sue merely because they could show that the original parties intended that they should benefit from the contract.

In order to reconcile the problems set out above, the Commission recommended that a third party should be able to enforce a contract in which the parties intend that he should receive the benefit of the promised performance and also intend to create a legal obligation enforceable by him. Thus a third party's rights could not be inferred from the fact that he would derive a benefit from the performance of the contract. Similarly the third party would not be able to sue on a contract that is simply made for his benefit – he would have to show that the parties intended to confer a legally enforceable obligation on him. Whether or not this intention exists is to be derived from the terms of the contract and the surrounding circumstances of the case. Thus it would not be necessary to name the beneficiary or even for the beneficiary to exist at the time the contract is made (as in the case of a pre-incorporation contract), though it has to be said that difficulties in identifying a beneficiary would presumably affect whether the parties to the contract could have intended to confer a legally enforceable obligation on a third party.

It can be seen immediately that the Law Commission considers that an objective test should be employed in determining the original parties' intentions *vis-à-vis* the ability of a third party to take action on the contract.

Benefits and defences

The Law Commission also considered what benefits would be conferred on third parties under the arrangements set out above. The Commission recommended that the rights created would only arise to the extent that the contract itself was valid and would be conditional on the other party performing his obligation under it. Thus a contract that is affected by misrepresentation, lack of formalities (where relevant) or frustration would also limit the rights of a third party. Similarly, if the promisee had failed to perform his own obligations under the contract, then the consequent rights of the third party would also be affected. The Law Commission gave an example here of an insurance policy taken out by a father in favour of his son and stated that the son could clearly not enforce the policy if his father had not paid the premiums due under it.

It was stated that, where rights are created in favour of a third party, that party should have the right not only to receive the promised performance of the contract from the promisor where that is appropriate, but also to pursue any remedies for defective performance of the contract. The Commission also considered that the third party would have the right to rely on terms in the contract which restrict or exclude the third party's liability as if he were a party to the contract.

With regard to defences, the Commission considered that the third party's rights would be subject to the promisor's defences, rights of set-off and counterclaims. The Commission, however, was undecided as to whether the promisee should be made a party to an action when the third party seeks to enforce a contract made for his benefit.

Variation and cancellation of contracts

It is clear that parties to a contract are entitled, subject to the provisions of the contract, to vary the terms of the contract or even to cancel it. The Commission considered that they should still be entitled to do so where third party rights arise, provided the parties expressly allow for such reservations on the rights of third parties. The Commission, however, was undecided as to whether variation or cancellation would be allowed where there was no such express provision. In considering this position the Law Commission examined several possibilities: thus it was considered that variation or cancellation would cease to be available once the third party adopted the contract, either expressly or by conduct; that variation or cancellation would be available until the third party accepted the contract or until he materially altered his position in reliance on the contract.

Creation of duties in third parties

The Law Commission Paper is centred on the conferment of benefits on third parties. However, the Commission also briefly examined the question as to whether parties to a contract could impose liabilities on third parties. It was considered that this should not be allowed except to the extent that the parties to the contract could impose conditions on the enjoyment of any benefits conferred on the third party by the contract. By way of example the Paper refers to the case of *Halsall* v *Brizell* [1957] Ch 169, in that it states that if a contracting party agrees to allow a third party to use a road across his land on condition that the third party keeps it in repair, the third party becomes subject to an obligation, though one that arises out of his own implied agreement rather than one that is imposed on him by the parties to the contract.

Conclusions

Undoubtedly the proposals for reform put forward by the Law Commission will answer many of the criticisms of the privity of contract rule, although the proposals themselves do create substantial difficulties in some situations – for instance, in relation to the variation and cancellation of contracts where third party rights arise. The double-intention criteria based on an objective test will tend to blur the point at which third party rights arise and, indeed, if applied to cases such as *Jackson* v *Horizon Holidays* may well produce a different result. It has to be said, however, that at the end of the day the proposals are a better alternative to the courts' struggling to manipulate existing legal principles in order to avoid the application of the present third party rule.

Further reading

Beale, Bishop and Furmston, *Contract – Cases and Materials* 2nd ed. 1990, Butterworths
Cheshire, Fifoot and Furmston, *The Law of Contract* 12th ed. 1991, Butterworths
Flannigan, 'The End of an Era (Error)', 103 *Law Quarterly Review* 564, 1987
Guest, *Anson's Law of Contract* 26th ed. 1984, Oxford University Press
Reynolds, 'Privity of Contract, the Boundaries of Categories and the Limits of Judicial Function', 105 *Law Quarterly Review* 1, 1989
Treitel, *The Law of Contract* 8th ed. 1991, Sweet & Maxwell

20 | Agency

INTRODUCTION

It was seen in the last chapter that a person cannot, as a general rule, enter into a contract with another so that rights and liabilities are conferred and imposed on a third party. It is, however, possible for a person, an agent, to act on behalf of another, the principal, in order to effect a contractual relationship between the principal and a third party. The latter point is particularly important since it must be emphasised that there is no contractual relationship between the agent and the third party and therefore there is no question of an exception to the doctrine of privity of contract being set up by virtue of the relationship between a principal, the agent and a third party.

Agency is an essential fact of business life and indeed it is questionable whether the business would exist without the doctrine of agency since non-human agencies such as companies, whilst having a separate personality, could not function without a human representative who acts on behalf of the company. This point also provides an indication of the fact that agency may arise quite independently of some other capacity a person may have in relationship to the principal. Thus an employee is the agent of his employer, a partner is an agent for the partnership, a person may be in a business as an independent contractor acting as a mercantile agent for several companies, and, indeed, a person can be an agent simply because he represents the interests of his principal, who has conferred on him the authority to act on his behalf.

THE CREATION OF THE AGENCY RELATIONSHIP

Agency by agreement

Where an agency arises out of an agreement between the principal and the agent then actual authority is said to be conferred on the agent. The actual authority may arise either expressly or impliedly.

Express authority

In general such authority may be given orally or it can simply be reduced to writing. In either case the normal rules of construction as to the terms of the agreement will apply in order to assess the authority of the agent.

In certain circumstances special formalities have to be complied with, thus, in the Law of Property (Miscellaneous Provisions) Act 1989, s. 1 stipulates certain requirements where the agency is arising out of the deed. Section 1(5) provides:

> Where a solicitor or licensed conveyancer, or an agent or employee of a solicitor or licensed conveyancer in the course of or in connection with a transaction involving the disposition or creation of an interest in land, purports to deliver an instrument as a deed on behalf of a party to the instruments, it shall be conclusively presumed in favour of a purchaser that he is authorised so to deliver the instrument.

The provision thus has the effect of deregulating the need for an agent to be appointed by deed where he is executing a deed involving the disposition or creation of an interest in land.

Implied authority

(a) *Generally.* Agency may arise from the conduct or relationship of the parties and indeed may arise despite the absence of an express agreement. In the latter case whether the implied agency exists or not is subject to an objective test. More usually implied authority arises out of an express authority since an agent's authority is not necessarily confined to those matters expressly referred to within the authority. The agent will have implied authority to carry out such acts as are ordinarily incidental to the performance of his duties under the express authority. Thus it was held in *Mullens* v *Miller* (1882) 22 Ch D 194 that an estate agent has implied authority to make representations and warranties relating to a property when conducting negotiations with a prospective purchaser.

(b) *Incidental authority.* This type of authority arises from the fact that authority may be implied to an agent from a particular trade usage or custom found in a particular market-place, such as the London Stock Exchange, or arising in a particular trade, profession or business. In these circumstances an agent is clothed with implied authority to perform such acts as are consistent with the trade usage or custom prevailing, provided that they are reasonable. Thus a custom would not bind a principal if it is inconsistent with the relationship that exists between the principal and his agent, as in *Blackburn* v *Mason* (1893) 68 LT 510 where a principal instructed a country broker to sell certain shares for him. The broker (agent) sold the shares to a member of the London Stock Exchange. The member alleged that there was a custom within the Exchange that a member who owed money to a country broker could set that debt off against the broker in his personal capacity for monies owed by the broker in respect of previous transactions. It was held that this custom did not bind the principal since it was unreasonable in that it resulted in a conflict of interest with regard to the agent's duties to the principal.

Before leaving incidental authority a word of warning needs to be issued since this type of authority is sometimes described as 'usual' authority. Unfortunately this term is seldom used consistently and some authorities have used it to describe apparent authority below. In this work it has been used to describe an authority that arises out of the case of *Watteau* v *Fenwick* (1893) 1 QB 346, though again some authorities place this decision within the bounds of incidental authority as described above. These approaches all have some degree of integrity but it is hoped that the structure adopted here, as in Treitel, Chapter 17 (8th edition) will aid one's understanding of this not particularly easy aspect of the topic.

Apparent authority

Generally

This type of authority, sometimes referred to as 'ostensible' authority, as well as 'usual' authority as described above, really forms an application of the doctrine of estoppel. It arises where a principal, whether by words or conduct, creates an implication that the agent is entitled to act on his, the principal's, behalf when in fact no such authority actually exists. An agent acting within this apparent authority will bind his principal to a third party despite the fact that he has no actual authority to do so. In other words, the principal has 'held the agent out' as having authority and is therefore estopped from denying this authority in order to avoid liability to a third party. The principle is illustrated by the case of *Spiro* v *Lintern* [1973] 1 WLR 1002 where a wife had been asked by her husband to employ an estate agent in order to enable his house to be sold. The estate agents employed found a purchaser and, acting on the instructions of the wife, they signed a contract of sale and handed this to the purchaser. The husband did not authorise the sale but nevertheless when he discovered the facts he took no action whatsoever. When the husband later attempted to deny the existence of a valid contract the court held that his conduct estopped him from sustaining the allegation as regards the non-existence of the contract.

The criteria needed for establishing apparent authority

The basic criteria needed for establishing apparent authority can be seen by reference to the judgment of Slade J in *Rama Corporation* v *Proved Tin and General Investments Ltd* [1952] 2 QB 147, where he stated:

> Ostensible or apparent authority which negatives the existence of actual authority is merely a form of estoppel and a party cannot call in aid an estoppel unless three ingredients are present (1) representations, (2) a reliance on that representation and (3) an alteration of his position resulting from such reliance.

(a) Representation. Whilst the representation may be either express or implied, it must produce a belief in the third party's mind that it is attributable to the principal rather than being merely the words or conduct of the agent, as held in *Attorney-General for Ceylon* v *Silva* [1953] AC 461. In certain situations the fact that apparent authority cannot arise out of the actions of the agent himself may present problems. For instance, a company can only act through its agents and on the face of things it would not appear possible for the principal, the company, to set up the representations needed to invest an agent with apparent authority.

> In *Freeman & Lockyer* v *Buckhurst Park Properties (Mangal) Ltd* [1964] 2 QB 480, a company had power within its articles of association to appoint a managing director. X, with the knowledge and approval of the board of directors, acted as the managing director, although his appointment was never confirmed. X entered into a contract on behalf of the company with a firm of architects. The company purported to disclaim liability under the contract on the basis that X had no authority to enter such a contract on behalf of the company. It was held that whilst X did not operate with actual authority, he was invested with apparent authority. The Court of Appeal found that the representations needed to support the apparent authority arose out of the actions and knowledge of the board who, whilst having actual authority themselves, had condoned the actions of X and held him out as possessing such authority. The company was thus bound by the contract.

The above circumstances also beg the question as to whether an agent, having actual authority, can enlarge the scope of his own authority by way of apparent authority. The House of Lords in *Armagas Ltd* v *Mundogas SA, The Ocean Frost* [1986] 2 All ER 385 stated not, since here the representation would arise from the agent himself rather than from that of the principal.

Whilst the representation can arise by either the intentional or the negligent actions of the principal it must nevertheless clearly present the agent as having authority to act.

(b) Reliance on the misrepresentation. In order to render the principal liable, the third party must show that he has relied on the representation. It was stated in *The Ocean Frost* that constructive notice of the representation is not enough, and that the third party must have actual knowledge of the representation. It follows that if the third party is unaware of the representation or has actual or constructive knowledge of the fact that the agent does not possess the authority to act, in spite of the representations made by the principal, he will not be able to enforce the contract against the principal, as was held in *Overbrooke Estates Ltd* v *Glencombe Properties Ltd* [1974] 1 WLR 1335.

(c) *Alteration of the third party's position.* The third party must have altered his position by relying on the representation. It seems to be unclear whether the third party must have altered his position to his detriment or not, as in promissory estoppel. Since the situation is more akin to proprietary estoppel than promissory estoppel some commentators consider that the third party has to act to his detriment.

Usual authority

As indicated earlier the meaning of the term 'usual authority' has created substantial difficulties since authorities are not consistent in their use of the expression. Some use it to mean implied actual authority, whilst others use it to describe apparent authority. As has been stated, in this work it is intended to use it in the sense used by Treitel (8th edition, p. 619) in order to aid understanding of all the material surrounding the various types of agencies already referred to. Treitel uses the expression to describe an authority that binds a principal to a contract entered into by his agent where that agent has no express, implied or apparent authority to act. The type of authority revolves around the decision in *Watteau v Fenwick* [1893] 1 QB 346. In the case Fenwick employed Humble as manager of his public house. Humble had been expressly forbidden to purchase cigars on credit, but Humble did so order cigars from Watteau. Watteau himself at the time of contracting was unaware of the existence of Fenwick and, indeed, it was Humble's name that appeared over the door as licensee. Furthermore the cigars were of the type normally supplied to such premises. It was held that Fenwick was liable since Humble was acting within the usual authority normally possessed by agents acting within that trade.

The decision is striking since, firstly, it is clear that any restriction placed on an agent by a principal will not bind the third party, unless he is aware of the restriction imposed by the principal. Secondly, it is clear that there is no question of liability arising under apparent authority since, as has already been seen, there must be a representation to the third party from the principal that the agent has authority to act, when in fact he does not. No such representation was, of course, present in the case.

The decision has been heavily criticised since one must ask why the principal should be liable in circumstances where he has not only not conferred authority on an agent but expressly restricted his authority in respect of purchasing the cigars. Similarly Watteau had not been misled by any representations made by Fenwick to the effect that Humble had such authority. It is sometimes thought that the decision is wrongly decided, though it may be that the case fulfils a commercial exigency in that it is incorrect that an innocent third party should suffer when a man of business, intent on maximising profits, and in order to avoid liability should rely on the fact that he has not been disclosed by the agent. Such reasoning might well have been in the mind of Wills J when he stated in the case:

> once it has been established that the defendant was the real principal, the ordinary doctrine as to principal and agent applies – that the principal is liable for all acts of the

agent which are within the authority usually confided to an agent of that character notwithstanding limitations, as between the principal and the agent, put upon that authority. It is said that it is only so where there has been a holding out of authority . . . But I do not think so. Otherwise, in every case of undisclosed principal, or at least in every case where the fact of there being a principal was undisclosed, the secret limitation of authority would prevail and defeat the action of the person dealing with the agent and then discovering that he was an agent and had a principal.

If this is the reasoning behind the case then it should be borne in mind that the principal does not necessarily suffer loss since he would of course have a right of indemnity from the agent himself.

Wills J makes reference to one important limitation on the operation of usual authority, that is, that its existence depends on the class or character of the agent and on the common understanding within the particular trade to which he belongs concerning the authority of agents. Usual authority does not therefore operate as a matter of general application and indeed could not operate at all where an agent does not belong to a particular trade or belongs to a trade which does not recognise the authority that the third party is attempting to attach to the agent. In *Daun v Simmins* (1879) 41 LT 783 it was decided that the manager of a tied public house could not have attached to him the usual authority to purchase spirits from anyone he liked. A manager's authority in this particular aspect of the trade was normally restricted, thus preventing usual authority from arising. Here the third party should have been put on notice to enquire into the authority of the manager. Since he did not do so the principal was not liable to the third party.

Wills J also made reference to the undisclosed principal, a doctrine which raises wider issues and which will be dealt with later on. The relationship of *Watteau v Fenwick* to this doctrine will also be discussed later.

Agency of necessity

The law sometimes confers the authority of an agent on an individual despite the fact that the principal has not consented to the granting of such authority. Such an agency often arises where, as a matter of urgency, a partner enters into a contract on behalf of another and without that other's consent. The use of this type of agency is strictly confined by the courts, which only allow such an agency where there is an existing contractual relationship between the two individuals. Historically the basis for such agency arose out of the merchant shipping business, at a time when communication with one's principal was wellnigh impossible, as in cases like *Couturier v Hastie*. The use of agency of necessity soon developed into areas beyond this specific situation. In *Great Northern Railway Co v Swaffield* (1874) LR 9 Ex 132 a horse had been transported by train but on its arrival no one appeared to receive it. The railway company, being bound to take reasonable steps to take off the animal and being unable to contact the defendant, placed it with a livery stable. It was held that the defendant principal was bound to pay the livery fees.

To establish agency of necessity it has to be shown that the agent had been unable to contact the principal in order to obtain instructions on how to act. In *Springer v*

Great Western Railway [1921] 1 KB 257 the plaintiff sent a consignment of tomatoes from the Channel Islands to London. The ship was delayed so that they arrived on the mainland three days late. A further delay of two days arose because of a railway strike so that the consignment could not be unloaded. When at last the consignment was unloaded the tomatoes were found to be bad and the railway company sold the consignment locally. No communication was made to the plaintiff even though this had been possible. It was held that the company were liable since they should have asked for instructions prior to selling the consignment.

It must be shown that the creation of the agency was both an actual and commercial necessity. In *Prager* v *Blatspiel Stamp and Heacock Ltd* [1924] 1 KB 566 an agent acting for the principal in 1915 bought a number of fur skins for £1,000. The skins were paid for by the principal but before they could be sent the German forces invaded Romania thus rendering transportation impossible, nor could the agent communicate with the principal. Some two years later the agent sold the skins which by this time had increased in value. It was held that the agent would be liable to the principal in damages since the sale had been completely unnecessary given that the skins, if stored correctly, would not have deteriorated.

Finally, agency of necessity will only arise if the agent had acted in a bona fide manner and in the interests of the parties concerned.

It should be noted that agency of necessity does not apply simply where a person voluntarily expends money in order to protect some interest of another. The principle is that one cannot compel individuals to take liabilities that have been incurred by others on their behalf whilst their backs have been turned. There is no contractual relationship here and any claim made would therefore have to fall within the law of restitution rather than agency.

Presumed agency

This type of agency is really a form of implied agency that arises out of cohabitation. It is afforded special status since there are vestiges of agencies of necessity and apparent authority within it. A wife is presumed to have the authority of her husband to pledge his credit for the necessary household items needed to maintain their station in life. The principle is not confined to married cohabitees and will arise in relation to mistresses. Whilst it has been traditionally based on female cohabitees there appears to be no reason why the principle does not apply equally to male cohabitees pledging the credit of a female cohabitee.

Once cohabitation has ceased the trader, in order to recover monies in respect of goods supplied on credit, would have to show that a husband, for example, had held his wife out as having authority to pledge his credit. It should be noted that the same considerations as relate to necessaries in minors' contracts apply equally here. Thus the trader would have to show that the goods bought were necessaries to the cohabitees' station in life and could only claim a reasonable sum and not necessarily the contract price.

For a husband to avoid liability he will have to rebut the presumption that his wife does not have authority to act. He may do this by expressly warning tradesmen not to supply his wife with credit, or he may be able to show that the items purchased by the wife were not necessaries in that she was already adequately supplied with such goods or that the goods in nature or price were extravagant having regard to their station in life or means. Finally, he may be able to avoid liability by showing that he expressly forbade his wife to pledge his credit. It should be noted, however, that if he has held his wife out as having authority then a private communication to his wife telling her to stop pledging his credit will not be sufficient to exclude his liability.

Ratification

If a duly appointed agent enters into a contract without the authority of his principal or if a person having no authority to act as an agent at all purports to act in such capacity, the principal may, nevertheless, decide to adopt, or ratify, the contract so that he will be bound by it. The act of ratification renders the principal liable as if he had entered into the contract *ab initio* since the principal's authority is said to 'relate back'. The principal will be bound whether the act of the agent is detrimental or beneficial to him and whether the liability arises in contract or in tort.

It has already been seen that only parties to a contract, acting either for themselves or by way of an authorised agent, can sue or be sued on it. Ratification forms an important exception to this rule. Lord MacNaghten in *Keighley, Maxted & Co v Durant* [1901] AC 240 stated it to be:

> a wholesome and convenient fiction [whereby] a person ratifying the act of another who without authority has made a contract openly and avowedly on his behalf, is deemed to be, though in fact he was not, a party to the contract.

Anson states the principle of ratification to be as follows:

> The agent must contract as agent, for a principal who is in contemplation, and who must also be in existence at the time for such things as the principal can and lawfully may do.

This principle requires further elaboration, however.

The agent must contract as agent

In other words, the agent must purport to act on behalf of a principal. If an agent purports to act on his own behalf then the principal is not capable of ratifying the acts of the agent. The most common example of this is where the agent fails to disclose the existence of the principal. An undisclosed principal cannot ratify the act of an agent. This proposition can be seen in the case of *Keighley, Maxted & Co v Durant* [1901] AC 240 where an agent bought corn at a price higher than he was authorised to do. Whilst he intended to purchase on behalf of his principal, he failed to disclose his agency to the seller. The undisclosed principal initially purported to ratify the actions of his agent but in fact refused to accept the corn when it was delivered to him. The seller sued but it was held by the House of Lords that his action should fail. The agent's actions were unauthorised and since the principal was undisclosed at the time of the contract, the principal was incapable of ratifying the actions of the agent.

In the normal course of things an agent would usually name his principal, though he need not go as far as this provided the principal is capable of being identified. Not declaring the agency at all or simply stating that one is contracting as an agent is not sufficient and the act of the agent could not be ratified in such circumstances.

The principal must be in existence

In order for ratification to take place there must have been a competent principal in existence at the time the agent entered the contract. In *Kelner v Baxter* (1866) LR 2 CP 174 the promoters of a company purchased a quantity of wine on behalf of a company which had not been formed at that time. When the company was formed it purported to ratify the contract entered into by the promoters. It was held that since the company was not in existence at the relevant time ratification was not possible and the contract could not be enforced against the company.

The liability of persons purporting to act on behalf of a company prior to its formation is now governed by the Companies Act 1985, s. 36(4), which provides:

> Where a contract purports to be made by a company or by a person as agent for a company, at a time when the company has not been formed, then subject to any agreement to the contrary the contract shall have effect as a contract entered into by the person purporting to act for the company or as agent for it and he shall be personally liable on the contract accordingly.

It should be noted that in the case of *Phonogram Ltd v Lane* [1982] QB 938 it was held that agents signing 'for and on behalf of' a company that had not yet been formed could not escape liability personally on the basis of the clause 'subject to any agreement to the contrary' within the above provision. Exactly what is meant by this expression continues to be unclear. (Note that s. 36(4) of the Companies Act 1985 was formerly embodied in the European Communities Act 1972, s. 9(2).)

The principal must be a competent principal

In other words the principal must have had the capacity to enter into the contract at the time the agent did so on his behalf. An enemy alien, for instance, is incapable of ratifying the actions of an agent if his capacity was so restricted at the time the agent entered into the contract.

The actions of the agent must be capable of ratification

It is not possible to ratify contracts which are void *ab initio* though this restriction on ratification does not apply where the contract was merely voidable, since here there is a valid contract until it is repudiated.

Knowledge of material facts

The actions of an agent are only capable of being ratified if the principal was aware of all the material facts.

Ratification in toto

The principal cannot choose to ratify some parts of the contract entered into by the agent on his behalf and not others. If the principal elects to ratify then he must ratify the whole agreement *in toto*.

THE EFFECTS OF AGENCY

The effect as between the principal and the third party

Where the principal is disclosed

Where an agent has express, implied or usual authority then the principal may sue and be sued on the contract with the third party. The agent has no further part to play, he disappears from the scene, leaving a contract between the principal and the third party. A similar situation also arises where the principal ratifies the actions of his agent, provided the criteria for the ratification are present.

Where the principal is undisclosed

(a) Generally.   It has been seen in our discussions of ratification that one of its central rules is that the agent must disclose the existence of the principal to the third party at the time he enters the contract, so that the principal is reasonably identifiable, before ratification becomes possible. It was, of course, the absence of this factor that prevented the third party from enforcing the contract against the principal in the *Keighley, Maxted* case, despite the fact that the principal initially purported to ratify the contract entered into by his agent.

Into the above situation an anomaly must be introduced – the doctrine of the undisclosed principal. The doctrine, which is peculiar to English law, states that where an agent acting within his express, implied or usual authority makes a contract on behalf of a principal, but does not disclose the existence of the principal to the third party, then, despite that fact, the principal can sue or be sued in respect of the contract. The doctrine forms an exception to the privity of contract rule but, unlike ratification, seems to be completely irreconcilable with that principle.

In the *Keighley, Maxted* case the House of Lords criticised the doctrine and refused to apply it, thus Lord Davey stated:

[T]he rule which permits an undisclosed principal to sue and be sued on a contract to which he is not a party, though well settled, is itself an anomaly, and to extend it to the case of a person who accepts the benefit of an undisclosed intention of a party to the contract would, in my opinion, be adding another anomaly to the law, and not correcting an anomaly.

Furthermore, Lord MacNaghten refused to allow the principle of ratification to be extended to situations where the agent had not disclosed the existence of the principal. He stated:

> Does the fiction [in respect of privity of contract in relation to ratification] cover the case of a person who makes no avowal at all, but assumes to act for himself and for no one else? . . . it would seem to exclude the case of a person who may intend to act for another, but at the same time keeps his intentions locked up in his own breast; for it cannot be said that a person who so conducts himself does assume to act for anybody but himself . . . But ought the doctrine of ratification to be extended to such a case? On principle I should say certainly not. It is, I think, a well established principle in English law that civil obligations are not to be created by or founded upon undisclosed intentions.

Whilst one can understand Lord MacNaghten's reluctance to extend ratification in that direction, since its principles are now well established, one has to ask why the undisclosed principal should not be bound, as he certainly was in *Watteau* v *Fenwick*, the facts of which are virtually analogous to those of *Keighley, Maxted*. Of course, in *Watteau* v *Fenwick* there was a finding of usual authority that did not seem to arise in the *Keighley, Maxted* case. *Watteau* v *Fenwick* was nevertheless considered to be exceptional, given that the agent was expressly forbidden to pledge the credit of Fenwick in relation to the purchase of the cigars. A significant matter in the decision, however, was the fact that a commercial expediency was fulfilled by the decision and this approach seemed to have the support of Wills J. It is this feature that could appear to justify the anomalous existence of the doctrine of the undisclosed principal. Thus in *Keighley, Maxted*, Lord Lindley stated:

> There is an anomaly in holding one person bound to another of whom he knows nothing and with whom he did not, in fact, intend to contract. But middlemen, through whom contracts are made, are common and useful in business transactions and in the great mass of contracts it is a matter of indifference to either party whether there is an undisclosed principal or not. If he exists it is, to say the least, extremely convenient that he should be able to sue and be sued as a principal and he is only allowed to do so upon terms which exclude injustice.

It would seem that the doctrine of the undisclosed principal also exists as a matter of commercial expediency, even though it runs contrary to the general principle of privity of contract. But how does such a doctrine arise? The doctrine is, it is suggested, similar in nature to that of vicarious liability in tort, since here too the third party may be completely ignorant of the existence of an employer yet may, nevertheless, maintain an action against him. One of the reasons often given as justification for the principle is the fact that the employer is normally better able to bear the loss, a factor which strikes a common accord with the comments made so far.

In conclusion, it may be suggested that whilst liabilities in respect of usual authority and those arising under the doctrine of the undisclosed principal have developed from differing backgrounds, the common theme seems to be based on rendering the principal liable, on the basis that he will be the one who profits from the actions of the agent and is thus likely to be better able to compensate the third party in respect of his losses. If this statement represents the true picture, it is suggested that the decision in *Keighley, Maxted* is incorrect and that the better solution would have been to find the principal liable and then allow him to claim an indemnity from the agent.

(b) *Factors preventing the operation of the doctrine.* The doctrine will not apply where the terms of the contract are inconsistent with the agency, as in *Humble* v *Hunter* (1848) 12 QB 310, where an agent entered into a contract for the charter of a ship in his own name and describing herself as 'owner'. It was held that this raised a sufficient inference that there was no principal, so that the principal was found not to be liable on the contract.

The doctrine will not apply where there is an express provision in the contract that the agent is to be the sole principal. The effect of such a provision renders the whole question of agency incompatible with the contract. The doctrine will not apply where the personal qualities of the principal, for instance, the identity of the principal, are such as to be of importance to the third party.

One case illustrating this point is that of *Said* v *Butt* [1920] 3 KB 497 where the plaintiff, a theatre critic, wanted to go to the first night of a particular play. He knew that the management of the theatre would not sell him a ticket since there had been differences between them in the past regarding his critical comments on their productions. The plaintiff employed a friend to purchase a ticket for him without disclosing his name. When the plaintiff was then refused admission he sued the theatre for breach of contract. It was held that his action would fail since the theatre had specifically reserved first night seats for special persons and therefore the personality element was considered to be an important and fundamental factor. The principle would seem to be that an undisclosed principal cannot enforce a contract if he is aware that the third party would not normally agree to contract with him. It should nevertheless be borne in mind that the basic rule, as stated in *Dyster* v *Randall & Sons* [1926] Ch 932, is that simply because a third party does not want to contract with the principal this does not prevent a valid and binding contract from coming into existence.

(c) *The effect of the doctrine of undisclosed principal.* Whilst the principal remains undisclosed the agent may sue and be sued on the contract by the third party. Once the existence of the principal becomes disclosed then the right of the agent to sue is lost. As regards the rights of the third party when the existence of the principal is revealed, he may elect to sue either the agent or the principal. Such election will arise when the third party unequivocally indicates against whom he is going to enforce the contract. Once the election is made then the third party cannot afterwards retract it and purport to sue the other person, as was held in *Clarkson, Booker Ltd* v *Andjel* [1964] 2 QB 775.

Where the third party enters into the contract with the agent believing him to be the principal, then the third party is entitled to set off any debts owed by the agent to the third party against the principal. Broadly, this equates with the rule that applies in assignment of contract, in that the principal takes the benefits of the contract entered into by the agent, but subject to any equities that might arise against the agent, as stated in *Cooke & Sons* v *Eshelby* (1887) 12 App Cas 271. In that case the agent acting for an undisclosed principal eventually sued the third party who claimed a right of set-off relating to a debt owed by the agent to the third party in respect of an account held in the agent's name. The third party admitted that he entered the contract with the agent without being aware that he acted for the principal. It was held by the House of Lords that the right of set-off should fail. In order to exercise the right the third party would have to show that he had enquired of the agent as to whether he was contracting on behalf of himself.

The effects as between the principal and the agent

Apart from the express and implied obligations that are imposed on the principal and the agent via their agreement with one another there exists a set of general duties that overlie the relationship that exists between the parties.

The duties owed by the agent to the principal

The relationship of the agent to the principal is a fiduciary one. The nature of the fiduciary relationship is wide and encompasses a range of duties within it. Thus, for instance, it is a duty of the agent not to subdelegate his authority to another person. The principle is sometimes summed up in the expression '*delegatus non potest delegare*'. The agent has a duty to act for his principal personally unless given the authority by the principal to subdelegate.

Similarly an agent must not put himself in a position where his own interests conflict with the duties he owes to his principal. He must, of course, not allow the duties he owes to various principals to conflict where, for instance, he acts as a mercantile agent. This particular duty raises a variety of issues. An agent must maintain the confidentiality of his principal's affairs. Converse to the duty of confidentiality is the duty to disclose all relevant information to the principal. Disclosure encompasses the duty to account for all monies received by the agent on behalf of the principal and to keep proper accounts of all transactions. Part and parcel of this aspect of the agent's relationship with the principal is the duty not to make a secret profit out of the relationship. In *De Busche* v *Alt* (1878) 8 Ch D 286 an agent was instructed to sell his principal's ship for not less than $90,000. With the consent of the principal the agent employed a sub-agent, the defendant. The defendant bought the ship himself for $90,000 and soon afterwards sold the ship for $160,000. The plaintiff, the principal, claimed that the defendant should account for the profit made by the sale. It was held that the defendant was the plaintiff's agent and that he was in breach of his duty to the principal and he was therefore compelled to account for the profit he had made.

The agent will have to account for any profits made by virtue of confidential information that comes his way because of his position as agent. In *Boardman* v *Phipps* [1967] 2 AC 46 agents acting on behalf of trustees acquired some shares for them, at the same time also purchasing some shares for themselves. It was held that despite the fact that there was no intentional wrongdoing on the part of the agents and that the principal trustees had not suffered any loss, the agents were bound to account for the profits made out of the transaction. From this position it is clear that where a profit is made from intentional wrongdoing then the agent will have to account for any monies accruing to him from his wrongful conduct. An agent will be required to account for any bribes paid to him. For this purpose a bribe is a commission paid to the agent without the knowledge of the principal. In *Boston Deep Sea Fishing and Ice Co Ltd* v *Ansell* (1888) 39 Ch D 339 a director of a company was paid a bonus by two other companies, of which he was also a director, in respect of orders placed with those companies by the first company. He was held to be liable to account for those commissions to the first company since they had been obtained by virtue of his position within the company.

Apart from duties which are clearly of a fiduciary nature there are other duties relating to the exercise of one's duty as an agent. An agent must, for instance, carry out his principal's lawful instructions and must do so with reasonable care and skill. The lack of a contract between the agent and the principal does not prevent the existence of such a duty. In the absence of a contract, a principal can rely on such a duty being imposed in tort, although the standard of care here is likely to be lower than would be imposed in a contract where the agent professes a special skill. The latter point makes a great deal of sense since it is clear that one would not expect a higher or the same level of care from a person who undertakes a commitment to act as an agent free of charge than from one whom one pays as part of a contractual relationship.

The duties owed by the principal to the agent

The duties owed by the principal to the agent largely revolve around the recovery of remuneration from the principal in respect of commission or expenses incurred by the agent by virtue of acting within his office. The main duties are:

(a) *The duty to remunerate the agent for his services.* Normally this duty will only arise where the principal has expressly or impliedly agreed to pay for the agent's services, though in the case of a professional agency the courts will often imply such a duty into the contract. The entitlement to remuneration only arises where the agent has fulfilled the requirements of the agency agreement. Where an agent is an employee the remuneration arises as part of his salary. Where, however, the agent is independent, or where the employee can earn a commission in addition to his salary, the commission only arises where the event on which it is payable actually comes about. Thus an estate agent on a 'no sale, no fee' basis is only entitled to his commission when a sale actually materialises. Where no such term is included in the agreement then the precise circumstances in which the commission becomes payable largely depend on the circumstances of the individual case.

(b) *The duty to indemnify the agent for liabilities incurred.* If an agent incurs liabilities or expenses in the performance of his duties to the principal, then the agent is entitled to be indemnified by the principal for those expenses or liabilities reasonably incurred by the agent. Such duty to indemnify the agent will also arise where the liability incurred by the agent arises by way of tortious liability, as in *Adamson* v *Jarvis* (1827) 4 Bing 66, where the principal instructed his agent, an auctioneer, to sell certain goods for him at auction. The agent sold the goods but in fact they were not owned by the principal and, as a consequence, the agent had to pay damages. It was held that the principal was liable to indemnify the agent in respect of the damages. The duty to indemnify does not arise where the liability incurred by the agent arose by way of an illegal act or where the liabilities were incurred by the agent through his own fault. Further the principal has no duty to indemnify the agent where the agent acted in an unauthorised manner.

(c) The agent's lien over his principal's property. An agent is entitled to exercise a lien over his principal's property, which is in the possession of the agent, in respect of debts owed by the principal to the agent arising out of the agency relationship. It should be stated that the right of lien is only a possessory right which gives the agent no right to sell the goods to settle the debt, and a court order is required to exercise such a right of sale. Since the right is a possessory one it is lost when the agent parts with possession of the goods. It is in this last instance that the right of stoppage *in transitu* arises, but before we discuss this right it should be noted that the agreement can preclude the arisal of the right of lien.

(d) The agent's right of stoppage in transitu. Should the agent lose possession of the principal's goods thereby precluding him from exercising his agent's right of lien, the agent may recover the goods by way of stoppage *in transitu*. Stoppage *in transitu* simply involves the agent ordering the carrier to return the principal's goods to himself, the agent, whereupon he immediately exercises his right of lien over the goods.

The effect of making settlement with the agent

The necessity here is to discover the respective liabilities of the principal or the third party where one of them pays money to the agent, with the intention of settling their respective debts, and the agent subsequently absconds with the proceeds. Will the third party or the principal be liable to pay again?

Settlement by the third party

If the third party settles with the agent, who fails to hand the payment to the principal, the normal rule is that the debt is not discharged and the third party remains liable on the debt to the principal. The rule is based on the presumption that an agent who is authorised to sell is not necessarily authorised to accept payment, as stated in *Butwick* v *Grant* [1924] 2 KB 483. The general rule may be overturned if the agent has actual authority to receive payment or where such authority is given to the agent by way of apparent authority or ratification by the principal. Where the general rule is overturned in this way the third party must nevertheless comply with the nature of the authority given to the agent. If, for instance, the agent is given authority to accept payment but only in the form of a cash payment, then the effect of the third party settling the debt by negotiable instrument will not discharge his liability to the principal.

Settlement by the principal

A similar general rule to that seen in the case of third parties, above, also applies in the case of settlement by the principal to the agent, in that the principal's liability continues in respect of the debt owed. The general rule may be overturned where the agent indicates that he looks to the agent alone for settlement of the debt, with the result that the principal pays the monies to the agent. Further the third party may be estopped from claiming the debt from the principal where he leads the principal to assume that the debt has already been discharged, as was held in *Heald v Kenworthy* (1855) 10 Ex 739. The latter exception cannot, however, apply where the principal is undisclosed since it was held in *Irvine & Co v Watson & Sons* (1880) 5 QBD 414, that estoppel cannot arise where the third party was unaware of the existence of the principal.

The effect as between the agent and the third party

The general rule is that the agent incurs no liability and acquires no rights on the contract that is concluded between the principal and the third party; there are, however, certain exceptions to this general rule.

The liability of the agent

(a) Where the principal is undisclosed. It has already been noted that should the agent contract on behalf of an undisclosed principal then the agent has personal liability on the contract since to all intents and purposes the agent appears to the third party to be the principal himself. Further, even if the principal subsequently becomes disclosed the third party retains an election as to whether to sue the now disclosed principal or the agent.

(b) Where the agent contracts in a personal capacity. Whether an agent has contracted in his personal capacity is largely a matter as regards the construction of the contract. The contract may be constructed in such a way that the agent as well as the principal will be a party to the contract. It has also been seen in the case of *Kelner v Baxter*, above, that an agent who contracts on behalf of a non-existent principal is presumed to have contracted in his personal capacity, though the situation in that case is now governed by statutory provision. This position, however, is also subject to the construction of the contract.

An agent who, while acting on behalf of the principal, makes a misrepresentation will be liable in damages in tort, either in deceit or negligent mis-statement. This liability does not extend, however, to liability under s. 2(1) of the Misrepresentation Act 1967, as was held in *Resolute Maritime Inc v Nippon Kaiji Kyokai* [1983] 1 WLR 857.

(c) Liability for unauthorised acts. If the agent purports to act for a principal but without having authority to do so, the third party may bring an action against him for damages on one of three grounds:

(a) negligent mis-statement;

(b) the tort of deceit;

(c) breach of warranty of authority.

With regard to **negligent mis-statement**, the agent may incur liability in tort where he fails to exercise due and reasonable care in representing either the extent of his agency or whether it exists at all.

With respect to the **tort of deceit**. The agent will incur liability in deceit if he was aware that he did not possess either the agency or the authority that he represents to the third party.

The legal basis for liability for **breach of warranty of authority** is somewhat confused. Some authorities consider that it stands outside the law of contract altogether and that its basis lies in the law of restitution. Others consider it to be the result of a collateral contract in which the agent warrants to the third party that not only does a principal exist but that the agent has his authority to act on his behalf. In *Collen* v *Wright* (1857) 8 E & B 647 the agent, purporting to act on behalf of his principal, Gardner, granted a lease of Gardner's land to the third party for 12 years. Gardner was able to show that the agent had no authority to grant a lease of such a long duration and as a result the action against him as principal failed. The third party then brought an action against the agent for breach of his collateral warranty that he had the authority to grant such a lease. Consideration for the collateral contract was apparently provided by the entry of the third party into the main contract.

Breach of warranty of authority has the advantage of carrying with it the strict liability inherent in the law of contract, and thus does not depend on the third party establishing the state of the agent's mind, as required in negligent mis-statement and the tort of deceit above. A further advantage is that the warranty is said to be a continuing warranty. The effect of this is that the agent remains liable despite the fact that whilst he originally had a valid authority at the time of the contract, this authority has either become invalid or ceased to exist without his knowledge.

The rights of the agent

The rights of the agent to sue on the contract arise in much the same way as his personal liabilities arose, as discussed above. If a person enters into a contract as a principal then he will be able to sue in that capacity despite the fact that he is described as an agent.

THE TERMINATION OF THE AGENCY

The agency relationship may be terminated either by the actions of the parties themselves or by operation of law. It should be noted that in certain circumstances the agency relationship is irrevocable.

By the actions of parties

Just like any other contract, agency is a consensual relationship and, just as in discharge by agreement, it can be ended by the agreement of the parties. Further, the agreement might contain a time stipulation, so that once the fixed time for the continuance of the agency has ceased the agency is automatically terminated.

It is possible to terminate the agency agreement by notice or revocation, though it should be noted that some agreements contain an undertaking that the agency will not be terminated until a particular period has expired or until the agent has carried out his duties under the agency. It should be carefully noted that this does not amount to an irrevocable agreement since the agreement can plainly be terminated in such circumstances, although the party breaking the terms of the agency agreement will be liable for breach of contract.

Where the agency arises by way of apparent authority the revocation will only be effective against third parties if they have been given notice of the termination of the agent's authority.

By operation of law

In certain circumstances the agency will be brought to an end by the operation of the law. This may arise in several situations.

Death

The death of the principal automatically terminates the agency, although the agent may remain liable to the third party for breach of warranty of authority, even if the agent is unaware of the death of his principal. The death of the agent terminates the agency.

Unsound mind

The effect of the principal or the agent becoming insane is to terminate the agency, although it is possible for an agent to bind an insane principal to a third party by way of apparent authority, as was held in *Drew* v *Nunn* (1879) 4 QBD 661. In *Yonge* v *Toynbee* [1910] 1 KB 215, however, the agent had no authority to act and bind his insane principal but was nevertheless held to be liable to the third party by way of breach of warranty of authority.

Bankruptcy

The bankruptcy of the principal renders him legally incapable, the effect of which is automatically to terminate the agency. The same is not necessarily true of the agent although it is unlikely he could sustain his position as agent when tainted with bankruptcy.

Frustration

Frustration will bring about the automatic termination of the agency just as in normal contractual rules.

Irrevocable authority

In a limited number of cases the authority of the agent is rendered irrevocable.

Powers of attorney

If the power of attorney is expressed to be irrevocable and is given to secure the interests of the donee of the power, in our case the agent, then the power of attorney will remain irrevocable for so long as the interest of the donee continues to exist, by s. 4 of the Powers of Attorney Act 1971. The power may be removed where the donee consents to its removal; the power does not, however, lapse on the death, bankruptcy, incapacity or dissolution of the donor of the power.

Personal liability incurred by the agent

If an agent incurs a personal liability or a personal loss by virtue of the exercise of his authority, the agency cannot be revoked by the principal without the consent of the agent. The rule is clearly desirable since otherwise the position of the agent would be severely prejudiced. There is one qualification to the rule, however in that for it to apply, the liability or loss must have been within the contemplation of the parties at the time the authority was conferred on the agent, as stated in *Read* v *Anderson* (1884) 13 QBD 779.

Authority coupled with an interest

The authority given to an agent will be irrevocable where the authority is coupled to a subsisting interest. This may arise where a principal authorises an agent to sell property and to deduct his fee from the purchase price, as in *Gaussen* v *Morton* (1830) 10 B&C 731. Here the principal has conferred an interest on the agent so that the agency cannot be unilaterally revoked by him, nor on his death or bankruptcy. It should be noted that the principle does not operate where the authority arises incidentally with respect to a subsisting agency. It was held in *Smart* v *Sandars* (1848) 5 CB 895 that the authority must be given with the specific intention of protecting the interests of the creditor.

The effect of European law on the agency relationship

The Commercial Agents (Council Directive) Regulations 1993 (SI 1993, No 3053) came into force on 1 January 1994 and made significant changes to the law of agency as it applies to self-employed commercial agents. The changes will affect existing as well as future commercial agency agreements and will imply certain rights and duties into these agreements. A principal will be unable to avoid the effects of the Regulations in his agency contracts, though certain provisions within the Regulations only apply where the agency contract does not deal with a particular issue. In these circumstances where the agency contract differs from the provisions contained in the Regulations, the agency contract will be interpreted in favour of the agent. Where a provision within an agency contract cannot be interpreted in this way then it will be void as from 1 January 1994 insofar as it is inconsistent with the duties imposed by the Regulations.

Defining a commercial agent

The Regulations do not encompass all agency contracts – only those where the appointee is a commercial agent, which is defined by Regulation 2 as 'a self-employed intermediary who has continuing authority to negotiate the sale or purchase of goods on behalf of another person (the "principal"), or to negotiate and conclude the sale or purchase of goods on behalf of and in the name of that principal'.

Certain persons are excluded from the definition: firstly, the expression 'commercial agent' 'shall be understood as not including in particular' officers of companies or associations making contracts on behalf of their companies or associations, insolvency practitioners or partners making contracts that are binding on other members of the partnership; secondly, the Regulations do not apply to 'commercial agents whose activities are unpaid', commercial agents operating on the commodity exchanges and Crown Agents; thirdly, the Regulations do not apply to commercial agents whose activities 'are to be considered secondary'. In order to decide whether an agent's activities are secondary, Regulation 2(3) makes reference to the Schedule, which in turn states that an agent's activities are secondary when 'it may reasonably be taken that the primary purpose of the arrangement with his principal is other than as set out in paragraph 2'.

Broadly speaking, the Schedule provides that the activities of a commercial agent will be considered to be secondary and therefore outside the Regulations where:

1   the principal is not the manufacturer, importer or distributor of the goods; or
2   the goods are not specifically identified with the principal in the market in question; or
3   the agent does not substantially devote the whole of his time to representative activities (whether for one principal or for a number of principals whose interests are not conflicting); or
4   the goods are normally available in the market in question other than by means of the agent; or
5   the arrangement is described as being other than one of commercial agency; or
6   'promotional material is supplied directly to potential customers'; or
7   persons are granted agencies 'without reference to existing agents in a particular area or in relation to a particular group'; or
8   'customers normally select the goods for themselves and thereby place their orders through the agent'.

Thus, unless the contrary is proved, agents acting on behalf of mail order catalogue firms in respect of consumer goods are presumed to fall outside the Regulations.

The rights and duties of commercial agents and their principals

Regulation 3(1) provides that a commercial agent in performing his activities 'must look after the interests of his principal and act dutifully and a good faith'. By Regulation 3(2) this general duty is supplemented in that it provides that a commercial agent must make proper efforts to negotiate and, where appropriate, conclude the transactions he is instructed to take care of. He must communicate to his principal all the necessary information available to him and comply with the reasonable instructions given to him by his principal.

From the above it will quickly be seen that these duties vary little from the position that already exists under the present common law. Regulation 4, however, imposes duties on principals that are rather more specific and onerous than those found in the common law.

By Regulation 4(1) a principal in his relations with his commercial agent 'must act dutifully and in good faith'. Under Regulation 4(2) a principal is required to provide his agent with the necessary documentation relating to the goods concerned and obtain the necessary information in order to enable the agent to carry out the terms of the agency contract. A principal must also notify his agent within a reasonable period should he, the principal, anticipate that the volume of commercial transactions is likely to be significantly lower than the agent could normally have accepted. A further duty is laid on the principal by Regulation 4(3) in that he is required 'to inform his commercial agent within a reasonable period of his acceptance or refusal of, and of any non-execution by him of a commercial transaction which the commercial agent has procured for him'. The essence of these provisions is that they will not only enable the agent to have some sort of guidance as to the extent of his future commission earnings, but also enable the agent to be aware of any omissions of his principal in completing a commercial transaction.

It should be noted that the above rights and duties are mandatory, since by Regulation 5 they cannot be contracted out of. Similarly, Regulation 13, which gives both the commercial agent and principal the right to receive from one another on request 'a signed written document setting out the terms of the agency contract including any terms subsequently agreed', can also not be contracted out by virtue of Regulation 13(2).

Express provisions as to remuneration and commission

If the agency contract does not specifically provide for remuneration (a situation that is likely to be fairly rare!), Regulation 6 provides that the agent is entitled to remuneration. The amount of remuneration is calculated according to the customary practice in relation to the goods the agent is buying and selling, together with the geographical area in which he is conducting his principal's business. Thus a commercial agent operating in Spain would be entitled to remuneration at the customary rates for that area. Should he wish to be remunerated at a higher rate, then he should negotiate that rate as an express term of his agency contract with his principal. If there is no customary rate, then the commercial agent is entitled to 'reasonable remuneration taking into account all the aspects of the transaction', an approach which is compatible with that of the common law, since there is no general customary practice with regard to the remuneration of agents in the UK.

Where an agent is paid commission in respect of commercial transactions, the Regulations provide that the rules governing payment should be categorised in two ways:

(*a*) *Transactions concluded during the agency contract.* Where a commercial transaction is concluded during an agency contract the commercial agent is entitled to commissions on such contracts if:

(i)   'the transaction has been concluded as a result of his action' (Regulation 7(1)); or

(ii)   'the transaction is concluded with a third party whom he has previously acquired as a customer', even if the order was not placed through that agent (Regulation 7(1)); or

(iii)   the agent 'has an exclusive right to a specific geographical area or to a group of customers and where the transaction has been entered into with a customer belonging to that area or group' (Regulation 7(2).

It can be seen, therefore, that an agent is not only entitled to commission on actual sales as in (i) above but also on passive sales as in (ii). The position becomes even wider in relation to exclusive agents, as covered by (iii), since here the agent is entitled to commission in relation to both passive and generic sales. In relation to (iii) it may be seen that this is a major departure from the common law position. This provides that if a principal accepts a transaction that is not the result of the efforts of his exclusive agent, then that agent may take action for breach of an express term. The result of Regulation 7(2) is that the principal would now be liable by virtue of an implied term. A further result of regulation 7(2) is that a principal would be obliged to pay commission to an exclusive agent despite the fact that the transaction was completed by the principal acting on his own behalf.

(*b*) *Transactions concluded after termination of the agency contract.* In these circumstances at common law the question of entitlement to commission would be a matter for express agreement. In Regulation 8, however, it is implied that commission is payable to a commercial agent if:

(a) the transaction is mainly attributable to [the agent's] efforts during the period covered by the agency contract and if the transaction was entered into within a reasonable period after that contract terminated; or

(b) in accordance with the conditions mentioned in Regulation 7 . . . the order of the third party reached the principal or the commercial agent before the agency contract terminated.

From the above it may be seen that a problem can arise as to whether the principal should pay the commission to his outgoing commercial agent or to his successor. Regulation 9 attempts to draw the line here by providing that the successor has no entitlement to commission under Regulation 7 if, because of Regulation 8, the commission is payable to the outgoing commercial agent. It should be noted, however, that Regulation 9 provides that the commission should be shared between the outgoing agent and his successor if this is 'equitable because of the circumstances'. No attempt is made within the provision to define or explain the term 'equitable' and therefore one can only assume that a discretion will be in a court to apportion the commission payable to the outgoing agent and his successor. A further important point that arises out of Regulation 9 is that a principal is liable to pay the correct sum due to the appropriate agent, though the principal may recover any sum paid to an agent if he has paid money to the other agent who is not in fact entitled to it.

By Regulation 10 commission becomes due when:

(a) 'the principal has executed the transaction; or (b) the principal should, according to his agreement with the third party, have executed the transaction; or (c) the third party has executed the transaction . . .'

or

by Regulation 10(2) '. . . at the latest when the third party has executed his part of the transaction or should have done so if the principal had executed his part of the transaction, as he should have.'

From this provision it may be seen that it is no longer possible for a principal to delay paying the commission merely because he himself has not yet been paid by the customer. By Regulation 10(3) commission is to be paid 'not later than on the first day of the month following the quarter in which it became due'. For this purpose (unless otherwise agreed by the parties) 'the first quarter period shall run from the date the agency contract takes effect, and subsequent periods shall run from that date in the third month thereafter or the beginning of the fourth month, whichever is the sooner'.

In relation to the assessment of the amount of commission due, Regulation 12 requires the principal to provide his commercial agent with a statement of the commission due and how the amount is arrived at. Further, if requested, the principal is under obligation to supply to his agent all information available to him in order to enable the agent to check the statement. Thus a principal may be required to provide extracts from his own accounts in order to assist the agent in making his own assessment of the commission that should be payable to him. Such disclosure is only avoided if it is in the public interest not to provide the relevant information.

Termination of a commercial agency

With respect to agency contracts that are agreed to run for a fixed period of time, Regulation 14 provides that such agencies will be converted to a commercial agency for an indefinite term should the parties continue to operate the agency after the end of the fixed period. Whilst this provision is no doubt intended to protect the agent's right to remuneration and commission, it may also have the effect of allowing a third party to enforce a contract against a principal as if there were an express agency agreement between the principal and the commercial agent, thereby avoiding the need to prove apparent or ostensible authority in respect of the agent's actions.

Where the agency contract is for an indefinite period of time, Regulation 15 allows either party to terminate the agency contract by the giving of notice. The period of notice depends on the length of time the agency contract has run. Thus, unless a longer notice is agreed between the parties, the period of notice will be one month for each year of the contract, up to a maximum of three months at any time after the start of the third year and all subsequent years. It should be noted that these provisions do not contradict the rules that govern notice to terminate contracts of employment, since an employee cannot be a commercial agent. Further, if a longer period of notice is agreed, the period to be given by the principal cannot be shorter than that to be given by the agent (Regulation 15(3)).

In relation to the rules relating to the termination of the agency contract, Regulation 16 provides that the above rules do not affect:

> . . . the application of any enactment or rule of law which provides for the immediate termination of the agency contract:
> (a) because of the failure of one party to carry out all or part of his obligations under that constraint; or
> (b) where exceptional circumstances arise.

The effect of this provision is that it is still open for a principal summarily to dismiss his commercial agent who is discovered to be taking a secret profit, such as a bribe. Similarly the provision preserves the effect of the doctrine of frustration.

Compensation for termination of the agency contract

One of the fundamental features of the Commercial Agents Regulations is that they provide for an agent to be entitled to compensation for loss suffered as a result of his agency contract being terminated. By Regulation 17 a commercial agent may claim compensation for damage resulting from termination of the agency contract. Damage is deemed to occur particularly in circumstances which:

> '(a) deprive the commercial agent of the commission which proper performance of the agency contract would have procured for him whilst providing his principal with substantial benefits linked to the activities of the commercial agent;' and/or
> '(b) have not enabled the commercial agent to amortize the costs and expenses that he had incurred in the performance of the agency contract on the advice of his principal.'

The agent is entitled to such compensation provided the agency contract has been terminated:

(i) by the principal, except as a result of a default by the agent which has justified immediate termination; or
(ii) by the agent because of circumstances attributable to the principal; or
(iii) by the agent as a result of his age, illness, infirmity or death.

The right to compensation is lost if the agent does not notify his principal of his intention to claim within one year of the termination of the agency contract (Regulation 17(9)).

In addition to compensation for damages a commercial agent may also seek an indemnity from his principal. The entitlement to indemnity is provided by Regulation 17 paras 3–5 and arises where the agent:

> . . . (a) . . . has brought the principal new customers or has significantly increased the volume of business with existing customers and the principal continues to derive substantial benefits from the business with such customers; and
> (b) the payment of this indemnity is equitable having regard to all the circumstances and, in particular, the commission lost by the commercial agent on the business transacted with such customers.

Regulation 17(4) provides that the amount of the indemnity 'shall not exceed a figure equivalent' to an indemnity for one year calculated from the agent's average annual remuneration over the preceding five years and, if the contract goes back less than five years, the calculation shall be based on the annual average for the period in question.

Restraint of trade

By Regulation 20(1) restraint of trade clauses are allowed so that a commercial agent's right to act as an agent may be restricted once his contract with his present principal is terminated. There are, of course, conditions attached to this provision in that the restraint of trade clause, to be valid, has to be in writing and limited to the geographical area and/or a group of customers and to the kind of goods covered by the agency contract. Furthermore, by Regulation 20(2) the restraint must not last for more than two years after the termination of the agency contract.

A rather more subtle means of controlling restraint of trade claims may be found in Regulation 20(3) which provides that other enactments and rules of law are preserved. Presumably, therefore, the common law requirement of reasonableness would also have to be satisfied in relation to the application of Regulation 20 in England and Wales.

Exclusive distributorship agreements

It can be seen that the Commercial Agents Regulations 1993 profoundly affect commercial agency contracts to the extent that principals will no doubt, on assessing the impact of the Regulations, consider redrafting their present contracts. Many principals will reconsider their use of commercial agency contracts and move towards using employees as representatives or adopting a franchise system for distributing goods to customers.

Many principals will, it is suggested, move towards adopting distributorship agreements, in which one party (the distributor) buys goods from a supplier in order to resell them to its own customers. There are thus two contracts, one between the supplier and the distributor and another between the distributor and the customer. Such arrangements have the advantage that they are regulated by the usual rules of contract and do not fall within the law of agency, and thus the distributor is not paid a commission but derives a profit in the mark-up between the buying and selling price of the goods. A further advantage that is not easily discernible is that where, in an agency agreement, a principal employs an agent to act on his behalf outside the United Kingdom but in other countries within the EC, the principal will have to account for VAT in the state where the agent conducts his business. This is not the case with distributorship agreements since here it is the distributor's responsibility rather than the supplier's.

In assessing whether to enter into a distributorship agreement rather than an agency contract, a supplier needs to take many factors into account, apart from those already indicated. Thus the size and nature of the supplier's business will be an important consideration, since a small company may not have the means to monitor an agency contract effectively given the Regulations already discussed. The fact that the activities of an agent will bind his principal is also an important factor if the supplier is operating in an area where his knowledge of trading conditions is limited or non-existent. In these situations it may be better for the supplier to enter into a distributorship agreement. On the other hand, if the supplier wishes to retain control of the sales and distribution process where, for instance, the supplier is a manufacturer of goods that are custom-built for the eventual customer, then an agency contract may be more appropriate.

It should be noted that distributorship agreements can take various forms. Thus, for example, a sole or exclusive distributorship agreement would arise where a particular distributor has exclusive rights of distribution within a particular geographical area. It is, of course, also possible for a supplier to limit the operations of the distributor by restricting sales to customers who meet the supplier's specifications.

Further reading

Beale, Bishop and Furmston, *Contract – Cases and Materials* 2nd ed. 1990, Butterworths
Cheshire, Fifoot and Furmston, *The Law of Contract* 12th ed. 1991, Butterworths
Guest, *Anson's Law of Contract* 26th ed. 1984, Oxford University Press
Treitel, *The Law of Contract* 8th ed. 1991, Sweet & Maxwell

21 | Assignment of contractual rights

INTRODUCTION

Assignment is a method by which a party to a contract transfers the benefits he has contracted to receive from the other party to a third party, who is himself able to enforce performance of the contract. There is no question of this situation breaking the privity of contract rule as discussed in Chapter 19 since a party is actually assigning his position to enforce the contract to the third party, the contract thus remaining essentially bilateral in character.

The right to enforce a contract is in fact a form of intangible property known generically as a 'chose in action', an expression which also encompasses property such as copyrights, patents, trade marks and actions in tort. It should be noted that the benefit assigned to the third party is not the material benefits that may result from the contract, but the right to enforce the contract. It should always be remembered that a contract is useless if it cannot be enforced and it is the fact of enforcement that produces the benefits from the contract. Thus the right to enforce the contract is a chose in action, since it is an intangible form of property that gives rights of action that may be claimed or enforced without the need for taking physical possession of the material benefits arising out of the contract.

This chapter will be concerned with the means by which this chose in action can be transferred voluntarily to another person. It is possible for involuntary assignment to take place either where a party to a contract dies or where he is declared bankrupt. In the case of death the contract survives both against and for the benefit of the estate, thus allowing the personal representatives of the deceased to sue or be sued on any contracts entered into by the deceased prior to his death, with the exception, of course, of those requiring personal services. In bankruptcy a person who is adjudicated bankrupt has all his property vested in the trustee in bankruptcy.

This property will also include any rights possessed by the bankrupt by virtue of any contract entered into by him. The effect is that if the trustee considers that the estate of the bankrupt may benefit from the contract being enforced he may take steps on behalf of the estate to enforce it. The ability of the trustee to enforce the contract varies, however, where the contract involves personal services since if there is a breach of contract after the commencement of the bankruptcy, the right to enforce the contract remains with the bankrupt. The trustee nevertheless has a subsequent power to intervene and take any monies recovered by the bankrupt which are not required for the maintenance of the bankrupt. Where the breach occurs before the bankruptcy proceedings the right to take action passes to the trustee, though this will not apply to actions in respect of the reputation or character of the bankrupt, despite the fact that such action might arise out of a breach of contract.

VOLUNTARY ASSIGNMENT AT COMMON LAW

At common law the general principle was that choses in action could not be assigned, with the exception of those involving the Crown and the assignments of negotiable instruments. The assignment of negotiable instruments, sometimes referred to as 'negotiability' is an important exception which is virtually a subject in its own right, so discussion of it will be left for consideration elsewhere, in a more specialised mercantile law environment. The undoubted reason for the attitude of the common law courts was the desire to preserve the privity of contract rule which they feared would be undermined if the ability of the parties to assign their rights under a contract became widespread. It should be borne in mind that whilst the third party assignee could not enforce the contract against the promisor at common law, there was, nevertheless, a binding contract between the assignee and the assignor. The result of this was that the assignee could sue the assignor for breach of contract.

Despite the general rule of the common law not to allow assignment there were means of avoiding the rule so that the right to enforce a contract could be undertaken by a third party.

Firstly, the promisee could always allow the third party to sue in his, the promisee's name. Usually the promisee would insist that the third party agree to indemnify him against the legal costs of maintaining the action against the promisor.

Secondly, the promisee could give the third party a power of attorney, the effect of which would be to allow him to maintain the action as a representative of the promisee. This method was not particularly satisfactory for the third party since, just as in the case of the first exception above, it could be revoked by the promisee at any time and in any event it would end automatically on the death of the promisee. The rights of the third party were thus not guaranteed.

Thirdly, it was possible for rights to be acquired by the third party by a process called 'novation'. Novation is basically a contract entered into between the promisee, the promisor and the third party whereby the benefits of the contract would henceforth be owed by the promisor to the third party. Realistically this is not an assignment since the enforcement of the contract by the third party is based on the existence of a new contract between himself and the promisor and thus he would have to provide consideration in order that the second contract be enforceable. This exception is subject to the disadvantage that the consent of the promisor would always be required for the novation to work.

In truth, none of the methods discussed is a true assignment but merely a transaction which has the same effect as an assignment.

VOLUNTARY ASSIGNMENT IN EQUITY

The problem of assignment at common law led to the development of a doctrine in equity which would permit the assignment of a chose in action whether or not it was in the nature of a legal or equitable chose. The means by which the assignment was accomplished and whether it could be enforced in the assignee's own name differed, however, according to whether the chose was equitable or legal and whether or not it was an absolute assignment.

The legal and equitable nature of the chose in action

Prior to the Judicature Acts 1873–75 a legal chose was one which could be enforced by action in law within the common law courts, for example, a debt due under a contract. Equity would recognise an assignment of a legal chose but was faced with a difficult predicament in that whilst it would allow the assignee to succeed against the promisor, it had no jurisdiction to prevent the assignor from subsequently claiming from the promisor a second time. If the assignor undertook such an action then the promisor would himself have to present an action before the court of chancery in order to prevent the second recovery. Equity side-stepped this predicament by compelling the assignor, on the petition of the assignee, to sue in his own name, or at least lend his name to the assignee, the result of which was to have all the interests of the various parties decided by the same court.

If the chose in question was an equitable one then the matter was somewhat simpler since the court of chancery enjoyed sole jurisdiction over the matter. Here the assignee could bring the action in his own name and was not required even to make the assignor a party to his action. The reason for this was that there was no claim capable of being asserted at law. This situation might arise because the parties never intended that legal rights would exist as in, for instance, rights arising under a trust. Alternatively the equitable chose might arise out of informality, where the parties have failed to comply with a formality required by the common law, for instance, they might have failed to use a deed or been parties to an ineffective deed. Finally the equitable chose might have arisen because the parties themselves only possessed equitable rights, in which case it would be impossible to carve a legal assignment out of an equitable interest.

With the passing of the Judicature Acts the above anachronism cried out for abolition. The main point of the legislation was to fuse the operation of equity and common law into a single system of courts and it was clearly incompatible to have the common law and equitable rules relating to equitable and legal choses being administered within the same courts. Section 25(6) of the Judicature Act 1873 provided for a new statutory form of assignment that would take effect in law. This statutory form of assignment will be considered later but it should be noted that it did not abolish assignment of choses in action in equity, which could and can still be fallen back on if the conditions required for a statutory assignment are not complied with.

Whether or not the assignment is absolute

Absolute assignment

An absolute assignment occurs where the assignor has assigned his entire interest in the chose in action to the assignee. This is not to say that the assignor must have completely relinquished all further interest in the subject matter of the chose. Thus it was held in *Hughes v Pump House Hotel Co* [1902] 2 KB 190 that an assignment of monies due under various contracts as security for an overdraft was nevertheless unconditional and absolute, despite the fact that the assignor's rights to the debts owing to him were capable of being reassigned to him when the overdraft facility was no longer required. The fact that the right to reassignment is express or implied has no effect on the absolute nature of the assignment.

Non-absolute assignment

If the assignor reserves certain rights in the chose in action in spite of the assignment then the assignment is said to be non-absolute. This may occur in three circumstances:

(a) The assignee decides not to transfer the entire chose in action;
(b) where the assignment is by way of a charge;
(c) where the commencement or the cessation of the assignment is conditional upon an uncertain future event.

The assignee may decide **not to transfer the entire chose in action**, as, for instance, if the assignor decides to transfer only part of his rights in a debt owing to him under a contract.

An assignment may be by way of a **charge**. Unlike a mortgage, which transfers an entire fund to the assignee, a charge only entitles the assignee to a payment out of the fund. In *Jones* v *Humphreys* [1902] 1 KB 10 a schoolmaster, in consideration for a loan of £15, assigned such part of his income and salary as was necessary to discharge the loan, together with interest, or any further sums for which he might in the future become indebted to the plaintiff. It was held that this was not an absolute assignment of the schoolmaster's salary since it was only mere security that enabled the lender to have recourse to the salary should the state of indebtedness render this desirable. The assignment merely amounted to a charge on the salary and was thus not absolute.

The assignment will not be absolute where **its commencement or cessation is conditional upon an uncertain future event**. In *Durham Brothers* v *Robertson* [1898] 1 QB 765 a firm of building contractors executed an assignment which read:

> Re Building Contract, South Lambert Road. In consideration of money advanced from time to time we hereby charge the sum of £1,080, being the price . . . due to us from John Robertson in completion of the above buildings as security for the advances, and we hereby assign our interest in the above-mentioned sum until the money with added interest be repaid to you.

It was held that this assignment was not absolute but conditional. There was no question of the whole of the debt being assigned to the plaintiffs unconditionally but only such a sum as was necessary to discharge the advances made, together with interest.

Anson seems to suggest that one method of testing whether or not the assignment is conditional is by having reference to the state of knowledge of the promisor. If he cannot be sure whether he is paying his debt to the right person or not without knowing of the state of the accounts between the assignor and the assignee, then the assignment will be conditional and not absolute. If, however, as in *Hughes* v *Pump House Hotel Co*, the assignment passes the entire interest as security and there is a proviso for reassignment when the loan is repaid, the promisor knows who he is to pay his debt to. The reason for this is that he will be given notice of the assignment and later, when the loan is repaid, he will be given notice of the reassignment, and the assignment will thus be absolute.

The requirements of an equitable assignment

(a) Joinder of the assignor in an action by the assignee. Before discussing this requirement in detail we should note that an equitable assignment merely assigns the equitable title to the assignee. The result of this is that generally the assignee must join the assignor as a party to his action to enforce the chose in action against the promisor. The requirement of joinder, however, differs according to whether the chose in action is legal or equitable and whether it is absolute or non-absolute, as the following classification indicates:

(a) the absolute equitable assignment of an equitable chose in action;
(b) the non-absolute equitable assignment of an equitable chose in action;
(c) the equitable assignment of a legal chose in action.

When there is an **absolute equitable assignment of an equitable chose in action**, the action is one which formerly could be dealt with exclusively within the court of chancery, so there is no need for the assignee to join the assignor in the action. The assignee can sue in his own name.

In a **non-absolute equitable assignment of an equitable chose in action**, as we have already seen, the assignor retains some interest in the chose in action. The consequence of this is that a court, in deciding the action between the assignee and the promisor, would not be able to make any adjudication of the rights and liabilities of the parties without having reference to the state of the accounts between the assignee and the assignor. The result is that the assignee must join the assignor into his action so that the court can come to a decision that will bind all the parties that are interested in the chose in action.

In an **equitable assignment of a legal chose in action**, whether the assignment is absolute or non-absolute, the assignee must in all cases join the assignor into his action. If the assignor refuses to allow this then the assignee can sue him as a joint co-defendant. It should also be noted that these rules also apply if the assignor is attempting to recover the balance of the monies owing to him by the promisor – the assignor must join the assignee into his action or treat the assignee as a co-defendant. The existence of these rules arose out of the procedural difficulties that occurred prior to the passing of the Judicature Act 1873, as already described above. Some authorities suggest other reasons but these are not particularly convincing.

(b) The form of the assignment. Since equity looks to the intent and not to the form then generally no particular form is required to give effect to an equitable assignment. This statement is, however, somewhat simplistic since statutory regulation has overlaid this basic premise. The requirements as to form differ:

(a) where there is an equitable assignment of a legal chose in action of personalty;
(b) where there is an equitable assignment of an equitable interest;
(c) according to the terms laid down in the Law of Property (Miscellaneous Provisions) Act 1985, s. 2(1).

Where there is an **equitable assignment of a legal chose in action of personalty**, the basic premise still presides, in that no particular form is required, and it is thus possible for such an assignment to take place orally. In *Thomas* v *Harris* [1947] 1 All ER 444 certain life assurance policies were handed by a father to his son, and at the same time it was requested that the proceeds that arose on his death be used to buy a tombstone for his grave. This was held to be effective as a valid assignment despite the fact that no notice of the assignment was given to the insurance company.

It should be noted that it is always possible for the contract itself to provide that any assignment must comply with a certain formality such as writing.

An **equitable assignment of an equitable interest** is void unless it complies with s. 53(1)c of the Law of Property Act 1925. This provides:

[A] disposition of an equitable interest or trust subsisting at the time of the disposition must be in writing signed by the person disposing of the same, or by his agent thereunto lawfully authorised by writing or by will.

It should be noted that this provision covers equitable choses in action comprising of both personalty and land.

The **Law of Property (Miscellaneous Provisions) Act 1985, s. 2(1)** provides:

A contract for the sale or other disposition of an interest in land can only be made in writing and only by incorporating all the terms which the parties have expressly agreed in the document or, where contracts are exchanged, in each.

The full extent of the effect of this provision has yet to be decided; suffice it to say that failure to comply with the provision will render the assignment void. It can be seen that the provision is almost analogous to s. 53(1)c of the Law of Property Act 1925 above and there should be no difference between the two provisions as they affect an equitable assignment of an equitable chose in action of land. It is suggested, however, that s. 2(1) will now require an equitable assignment of a legal chose in action of land to be writing.

Despite the fact that certain types of equitable assignment are required to be in writing there is no requirement as to the form of that writing. The writing itself need not be expressed to be an assignment. In *William Brandt's Sons & Co* v *Dunlop Rubber Co* [1905] AC 454, Lord MacNaghten stated:

An equitable assignment does not always take that form. It may be addressed to the debtor. It may be couched in the language of a command. It may be a courteous request. It may assume the form of mere permission. The language is immaterial if the meaning is plain. All that is necessary is that the debtor should be given to understand that the debt has been made over by the creditor to some third person.

It can be seen from the above that the writing encompassing the assignment can be directed to either the debtor (promisor) or the assignee.

(c) Notice. Notice may be either to the assignee or to the promisor (debtor).

An assignment is ineffective unless the assignor or someone acting on his authority has **communicated it to the assignee**. It is not certain why this requirement is particularly necessary since it was stated in *Standing* v *Bowring* (1885) 31 Ch D 282 that a person can have property assigned to him without his knowledge, although this is subject to an implied right to repudiate the assignment when he gains knowledge of it.

The basic rule in **notice to the promisor (debtor)** is that notice of an equitable assignment to the debtor is not required to perfect the title. There are, however, sound reasons why such notice should nevertheless be given to the debtor.

Firstly, should the debtor make any payments to the assignor in ignorance of the assignment, the assignee will nevertheless be bound with respect to those payments. He will not, for instance, be able to recoup from the debtor any monies lost by reason of the assignor absconding with monies paid to him by the debtor in ignorance of the assignment.

Secondly, by virtue of the rule in *Dearle v Hall* (1828) 3 Russ 1, an assignee should give notice to the debtor in order to preserve his rights of priority over any competing assignees that might exist. Failure to give notice will mean that an assignee will lose priority to another later assignee who has given notice to the debtor.

The form of the notice, as already stated, is largely irrelevant, except that in *The Balder London* [1980] 2 Lloyd's Rep 489 it was stated that the notice must clearly and unconditionally direct the debtor to pay or transfer the benefits under the contract to the third party as an assignee, rather than in some other capacity such as, for example, an agent for the promisee/creditor. If the notice does direct the debtor to pay the monies to a third party as an agent of the promisee/creditor then he will not be liable to the assignee should he pay the money to the promisee/creditor.

(d) Consideration. The question of whether consideration is needed for an effective equitable assignment is universally accepted as one of great difficulty. It should be noted that this is not an issue that may be raised by the debtor/promisee since he is bound to pay the debt or transfer the benefits under the contract whether or not the assignment is gratuitous. All the debtor/promisee is concerned with is to whom he must pay his debt, and so on, in order to avoid becoming liable a second time for the same obligation.

The problem we are then faced with is whether, as between the assignor and the assignee, there is a need for the equitable assignment to be supported by consideration. The basic premise of equity is summed up in the maxim, 'equity will not assist a volunteer', but this is too wide since consideration is not an essential requirement in all situations. Before we consider voluntary assignments it should be stated that no problems arise where the assignment is supported by consideration, since on basic contractual rules the assignment is enforceable by and against the assignor and the assignee. Where the equitable assignment is voluntary the solution largely depends on whether the transfer is 'complete and perfect' or not, as the case may be.

To render a transfer 'complete and perfect' everything that needs to be done to effect the transfer or assignment must have been done. Thus, just as to render a gift of a chose in possession (that is, tangible property) complete, the actual property must be handed over to the donee, so that nothing remains to be done to give effect to the donor's intention, so the same is also true in the case of a voluntary equitable assignment of a chose in action. In the latter case all the formalities to give effect to the assignment of the chose in action from the assignor to the assignee must have been carried out. Failure to make the voluntary assignment complete and perfect will render the assignment invalid since 'equity will not perfect an imperfect gift'. In *Milroy v Lord* (1862) 4 De G F & J 264 Lord Turner expounded the principle in the analogous situation of voluntary settlements as follows:

> In order to make a voluntary settlement valid and effectual, the settlor must have done everything, which according to the nature of the property comprised in the settlement,

was necessary to be done in order to transfer the property and render the settlement binding upon him.

The effect of the above on the various types of voluntary equitable assignments differs according to whether they are:

(a) an agreement to assign a chose in action;
(b) assignments of an equitable chose in action;
(c) assignments of a legal chose in action.

An **agreement to assign a chose in action** relates to a future arrangement and clearly this is not capable of being 'completed and perfected' until the time of execution of the assignment arises. Such agreements then must be supported by consideration. The same is also true of an assignment of a future chose in action, since it was held in *Glegg* v *Bromley* [1912] 3 KB 474 by Parker J that 'nothing passes even in equity until the property comes into existence'. Consideration is thus required in respect of an assignment of such an interest.

In **assignments of an equitable chose in action**, if the assignor has done everything in his power to effect the transfer of the equitable chose in action to the assignee then the voluntary assignment will be valid. At that point the assignee is in a position to enforce his right to the chose in action since, as was stated in *Voyle* v *Hughes* (1854) 2 Sm & G 18, 'an assignment without any valuable consideration is not a mere agreement but is an actual transfer of the equitable right'.

Assignments of a legal chose in action pose the particular problem of whether a voluntary equitable assignment of a legal chose in action can ever be 'complete and perfect'. The position here formerly was not clear since such choses in action had to be enforced within the common law courts by the assignee seeking the help of equity to compel the assignor to allow the assignee to sue in his, the assignor's, name. Since collaboration of the assignor was needed to enforce the chose in action, the equitable assignment could not be said to be 'completed and perfected' and therefore consideration was required. Since the procedure now is that the assignee can simply add the assignor as a co-defendant if he refuses to collaborate with the assignee in allowing him to sue in the assignor's name, it would seem that the absolute assignment of a legal chose in action is valid despite the lack of consideration.

STATUTORY ASSIGNMENT

Generally

It was stated earlier that s. 25(6) of the Judicature Act 1873 introduced a general form of statutory assignment. This form of assignment is now contained in s. 136(1) of the Law of Property Act 1925. This provides:

Any absolute assignment by writing under the hand of the assignor (not purporting to be by way of charge only) of any debt or other legal thing in action, of which express notice in writing has been given to the debtor, trustee or other person from whom the assignor would have been entitled to claim such debt or thing in action, is effectual in law (subject to equities having priority over the right of the assignee) to pass and transfer from the date of such notice:

(a) the legal right to such debt or thing in action;

(b) all legal and other remedies for the same; and

(c) the power to give a good discharge for the same without the concurrence of the assignor.

It should be noted that s. 136 has not abolished equitable assignments and these will continue to exist where an assignment does not comply with the requirements of s. 136. In truth all the provision has done is to allow the rights of the assignee to be exercised in a more direct manner so that he can sue in his own name without the need for joinder of the assignor arising, as stated in *Tolhurst* v *Associated Portland Cement Manufacturers (1900) Ltd* [1903] AC 414.

Care must be taken in construing the words 'any debt or other legal thing in action' in s. 136(1). At first sight this appears to confine the statutory form of assignment to legal choses in action, that is, those choses in action which were formerly only enforceable within the common law courts. This provision has, however, been interpreted by the courts as including equitable, as well as legal, choses in action.

The provision does not require consideration to have been provided by the assignee in order to allow him to sue in his own name.

The essentials of a valid statutory assignment

The assignment must be absolute

The difference between absolute and non-absolute assignments has already been considered. If the assignment is conditional and non-absolute then the parties will have to fall back on the use of an equitable assignment for the assignment to be valid.

The assignment must be in writing

Whilst the assignment must be in writing and signed by the assignor, there are no provisions as to the contents, though clearly the writing must inform the debtor to pay or hand the benefit of the contract to the assignee, as an assignee and not merely as an agent of the assignor. Apparently if the date or the amount of a debt which is the subject of an assignment is incorrectly stated, then the assignment will be invalid. It would seem that the main point is that the terms of the assignment must be stated with a sufficient degree of certainty.

Notice of the assignment must be given to the debtor/promisor

It was held in *Holt v Heatherfield Trust Ltd* [1942] 2 KB 1 that notice takes effect when it is received by the debtor/promisor. The postal rules, for instance, have no application here.

OTHER FACTORS AFFECTING ALL TYPES OF ASSIGNMENTS

Priority of assignments

The problem that arises here occurs where an assignor decides to make two or more assignments of the same chose in action to two or more assignees. This in itself presents no difficulty, but if it transpires that monies owed under the chose in action by the debtor are insufficient to meet the respective claims of the various assignees then the question of priority will arise.

The ranking of priority is determined by the rule in *Dearle v Hall* (1828) 3 Russ 1 which provides that assignees will rank in accordance with the dates on which notice of their respective assignments were given to the debtor. Thus an assignee who fails to give notice to the debtor will lose his priority to a subsequent assignee who, having no knowledge of the first assignee's interest, gives notice to the debtor prior to the first assignee.

The notice may be made orally unless the interest that is being assigned is either an equitable interest in land or personalty when s. 137(3) of the Law of Property Act 1925 requires the notice to be in writing.

Where the interest to be assigned is an equitable interest under a trust fund then the assignee should give notice to all the trustees of the trust, though this not a mandatory requirement.

Assignees take 'subject to equities'

When an assignee takes the assignment of the benefits of the contract from the assignor he also takes the risk of any defences that may be available to the debtor/promisor against the assignor should the assignee have to take action against the debtor/assignor. The assignee is thus said to take the assignment 'subject to the equities' of the debtor/promisor.

The expression 'subject to equities' needs careful consideration since it is not confined solely to equitable remedies that may be available to the debtor. It will include common law remedies, so that any damages accruing to the debtor by virtue of a counter-claim may be set off against the assignee, provided they arise out of the contract which is the subject of the assignment, as stated in *Newfoundland Government v Newfoundland Railway Co* (1888) 13 App Cas 199. Further, the debtor is entitled to make use of any rights arising out of mistake, misrepresentation or breach of contract perpetrated by the assignor.

With regard to the latter point also, some care needs to be exercised since the debtor cannot raise against the assignee any personal claims he may have against the assignor. This problem is particularly prevalent in claims of fraud that may have accrued against the assignor by the debtor. The problem is well illustrated by the case of *Stoddart* v *Union Trust* [1912] 1 KB 181 where the Union Trust was induced into a contract to buy a newspaper by the fraudulent misrepresentation of a person named Price. The purchase price was £1,000, of which £200 was payable immediately and the rest by instalments. Price assigned the £800 debt to Stoddart who took it without knowledge of the fraudulent actions of Price. The Union Trust were subsequently sued by Stoddart for the monies owing, but they counter-claimed for damages exceeding the £800 on the basis of the fraud that had been perpetrated on them by Price. They therefore claimed that they owed Stoddart nothing. It was held by the Court of Appeal that they could not owe Stoddart nothing since the claim represented a personal claim against Price and did not arise out of the contract being enforced by Stoddart. An anomaly occurs here since Stoddart was then in a better position than Price would have been under the same contract and this is clearly to the detriment of the debtor, the Union Trust. It may be that the Union Trust should have sought the rescission of the contract rather than merely damages, since this action would tend to strike at the existence of the contract itself rather than at the more personal liability of the assignor to pay damages.

Where the equities accruing to the debtor arise out of a separate contract or transaction from the contract that is the subject of the assignment, the debtor cannot set off those equities against the assignee. The only exception to this is if the independent claim accrued before the debtor had notice of the assignment to the assignee. It can therefore be seen that the serving of notice of the assignment by the assignee to the debtor is particularly important in this context and certainly, in order to prevent the debtor setting up fresh equities against the rights of the assignee, as indicated in *Roxburghe* v *Cox* (1881) 17 Ch D 520, should not be delayed.

It can be seen from the above rules that great care needs to be exercised by the assignee when he decides to accept an assignment from the assignor, since he could be acquiring an interest in a chose which is far less valuable than it appears on the face of things. Thorough investigation of the circumstances in which the chose in action arose is highly desirable.

Rights which are non-assignable

Express exclusion of assignability

The contract entered into by the original parties may expressly provide that the contract is not capable of being assigned. Any subsequent assignment is invalid as it affects the debtor, though it is effective between the assignor and the assignee.

Rights of action

A right to sue for damages, sometimes described as a 'bare right of action' cannot be assigned since this is contrary to the rules relating to champerty and maintenance. Whilst this principle has been affirmed in the case of *Trendtex Trading Corporation* v *Crédit Suisse* [1982] AC 679, the House of Lords declared that such a right may be assignable where the assignee has a genuine legitimate interest of a financial or commercial nature in taking the assignment and subsequently enforcing the right in question. An example would be where the purchaser of land is able to sue the vendor's tenants for any breach of covenant that had arisen prior to the sale. These rights of the purchaser of the reversion of the lease are now contained in s. 141 of the Law of Property Act 1925, though here the right to sue the tenants only extends to the situation where there has been a breach of a covenant that 'has reference to the subject matter of the lease', that is, the covenants affect the landlord qua landlord and the tenant qua tenant rather than merely being personal in nature.

Personal contracts

If the contract involves the use of a personal skill or confidence then the parties can insist on the contract being performed personally by the other party. The reason for this is that the personal performance forms the essence of the contract and to allow assignment would be to alter the very nature of the contract itself without the consent of the other party. In *Griffith* v *Tower Publishing Co Ltd* [1897] 1 Ch 21 it was held that a contract by an author to write a book for a publisher amounted to a personal contract so that the author could restrain the publisher from assigning the contract to another. The logic here is that the author entered into the contract with the publisher on the basis of the latter's skill and judgment in that capacity.

Public policy

As we saw in Chapter 12, the law does not allow a public servant to assign his salary and similarly it does not allow a wife to assign her rights to maintenance on grounds of public policy.

ASSIGNMENT OF LIABILITIES

The general rule is that it is only the benefits of a contract that are assignable, not the burdens, unless the consent of the promisee is first obtained. The reasoning here is that it should not be possible to compel the promisee to accept performance of the contract from someone other than the promisor. It is nevertheless possible to achieve this position by novation since this results in the original contract being rescinded with the mutual agreement of the promisor and promisee, and a new one being substituted between the original promisor and the new promisee.

Further reading

Beale, Bishop and Furmston, *Contract – Cases and Materials* 2nd ed. 1990, Butterworths
Cheshire, Fifoot and Furmston, *The Law of Contract* 12th ed. 1991, Butterworths
Guest, *Anson's Law of Contract* 26th ed. 1984, Oxford University Press
Treitel, *The Law of Contract* 8th ed. 1991, Sweet & Maxwell

Index